W9-BXS-999

THE
COLLECTED
POEMS

1952-1990

POEMS TRANSLATED BY:

Antonina W. Bouis
Arthur Boyars
James Dickey
Vera Dunham
Geoffrey Dutton
Lawrence Ferlinghetti
Simon Franklin
Michael Glenny
Ted Hughes
Eleanor Jacka
Anthony Kahn
Edward Keenan
Stanley Kunitz
Peter Levi
Herbert Marshall
Igor Mezhakoff-Koriakin
Robin Milner-Gulland
James Ragan
George Reavey
D. M. Thomas
Albert C. Todd
Tina Tupikina-Glaessner
John Updike
Daniel Weissbort
Richard Wilbur

THE
COLLECTED
POEMS

1952ı1990

Yevgeny Yevtushenko

Edited by Albert C. Todd
with the author and James Ragan

A John Macrae Book
HENRY HOLT AND COMPANY   NEW YORK

Library of Congress Cataloging-in-Publication Data
Yevtushenko, Yevgeny Aleksandrovich, 1933–
[Poems. English]
The collected poems, 1952–1990 / Yevgeny Yevtushenko ; edited by
Albert C. Todd with the author and James Ragan.—1st American ed.
p.   cm.
Poems translated from the Russian.
ISBN 0-8050-0696-6
1. Yevtushenko, Yevgeny Aleksandrovich, 1933–   —Translations,
English.   I. Todd, Albert.   II. Ragan, James, 1944–   .
III. Title.
PG3476.E96A275   1991
891.71′44—dc20
90-44794
CIP

Henry Holt books are available at special discounts for bulk purchases for
sales promotions, premiums, fund-raising, or edu-
cational use. Special editions or book excerpts can
also be created to specification.
For details contact: Special Sales Director,
Henry Holt and Company, Inc., 115 West 18th Street,
New York, New York 10011
FIRST EDITION
Book design by Claire Naylon Vaccaro
Printed in the United States of America
Recognizing the importance of preserving the written word, Henry Holt and
Company, Inc., by policy, prints all of its first editions on acid-free paper.∞
10 9 8 7 6 5 4 3 2 1

Grateful acknowledgment is made to the following for use of translations included
in this volume: Marion Boyars Publishers, selections from *The Face Behind the Face*
(copyright © 1979 by Marion Boyars Publishers, Ltd.); Doubleday, selections from *Stolen
Apples* and *From Desire to Desire* (translation copyright © 1971 by Doubleday, a division
of Bantam Doubleday Dell Publishing Group, Inc., and copyright © 1968 by Curtis
Publishing Company; translation copyright © 1976 by Doubleday, a division of Bantam
Doubleday Dell Publishing Group, Inc.); E. P. Dutton, selections from *Yevtushenko Poems*;
George Reavey and October House, selections from *The New Russian Poets*; Sun Books,
selections from *Kazan University and Other New Poems*; D. M. Thomas, *A Dove in Santiago*
(translation copyright © 1982 by D. M. Thomas); Robin Milner-Gulland and Peter Levi,
selections from *Selected Poems* (copyright © 1962 by Robin Milner-Gulland and Peter
Levi); Tina Tupikina-Glaessner, Geoffrey Dutton, and Igor Mezhakoff-Koriakin, se-
lections from *Bratsk Station and Other New Poems*; Daniel Weissbort, selections from
Ivan the Terrible and Ivan the Fool (English translation copyright © 1979 by Daniel
Weissbort); George Reavey and E. P. Dutton, selections from *Yevtushenko's Reader*;
Stanley Kunitz, "Hand-rolled Cigarettes"; Antonina W. Bouis and Penguin USA, "The
Accidentless Captain" and "Provideniia Bay"; Ted Hughes, "Safari in Ulster."

CONTENTS

Introduction   *xv*
A Note on the Translation   *xxiv*

1952–1955

Lies   3
Train Car   4
The Depth   5
You Are Great in Love   6
The Third Snow   6
"I wander . . ."   8
"In every instance . . ."   9
Boots   10
Weddings   12
"The window looks out onto . . ."   14
Last Side Street   15
On a Bicycle   16
Envy   19
Prologue   20
"I am a purse . . ."   22
Idol   23
Fury   24
Gentleness   26
The Park   26
"In a red woolen cap . . ."   28
Zima Junction: A Poem   30

1956–1962

"I don't understand . . ."   61
"What a rude sobering . . ."   62
"Cowards have . . ."   63
Ice   63
"I congratulate you, Momma . . ."   64
"Poetry is a great power . . ."   65

"My love will come..." 66
"Damp white imprints..." 66
"I don't know what..." 67
Momma 68
They Killed Someone! 69
"The square..." 71
Letter to One Writer 72
"Again a meeting..." 73
"Here is what..." 74
"When I think of Aleksandr Blok..." 75
My Dog 76
Loneliness 77
"The icicles' delicate chime..." 80
Smiles 81
Assignation 82
In Memory of the Poet Xenia Nekrasova 84
Incantation 85
"I am older by..." 86
The Incendiary 88
Let's Not... 89
Secret Mysteries 90
"They shuffle..." 92
Pasternak's Grave 93
Our Mothers Depart 95
Honey 96
The American Nightingale 98
Encounter 99
Talk 101
Babii Yar 102
Irpen 105
Irony 107
Girl Beatnik 108
"No people are..." 109
"Professor..." 110
The Dead Hand of the Past 112
The Heirs of Stalin 113
Fears 115

1963–1964

People Were Laughing Behind a Wall 119
"Early illusions are beautiful..." 120

The Third Memory 121

The Sigh 123

Picture of Childhood 124

Nefertiti 126

The Far Cry 128

The Hut 129

The Mail Cutter 131

Perfection 133

Wounded Bird 134

"Citizens, Listen to Me..." 136

"No, I'll not take the half..." 138

Love's Maturity? 138

And So Piaf Left Us... 139

Hand-rolled Cigarettes 141

A Ballad about Seals 142

Why Are You Doing This? 144

Ballad about Drinking 145

White Nights in Archangel 148

Ballad about Mirages 149

"We can't stand..." 150

A Very Special Soul 151

Pitching and Rolling 152

The City of Yes and the City of No 154

A Ballad about Benkendorf, Chief of Gendarmerie... 156

Sleep, My Beloved 157

Bratsk Hydroelectric Station (Selections) 160

1965–1967

"White snow is falling..." 179

Mating Flight of the Woodcock 180

A Superfluous Miracle 181

Autumn 182

"The first presentiment..." 183

Kamikaze 184

Coliseum 186

The Confessional 190

Procession with the Madonna 191

Letter to Paris 193

A Hundred Miles 195

Letter to Yesenin 197

Italian Tears 199

The Stage   204

"Poetry gives off smoke . . ."   207

Dwarf Birches   209

The Torments of Conscience   210

Old Women   212

In Memory of Akhmatova   214

"I fell out of love with you . . ."   217

The Ballad of the Big Stamp   218

"The old house . . ."   221

"The snow will begin again . . ."   223

Yelabuga Nail   224

Belly Dance   225

The Mark of Cain   228

Love in Portuguese   231

When They Murdered Lorca   232

Barcelona's Little Streets   234

Happiness Andalusian Style   235

The Revue of Old People   236

Black Banderilla   238

"I dreamed I already . . ."   240

Stolen Apples   241

An Attempt at Blasphemy   243

In a Steelworker's Home   244

My Handwriting   247

Ballad of the Running Start   248

"Hurry is the curse . . ."   250

Monologue of a Poet   252

Monologue of an Actress   254

A Ballad about Nuggets   256

New York Elegy   259

Monologue of a Blue Fox   260

The Restaurant for Two   263

Cemetery of Whales   265

Smog   267

On the Question of Freedom   271

1968–1972

Monologue of a Restorer   275

Ballad about Sausage   277

Knowing and Not-Knowing   279

"Light died in the hall . . ."   280

The Streetcar of Poetry 281
Gratitude 282
Russian Tanks in Prague 284
The Art of Flower Arranging 285
Thanks 287
Marektinsky Shoals 288
A Special Vantage Point 291
Russianness 292
The Singing Dam 294
The Grave of a Child 297
Come to My Merry Grave 298
Unrequited Love 300
The Salty Hammock 302
A Moment Half-Winter, Half-Fall 304
Keys of the Comandante 305
My Peruvian Girl 308
Satchmo 310
Son and Father 312
The Family 313
Tips of Hair 314
Pompeii 315
A Childish Scream 317
A Few Tender Days 318
Kompromise Kompromisovich 319
Vietnam Classic 321
Who Are You, Grand Canyon? 323
Wolf House 328
Two Blacks 334
Saints of Jazz 336
From Desire to Desire 337
I Would Like 342
Kazan University: A Poem (Excerpts) 346
Under the Skin of the Statue of Liberty: A Poem (Excerpts) 358

1973–1975

An Old Friend 369
The Drunken Cow 370
Love Is Always in Danger 372
Wisdom and Folly 374
A Father's Ear 375
The Face Behind the Face 376

For Your Attention 377
Epistle to Neruda 378
Wounds 380
Memento 381
Mother 382
"When I cast off for ..." 383
Lament for a Brother 384
Russia 386
Malachite Frog 386
Interconnection of Phenomena 388
Metamorphoses 389
Verbosity 390
"A drop fell ..." 391
Potato Flower 392
Hope 393
A Tear 394
The Ringing of the Earth 395
But Before ... 396
Iron Staircase 398
The Easter Procession 399
Memory's Revenge 401
To Beginners 402
Alder Catkin 403
"In moments of ..." 406
The Wild Ass's Skin 407
"Once people ..." 408
Safari in Ulster 409
Snow in Tokyo: A Japanese Poem 417

1976–1978

Good-for-nothing Places 439
Long Life 442
Woman Midget 443
Tomorrow's Wind 445
Gogol's Mistake 448
Across Eight Thousand Kilometers 450
"When the clover field stirs ..." 451
Insurance Agent 453
Don't Disappear 455
Nice People 456
Moscow-Ivanovo 457

The Unexpressed 459
Psychotherapy 462
On Modesty 463
Monologue of a Loser 464
To Charlie Chaplin 465
The Art of Ingratiating 467
"O Georgia..." 468
"No, literacy is not..." 469
Russians and Jews 469
Ivan the Terrible and Ivan the Fool: A Poem (Excerpt) 470
A Dove in Santiago: A Novella in Verse 477

1979–1985

"Moscow believed..." 521
Designers of Spiderwebs 522
Directness 522
Two Pair of Skis 523
Back Then 525
Maternity Floor 529
On What Is Life Spent? 531
Final Faith 534
Momma and the Neutron Bomb: A Poem (Excerpt) 535
Guardian of the Hearth 539
Flowers for Grandmother 541
"A small dish..." 543
Afghanistan Ant 545
My Universities 545
Violets 548
Meditations at the Back Door 550
Murder 552
You Still Haven't Returned 553
"What right..." 555
Eight-year-old Poet 555
Being Late 557
Trumpet 559
Disbelief in Yourself Is Indispensable 561
To Incomprehensible Poets 563
Comradesbutwhatifers 564
A Half Blade of Grass 568
A Distant Relative, or Désespoir: A Poem 569
Fuku: A Poem (Excerpts) 575

1986–1990

"We should be stingier…" 597

Antedeluvian 598

Zoya Osipova 600

Siberian Wooing 602

Aldan Girl 604

Farewell 606

Fireflies 608

Requiem for *Challenger* 610

The Last Attempt 611

Stalin's Funeral 612

The Peak of Shame 613

Russian Koalas 615

The Accidentless Captain 618

Monuments Still Not Built 619

Personal Letter from the Generalissimo 621

Provideniia Bay 623

We Can't Go On 625

Vendée 626

The Apple Trees of Drobitskii 627

A Striking Heart 631

Half Measures 633

Russian Writers and Historical Figures Frequently Referred to in the Poems
635

Rivers and Geographic Names Frequently Referred to in the Poems
637

Previous Translation Sources 639

Bibliographic Data 641

About the Editors 661

· · · *This symbol is used to indicate a space between stanzas of a poem wherever such spaces are lost in pagination.*

⚬——ᵥ *This symbol is used to indicate missing portions of a poem in excerpts.*

INTRODUCTION

Yevgeny Aleksandrovich Yevtushenko was blessed and permanently marked by family and childhood. He was born deep in the vast hinterland of Siberia just outside the small Trans-Siberian railroad town of Zima (which means "winter" in Russian, from the Buriat word for "prisoner") Junction, not far from Lake Baikal, whose enormous canyon was filled with icy, crystalline water. The birth was registered in Zima, July 18, 1933. His mother was and is a warm and generous socialist-humanist worker, who, until recently, sold newspapers from a Moscow kiosk; his father a geologist who wrote verse and recited poems to his son from memory. If his son didn't understand something it was explained through the beauty of rhythm and the power of imagery. In this way he learned not only Pushkin and Lermontov but contemporary giants, including Pasternak and Akhmatova, and foreign poets, especially Burns and Kipling.

The family moved to Moscow when he was a child, but Yevtushenko—Zhenia, as he is still called—was evacuated from Moscow back to Siberia and put in the care of his grandmother in Zima Junction during World War II. Having spent his most crucial childhood years there, he considers it to be his native land and spiritual birthplace.

Siberia—few things are so fundamental to Yevtushenko's vision and sensibility. It runs openly through countless pages of his verse. Zima is not only a railroad junction, it is located on the Oka River, which merges with the mighty Angara that alone flows out of Lake Baikal.

Clearly, the physical world plays a major role in shaping an artist's work. The rivers of Russia, for example, are a geographic specific to Yevtushenko and also vital to the development of Russian history and culture. Uniting the immense land mass by providing the easiest transport over Russia's great distances, the country's magnificent rivers are a cruel irony of nature. In European Russia they flow into land-locked seas, the access from which (to the world's oceans) is blocked by other nations. The formidable rivers of Siberia, like those in the north of European Russia, flow into the frozen Arctic Ocean. Hence this vast land empire united by rivers is at the same time marooned. Stemming from childhood experiences in Zima, Yevtushenko's lifelong passion for the rivers, recorded in a large number of poems, is a devotion that turns inevitably to tragedy as Russian history unfolds. Rivers, used and abused, are seen as sources of thwarted power and wealth, and finally as roads to brutal enslavement, escape from which can lead only to arctic wilderness.

From Yevtushenko's own testimony in his *Precocious Autobiography* and the internal evidence of his poetry (as well as his new film, in production as these lines are being written) we can see the impact of Stalin's funeral on his life's work. He viewed firsthand the chaos that trampled some 150 people to death in the crowd on Trubnaia Square in 1953 on their way to view Stalin's body.

When trucks barred the crowd's escape, the police officer in charge explained, "I have no instructions." Though previously as blind as the next man to Stalin's crimes, it was the funeral of Stalin that caused young Yevtushenko to begin to recognize the monstrous lie the nation had been living. Even in death the dictator caused the deaths of innocent people. "For *he* is the one who taught us to walk over people." In time Yevtushenko would understand this more fully by acknowledging that "Stalin's greatest crime was not the arrests and the shootings he ordered. His greatest crime was the corruption of the human spirit." To deal with this legacy became Yevtushenko's overriding creative motivation. It would be difficult to find anywhere a more consistent creative life. In America a young man so driven would have found a career as a preacher or, perhaps, in politics. In Russia poetry was the more natural and fortunate outlet for the talents of a new generation of fiery idealists (Yevtushenko, Akhmadulina, Voznesensky, Brodsky, Rozhdestvensky, and the slightly older Okudzhava), which found opportunity in the chaos and confusion of the post-Stalin years. They found ready audiences in schools, factories, and most of all, on street corners. By no apparent decision of authority, but rather by a default of political power as the nation caught its breath after the tyrant's departure, uncensored young voices spoke to crowds that grew quickly into hundreds, then thousands and tens of thousands in city squares and sports stadiums. Electrifying, audacious voices of youth touched strings of conscience and hope by speaking verse of simple truth, often about the most ordinary things, and with increasing boldness about things so long unspoken they seemed like new discoveries and moral revelations of great wisdom.

The cunning of the state was not to boost the importance of what undoubtedly was bewildering to all by open opposition and repression. Rather it sought to defuse the danger by absorbing it and giving it sanction. Yevtushenko's poems, "Babii Yar" and "The Heirs of Stalin," for example, would be published, uncensored, perhaps because they were useful in enhancing Khrushchev's anti-Stalin strategy. They were published as written only once. Khrushchev's brief bloom would be replaced by the gray, tedious times of Brezhnev, which Yevtushenko aptly characterized in a poem dedicated to Robert Kennedy:

> You ought to tremble with a ghastly shudder
>
>   at a cozy dinner—
> for the brown horror
>   is shoving its way behind the grayness.

The new cunning of honest writers was to evade the restraints of censorship by Aesopian language, by double meanings which the skilled Russian reader could extract between lines, by substituting the names of other lands when the Soviet Union was the real subject, by samizdat editions, or, when all else failed, by publishing abroad. To publish abroad anonymously offered the writer complete freedom to say whatever one wanted. The more critical a work was of the Soviet Union the greater its celebration in the foreign press, but the less likely it would be known at home. At the time of their arrest and trial the pseudonyms of Abram Tertz and Nikolai Arzhak for Andrei Sinyavsky and Yurii Daniel were almost totally unknown in the USSR while their writings were known on major university campuses in the West. The state's attempt to make an example of them by a show trial backfired: the intelligentsia's indignation at the harsh injustice meted out united an opposition that forged the modern dissident movement in the Soviet Union. To evade the censor by emigration has been an age-old temptation for writers who have been denied free expression in their native language. Yet, as Bruce Chatwin said of Václav Havel, "we learn that the true heroes of our time are those who stay the course." Yevtushenko expresses it:

> Save yourself, poet,
> > eternally wounded bird,
> equally from the butcher's caresses and tortures.
> The interminable dilemma!
> To go to Liubianka was terrifying,
> > to be free—shameful.

Freedom by emigration—yes, but only with the painful and disabling loss of language and country. Poets have had a distinct advantage over other artists through readings of material unpublished and therefore uncensored, which could become known to multitudes, thanks to the prodigious Russian memory for lines of verse. Of course this technique had to be exercised with great caution. For example, even though "Babii Yar" was not to be reprinted it was read to appreciative audiences, as was "Dwarf Birches," which had been printed only once in an obscure Siberian journal; other poems such as "Russian Tanks in Prague" could be read only to intimate, trusted friends.

Life along the Trans-Siberian railroad implicitly reminds Russians of life elsewhere. It is as if the land-locked rivers of Siberia were seeking ways out of nature's imprisonment. Yevtushenko's Zima Junction told him to:

> Hang on, watch closely, listen carefully,
> and explore, explore.
> > Travel the whole world over.

Because of the international acclaim for "Babii Yar" and "The Heirs of Stalin" Yevtushenko was invited to travel the entire world. Cycles of poems about the United States, Latin America, Europe, and Asia, alive with the double meanings dear to the astute Russian reader, followed his travels. The real cunning of history, however, was to be the impact on the early audience of the fresh air of truth and the hopes for national renewal expounded by the young generation of poets soon after Stalin's death. It would be impossible not to consider it among the formative influences for the poets who have now come to maturity in the Soviet Union. No two themes are so consistently present in Yevtushenko's work from the beginning as the call to a restructuring of self and society and the indispensability of free expression.

Confession, grappling with self-understanding, is the impetus behind most of the poems that are mistakenly understood to be merely social or political. His sharpest attacks on moral cowardice begin with a struggle within his own conscience. Though a proud man he is most distinguished by a capacity to feel shame for himself, for his own failures and insensitivities even before he exposes them in the deeds of others. That there is a way out, a reason to hope for a better world is present in much of his verse, often in the awkward prophetic motif of messianic expectations harbored by the universal boy (or girl) who will rise up.

> They're zealously concerned for everything,
> and live with their doubts in the open,
> as stepsons they won't keep silent
> when real sons would.
>
> . . .
>
> I can't forget there is somewhere a boy
> who will achieve far more
> than I.
>
> . . .
>
> The Russian paradise
> brims with tears.
> but a boy will come—
> he will appear again—
> and with justice he will say
> "Arise..."

Yevtushenko's emotions respond swiftly, spontaneously, and authentically to experience, particularly to the discovery of specific instances of evil and injustice. "Babii Yar" is a case in point. The poem's history characterizes much of Yevtushenko's poetic life. When shown the unmarked site of that terrible atrocity against Jewish citizens in the suburbs of Kiev by Anatoli Kuznetsov, who as a boy had witnessed the massacre and would later record it in his own book, Yevtushenko immediately composed his poem. After reading it to an old friend and sometime mentor, Aleksandr Mezhirov, he was advised not to read it publicly or try to publish it as it would be misunderstood and resented by Jew and anti-Semite alike. Characteristically, following his own instincts for what is right, he read it to a stunned public audience, which according to eyewitnesses exploded with approval. Coincident with Khrushchev's political strategy of unmasking Stalin, whose last political act was the infamous "Jewish doctor's plot," the poem was approved for one-time publication in *Literaturnaia gazeta*. It was impossible to reprint it in the numerous collections of Yevtushenko's poetry that followed until his three-volume collected works in Russian were assembled in 1983, and then only with the editorial inclusion of a footnote explaining that not only Jews but others had perished in the Nazi slaughter outside Kiev. The poem has been marked by the bizarre phantoms and paradoxes that haunt Russian literature. Kuznetsov was to launch his own career as a writer with his historical account of the event and then persuaded the KGB of his ability to report alleged subversive activity by Yevtushenko in order to gain permission to travel abroad to defect and once there declare his allegation false. Ukraine, where Babii Yar is located, refused to invite Yevtushenko to read anywhere on its territory until *perestroika*. Some Ukrainian emigrants to the West, the offspring of collaborators with fascism, have been vociferous and ugly in their several attempts to interrupt Yevtushenko's poetry readings in the United States. Once, during a reading in Minneapolis, six hulking youths rushed onstage, physically throwing him from the podium and assaulting him with kicks and fists. Yet the Ukrainian city of Kharkov would, in 1988, elect him their National Deputy. Sympathetic admirers in Israel attempted to invite him to Israel but were prevented from doing so by the Israeli Communist Party— until 1988.

Dmitri Shostakovich composed his Thirteenth Symphony on the lines of "Babii Yar" and three other Yevtushenko poems. The premiere on December 18, 1962, was greeted by thunderous applause. Such enthusiasm was viewed with apprehension by the Kremlin, where a strident ideological meeting had taken place the day before. The second performance was to be canceled unless "Babii Yar" was altered. Four lines of text were changed at the beginning and words were substituted in the final four lines to celebrate Russia's victory over fascism in World War II. Poet and composer were jointly compelled *on this occasion* to agree to the changes. Nevertheless, it gave rise to a rumor that Yevtushenko himself had written and was reciting a different version of "Babii Yar" in the Soviet Union than elsewhere. Some Russians living in the United States would fall victim to this disinformation and themselves contribute to the lie by writing a letter to *The New York Times* avowing that a compromised version of "Babii Yar" was published in *Literaturnaia gazeta*, a statement they should have recognized as false. Further, the memoirs of one musician (recorded in conversations some years later) falsely reported a meeting with Shostakovich at which a new version of "Babii Yar," "double in size," was produced and later published in *Literaturnaia gazeta*. This was a complete fabrication. The version with the eight altered lines was printed only once with the score of the symphony. Only one version of the poem—the original, authentic version— has ever been published or read by Yevtushenko *anywhere*. We have searched *Literaturnaia gazeta* and the Russian *Chronicle of Newspaper Articles* for some source to this story. The ability to manipulate or let others manipulate our memory seems the only explanation unless we assume someone printed a fake single copy of *Literaturnaia gazeta* to deceive the musicians and others and to induce their political cooperation.

The house of Russian literature has often been strangely divided against itself. The traditional destructive divisions between individual writers have been brought to a painful extreme in the conflicts between émigré, dissident, and writers legally published in the USSR. The healing of literature is indispensable to the healing of the nation. One of the tragic consequences of the Stalin legacy is that its central principle of rule is still alive—the principle that horizontal connections between people must be destroyed, that all bonds, all trust, all obligations must be vertical—upward toward the leader, the state, the party. The quarrels, the bruised egos that are so pained, the mean-spirited resentments, the petty feuds that keep Russians divided from each other, often fueled by KGB disinformation, have unfortunately kept alive the legacy of Stalin. Occasionally the foreign press, especially in this country, has been duped in the process.

Yevtushenko's greatest weakness as a poet is his swift response to life, which seems to compel him to write about almost everything he experiences. Because the seduction of the next experience is always anticipated, there is little time to reflect and rework his inspiration to the highest level of refinement. Yevgeny Vinokurov, a poet and friend, has written of this:

> Characteristic of him as a poet is an elevated, ten-times-multiplied sense of daily life, of existence. He is a poet of life, I would say, a poet of Her Royal Majesty Life. He sees the world in detail, protruding sharply in stereoscope, palpably concrete; with his nerve endings he experiences the physicality of the world. He writes of himself: "A hungered insatiability reared me, a craving thirst nursed me."

The raw edge of the blade of experience and the rough texture of life itself are honestly reflected and preserved in his unpolished and uninhibited directness. He is a prodigious worker whose activity a young scholar (assisting him with research for his *Anthology of Russian Poetry*, published regularly in *Ogoniok*) characterized as "exhausting and unbelievable." Yevtushenko has published forty-six collections of poetry (including two slightly different three-volume collected works) in Russian in editions of 100,000 and continues to reach new heights of popularity (the true size of at least one edition was concealed by more than half its number to avoid complaints from other writers). In addition there are novels, short stories, essays, screenplays (two of which became movies he directed himself); symphonic pieces and dozens of popular songs have been written to his verse.

Despite the celebrated political and social significance of his writing, his most central themes are lyrical, confessional explorations of the definition of self and what it is to be a poet. It is a commonplace, and misleading, simplification to say that a poet's only true biography is his poetry. Yet ultimately Yevtushenko will be judged as a poet, a popular people's poet in the tradition of Walt Whitman. Yevtushenko's rediscovery of folk rhymes and his deliberate use of rich conversational language, in vocabulary and intonation, make his verse immediately comprehensible to readers and, as with a haunting melody, often difficult to forget. Music was part of his earliest childhood experiences. When only a boy he rode the Trans-Siberian railroad to earn kopecks, entertaining wartime passengers by singing and dancing.

A lover of narrative art, Yevtushenko tends to tell stories in his poems with plots drawn from life. Yet a natural parallel feeling for aphorism combines with his broad use of folk language to make his poetry sparkle with what appear to be authentic folk sayings and proverbs that are often in reality his own creation.

The poem "Russia," first published without any title, gains its harsh significance only when the title is added and we can appreciate its view of his nation's liabilities. His first poem about America, "American Nightingale," sounds the theme of brotherhood and the need for understanding among nations and people, which has become a *leitmotiv* in much of his verse. His relationship to American immigrants involves a spiritual kinship, which was manifest twenty-two years ago. At the studio of Ben Shahn when the poet was enroute to a reading at Princeton University, Shahn apologized for being unable to attend and asked if Zhenia would read a poem for him. Even in an inadequate, simultaneous translation, "A Hundred Miles" produced a profound response: Shahn went immediately to his studio to bring forth his latest drawing of a bent, lonely man in a field, which he had titled "A Hundred Kilometers from the City of Our Hopes." With excitement he explained that the idea of his drawing was fully developed in Yevtushenko's poem, whose first line reads "A hundred miles from the capital of all hopes."

Because Yevtushenko chose to stay the course: to live and write in Soviet Russia despite the constraints that accompany unfreedom, he has been criticized in the West—mostly by émigré writers cut off from their native land and language. The suggestion implicit in their criticism is that Yevtushenko has not served the cause of free expression. The facts are otherwise, and a brief summary follows to indicate a few of the poet's extraliterary entanglements, many of which inform the poems in this collection.

· Before the appearance on the political stage of either Solzhenitsyn or Sakharov and beginning in 1954, his was the first voice against the twin evils of Stalinism and anti-Semitism.
· In 1957 he was expelled from the Literary Institute because he publicly defended *Not by Bread Alone*, the novel by Vladimir Dudintsev that first dared to criticize the Soviet bureaucratic system.

- In 1962 in a public meeting of writers and artists with Khrushchev, he spoke vigorously in defense of artistic freedom in painting and sculpture, reminding Khrushchev that the police power of the state could no longer be employed to force socialist realist art on the people.
- In 1966 he joined and encouraged other writers in letters of protest against the trial of Sinyavsky and Daniel.
- Over the years he has jeopardized himself by seeking the release of imprisoned writers, including Anatoli Marchenko (the first to write about post-Stalin camps and the last dissident to die in prison in December of 1986). Lev Timofeev, Felix Svetov, Natalia Gorbanevskaya, Irina Ratushinskaya, and Joseph Brodsky.
- On seven separate occasions he intervened with the government in defense of Solzhenitsyn's right to express his views of Russian history and religion.
- When Solzhenitsyn was arrested in 1971 Yevtushenko called the head of the KGB, Yurii Andropov, to declare: "I will die on the barricades if Solzhenitsyn is imprisoned again." In a telegram he sent a similar message to Brezhnev.
- On the fateful day of August 23, 1968, he sent a telegram to Brezhnev protesting the invasion of Czechoslovakia. His poem of protest was circulated secretly.
- "Afghanistan Ant," a poem condemning the Soviet invasion and war, was widely circulated.
- Yevtushenko is one of the founders and vice presidents (Sakharov was the president) of the anti-Stalin "Memorial Society" dedicated to building a memorial to the victims of Stalinism.
- As a National Deputy from Kharkov during the first Congress of Deputies he declared in a speech his opposition to the Communist Party's monopoly of power.
- As a vice president of the newly founded PEN Center in Moscow he wrote the declaration supporting the independence of Lithuania that was adopted by twenty-five PEN centers worldwide.
- Upon receiving the State Prize for Literature in 1984, he wrote his declaration against censorship in any form.
- Based on his various speeches at the Writers' Union congresses, he has been characterized as an enemy of the party and writers protected by the state.

Yevtushenko has always been clear in his own thinking that the real struggle is against a deeply rooted spiritual failure, which might be diagnosed best by philosophers or religious thinkers. As Boris Shragin, a recent emigrant from Moscow, writes:

> ... the evil lies not in the prevailing ideology or the political system, but in the national tradition in which all participate to some degree. If a national renewal is conceivable at all, it must begin with a spiritual change, an alteration in the attitude toward life of individuals, not of the masses.

Poetry has selected Yevtushenko as surely as he has selected it: "A choice," he explained, "that has no mercy, but is surely redemption."

The selections in this book are Yevtushenko's own. For years he was urged to prepare a list of suggestions for the contents of an English collection of his poetry that would survey fairly his long career. This became a particularly appropriate undertaking, and perhaps one that could be handled with more care and perspective, after the Russian publication of his collected works in three volumes in 1983–84 and in a different three volumes in 1987. His selection has been carefully examined and amended, mostly by reduction, to provide a representative selection of the full range of his poetic work: long *poemy*; intimate lyrics; biographical, love, pastoral, elegiac, and didactic verse; and the celebrated poems of political and social protest. It includes many of his poems about America, both because of their intrinsic interest for the American reader and because, when read between the lines, they are often also about Russia. Yevtushenko's work has been widely translated into English and published in a variety of collections in England, the United States, and Australia. Some poems exist in two or three translations and it has often been difficult to choose among them. The editors are responsible for the final choices. All existing translations have been rigorously examined and revised where appropriate. A substantial body of older poems not previously available in English have been translated.

—Albert C. Todd

A NOTE ON THE TRANSLATION

A waggish poet and translator once remarked that the only thing lost in translation is the money. Others, more sober-sided, have suggested it's the poetry itself that is lost.

The poets, translators, and editors who have contributed to this ambitious volume recognize that poetic translations are, at best, adaptations or imitations of the originals. Because Russian and English (unlike French) are stressed languages, some of the power of the original verse survives here; but as Russian words rhyme more easily and the language does not employ articles, Yevtushenko's Russian poems are more compact and muscular than their English interpretations. William Jay Smith has said that Russian poems occasionally burst into English bloom "like Japanese paper flowers put into water—and frequently with the same monstrous results." Because many world-class poets—their names appear on p. iii—intervened in these English imitations, we believe that the more garish blossoms have been pruned. For this Yevtushenko expresses special thanks to each of them, and to the editors and early readers—especially Nina Bouis and Tess Gallagher—who have made a good many of his poems freer than they have ever been in any translation.

The poems are arranged in chronological order according to the date of writing (exceptions to this rule are made in the case of long poems, which appear at the end of each part), which at times, because of pre-*glasnost* censorship, precedes the date of first Russian publication by many years. Each date is noted, along with translation credit and, where necessary, information on historical figures, rivers, and place names. These annotations have been provided by Albert C. Todd, the book's chief translator, with information supplied by Yu. S. Nekhotoshov and Masha Yevtushenko.

From Pushkin through Mandelstam and Pasternak, Tsvetaeva, Mayakovsky, and Akhmatova, to Yevtushenko himself, it would appear that Russian poetry, especially spoken verse, cannot be repressed, even in the darkest of times. It is fitting that this volume—the collected work by the world's best-known living Russian poet—appears approximately one year after the Eastern European revolutions of 1989 and thirty-one years after unauthorized public readings in a Moscow sports stadium by three courageous young artists named Yevtushenko, Akhmadulina, and Voznesensky thrilled fourteen thousand Soviet citizens, their thunderous applause a clear signal that poetry is indeed the language of people who crave freedom.

—John Macrae III

To defecate life of its misery and its evil was the ruling passion of his soul; he dedicated to it every power of his mind, every pulsation of his heart. He looked on political freedom as the direct agent to effect the happiness of mankind; and thus any new-sprung hope of liberty inspired a joy and an exultation more intense and wild than he could have felt for personal advantage. Those who have never experienced the workings of passion on general and unselfish subjects cannot understand this; and it must be difficult of comprehension to the younger generation rising around, since they cannot remember the scorn and hatred with which the artisans of reform were regarded some few years ago, nor the persecutions to which they were exposed.

—Preface by Mrs. Shelley
to Second Collected Edition
of *Poetical Works of Percy Bysshe Shelley,* 1839

1952⁄1955

People are really talking now.

Lies

Lying to the young is wrong.
Proving to them that lies are true is wrong.
Telling them
              that God's in his heaven
and all's well with the world
                            is wrong.
They know what you mean.
                        They are people too.
Tell them the difficulties
                    can't be counted,
and let them see
              not only
                      what will be
but see
      with clarity
                  these present times.
Say obstacles exist they must encounter,
sorrow comes,
              hardship happens.
The hell with it.
              Who never knew
the price of happiness
                    will not be happy.
Forgive no error
              you recognize,
it will repeat itself,
                    a hundredfold
and afterward
              our pupils
will not forgive in us
                    what we forgave.

1952

*TRANSLATED BY ROBIN MILNER-GULLAND AND PETER
LEVI (REVISED)*

Train Car

A train car, which had seen the world,
stood on a slope of cinders,
grass up to the buffers,
its wheels grown into the enbankment.
It had become a house where people lived.
Though for a time unfamiliar,
they warmed up to it, fixing up a stove
in order to be warmer,
adding wallpaper,
then geraniums in the window.
They put in chests of drawers
and thumbtacked to the wall
postcard pictures of a breaking surf.
They wanted appearances
so that in geraniums and wallpaper
it might not remember it was a train car.
But memory being implacable,
the car would not sleep
when in flames, whistles, and clumps of smoke
trains
     flew
        by.

Their breathing touched it.
And the trains on their route
whistled as though
they might lure it along.
No matter the strength expended,
it could not budge its wheels.
The ground had grabbed them,
and goosefoot had locked them in.
But there had been days when through thickets,
wind, songs, and flames
it had flown off in search of happiness,
shaking wattle fences with its voice.
Now it will dash off nowhere.
Now it will not go from this place.

. . .

Immobility is retribution
for youthful flight.

1952

TRANSLATED BY ALBERT C. TODD AND JAMES RAGAN

The Depth

To V. Sokolov

The bellow of a steamer in the morning
woke the coniferous distances,
and we stood on deck,
spellbound by the Angara,
gazing straight to the river floor,
where the painted rocks gleamed
through a bright green dimension.
We could not trust our eyes.
It seemed at times in our passage
that we could reach over the side
and with our fingertips touch bottom;
for depth could not be gauged
in that transparency of water.
Of course I know that danger lurks
in the placidity of the wave,
and that the clearest purling stream
may be the shallowest.
But deepness isn't all.
I wouldn't give a tinker's damn
for a stupid stagnant pond
where the eye sees nothing plain.
Let me be like the flow of a river
obliquely struck by sunset glow,
as deep and measureless,
with each
        small pebble
               shining through!

1952

TRANSLATED BY STANLEY KUNITZ WITH ANTHONY KAHN
(REVISED)

You Are Great in Love

You are great in love.
                    You are bold.
My every step is timid.
I'll do nothing bad to you,
but can hardly do you any good.
It seems you are
                    leading me
off the beaten path through a forest.
Now we're up to our waist in wildflowers.
I don't even know
                    what flowers they are.
Past experience is of no help here.
I don't know
                    what to do or how.
You're tired.
                    You ask to be carried in my arms.
Already you're in my arms.
"Do you see
                    how blue the sky is?
Do you hear
                    what birds are in the forest?
Well, what are you waiting for?
                                    Well?
                                    Carry me then!"
And where shall I carry you? ...

1953
TRANSLATED BY ALBERT C. TODD

The Third Snow

To S. Shchipachev

We watched through the window how the lime trees
darkened in the back of the yard.

6

We sighed; again it hadn't snowed,
and it was really high time.

And then the snow started toward evening.
Abandoning altitude
it flew where the wind blew it
and wavered with doubt in the air.

Multilayered and fragile,
it was itself embarrassed and confused.
Tenderly we took it in our hands
and wondered: "Where did it go?"

It reassured us: "There will be
a real snowfall here for you.
Don't worry—I'll melt,
don't be upset—I'm on my way . . ."

A new snow came in a week.
Not a snowfall—a deluge,
pounding our eyes like a blizzard,
reeling clamorously at full power.

In its stubborn intransigence
it wanted to win a victory,
so everyone agreed it was good
only for a day or two.

But itself reckoning it was that kind,
it didn't stand its ground and gave up,
and if it didn't melt in your hands
it began to thaw underfoot.

And all the more often with alarm
we stared again at the horizon:
"When will there be the real one?
After all it has to come."

And somehow rising sleepily in the morning,
still knowing nothing,
in astonishment we suddenly stepped
into it through the opened door.

. . .

It lay before us deep and pure
with all its soft simplicity.
It was modestly fluffy
and assuredly deep.

It lay on the ground and on the roofs,
stunning everyone with its whiteness,
and was truly magnificent,
and was truly beautiful.

It snowed on in the morning din,
to the drone of cars and horses' snorts,
and didn't melt underfoot,
but only became more compact.

It lay all fresh and shining,
and the city was blinded by it.
It was the one. The real one.
The snow we'd waited for had come.

1953
TRANSLATED BY ALBERT C. TODD

"I wander..."

I wander in the crazy bustling capital
above the sprightly April river,
subversively illogical,
inexcusably young.

I take tramcars by storm,
enthusiastically tell someone lies,
and running after myself
never do catch up.

· · ·

I'm startled by big-flanked barges,
by passing planes, by my own poems...
They have endowed me with wealth
without saying what to do with it.

1954

TRANSLATED BY ALBERT C. TODD

"In every instance..."

In every instance some boy turns up,
one of those to whom fate did not give talent,
and the thing they worship
nags sharply back at them like a stepmother.

They feel it sharply, struggling
year after year for their rights,
but, as before, their words
have young, treacherously pink cheeks.

They're zealously concerned for everything,
and live with their doubts in the open,
as stepsons they won't keep silent
when real sons would.

Alien to them are the lovers of quiet,
those who would flee from themselves.
They feel with all their skin what's needed
but don't know how to help.

When the lack of talent struggles
clumsily to fight for the truth,
ruining its own cause by lack of talent—
at such times I am ashamed of talent.

1954

TRANSLATED BY ALBERT C. TODD

Boots

To K. Vanshenkin

Our railway car was like a gypsy camp.
Raucous shouting everywhere.
The left platform stuffed with hay,
sailors sleeping like gods.
"Marusya," someone bellowed softly.
A red-haired cat gulped cabbage soup.
A somber fellow was being taught
never to cheat at cards.
Hamming it up wasn't new to me
and I became famous in those circles
thanks to my tall American boots.
One
    after another
                took me by the elbow,
asking me to sell them,
              but I
only let them pat them,
and tap them on the soles.
But below me,
            on the way to some Yetkul,
a boy my age
with a thick head of hair,
                  was traveling
barefoot, in enormous riding breeches.
And so what,
        if I have boots,
and he is barefoot,
           well, so what! —
but for some reason I tried
to look at him less often . . .
I don't remember
          in just what place
our train stopped for five minutes.
The whole car was excited by the news:
"Brothers,
        they are giving out something!"
Half asleep, dimly cursing everything,

I wanted to put on my boots,
but someone screamed, running by:
"You're going to be late!

                    Get a move on!"
I ran off,

        but in the frightening din
by the station stall,
in the distance,

           and with my boots,
I caught sight of that boy.
Took off in a storm after the thief.
I was righteous in mighty anger.
I jumped from one car buffer to another,
tearing my pants on something.
Chased after him with all my strength.
I pinned him to a train car
where giving back my boots in silence,
he suddenly burst out crying and ran away.
And I

      in a kind of shock
stared and stared through the slanting rain,
as he ran

          over the raw ground
of autumn,

         crying,

           barefoot . . .
Then the imposing, portfolio-carrying,
chief old resident of the car
offered me half a glass
of Novosibirsk port wine.
Girls patched my pants
assuring me that it was not serious,
and out the window

              power lines
flew up

      and then dove down.

1954

TRANSLATED BY ALBERT C. TODD

Weddings

To A. Mezhirov

Weddings in days of war,
false cheating comfort,
those hollow phrases:
"He won't get killed..."
On a snowbound winter road,
slashed by a cruel wind,
I speed to a hasty wedding
in a neighboring village.
Gingerly I enter
                    a buzzing cottage,
I, a folk dancer of repute,
with a forelock dangling
from my forehead.
All spruced up,
                    disturbed,
among relatives
                    and friends
the bridegroom sits, just mobilized,
distraught.
Sits
    with Vera—his bride—
but in a day or two
he'll pull on a gray soldier's coat
and, wearing it, leave for the front.
Then with a rifle he will go,
tramping over alien
                        soil;
a German bullet, perhaps,
will lay him low...
A glass of foaming home brew
he's not able yet to drink.
Their first night together
will likely be their last.
Chagrined, the bridegoom stares,
and with all his soul in anguish
cries to me across the table:

"Well, go on, why don't you dance!"
They all forget their drinking,
all fix me with goggling eyes,
and I slide and writhe,
beating a rhythm with my hooves.
Now I drum a tattoo,
                    now drag my toes
across the floor.
Whistling shrilly,
            I clap my hands,
leap up near the ceiling.
Slogans on the wall fly past,
"Hitler will be kaput!"
But the bride
            scalds
her face
        with tears.
I'm already a wet rag,
barely catch my breath . . .
"Dance!"—
            they shout in desperation,
and I dance again . . .
Back home, my ankles
feel as stiff as wood;
but from yet another wedding
                    drunken guests
come knocking at the door once more.
Soon as mother lets me go,
I'm off to weddings once again,
and round the tablecloth anew
I stamp my feet and bend my knees.
The bride sheds bitter tears,
friends are tearful too.
I'm afraid for everyone.
                    I've no desire to dance,
but you can't
        not dance.

1955

TRANSLATED BY GEORGE REAVEY (REVISED)

"The window looks out onto..."

To L. Martynov

The window looks out onto the white trees.
The schoolmaster looks out at the trees,
For a long, long time he looks at the trees,
breaking chalk slowly in one hand.
It's only—
        the rules of long division.
And he's forgotten them—
            the rules of long division.
Imagine—
       not remembering—
             long division!
A mistake!
      Yes!
         A mistake on the blackboard!
We all sit today in a different way,
and listen and watch with a different attention,
yes and it could not today be any different,
and we need no prompting about it.
The schoolmaster's wife has left him.
We know not
       where she has gone,
we do not know
       why she has gone,
what we know is his wife has gone away.
In a suit neither new nor in fashion,
as always, neither new nor in fashion,
yes, as always, neither new nor in fashion,
the schoolmaster goes downstairs to the cloakroom.
He fumbles long in his pocket for a check:
"Well, what's wrong?
         Where is the check?
Perhaps
    I never picked up my check?
Where did it go?"
       He rubs his forehead.
"Oh, here it is!...
      It's obvious,
        I'm getting old."

Don't argue, Auntie Masha,
                    I'm getting old.
You can't do much
                    about getting old."
We hear the door below
                    creaking behind him.
The window looks out onto the white trees
onto the tall wonderful trees,
but now we are looking not at the trees,
we look in silence at the schoolmaster.
He leaves,
            back bent,
                        clumsy,
somehow helplessly clumsy.
I ought to have said—
                    wearily clumsy,
beneath the snow falling softly in the silence.
And like the trees,
                he becomes
                            white.
Yes,
        like the trees,
                    perfectly white.
A little more—
                and he will be so white
that among the trees
                    he won't be seen.

1955

TRANSLATED BY ALBERT C. TODD

Last Side Street

Really, it's Last Side Street,
in whose house, with stench like a tavern,
I act the smart aleck in front of a fool
and become more the fool.

                . . .

Why be a poet—just to embrace
a philistine on a big soapbox?
And comic, like a bast shoe in fashionable slippers,
I've fallen into the clutches of Mother Moscow.

Here in a room of wine goblets and cheval glass,
poetry is not saved by the lure of the bed.
Last Side Street. House number thirteen.
There is nowhere else to go.

1955–1975
TRANSLATED BY ALBERT C. TODD

On a Bicycle

At dawn I wake
my two-wheel friend.
Mother shouts from bed:
"Mind you don't clatter on the stairs!"
I walk him down;
he springs from step to step.
If you pat his tires flat-handed—
he'll bounce your hand.
I mount with a careless air—
as light a landing as you'll encounter!
Out of the gates I ride
to meet the Sunday world,
rolling along asphalt,
gladly pressing down the pedals,
speeding fearlessly,
I ring,
     ring,
         ring . . .
Clear of Moscow I frighten
a one-eyed cock with a broken tail,
give a tow-haired boy a spare valve,
drink brown kvass.*

In the town of Kuntsevo in a cloud of dust
I lean my back against
the sun-warmed kvass tank.
The girl who's serving gives me
a handful of damp change,
won't say her name.
"You're the sly ones, all you boys."
I smile. "So long!"
Riding to the cottage of a friend,
again I gather speed
and swish on down the road.
My friend's unhappy
whittling a big stick
in the shining grass
     beside his garage.
"They've stolen the balls!" he says,
       "Infuriating!"
and scolds his housekeeper:
"My caretaker too . . .
     She's a fine one!"
Best to be silent.
I have a look at his broad, strong shoulders.
Even when talking to me
he's always thinking about something.
He finds it hard.
The war was easier.
Life goes on.
Youth ended when the war ended.
He says:
"There's the shower.
    Here, take this,
       dry yourself."
We wander through a grove of forest
cursing films and poems.
Then at lunch
on the cool, silent terrace
sitting with my friend and my friend's wife,
I drink the long taste of the dry wine.
Soon I say:
"So long, Galia and Misha."
He comes out the gate,
his wife leaning on his shoulder.
For some reason I believe:

He can do it,

        he'll write . . .

Well, if he can't,

I don't want to know about it.

I tear along!

I'm incapable of breaking

with the cheerfulness that's inherent.

I overtake trucks on the road

in a single swoop,

fly behind them

in the cut-open space,

hanging on to them

going up steep hills.

I know myself

        it's dangerous!

I love the risk!

Hooting nervously,

they tell me:

"We'll give you a hand on the hills,

give you some speed, after that

you race on your own."

I race as fast as I can

pelting cockily a flurry of jokes.

Just don't you look

at how crazily I speed—

it's the fashion.

I know

      I ride badly,

someday I'll learn how to ride.

I spring down at a deserted

ancient lodge

        by the roadside,

break off a cluster of bird cherry

                 in the ringing forest,

and, twining it with ivy onto the handlebars,

I fly on,

       parting the bouquet with my face.

I return to Moscow,

not quite worn out,

switch on the table lamp,

switch off the overhead light.

I put my bird cherry into water,

set the alarm for eight o'clock,

sit at the table,
            and write
                    these lines.

1955

TRANSLATED BY ALBERT C. TODD

*kvass: Sour drink made of rye bread or flour with malt.

Envy

I envy.
        This secret
I have not revealed before.
I know
        there is somewhere a boy
whom I greatly envy.
I envy
        the way he fights;
I myself was never so guileless and bold.
I envy
        the way he laughs—
as a boy I could never laugh like that.
He always walks about with bumps and bruises;
I've always been better combed,
                                intact.
He will not miss
                all those passages in books
I've missed.
            Here he is stronger too.
He will be more blunt and harshly honest,
forgiving no evil even if it does some good;
and where I'd dropped my pen:
                            "It isn't worth it!"—
he'd assert:
            "It's worth it!"—
                            and pick up the pen.
If he can't unravel a knot,
                        he'll cut it through,

whereas I can neither unravel

                                nor cut through.

Once he falls in love,

                        he won't fall out of it,

while I keep falling in

                          and out of love.

I'll hide my envy.

                    Start to smile.

I'll pretend to be a simple soul:

"Someone has to smile;

someone has to live in a different way..."

But much as I tried to persuade myself of this,
repeating:

                "To each man his fate..."

I can't forget there is somewhere a boy

who will achieve far more

                    than I.

1955

TRANSLATED BY GEORGE REAVEY

Prologue

I'm many-sided.

                  I'm overworked,

and idle too.

I have a goal

               and yet I'm aimless.

I don't, all of me, fit in;

                 I'm awkward,

shy and rude,

nasty and good-natured.

I love it,

           when one thing follows another

and so much of everything is mixed in me:

from west to east,

from envy to delight.

I know, you'll ask:

               "What about the overall goal?"

There's tremendous value in this all!
I'm indispensable to you!
                                    I'm heaped as high
as a truck with fresh-mown hay!
I fly through voices,
                    through branches,
                                        light and chirping,
and butterflies flutter in my eyes,
                                    and hay pushes out of cracks.
I greet all movement! Ardor,
and eagerness, triumphant eagerness!
Frontiers are in my way.
                            It is embarrassing
for me not to know Buenos Aires and New York.
I want to walk at will
                        through London,
and talk with everyone,
                            even in broken English.
I want to ride
                through Paris in the morning,
hanging on to a bus like a boy.
I want art to be
                    as diverse as myself;
and what if art be my torment
and harass me
                on every side,
I am already by art besieged.
I've seen myself in every everything:
I feel kin to Yesenin
                    and Walt Whitman,
to Mussorgsky grasping the whole stage,
and Gauguin's pure virgin line.
I like
        to use my skates in winter,
and, scribbling with a pen,
                            spend sleepless nights.
I like
        to defy an enemy to his face,
and bear a woman across a stream.
I bite into books, and carry firewood,
pine,
        seek something vague,
and in the August heat I love to crunch
cool scarlet slices of watermelon.

I sing and drink,

        giving no thought to death;
with arms outspread

        I fall upon the grass,
and if, in this wide world, I come to die,
then it's certain to be

        from sheer joy that I live.

1955

TRANSLATED BY GEORGE REAVEY (REVISED)

"I am a purse..."

I am a purse

        lying on the road,
alone here in broad daylight.
You don't even see me, people.

        Your feet
walk over and around me.
And don't you

        understand anything?
And don't you, really,

        have eyes?
That dust,

        that you yourselves raise,
conceals me,

        so clever

        of you.
Look more closely.

        Only a glance is needed.
I'll give everything to you,

        all that I treasure.
And don't look for my owner.
I laid myself on the ground.
Don't think

        they'll suddenly pull a string,
and above the crooked fence not far away
you'll see some little Nina,

saying with a laugh:
                    "They fooled you!"
Don't let a humiliating laugh and some faces
in a window somewhere scare you.
I'm no fraud.
                    I'm the real thing.
Just look inside me!
I'm afraid of one thing,
                    to your disfavor:
that right now,
                    in broad daylight,
I won't see
            the one I wait for,
that the one who should
                    won't pick me up.

1955

TRANSLATED BY ALBERT C. TODD

Idol

Down in the pine needles
in the snowstorm-stogged ravine
an Evenki idol stands
fixing his eyes on the taiga.

Aggressively squinting,
he watched until the time came
when Evenki women started
hauling presents to him.

They brought him mukluks and parkas,
they brought him honey and fur,
figuring that he'd pray
but mainly think for them all.

In the dark assurance
that he'd understand,

they'd smear his mouth
with warm deer blood.

But what could he do, the phony
little god,
with his fierce, wooden
whittled-down soul?

Now he's looking through the branches,
abandoned and dead.
No one believes in him;
no one prays to him.

Did I dream this up? At night
in his ravine, far off yonder,
he sets his eyes
on fire, overgrown with moss,

and, listening to the snowstorm
blast down, licks
his lips. Lord, I know it.
He wants blood.

1955

TRANSLATED BY JAMES DICKEY WITH ANTHONY KAHN

Fury

Kindness should have fists.
—M. Svetlov (in conversation)

They tell me,
            shaking their heads:
"You should be kinder ...
                        You are somehow—furious."
I used to be kind.
            It didn't last long.
Life was breaking me
            hitting me in the teeth.

24

I lived
    like a silly puppy.
They would hit me—
        and again I would turn the other cheek.
I'd wag my tail of complacency,
        and then, to make me furious,
someone chopped it off with a single blow.
And now I will tell you
    about fury,
about that fury
    with which you go to a party
and make polite conversation
while dropping sugar into your tea with tongs.
And when you offer me more tea
I'm not bored—
    I merely study you.
I submissively drink my tea from the saucer,
and, hiding my claws,
    stretch out my hand.
And I'll tell you something else about fury.
When before the meeting they whisper:
    "Give it up . . .

You're young,
    better you write,
don't jump into a fight
    for a while . . ."
Like hell
    I'll give in!
To be furious at falsehood—
    is real goodness!
I'm warning you—
    that fury hasn't left me yet.
And you ought to know—
    I'll stay infuriated for a long time.
There's none of my former shyness left in me.
After all—
    life is interesting
    when you're furious!

1955

TRANSLATED BY TINA TUPIKINA-GLAESSNER, GEOFFREY DUTTON, AND IGOR
MEZHAKOFF-KORIAKIN (REVISED)

Gentleness

How and in what year did this come into fashion:
"Deliberate indifference to the living,
                 deliberate cultivation of the dead"?
People's shoulders slump,
                      they get drunk sometimes,
one by one
         they quit,
and orators at the crematorium
speak words of gentleness to history . . .
What was it took life from Mayakovsky?
What was it put the gun between his fingers?
If with
        that voice of his,
                 with that appearance—
if ever they had offered him in life
               some crumbs of gentleness.
People alive—
         are troublemakers.
Gentleness
       is a posthumous award.

1955

TRANSLATED BY ROBIN MILNER-GULLAND AND PETER LEVI (REVISED)

The Park

People are really talking now.
Those sloshed on conversations,
shout noisily, whimper noisily,
and from time to time grow noisily silent too.

The topics unnerve me.
I'm pale, with hollows under my eyes.
In a sweat from these disputes,
I'd rather walk in the park.

              • • •

I'm ready to climb a wall,
fearful of cerebral phenomena,
more at ease should some bumptious emcee
invite me up onstage.

I'll solve all the charades
and, rewarded with two balloons,
I'll come off the stage luxuriating
and release them in the garden.

I'll strap on roller skates
and mumble a song about something
that Montand sings well,
and idolize a fountain.

And with an itch to be gently rocked,
cherishing my blissful sloth,
I'll take some Czech salami
and a mug with spilling foam.

But two men are sitting there
arguing about the problems of the age.

One screams about the danger
of open criticism here,
that there are enemies all around,
that the time is not right.

The other—that everything is wretched,
that lies breed only lies
and, no matter what time seems right,
we won't reach truth through untruth.

I light up again, get up,
take off anew to the fountain,
stumble into one conversation, then another . . .
No, I won't put my foot in the park again.

Constant conjecturing: a doctor
that complains to his wife in a boat,
and a woman on a motorcycle thinking vertically
of flying horizontally along a wall.

. . .

On a floating restaurant cozily unstable,
in avenues where gardens murmur,
on painted hobbyhorses—
there are thinkers everywhere.

Rambling walks at times are fatal!
People drink absorbed in thought,
fountains, gurgling, absorbed in thought,
beat our mugs absorbed in thought.

Young girls' bangs are absorbed in thought,
and the night, seriously absorbed in thought,
recites, like doubtful rosary beads,
the cars of the "Devil's Wheel..."*

1955

TRANSLATED BY ALBERT C. TODD AND JAMES RAGAN

Devil's Wheel: A Ferris wheel–type amusement park ride.

"In a red woolen cap..."

In a red woolen cap and inadequate overcoat
a lad comes out of the gate.
He takes an icicle that tastes of the roof
between his freezing teeth.

He steps over puddles
and smiles when he looks up at the dawn.
Who does he love? Who has he made his friends?
What does he want from life?

They skillfully tried to distract him
from the aching questions "how come?"
Diligently critics expounded
on the absence of conflict to him.

Someone assured him ponderously
that the road was smooth and exact,

though a string of contradictions
might have led to disbelief.

He stood square. His eyes were never hidden.
He will forget nothing.
His avowed enemy is all untruth
and it can't hide from him.

Insinuating itself in people,
the lie rots its own by stealth,
displacing great truth
with a shameful farce.

It brands people with the harshest verdict.
Following the daily tabloid's example,
oversaturated with syrup,
a lie inflates its carbonated rapture.

Year by year now things are getting harder.
The lie and the twists cannot conceal
what was created by the people,
in the name of the truth, and not of the lie.*

But all its tricks and smiles,
its ingratiation and its quickness
are for that lad evidence
that unmasks the lie's face.

The lad comes out of the gate
into the enormous brightly colored commotion.
Cap dripping with thawing snow,
he roams the noisy streets.

And all around him, with pain and mirth,
people think and grieve alike—
and desire the same as he,
crunching the same spring ice.

1955

TRANSLATED BY ALBERT C. TODD

*This eighth stanza was cut from the two-volume selected works in 1975 as well as both three-volume editions of the collected works in 1983–84 and 1987 and was last printed in *Vzmakh ruki* in 1962.

Zima Junction: A Poem

We grow more candid as we grow up.
There is fate to thank for that.
And changes in life coincide
with major changes in ourselves.
If we see people differently
than we saw them before,
                              if we discover
something new in them,
                              then that means
it surfaced first in ourselves.
Of course I haven't lived all that much,
but at twenty I reassessed everything—
what I said,
                 and wasn't supposed to say,
what I didn't say,
                         and should have.
I saw that often I'd lived cautiously,
that I had thought, felt, and desired too little,
that life had been easy—
more noble impulses than action.
But there is always the recourse at such a time
of marshaling new plans and strengths
by touching again the ground where
once barefoot you'd kicked up dust.
This thought, which at first seems very ordinary,
helped me everywhere:
that somewhere near Lake Baikal awaits
a rendezvous with you, Zima Junction.

I wanted to get back again to familiar pines,
to witnesses of those former times
when to Siberia for a peasant revolt was banished
my great-grandfather and others like him.
Hither
          through mud and rain
                                         from far away
to regions of cobwebbed trunks

they drove them with wives and tiny children,
peasants from Zhitomir province.
They dragged themselves along, trying to forget much
that each prized more than life.
The guards watched warily,
their hands heavy with veins.
The noncom trumped hearts with clubs,
but my great-grandfather pondered the night long,
lighting with his fingers, as only peasants can,
his pipe with coals from the fire.
Of what did he think?
                    He wondered how
this unfamiliar region would receive them.
Would it welcome them, or perhaps not,
only God knows what it's like there!
He didn't believe the stories and tall tales.
(Where and when had people ever lived like princes?)
He didn't trust the anxious thoughts
that came on suddenly, uncheering—
after all one can plow and plant,
no matter what it's like, it's land.
What's ahead?
              March on!
                          You'll find out there.
A lot of walking before it's over.
But where is she now,
                    Ukraine, beloved mother?
The road back cannot be found.
Yes, the way to the nightingale
that sings sweetly at daybreak is silent.
All around us there's no way through
for neither riders nor those who walk,
for neither riders nor those who walk,
for neither fugitive, nor wood-goblin.

Peasants, against their will new settlers,
surely had to consider
this region's foreign soil
a hapless fate for them.
It would seem, they accepted it
with great reluctance:
You see, a stepmother, even with a kind heart,
is, understandably, after all, not one's mother.

But crumbling this earth in their fingers,
giving their children to drink of its waters,
relishing it, they understood:
                              It's our own!
They felt:
            'Tis ours by blood,

                    ours . . .
Then once again, step by step, they crawled back
into the poor man's yoke of bitter existence.
Is the nail guilty
                    that it sinks into the wall?
They pound it in with an ax head.
Daybreak wakes them not with roosters—
a rooster sits inside each one.
However much they bend their backs, it turns out:
they didn't eat the grain, the grain ate them.
By threshing, mowing,
                        cleaning the pigsty,
at work in field, house, and barn,
truth would be in abundance, where grain was abundant,
and that would be quite enough,
                            it seemed to them.
And my great-grandfather who believed
in grain as he believed in God,
who knew crop failures without number,
probably dreamt about this truth,
and not about the one that came.
It had little to do with great-grandfather's truth.
There was something new, something of us in it.
Mama, a nine-year-old girl,
encountered it in nineteen nineteen.
One autumn day, during shooting that was growing more intense,
a young cavalryman appeared on a hillock,
crouching to his horse's withers,
                            a red forelock bouncing
under a fur cap with a tin star.
Racing behind him in a maddened charge
over the creaking old bridge,
horses burst into the Junction
and sabers quivered in the air.
There was something good and simple in what
already had been won for certain,
even in this, that when the Cheka* commissar came,
there were no more raids by marauders,

even in the company comic in the overheated club
doing imitations
of how the enemy looked,
and in the way the lodger, the redheaded cavalryman,
frenziedly
polished
his boots.
He fell passionately in love with the schoolmistress
and wandered about not himself,
and talked with her about all sorts of things,
but most of all
about the world's hydra monster.
A master of theory as he was of his saber
(in the opinion of his squadron),
he proclaimed that ideas were everything,
and if there is no bread,
to hell with it.
He insisted, blustering with enthusiasm,
backed up with quotations and fists,
that we had only to shove the bourgoisie in the ocean,
everything else
was kids' stuff.
And life thereafter will be a cinch:
Fall in line,
unfurl the banners,
sing the "International,"
into the sun with trumpets,
and all in flowers,
a straight path to the Commune!
And the redheaded cavalryman, abrupt as "either-or,"
stuffed his saddlebags with oats,
mounted his horse,
and jauntily said
to the schoolmistress:
"We'll see each other again ... So long!"
Standing tall in his stirrups,
he looked
to where it smelled of gunpowder,
and his horse bolted
with him to the east,
shaking his forelock tied with ribbons and burdock ...

I grew up there,
and, when playing hide-and-seek—

uncatchable, no matter who was "it"—
we peered out through bullet holes
in an old barn.
We were living in a world of kids' pranks and sweet rolls
when, standing on the lead tank,
through binoculars Guderian's† eyes devoured
Moscow with its Bolshoi Theater and Kremlin.
Carelessly forgetting threats of low marks,
we tore away from lessons across the school yard,
ran through fields to the Oka,
broke open an old money-box,
went to look for green grasshopper larvae,
and baited wet hooks.
I fished,
      glued together paper kites,
and bareheaded often
wandered alone,
        chewing a clover stem,
in sandals washed clean by the grass.
I went past the black plowed fields,
           the yellow hives,
and watched how luminous clouds slightly stirred,
half drowning in the horizon.
And, passing the outskirts of a camp,
I used to listen to the neighing of horses,
then peacefully and tiredly fall asleep
in hayricks turned dark by the rain.

Later in Moscow I lived almost without a care in the world,
though life,
      presenting no big obstacles,
seemed uncomplicated to me, only because,
what was complicated
      was solved for me.
I knew that harmonious answers would be given
to everything, both how? and what? and why?
but of a sudden it felt necessary
to answer these questions for myself.
I would go on from where I started,
since complexity had come on its own,
and disturbed by that, and nothing else,
I set off for Zima Junction.

        • • •

Into my native pine forest,
to those long-trodden streets,
I took my complexity of today
to former simplicity to take stock.
Trying to stare at each other
in an unequal mutuality of offenses,
Youth and Childhood
                    stood face to face
and waited long:
                    Who would start talking?
Childhood spoke first:
                    "So, then . . . hello.
I barely recognized you.
                    It's your fault.
Once when I often used to dream about you
I thought you'd be quite different.
I tell you openly, you worry me,
you're still in heavy debt to me."
Youth asked:
                    "Well, but will you help?"
And Childhood smiled:
                    "I'll help."
They said good-bye, and, stepping cautiously,
watching the passersby and the houses,
I strode out happily and uneasily
through that very important—
                    Zima Junction.
I had worked out in advance the assumption,
that if its circumstances hadn't gotten any better,
they couldn't have gotten any worse.
But somehow the Corn Exchange seemed less big,
as did the drugstore and the town park,
as if everything had become much smaller
than it had been nine years ago.
And, by the way, I didn't grasp at first,
ranging in wide circles,
that the streets hadn't become shorter
but my stride was simply longer.
Here I had once lived, as in my own apartment,
where, without turning on a light,
in three or four seconds I could find
without stumbling the dresser or bed.
Maybe circumstances had changed,

and maybe the absence had been too long,
but now I bumped awkwardly
on everything I used to slip around by habit.
Here everything caught my eye:
the fence with the obscene inscription,
the drunk slumped against the tea-room,
and the quarrel in line at the store.
It would be okay if this were just anywhere,
but this was here, in my native place,
where I had come for strength,
for courage, for truth and goodness.
A driver was cursing the town council,
hot tempers were fighting while someone laughed,
burdocks listened dustily to all of it,
never moving an ear.
I was expecting something else, something I needed,
which would drown my face with freshness,
when I approached the gates of my home
and turned the iron ring.
And for sure, at once, from the first exclamations:
"He's here!" "Zhenka" "Ooh, have some sweets!"
from the embraces, kisses, reproaches:
"And couldn't you have sent a telegram?"
from the threat:
                    "We'll heat the samovar right away!"
from recollections: "How many years has it been!"
just as I expected, my hesitation vanished,
and things became peaceful and clear to me.
Aunt Liza, full of anxiety,
made a firm proposal:
"You need to wash up from the trip,
I know what those trains are like..."

Already tureens and skillets were to be seen,
the table was already being dragged to the yard,
and I ambled among the dove-gray onion shoots
singing, to fetch the water.
Bending over with a Cossack song I wakened the well
that smelled of my childhood
and from it, bumping on the walls,
flashing its wet chain, came the bucket...
And soon, as an important Moscow guest,
amid questions, toasts, and bustling,
in a clean shirt with hair slicked down,

I sat in a circle of radiant relatives.
I'd grown too soft for the great Siberian dishes
and gazed with longing on their abundance.
My aunt said:
          "Have another gherkin.
What do they feed you in Moscow?
You're not eating a thing! It's not decent . . .
Have some dumplings . . . Do you want some squash?"
And my uncle:
             "I suppose you're used to Stolichnaya vodka?
But let's drink our local 'branch'!
Come on, come on . . .
             But all the same I'd admit
it's not good at your age!
And who's been teaching you?
             Look at that, down in one gulp!
Well, God grant it's not your last!
             Cheers!"
We drank and chattered with animation,
joked about everything,
             but when my sister suddenly
asked whether I was in the Hall of Columns in March,‡
everyone grew serious all around.
We began to speak of vital matters
of which that year was full,
and of its events that occasioned
a lot of reflection and worry.
My Uncle Volodia pushed away his glass:
"Nowadays everyone is like the philosophers.
It's the times we live in.
             People are thinking.
Where, what, how—answers don't come running.
It turns out those doctors are innocent?§
Why then did they hurt people so?
A scandal for all Russia, of course it is,
but all because of that scoundrel Beria . . ."
Incapable of smooth rhetoric,
             he talked to me,
of what disturbed him those days:
"You live in Moscow.
             It must be clearer there to you.
Explain it all to me in proper order!"
As we say, he grabbed me by the buttons,
absolutely not embarrassed by anyone,

he rolled himself a cigarette,
and waited for my answer.
But I think that, really, it wasn't wrong
to say calmly
           to my uncle waiting with difficulty,
as if it all had been clear to me long ago:
"I'll explain later."
They made up my bed, as I requested,
                       in the hayloft.
I lay down and listened long to the night.
A concertina was playing.
               Somewhere there was dancing,
and no one had any power to help me.
It grew colder.
           Without a mattress it was prickly.
The loft rustled and stirred,
and my younger brother Kolka
tirelessly kept me from sleep.
He began a stored-up conversation—
what's pineapple, a fruit or a vegetable?
do I know the dynamo goalie Khomich?
and had I never seen a helicopter? . . .
In the morning I stretched a little,
and sat down on sacks by the loft.
The dawn
        rising in the east
                 remained
on the crimson combs
           of cockerels.
The daybreak mist was growing thin,
houses
      swam in the distance,
and starling-houses
            on long poles
pushed themselves ponderously up from the ground.
Cows moved sedately along the streets,
an old herder cracking his whip from time to time.
Everything was strong, harmonious, and healthy,
and there was no desire to think about anything.
Forgetting breakfast and not listening to reproaches,
lightly clad, pockets stuffed with bread,
as when I used to play hooky from school,
just the same way now, I ran off to the river.
Getting my feet stuck in the warm silt

I made my way to the old willow on the bank
and lay down on the sand in its shade.
The Oka stirred before me evenly.
Logs floated past without haste,
bumping each other now and then.
The sounds of distant horns were heard.
Mosquitoes buzzed.

                Nearby
a gray-haired trackwalker, trousers rolled up,
was standing on a rock with a fishing rod
and angrily furrowed his brow at me
trying to express with his look:
"What's he doing here?

                        Well, okay, he doesn't fish himself,
but he doesn't let others fish . . ."
After searching my face thoroughly,
he approached.

           "It can't be?

                  Hold on! . . .
But aren't you Zina Yevtushenko's son?
And I look at you . . . Daresay you've forgotten me . . .
Well, God be with you!

               Come from Moscow?

                       For the summer?
But let me make myself at home . . ."
He sat down beside me,

                 unwrapped a newspaper,
took out a crust of bread, tomatoes, salt.
I got tired from answering his questions.
He had to know everything:
what kind of stipend did I get,
when will they open the Exhibition again.
He was an obstinate, prickly old man
and quickly started provocative talk,
that young people used to be better,
that the Komsomol today was painfully boring.
"I remember your mother at seventeen,
the boys were after her in flocks,
but they were afraid—

               they couldn't keep up
with such a tongue, and barefoot too.
I remember

       such ones

          as she,

in army coats cut down for size,
at political meetings they shouted till dark
that pleated hair was a bourgeois leftover.
They used to spout off threateningly,
always full of ideas of some sort, for instance,
in all seriousness they'd suddenly raise the issue
of the 'socialization' of children!...
A lot of it, of course, was ridiculous
and truly sometimes even harmful,
but I'll say this:
               It worries me
that you don't have their passion.
And the main thing is,
                     contradict me if you want to,
you don't think like young people.
And people, my friend, are always
the same age as their thoughts.
There are young people, but youth in them...
Why argue?
               Look at my nephew—
he won't reach twenty-five this winter,
but you wouldn't think he's less than thirty.
What happened?
                 He was a boy, like any other,
and, you see, he was elected to the district council.
He sits there, a green kid, steamed up in debate,
and bangs his bossy fist.
He changed his walk.
                 There's iron in his look.
And as for his speeches, now he's sure
that words aren't for the sake of business,
but business exists for the sake of words.
Everything's smooth and obvious in those speeches...
What sort of young person is that,
                     what sort of ardor?!
Because it isn't respectable, you might say,
he gave up football, and girls.
Well, now he's respectable, but what else is there?
Where's the questioning,
                 the straight honesty of disagreement?
No, youth is not what it used to be,
and the fish also
           (he gave a sigh)
                 they're not the same either...

Well, we've sort of had our dinner,
brother, let's try a worm..."
And, smacking his lips, in a minute he was taking
a splendid carp off his hook.
"Well, took a bite, did you? Here's the reward!"—
he glowed with delight, admiring the carp.
"Weren't you just saying that fish aren't the same..."
He replied shrewdly:
                    "Wasn't talking about all of them..."
And smiling, he shook his finger at me,
as if to say: "Keep in mind:
this carp, brother, ended up on a hook,
and I don't propose to end up the same way..."

Eating my aunt's thick hearty soup
I became feeble and incoherent in discussion.
Why did I keep remembering that old man?
There's no shortage of them!
My aunt grumbled:
                    "I'm not your mother-in-law,
why are you so gloomy and depressed?
Snap out of it, lad! Don't be so complicated.
Come on, let's go berry picking."
Three women and two short-haired little girls
and I...
            The truck bed stuffed with hay flew
through the broad murmuring fields.
And watching the fleeting mowing machines,
the horses,
            the ears of corn,
                        the caps,
                                the kerchiefs,
we got rolls from our baskets
and drank fresh milk.
From under the wheels quail shot up
splitting and deafening the eardrums.
The world was a hubbub of fluttering greenness.
And I—I listened and listened, and watched.
Small boys were throwing stones beside a stream,
and the blazing sun burned,
but clouds were piling up watery drops,
shifting and breathing heavily.
Everything became misty and silent,
the kolkhoz farmers were already climbing into hayricks,

and without looking back we flew into the downpour,
and we and the downpour and the flashes of lightning
careered together into the woods!
We sensibly reorganized the truck bed,
raking up piles of hay
to cover ourselves . . .
                         Only one didn't,
a forty-year-old woman.
The whole day she had stared tiredly,
eating unsociably in silence,
and suddenly now she roused herself, stood up
and became young and full of youth.
She pulled the white kerchief from her hair,
full of a crazy, frolicsome spirit,
shook her shoulders and started to sing,
wet and joyful:
"Barefoot through the dark forest
the young girl runs.
Doesn't touch little berries
but picks big ones."
She stood with a proud head,
both heart and eyes
                         looking only forward,
her face lashed
                    with wet pine needles
eyelashes laden
                    with tears and storms.
"What are you doing?
                         Fool, you'll catch your death . . ."
My aunt tugged and pulled at her.
But she gave herself wholly to the rain,
and the rain gave itself to her.
She threw back her hair with a dark hand,
and looked into the distance,
                              as though there,
while singing,
                    she could see what
all the rest could not.
To me it seemed
                    that there was nothing else in the world,
only this
          crowded flying truck bed,
there was nothing—
                    only the lashing wind coming at us,

the downpour of rain,

                 the woman singing . . .

We settled ourselves in a barn for the night.

In the low barn

            the stifling smell

of sheepskin, dried mushrooms,

grain, and red whortleberries soaking.

Tied bunches of birch branches breathed with green leaves.

In the gliding beams of light and dark

horse collars shifted darkly

like bats under the roof.

I couldn't sleep.

            Faces were barely visible

and the whisper of women was audible in the dark.

I strained to listen:

           "Ah, Liza, Liza,

you don't know what my life is like!

Yes, we have rubber plants, and well, a Dutch oven,

even a good zinc roof,

everything cleaned,

           scoured,

              polished,

and the children and my husband,

                 but doesn't the soul count?

And it's somehow cold, fiercely cold . . .

My mother asks:

            'What's bad about your Piotr?

He doesn't beat you,

           doesn't fool around,

drinks, of course,

           but who doesn't nowdays?'

Ah, Liza!

        He comes home drunk at night,

growls, ain't I his forever,

and turns me over roughly

             and—without a single word,

as if I weren't a person at all.

I remember, I used to cry and not sleep,

now I know how to go to sleep.

What have I turned into . . .

            Everyone thinks I'm forty,

but, Liza, I'm

        only thirty-five!

What will become of me?

I've no more strength . . ."
If only I had someone I really loved,
how I would take care of him.
He could beat me, if only he loved me!
I'd never think of going out
and I'd make the house beautiful.
I'd wash my darling's feet
and would drink the water after . . ."
Yes, she was the one who through the rain and wind
flew young and full of youth,
and I—
    I had envied her,
        I had believed
that audacious unconcern.
The conversation grew quiet.
        The creak of the well
reached us, then ceased. Everyone in the village was down,
and only wheels sloshing with satisfaction hub-deep
in the roadway mud could be heard.
A young boy in a jacket stretched over a T shirt
woke us early in the morning.
His nose was aggressively sunburned
and he held a copper teapot in his hand.
He looked disdainfully at me,
        my aunt,
at all those sweetly asleep on the floor.
"Citizens, aren't you going out for berries?
Why, then, are you sleeping?
        I don't understand you . . ."
A straggling cow wandered after the herd.
A barefoot woman was chopping wood.
A rooster crowed.
    We left the village.
The deafening din of grasshoppers filled the meadows.
Shafts of immobile carts reared upward
and over the earth a blue beyond belief.
First we passed open fields,
        then undergrowth in the woods
glistening with the cold of suspended morning dew,
with birds solicitously bustling.
Bright red sour berries beckoned in the grass,
here and there smoky tender raspberries reddened in bushes.
Bilberries pulled us down on pine needles,
red whortleberries burned our feet,

but we were after the best of the berries,
wild strawberries that grow in the deep woods.
Up ahead someone suddenly called out wildly:
"Here they are! And I can see some others!..."
Oh, the joy of simply picking greedily!
The sound of the first berries plopping in the bucket!
But our young guide pulled us up
and we had to submit to him:
"Ekh, citizens, you just make me laugh!
We haven't even got to the berries yet..."
And suddenly a meadow broke through the thick trees
with a drunkenness of sunlight, berries, and flowers.
It dazzled our eyes.

        In amazement
we just breathed out: "Ooh."
The strawberries were numbing, their smell terrifying.
Rattling pans, we ran to them
and fell down,

        lying in them drugged,
picking them from their stems with our lips.
The hillocks were smoking with downy grass,
the forest humming with midges and pines.
And I...

        I quickly forgot about the berries.
My eyes were again on that woman.
In her movements joy alternated with pleasure.
Her white kerchief slipped down on her brow.
She was picking strawberries and laughing,
laughing,

        but, well, I was incredulous.
Reflecting with dismay and embarrassment,
I got up from the warm and crumpled grass,
poured my berries into someone's bucket,
and wandered off the path through the forest.
I subtracted nothing from memory
and calculated everything that was there.
I came out of the echoing pines into a stand of wheat
and closed my eyelids at its feet.
I opened my eyes.

        Saw a bird in the sky.
Sat down on a dry, stalky bed.
Fingered the ears.

        And asked the wheat
what to do to make everyone happy.

"How do we do it, wheat?

Wheat, you're wiser than . . .
I'm ashamed of my pitiful helplessness.
Perhaps I just don't know how,
and perhaps I'm no good and not suitable . . ."
The wheat answered me
scarcely moving its head:
"You're neither bad nor good—
just very young.
I accept your question,
but excuse my muteness.
It's sort of like I don't understand
and cannot answer . . ."

And I followed the railroad track,
passed wagons smelling of tar,
and met a happy-looking fellow
covered with dust, snub-nosed, and small.
He was hungry,

young, and barefoot,
thriftily carrying his shoes
on a slender birch stick.
With ardor he told me all sorts of things—
that the harvest was in full swing,
that the kolkhoz director, Pankratov,
was doing shocking things.
He said:

"I'm not going to kiss ass.
I'll leave.

I'll find out the truth.
If the Zima bosses won't help—
I'll go to Irkutsk . . ."
Suddenly from nowhere a car appeared.
Riding in it with a briefcase—

symbol of his office—
a canvas-clothed citizen

in a jeep,
as though he were sitting

in a presidium.
"You want your mother to start crying?
The hero

is charging off

to Zima?
Just mention Pankratov again

46

and you'll find out what's what..."
And he sped away.
                    I didn't perceive
any sober force in him at all,
but in the young boy with iron belief,
without a car, barefoot, and angry.
We said good-bye.
                    He went on, looking small,
feet drowning in the dust,
shoes on the slender stick,
for a long time
                    swinging in the distance.
Two days later we got ready to leave for home in the morning,
still tired,
                    on a small truck going our way.
The head of the house saw his guests off.
There were handshakes and warm good-byes.
He told us
                    to come back often,
and we told him
                            to come visit us.
He was a tough, dignified old man,
a genuine Siberian lumberman!
He filled up the truck unhurriedly from a bucket
with a cloth tied over it as filter.
The morning stars were fading in the sky,
and under the swimming, changing blue above
our little truck moved onto the road
with young grass clinging to the tires...
The old man waved.
                    For sure he knew many secrets!
The taiga he knew inside and out,
but what I learned in his barn
remained a secret to him.
I won't slobber on about it...

Better
        about how it was back at home,
                                    how at daylight
I got up,
        drank milk,
and that was the last anyone saw of me,
how a strip of steppeland shimmered with green
surrounded by the taiga on both sides,

47

when I wandered,
                    stepping carefully
along the moving shadows of clouds.
At times I went to the woods
                         with a double-barreled shotgun.
Of course, it made little sense,
but I wandered about carrying it pensively.
I sat down in the shade and calmly examined the barrel.
I thought of much,
                    thought even about you,
my uncles,
               Volodia and Andrei.
I love both.
          Now Uncle Andrei—
                         he's the elder ...
I love the way he sleeps,
                    worn out with troubles,
                                   barely alive,
how he washes,
                    rising very early,
how he picks up other people's children.
He runs the local garage,
smeared with grease,
                    eternally enraged,
he dashes around, his big forehead hunched over
in a car named Billygoat.
He would suddenly quarrel with someone at home
and disappear in the country for a day or two,
and then come home,
                    exhausted,
                              benevolent,
smelling of gasoline and the taiga.
He loves to shake people's hands until they crack,
and playfully in fights to throw people down by twos.
He knows how to do everything cheerfully and with taste:
from sawing logs
                    to sprinkling salt on black bread ...
But my Uncle Volodia!
                    How marvelously
in his hands a plane became a daring thing
as he shook the wood shavings out of his hair
ankle-deep in golden foam!
What a carpenter!
                    Ah, what a carpenter!

Well, and a storyteller—
                    what a past master!
How many times I listened standing in the barn,
or sitting on the edge of the bench,
how a cook got shot for being dishonest,
how fighting men passed through a village,
how a woman named Francesca
from Petersburg sang a song to them . . .
My uncles—
            my own people!
How wonderful it was until
a neighbor woman told me:
                    "Andrei
fools around with the wife of one of the drivers.
You ought to tell your aunt with a poem.
But what for? She'll find out on her own.
And Volodia—
            he's a fine carpenter,
but he's a drunk—
                All Zima knows about it."
She hammered at me like a woodpecker
that I ought to show some interest.
I didn't.
        But my younger uncle
suddenly mysteriously disappeared somewhere.
People kept coming the whole time wanting
toys and sofas repaired.
They were told simply and briefly:
"He's away for the week.
                    On business."
And all of a sudden the neighbor biliously screamed out,
shoving her sharp nose through the gate:
"Zhenka, they're ashamed in front of you.
Your uncle is just laid out—
                    on a binge.
You've got to learn, my little student, all about life.
Come on with me!"
                And joyfully and wickedly,
as if she were mistress of the house,
she took me to the larder.
There my uncle lay in his underwear
fuming solid vodka
and trying to sing "Little Apple"
to the tune of "Sulik."

Seeing us, he half got up with a pitiful expression,
confused, already sober,
and said quietly to me:

        "Ah, Zhenka my dear,
do you understand how I love you? . . ."
I couldn't stay and watch him like that.
He had opened old wounds in me anew;
I lost the desire

        to eat at home
and went to the tearoom alone.
The Zima tearoom was hot, breathing of summer.
Behind the kitchen they were noisily slaughtering piglets.
Trays and faces flashed by,

        flypaper hung in the windows
stuck all over with flies.
A shortsighted teacher noisily fumbled with the menu,
a kolkhoz girl grumbled about the thin soup,
and a woodcutter's huge swarthy hand
tapped a glass with a fork by habit.
The Zima tearoom was unusually noisy,
a surge of flying waitresses.
Drinking tea in chance conversation
with a man with glasses and a fat face,
quite intelligent, judging from everything,
and suddenly we are laying our souls bare.
He called himself a Moscow journalist
who'd come to Zima to do a feature.
Treating me to a cranberry-marinated vodka
and waving away the tobacco smoke
he answered me:

        "Hey, my dear young innocent,
I used to be exactly the same myself!
I wanted to find out what came from where,
thinking then that I could handle anything.
I strove to analyze and I fought
to reconstruct the times the way I wanted.
I too was a troublemaker and pushy
and didn't want to feel sorry before my time.
Then—

        my novel wasn't published,
then—

        a family and you have to live somehow.
Now I scribble for newspapers, and not the worst, by the way.
Took to the bottle and became, they say, gloomy.

Don't write now . . .
                         just a custodian of thoughts.
Sure there are changes, sure,
                         but behind the speeches
a nebulous game goes on.
We memorize today
                    what we were silent about yesterday,
we're silent today
                    about what we did yesterday . . ."
But in his glances measuring his neighbors,
as in his rote repetitions of what was bad,
I saw only a peevish lack of faith,
I didn't believe him. Believing is loving.
"Oh, hell, I've forgotten about my article!
I must get to the sawmill. Time to go.
The cooking here is unbelievably bad . . .
                         But anyway,
what could you expect! What a hole this is . . ."
He wiped his lips with a paper napkin
and, noticing my heavy look:
"Ah, yes, you were born here, excuse me!
I forgot . . . Forgive me, my fault . . ."
I was paying with interest for my reflective mood
and I wandered through the taiga, listening to the pine branches.
And Andrei said to me:
                         "If only I could find a prescription
to cure you.
          Ekh, you silly boy!
Come to the club with us.
                         Today there's
an Irkutsk Philharmonic concert.
Everyone—everyone is going. We all have tickets.
Look how crumpled your trousers are . . ."
And very quickly I was on my way, submissively dressed up
in a shirt still warm from the iron.
And by my sides, moving in solemn gait,
carefully taking care of their boots,
my very decorous uncles
smelling of cologne, vodka, and shoe polish.
The star of the program—pink torso
Anton Bespiatykh—Russian folktale hero.
He did everything! Straining magnificently
he lifted a bundle of weights with his teeth.
He leaped between sharp swords,

played a waltz elegantly on a violin.
Juggled bottles, balls,
and elegantly dropped them on the floor.
He strewed out kerchiefs inexhaustibly,
tied them all into one, pulled it apart,
and on the kerchief an embroidered dove of peace—
the ideological climax to the show.
And my uncles applauded . . . "Look at that, what a trick!
He's really good . . . But just look, look!"
and I . . .

      I too clapped a little,
otherwise they'd be offended.
Bespiatykh bowed and flexed his muscles . . .
We went out into the dark night.
"Well, what about the concert, nephew, what do you think?"
But I wanted to be alone for a while.
"I'm going for a walk . . ."
                "You're hurting us.
And everyone in the family wonders about it:
you're absolutely never at home.
Have you got a romance going in Zima?"
I walked alone, silent, and unnoticed.
My thoughts were down to earth, no fantasies.
Well, that concert—good luck to it!
I've seen enough of them!
So many antiquated stunts
but with new, expensive staging,
and at so many similar shows
applauded others, though not too much.
I've seen so many elaborately painted spoons
when you can't find barley to make soup,
and I've thought about what's true and false,
and the metamorphosis of the authentic into a lie.
Think on it.
      We are all guilty
for masses of trivial irritations,
for vacuous verses, for endless quotations
in the standardized endings of speeches . . .
I thought of many things.
          There are two types
of love.
Some flatter their loved ones,
no matter how much they offend,
they forgive, and don't even want to think.

We've endured so many "after-temporary-disappointments"
in our recent history.
We don't need a blind love for Russia,
but a thinking, steady love.
Let's think about the big and the small
in order to live profoundly, to live not just somehow.
A great thing cannot be a deception
but people can betray it.
I don't want to justify what is weak,
nor am I going to excuse those people
who want to fritter away the prophetic insights of Russia
like trivia of gossip.
Let vanity be the lot of the weak.
It's easier to live, blaming others for everything.
Not weakness,
                    but great and glorious things
Russia expects from me.
What do I want?
                    I want to fight with courage,
but so that in everything that I fight for,
truth alone will be on fire,
for which I will never waive my rights.
So that wherever I may go,
                            over the searing steppe,
or the undulations of rust-colored sand,
stirring banners—
                    overhead,
the feel of the flagstaff—
                            in my palms.
I know there is a hesitation
                        that comes from lack of faith.
Our hesitations
            come from love.
Our disclosures are in the name of truth—
in the name of those who lay down their lives for it.
We don't want to live
                    the way the wind blows.
We are going to get into the whys and wherefores.
Greatness is calling.
                    Let's think.
Let's be equal to it.
Thus I wandered by a long strange route
over the noisy wooden sidewalks.
The shutters of houses were squeaking.

Young girls ran past me talking loudly.
"In love, he says . . .

                    Rimma, what should I do?"
"D'ya love him?"

                 "D'ya think I'm crazy?"
I walk on farther.

               The settled mist lay all about.
The unsleeping might of locomotives, rails, and fire
revealed itself to me.
Half-visible piles of iron filings glimmered.
Little shunting-engines with ridiculously huge stacks
now wheezed noisily,

                now braked with a scream.
Hammers thundered.

              Muscles on the shoulders
of tenacious lads rippled
and white teeth showed through black grease.
With aggressive sharpness,
hissing clouds burst
from under wheels,
rails and black sides of engines
glittered coldly.
Skillfully rolling a cigarette for a pal,
with a flag stuck under arm, a signalman sighed:
"Late from Irkutsk again.
And Vaska's splitting up, did you hear?"
Peering and remembering
I suddenly froze;
in an oil-stained coat,
stepping as by habit across the rails,
came a young lad with a suitcase.
It can't be! . . . It's him . . . Vovka Drobni!
I thought he left Zima.
I went up to him and said in a sepulchral voice:
"It seems to me we're acquainted!"
He recognized me. Smiled. Still just the same Vovka,
only now without Defoe under his belt.
"Haven't lost your ugly mug, Zhenia . . . Skinny as a sardine.
Still writing rhymes? Should have come to us in the depot . . ."
"Do you remember our revenge
on Pietka Sinelnikov for his deals?"
"And singing to the soldiers in the hospital?"
"And that girl you were going to marry?"
I wanted us to talk on and on,

tell him everything—
                    the joy and the longing:
"But you must be tired, you're coming from work, Vovka..."
"Knock it off, let's go to the Oka!"
The path led through the night shadows,
covered with bare footprints, boot and shoe tracks
between the tall umbrella shapes of vegetation,
and huge pewter-colored burdock.
I talked freely and anxiously
about everything I'd been thinking,
                    and swore a lot.

My old classmate listened carefully
and said nothing in reply.
The two of us followed the small path.
Already we were being drawn on by the moldy willows,
the sand, and fish, the wet bark,
a fisherman's smoking campfire...
                    The Oka was near.
We swam in the deep, black water.
"Well, now," he screamed, "don't make a mess of things."
And I forgot some things for no reason
and remembered other things by chance.
Later we sat on the moonlit riverbank,
our thoughts rocked by the gentle water,
and somewhere not far off in a misty meadow
horses roamed, neighing now and then.
I thought, as I looked at the water,
about much I was guilty of myself.
"Do you think it's only you?"
                    Vovka said.
"Everyone considers it today, brother.
Don't sit like that, your jacket'll get rumpled...
What a character you are, have to tell you everything!
Everything is going to be found out and understood in time.
Here we've got to think long and hard.
                    Don't rush things?"
The nighttime hooting was far away,
and my buddy got up from the ground:
"That's how it is,
                    and there's work to be done.
Time to get home.
                    Tomorrow, brother, it's eight for me..."
It dawned...
        Everything seemed younger,

the night disappeared into nothing,
and for some reason it got a little colder,
and the outlines took on color.
Some rain came, barely a drop or two.
The two of us strode together,
and somewhere Pankratov was still driving around,
in his self-satisfied jeep,
carelessly and ponderously sermonizing.
But across land

           that was spattered with dew,
walked an angry lad,
with a gay birch stick,

              barefoot and stubborn . . .

It was a day like any other,

               neither hot, nor cold,
but so many pigeons overhead!
And I was somehow very good,
somehow very, very young.
I was leaving . . .

          I felt sad, clean
and sad, probably because
I had learned something about life,
but still didn't know

         what it was.
I drank vodka with my relatives to my relatives.
Went for a walk around Zima one last time.
It was a day like any other . . .

             In shimmering colored specks
of light the earth's trees radiated their foliage green.
Young boys were throwing coins against a wall,
trucks stretched out in a line,
women were trading at the bazaar
in cows, whortleberries, and bird cherries.
I went on sad and free,
passing the last block,
climbed a sunny hill
and stood there for a long while.
From above I saw the station building,
barns, haylofts, and houses.
Then the voice of Zima Junction spoke to me.
Here is what it said:
"I live modestly, crack nuts,
quietly steam with train engines,

but I also think a lot about the age,
love it and suffer from it.
You are not the only one in the world like this now,
with your searching, planning, and struggle.
Don't worry, my son, that you haven't answered
the question that was given to you.
Hang on, watch closely, listen carefully,
and explore, explore.
                    Travel the whole world over.
Yes, truth is good,
                    but happiness is better,
but nonetheless without truth there is no happiness.
Go about the world with a proud head,
with everything facing forward—
                              both heart and eyes,
and your face—
                    lashed with wet pine needles,
and on your eyelashes laden—
                         with tears and storms.
Love people,
         and discriminate among them.
Remember:
         I've got my eye on you.
But if there's trouble—
                    come back to me . . .
Go!"
         And I went.
                    And I keep on going.

1955
Zima Junction — Moscow
TRANSLATED BY ALBERT C. TODD

---

*Cheka: Popular name for the original secret-police organization established by Lenin following
the October Revolution.
†Guderian: General Heinz Guderian, famed German Panzer commander.
‡Hall of Columns: Stalin's body lay in the historic Hall of Columns in Moscow for three days in
March 1953 for public viewing before his funeral.
§Doctors: Prominent Jewish doctors were arrested in the last months of Stalin's life and charged
with a plot to poison principal Soviet leaders. Their innocence was established only after Stalin's
death.

1956⁄1962

that time
        so strange,
                when
simple honesty
        looked like courage!

"I don't understand..."

I don't understand
               what's come over me.
Exhaustion, perhaps—
                 perhaps, it's exhaustion.
I'm so easily worried,
             and I grieve,
and blush without cause
               to blush.
It was in a Moscow shop not long ago it happened,
yes, in a Moscow shop
               amid the steady din
                      and rumbling.
A saleswoman with straggly curls,
with inept but nice hands,
measured the inches of my neck.
Not prone to sentiments before,
I now stared hard,
             and pain pinched my heart,
and pity,
       you must know,
               pure pity
I felt for her clean, exhausted hands,
her smock
       and straggly curls.
Here's the book . . .
             I intend to read!
A chapter—
       just
           an ordinary chapter,
but I can't read—
             in a mist of tears
my eyes won't let me.
I've confused all things with myself.
I retire into my shell,
               fear art like fire.
Visions of *The Bicycle Thief*,
             of *Peer Gynt*,
seem, all of them, now
           to apply to me.
People mumble on

and I can't cope with it,
that I'm no good,
          that I have a weak link with life.
But if I connect with so many things,
I must, apparently, stand for something,
                    have some value?

And if I stand for nothing,
why then
          do I suffer and weep?!

1956

TRANSLATED BY GEORGE REAVEY (REVISED)

"What a rude sobering . . ."

What a rude sobering up comes and
how harsh our conscience is to us later,
when, in a moment of candor at the table,
we don't notice the enemy slipping in.

But it's terrible to have learned nothing
and in the fervor of vigilance again
to attribute unsavory motives
to astonishing though pure immaturity.

Zeal in suspicion has no merit.
A blind judge doesn't serve the people.
More terrible than mistaking an enemy for a friend
is the haste to mistake a friend for an enemy.

1956

TRANSLATED BY ALBERT C. TODD

"Cowards have..."

Cowards have small possibilities.
Fame is not won through silence,
and cowards,

out of caution,
are at times obliged to show courage.

Thus adders hustle to be hawks;
sensing the way the wind is blowing,
they adapt themselves to courage
just as they had adapted themselves to lies.

1956
TRANSLATED BY GEORGE REAVEY

Ice

I can make you out with difficulty.
What tricks the water has played all around!
We've been parted by the ice.
Now we are on different sides.

The houses and woods have grown gaunt.
A maple sways pale, emaciated.
After settling on the water, our voices
will move quietly on with the water.

The ice floe groans and sinks in the struggle,
and you are slender like a piece of ice far away,
and carried toward you in the river current
is a scrap of the pathway.

1956
TRANSLATED BY ALBERT C. TODD

"I congratulate you, Momma..."

I congratulate you, Momma,
>> on your son's birthday.

You worry about him,
>> and your worry is great.

Here he lies,
> so gaunt,
>> large and untidy,

married unwisely,
>> unprofitable for the home.

You gaze on him
> with eyes bright and misted...

Congratulations, Momma,
>> on the birthday of your worry!

You have made him a present
>>> of his ruthless love for this age,

a hard,
> proud faith
>> in the Revolution.*

You gave him neither fame
>> nor riches,

but you've given him instead
>> the ability not to fear.

Open windows then
> onto the leaves
>> and warbling birds,

awake his eyes
> with a kiss.

Make him a present
> of a notebook and inkstand,

give him his fill of milk
>> and speed him on his journey.

1956

TRANSLATED BY GEORGE REAVEY (REVISED)

---

*Lines fourteen through eighteen, published in *Iabloko* and *Vzmakh ruki* (1962), were cut from the two-volume selected works and both three-volume collected works.

"Poetry is a great power..."

Poetry is a great power.
The authority of empires, driven mad,
threatened it so many times,
but it was the rulers who perished.

Poetry is a kingdom
in which the truth rules in every city,
where one is judged both for poverty and riches,
where the ruler is whoever becomes its slave.

It has large and small buildings,
fences of lies, and groves of goodness,
and plain, honest plants,
and red poisonous belladonnas.

And the higher one goes, the more singular
the fruits of its great labor—
cities standing turbulently
above the petty bustle of towns.

Poetry, your capital is Pushkin
with a crazy Moscow dash of sin,
church bells of white stone poems
ringing over the hurried, intemperate crowd.

Here is Lermontov city beneath pale stars
darkening in the sound of raindrops and hoofbeats
with tragic outlines of dwellings
and irony of silent dead ends.

Yesenin village looks through quiet birches
at distant morning roads.
Mayakovsky city bellows and smokes.
Snowy, severe, and passionate—the city of Blok.

In your country, poetry, so insouciant at first glance,
is widows' blood and tears,

and Pasternak, the eternal suburb
of future great cities.

1956–1970

TRANSLATED BY ANTONINA W. BOUIS

"My love will come..."

To B. Akhmadulina

My love will come,
will fold me in her arms,
will notice all the changes,
will understand my apprehensions.

From the pouring dark, the infernal gloom,
forgetting to close the taxi door,
she'll dash up the rickety steps
all flushed with joy and longing.

Drenched, she'll burst in, without a knock,
will take my head in her hands,
and from a chair her blue fur coat
will slip blissfully to the floor.

1956

TRANSLATED BY ALBERT C. TODD

"Damp white imprints..."

Damp white imprints dog the feet;
snowbound trolley, snowbound street.
Her tip of glove to lip and cheek,

"Good-bye." Go.
Deathly, into soaring snow
and stillness, as expected, go.
A turn:
            the plunge into the metro.
A blare of lights. A melting hat.
I stand, am spun in drafts, see black,
take the tunnel, train, and track,
sit and wait as others sat,
touch cold marble, chill my hand,
and, heavy-hearted, understand
that nothing ever really happened,
ever would, ever can.

1956

TRANSLATED BY ANTHONY KAHN

"I don't know what..."

I don't know what he wants,
but I know—he's not far off.
He's somewhere near, walking close by,
clutching an apple in his hand.

While I expend my strength in vain,
he walks about and does not tire,
like everyone in a trolleybus he passes on
change wrapped in a ticket.

He watches, catches the slightest sound,
lets nothing slip by,
without understanding his own
enormous predestination.

Everything in the world awaits him,
desires and yearns for him, unrecognized,
and he just strolls about the streets,
crunching a firm apple.

                    .   .   .

But I quail before that moment
when, having understood his rights,
he'll rise up, recognized, above the world
and speak new words.

1956

TRANSLATED BY ALBERT C. TODD

Momma

It's been too long since Momma sang,
and when would she have time!
Does she have so little to do
that there is time for everything!

On birthdays during
the clicking of glasses and conversation
her friend, the old actor,
sits down to the piano.

With a joke she dilutes her sorrow,
and searches for the music sheets,
searches and turns red
from shyness and from wine . . .

They will clap respectfully
and say:
          "Well done!"—
but Momma will run to the kitchen
with a face grown older.

Once she had given concerts
face to face with fighting men
in austere,
              frontline forests,
tall as a church.

Momma's hands were frozen,
her head heavy, and still

the sounds would swell
as pure as the silence.

The driver's horses,
turned gray from the cold,
twitched their ears as they breathed
and reflected on themselves.

The saddle blankets were vaguely white.
There had been a snowfall—
you can't tell the blankets apart:
the officer's from the soldier's . . .

Momma brings out the wine
and spreads out the feast.
The courteous guests ask
Momma to sing something.

Momma,
      I beg you,
            don't . . .
You'll blame yourself later.
It's not your fault—
the guests must understand.

Let the radio phonograph do the singing
and the glasses ring as they come together . . .
Momma,
      don't sing, for God's sake!
Momma,
      don't torture me!

1957

TRANSLATED BY ALBERT C. TODD

They Killed Someone!

I recall that distant dry river gulch,
the dilapidated, rotting little bridge,

and the woman flying over it on a bay mare.
In a dark cloud of dust,
pale-cheeked and unattractive,
she screamed out:
"They killed someone!"
I cannot forget as long as I live
how people ran after her
dropping their scythes in the grass.
He was lying, forlorn and strange,
on the far side of a small hill,
with an imperceptible wound under his last rib.
Guiltless, he had been murdered
by someone at the crossroads . . .
I recall the darkness of the mud
and hear the clatter of hooves.
In dreams I see
the woman in her cloud of dust.
"They killed someone"—
tears my heart inside.
I find it hard to live in the world,
hard to have heard that scream.
I am not yet used
to human death.
More than once I have seen,
deplore it though we might,
the imperceptible destruction
of the human soul.
Watching a senior comrade
in the midst of daily bustle,
it terrifies me to divine
his features hardened in death.
I am not strong enough.
Clenching my teeth, I remain silent.
"They killed someone!"—
I all but scream it out.

1957

TRANSLATED BY ALBERT C. TODD

"The square..."

The square had stately scattered the leaves.
The dawn was breaking, cold and sober.
By the door with the sign in black
the sleeping watchman bristled on a chair.
A potbellied street cleaner swirled by,
thrusting out its white whiskers.
I stepped out into this vaguely perceived world
and, turning up my collar tiredly,
my wrist remembered a forgotten watch.
Enfeebled and lonely,
I returned nonetheless. I remember
how, in her Japanese kimono, the woman
opened the door to my first knock,
startled but composed: "You're back?"
There was in her whole being
a mocking sensible weariness,
which neither warmed nor burned.
"You decided to stay? A change in the rules?
A fresh beginning?"
"Just for a minute. I left my watch."
"Ah yes, the watch, but of course, the watch..."
On the chair by the ottoman a box of makeup,
a notebook with a new role, a volume of Graham Greene,
a rosy celluloid naked doll.
"Here's your watch. I'll put it on you..."
And with a voice concealing hope
and also pain: "Will you call me?"
...I walked wearily along the Neglinnaya.
Everything slept: the yawns of janitors,
watermelons in long wooden boxes,
locks on boot-black cabinets.
Everything looked mystic and obscure—
both the square with its low, twisted fence,
and the faucets wound with rags
on carts with carbonated water.
Scoffing taxi drivers on a break
stood in a circle. Someone, dead drunk,
knocked on the restaurant "Uzbekistan,"
where, of course, they turned him away...

Keen-nosed cats ambled along the fence.
I walked on and on . . . Suddenly a shout:
"Got a smoke?"—with a hazy pale glance,
both strange and familiar.
We set off side by side, our path the same.
I saw he didn't know how to smoke at all.
Twenty-five or twenty-eight,
but no more than thirty.
And I understood the unsociable melancholy
by which we were linked,
that he was also tortured
for leaving someone unloved.
And I saw in this strange double,
as though in my own cruel diary,
the clash of kindred thoughts,
and our pain, trembling into being.
On my forehead are such wrinkles,
cruel for all that happens with me,
while in my soul in unequal skirmish
old age and youth come together,
a clash that occurs ever less often.
Youth wants not to retreat, but,
winning inch by inch,
old age sullenly advances.

1957

TRANSLATED BY ALBERT C. TODD AND JAMES RAGAN

Letter to One Writer

You've betrayed again. Didn't hold out again.
Habit of former years compelled you,
and no matter how you console yourself,
the circle's closed. There's no going back.

Hasn't a little burden piled up
on your conscience? How can you sleep at night?
I understand untalented cowards,
but you—what did you have to fear?

. . .

With real talent you've been a coward.
You've inspired yourself with lying phrases,
and, though you've put on weight, are still handsome,
you've been deceiving us with your dignity.

But the lie has lost its charm.
With cold suspicion those in charge
follow your new shifts and changes,
as young people do with mocking contempt.

1957

TRANSLATED BY ALBERT C. TODD

''Again a meeting . . .''*

Again a meeting, noisy, dying,
                half colloquium,
                        half co-lying.
Obedient hands
          raised to vote,
is there no sob of sentiment
                  in your throat
when making
         a charming deal
to dismember friends
              on the wheel?
What kind of minority
             honestly stands?
Only two hands,
         only two hands.
A minority has courage,
             the majority reeks.
They are not Bolsheviks,
            just bullshitviks.
They are not soldiers
         of revolutions.
Just soldiers
       of resolutions.
You, my friends,
         are silent with reason.

But cowardly silence
                    also is treason.
Oh, majority, majority,
                    creators and victims of fraud,
so many times you've
                    tortured, corrupted,
you have no right
                    to be our god.
The nonruling minority
                    has no authority.
On so many cowards I see
                    an invisible life vest.
But how powerless is the dishonest assent
                    of the majority.
And how powerful is
                    minority's honest protest.

1957

TRANSLATED BY ALBERT C. TODD WITH THE AUTHOR

*The notorious meeting of the Writers' Union in Moscow in 1957, when Vladimir Dudintsev was criticized for his novel *Not by Bread Alone*, which, following Ilia Ehrenburg's novelette *The Thaw*, became the second signal for change in the immediate post-Stalin era.

"Here is what..."

To B. Akhmadulina

Here is what is happening to me:
my old friend doesn't come to visit,
and in idle vanity
come various folk, not those who should.
And he
          goes about somewhere not with those he should
and he understands that too,
and our discord is not cleared up,
and both of us suffer from this.

Here is what is happening to me:
Not the right girl at all comes to visit,
she puts her hands on my shoulders
and steals me from another.
And that one—
                    tell me for God's sake,
on whose shoulders does she put her hands?
That one
            from whom I was stolen.
in vengeance also will begin to steal.
She won't respond immediately this way,
but will live in a struggle with herself
and unaware will select
someone superfluous for her.
Oh, how many nervous
                    and unhealthy,
unnecessary involvements,
                        unnecessary friendships!
Something rabidly desperate in me!
Oh, somebody,
            come,
                    break up
the conjunction
            of people alien to one another
and the estrangement
                    of souls that are kindred.

1957

TRANSLATED BY ALBERT C. TODD

"When I think of Aleksandr Blok..."

When I think of Aleksandr Blok,
and grow nostalgic for him,
I then remember not some line of verse,
but a bridge, a carriage, and the Neva.

· · ·

And above the voice in the night
a rider's figure is clearly etched—
the circles beneath his startling eyes,
and the black silhouette of his frock coat.

Lights and shadows fly to meet him,
stars are splintered in the roadways,
and the waxen fingers of his clasped hands
show something higher than dismay.

And as in an enigmatic prologue,
whose meaning is deep and troubled,
a mist envelops the rattling carriage,
the cobblestones, the clouds, and Blok ...

1957
TRANSLATED BY GEORGE REAVEY (REVISED)

My Dog

Squeezing his black nose on the windowpane
the dog waits and waits in vain.

I bury my hand in his fur,
I too am waiting just for her.

You remember, dog, there was a time
when there lived here a woman sublime.

Who in the end was she to me?
Not as wife or sister would be.

But sometimes, it seems, a daughter
who needs help from me, her father.

She has gone. You've settled down.
No other women will be around.

.   .   .

My splendid dog, good at everything, I think:
What a pity it is that you don't drink.

1958

TRANSLATED BY ALBERT C. TODD

Loneliness

How ashamed one is alone at the movies
with neither a wife, nor lover, nor friend,
where the shows are short
and the waiting long!
How ashamed one is
                          in that private war of nerves
with the derision of couples in the lobby
to munch a pastry, blushing, in a corner
as if from depravity ...
Embarrassed by loneliness,
                          out of longing
we fling ourselves into all forms of company,
and pointless friendship's enslaving obligations
pursue us to the grave.
Companionships form themselves foolishly,
for some to drink and drink,
for others, trendy clothes and dolls,
while others
              argue round supposed ideas,
but if you look carefully
                          all have the same traits.
Varied are the forms of vanity!
First one,
          then another noisy companionship ...
From how many have I managed to escape—
                                        there's no counting!?
How often in a new trap
have I left
          some fur behind?!
You, the desert's freedom,
are ahead ...

But who the devil needs you!
You're enticing,
                    but just as loathsome
as an unloved and faithful wife.
And you, my beloved?
                         How are you getting on?
Are you rid of vanity's affliction?
To whom do your slanting eyes belong now,
and your shoulders luxurious and white?
You think that I am vindictive, no doubt,
that I'm in a taxi now racing somewhere,
but even if I rush,
                    just where am I to get out?
No matter what, I can't get free of you!
With me, women retreat into themselves,

                                      sensing
that they are now so foreign to me.
I lay my head on their laps,
but not to them,
                    to you I belong . . .
Not long ago while seeing a girl
in a moldered house on Sennaya Street,
I hung my coat on pathetic antlers.
Under a one-sided Xmas tree with lusterless lights
shining like miniature white slippers,
the woman sat
                    austere as a child.
I had been so easily permitted
to visit,
          that I was self-assured
and intoxicated with being chic—
Forgetting flowers,
                    I brought wine.
She was silent
                    and two earrings,
two transparent drops,
                         quite like orphans
sparkled in her rosy earlobes.
And, like an invalid, gazing incomprehensibly
while raising her childlike body,
she said obscurely:
                    "Go away . . .
                         Please don't . . .
I can see

you're not mine,
                    but hers . . ."
One young girl loved me
with the wild ways of a child,
with a flying forelock
                    and eyes like bits of ice,
pale from fear
                    and from gentleness.
We were in the Crimea,
                    and the girl,
beneath the magnesium lightning
                    of a night storm
whispered to me:
                    "My little one!
                              My little one!"—
covering my eyes with her palms.
Everything around was terrifying
                    and exulting,
both the thunder
                    and the sea's deaf and dumb moans,
and suddenly,
                    filled with feminine intuition,
she cried out to me:
                    "You're not mine!
                              Not mine!"
Farewell, my beloved!
                    I'm yours,
                              morosely,
                                        faithfully,
and loneliness
                    of all faithfulness is the most faithful.
Let not the parting snow from your mitten
melt on my lips forever.
Thanks to women,
                    beautiful and unfaithful,
that it was always so fleeting,
that their "Good-byes!"
                              were not "Au revoirs!"
that in their mendacity, so regally proud,
blissful suffering gives us as well
the beautiful fruits of loneliness.

1959

TRANSLATED BY ALBERT C. TODD AND JAMES RAGAN

"The icicles' delicate chime..."

The icicles' delicate chime
is so much like a moan,
like a faint moan in a dream
when that dream is so sweet.

But a woman is hurrying.
Almost amused
that she hurries so,
and a little frightened.

Courageous high heels
go clop-clop on the ice,
and her shaggy cap
is rakishly askew.

And behind her back—neither torments,
nor anyone's faces, nor hands,
nor meetings, nor partings—
only that masterful sound!

The young boy waits for her,
fever-chilled and burning.
And here she comes—
the way one comes to die.

The young boy is too old.
He became that way early.
Already he's surrendered full force—
like her he's tired.

Two different woes, two miseries,
helplessly proud,
in silence embarrassed,
as if they had to keep mum.

Two of them—not one,
everything constrained,
but haughtily and darkly,
through the gaping window,

. . .

as through an open hatchway,
that melancholy aching sound,
flies out of March
like tears, pure sound.

And hands take hold of hands,
and to the lips a lock of hair,
all this is not a game
but dying together.

But this death hour
is a birthing hour.
And like a funeral song
it proclaims us,

flying from all sides,
like a faint moan
when a dream is so sweet,
that icicles' delicate chime!

1959

TRANSLATED BY ALBERT C. TODD

Smiles

At one time you had so many smiles:
astonished, rapturous, roguish smiles,
sometimes a little sad, but all the same, smiles.

Now there's left not even one of your smiles.
I'll find a field deep with hundreds of smiles.
I'll bring you a handful of the loveliest smiles.

But you'll tell me that now you don't need any smiles,
that you're so tired of others' and my own smiles.
I too am tired of others' smiles.

. . . .

I too am tired of my own smiles.
I have so many defensive smiles,
making-me-still-more-unsmiling smiles.

But in reality I have no smiles.
You, in my life, are the last of my smiles,
a smile on whose face there never are smiles.

1959

TRANSLATED BY HERBERT MARSHALL (REVISED)

Assignation

No, No! Believe me!
                    I've come to the wrong place!
I've made a god-awful mistake! Even the glass
in my hand's an accident,
                        and so's the gauze glance
of the woman who runs the joint.
                            "Let's dance, huh?
You're pale . . .
            Didn't get enough sleep?"
And I feel like there's no place
to hide, but say, anyway, in a rush
"I'll go get dressed . . .
                    No, no . . . it's just
that I ended up out of bounds . . ."
And later, trailing me as I leave:
                        "This is where booze gets you . . .
What do you mean, 'not here'? *Right* here! Right here every time!
You bug everybody, and you're so satisfied
with yourself about it, Zhenichka,*
you've got a problem."
                    I shove the frost of my hands
down my pockets, and the streets around are snow,

deep snow. I dive into a cab. Buddy, kick this thing! Behind
                                                    the Falcon
there's a room. They're supposed to be waiting for me there.
She opens the door,
                    but what the hell's wrong with her?
Why the crazy look?
                        "It's almost five o'clock.
You sure you couldn't have come a little later?
Well, forget it. Come on in. Where else could you go now?"
Shall I explode
            with a laugh
                        or maybe with tears?
I tell you I was scribbling doggerel,
                        but I got lost someplace.
I hide from the eyes. Wavering I move backwards:
"No, no! Believe me! I've come to the wrong place!"
Once again the night,
                    once again snow
and somebody's insolent song,
and somebody's clean, pure laughter.
I could do with a cigarette.
In the blizzard Pushkin's demons flash past,
and their contemptuous, buck-toothed grin
scares me to death.
                And the kiosks,
and the drugstores,
                    and the social security offices
scare me just as much . . .
                    No, no! Believe me! I've ended up
in the wrong place again . . .†
                    It's *horrible* to live
and even more horrible
                    not to live . . .
                            Ach, this being homeless
like the Wandering Jew . . . Lord! Now I've gotten myself
into the wrong century,
                    wrong epoch,
                            geologic era,
                                    wrong number.
The wrong place again.
                    I'm wrong.
                            I've got it wrong . . .
I go, slouching my shoulders as I'd do

if I'd lost some bet,

            and ah, I know it ... everybody knows it ...
I can't pay off.

1959

TRANSLATED BY JAMES DICKEY WITH ANTHONY KAHN

*Zhenichka: Diminutive familiar form of Yevgeny.
†The next twelve lines were cut after the first publication.

In Memory of the Poet
Xenia Nekrasova

I'll never forget about Ksiusha,
Ksiusha,

        who looked so like a ninny,
with her squinting eyes,

              her pockmarks.
And how was she to blame?

             Her blame
lay in her pockmarks,

           her squinting eyes,
and the unsightly dresses she wore.
What did she really want of us?
A kindly smile,

        a glass of lemonade,
that we print her verse from time to time
and accept her, Ksiusha, as a writer.
In general, we gave her the lemonade,
but as for the kindly smile—

             hardly that.
We even paid her an occasional small fee,
but we wouldn't accept her as a writer,
because our moral guardians
had decided:

       "She isn't normal."
Thus, our Ksiusha lay in her coffin.
She held her hands clasped on her belly,
as though she were gently protecting
an infant inside.

You,
> who are so revoltingly normal,
you
> are abnormal from birth.
Why do you strut your incorporeal bodies,
you people,
> pregnant only with barrenness?
You shall not be forgiven on poor Ksiusha's account.
You'll have to answer for Ksiusha's soul.*

1959

TRANSLATED BY GEORGE REAVEY (REVISED)

*The line sequence was slightly rearranged and a total of seven inconsequential lines were dropped after the first publication.

Incantation

Think of me on spring nights
and think of me on summer nights,
think of me on autumn nights
and think of me on winter nights.
Though I'm not there, but somewhere gone,
far from your side, as if abroad,
stretch yourself on the long cool sheet,
float on your back, as in the sea,
surrendering to the soft slow wave,
with me, as with the sea, utterly alone.

I want nothing on your mind all day.
Let the day turn everything upside down,
besmudge with smoke and flood with wine,
distract you till I fade from view.
All right, think of anything by day,
but in the night—only of me alone.

Over the locomotive whistles, over
the wind, ripping the clouds to shreds,
listen to me, for pity's sake:

Show me again, in the narrow room,
your eyes half-shut with ecstasy and pain,
your palms pressing your temples till they ache.

I beseech you—in the stillest stillness,
or when the rain patters on your roof,
or the snow sparks on your windowpanes,
and you lie between sleep and waking—
think of me on spring nights
and think of me on summer nights,
think of me on autumn nights
and think of me on winter nights.

1960

TRANSLATED BY STANLEY KUNITZ WITH ANTHONY KAHN

"I am older by . . ."

I am older by your thirty-three years,
and all that has ever happened to you,
what you remember and what you forgot,
is concealed like a stone inside of me.

Inside me your father is murdered,
inside me your mother is dragged to interrogation,
inside me your childlike eyes grow dim
when there's no medicine to be found.

Inside me you look at yourself for the first time,
in the mirrored depths, not of a child, but a woman.
Inside me, in timidly fearless bliss,
you give cold lips without loving.

But later you love, and maybe not,
but later you don't love, and maybe you do,
and leaves and the moonlight you exchange for crowds,
and a sticky-from-vodka parquet floor.

. . .

In sewing and English you seek barriers.
You throw yourself nervously into some book.
You flee to Beethoven and Grieg like a church,
pleading with a moan for the organ's sanctuary.

But they don't let you hide yourself anywhere.
They send you back kulak-like* to your daily life,
and, seeing in you no repentance,
they beat you kulak-like—not to death.

You silently sob alone in the quiet,
hatefully ironing shirts and socks,
and in the March night, with unseeing eyes,
as in a dream you come to me.

Then you are ill, and bending over you,
doctors conjure like white magicians,
and in the windows, already quite like May,
April birds vie with each other in din.

Twice you reached the very last line,
but still you fight on, even when despairing,
and afterward emerge, so fragile and reeling,
as though any moment you'll break.

I live with twofold pain and anxiety.
I live with your hearing, your sensing of all,
I live with your seeing, your tears,
your words, and your silence.

My being is two beings in one.
Two pasts with their weight bend my shoulders.
Two lives are in me—both mine and yours.
And in order to kill me, two bullets must come.

1960

TRANSLATED BY ALBERT C. TODD

---

*kulak: Prosperous farmers who were brutally forced into collective farms and "liquidated" as a
class in the 1920s. Countless numbers were executed.

The Incendiary

You are completely free of affectation:
silent you sit, watchfully tense,
just as silence itself pretends to nothing
on a starless night in a fire-gutted city.

Consider that city—it is your past,
wherein you scarcely ever managed to laugh,
now raging through the streets, now sunk in self,
between your insurrections and your calms.

You wanted life and gave it all your strength,
but, sullenly spurning everything alive,
this slum of a city suffocated you
with the dreary weight of its architecture.

In it every house was shuttered tight,
in it shrewdness and cynicism ruled,
it never hid its poverty of spirit,
its hate for anyone who wasn't broken.

And so one night you burned it down
and ran for cover, frightened by the flames,
till chance produced me in your way, the one
you stumbled on when you were fugitive.

I took you in my arms, I felt you tremble,
as quietly your body clung to mine,
not knowing me or caring, but yet,
like an animal, grateful for my pity.

Together then we left . . . Where did we go?
Wherever our eyes, in their folly, took us.
But intermittently you had to turn
to watch your past ominously burning.

It burned beyond control, till it was ashes.
And I remain tormented to this day
that you are drawn, as though enchanted,
back to that place where still the embers glow.

You're here with me, and yet not here.

In fact you have abandoned me. You glide
through the smoldering wreckage of the past,
holding aloft a bluish light in your hand.

What pulls you back? It's empty and gray there!
Oh, the mysterious power of the past!
You never could learn to love it as it was,
but yet you fell madly in love with its ruins.

Over what's left where once she set her fire
the incendiary cries like a little child.
Ashes and embers must be magnets too.
How can we tell what potencies they hold?

1960

TRANSLATED BY STANLEY KUNITZ WITH ANTHONY KAHN (REVISED)

Let's Not...

Let's not...
        Everything's ghostly—
                        the blank windows watching,
the snow reddening behind the stoplights of the cars.
Let's not...
        Everything's ghostly, lost in mist,
like a garden in March emptied of men and women,
                                        paraded by shadows.

Let's not...
        I stand by a tree,
                        not speaking, undeceiving,
facing
        the double glare of the headlights,
and with a quiet hand touch
                        but do not break
the tender icicle imprisoning a twig.
Let's not...
        I see you in the sleepy, reeling trolley
with spectral Moscow rocking in the window,

your cheek propped on a child's wool mitten,
thinking of me with a woman's rancor.
Let's not ...

       You'll be a woman soon enough, subtle and worn,
hungry for praise, for the balm of a caress;
it will be March again,

          a callow boy will whisper in your ear,
your head will whirl inconsolably.
Let's not ...

      for both your sakes,
don't stroll with him down the slippery path,
don't place

     your insubordinate hands
upon his shoulders,

        even as I do not place them today.
Let's not ...

       Oh, disbelieve, like me, in the ghostly city.
Be spared

    from waking in the wasteland,

           terrified.
Say: "Let's not ..."

     bending your head,
as I this moment

    say

      "Let's not ..."

        to you ...

1960

TRANSLATED BY STANLEY KUNITZ WITH ANTHONY KAHN

Secret Mysteries

Adolescent mysteries melt away
like mist upon the shore ...
The Tonyas and Tanyas were all mysteries
even with cold sores on their legs.

Stars and animals were mysteries.
Mushrooms under aspen trees

and doors creaking mysteriously—
only in childhood do doors creak that way.

The world's riddles rose up
like balloons from the mouth
of some seductive fakir
full of crafty schemes.

Enchanted snowflakes
fell in fields and woods.
Enchanted laughter
danced in young girls' eyes.

Mysteriously we whispered something
on the mysterious ice of a skating rink,
mystery touching mystery,
hand touching hand . . .

Unexpectedly maturity caught up with us.
His dress coat worn to holes,
the fakir went on tour
in someone else's childhood.

We, as grown-ups, are forgotten.
Ah, fakir, you're a faker!
So unmysterious it hurts,
snow falls on our shoulders.

Where are you, bewitched balloons?
There's no mystery to our mourning.
Others are unmysterious to us,
and we're unmysterious to them.

And if some hand by chance
caress us lightly,
it still is only a hand and not a mystery,
a hand, understand, only a hand.

Oh, give me a mystery, some simple mystery,
a secret mystery—silence and timidity—
a fragile mystery, a barefoot mystery . . .
just one sweet secret mystery!

1960

*TRANSLATED BY LAWRENCE FERLINGHETTI WITH ANTHONY
KAHN*

"They shuffle..."

They shuffle and mumble in the train's berth
and raucously invite people to a shindig.
And while it softly shakes up the chess game,
I write on as quietly

as the darkness falling
on what was today's light
and the gradual enthronement
of the breathing around me.

You came to me not out of joy—
you hardly remember that—
but from some kind of shared equality
of hauntingly shared silence.

You came out of desperation.
Merry, rational beyond your strength,
you left the past behind,
to return again into the past.

And, smiling somehow brokenly,
and crying somewhere within,
you offered salty olive pits
to me with your lips.

And, rushing ever more unneedingly
toward a nonexisting depth,
from two miseries, like children,
we wanted to make at least one joy.

Here with a green notebook
I lie on the upper bunk.
The salty olive pits
I still keep behind my cheek.

I am going away from this bottomlessness,
as though there is a bottom to something.
I am going away from this homelessness,
as though for me there is a home.

You are on some other train

on the move to other destinations.
Forgive me, you who are always late,
that I was always late as well.

Still my perceptions
pour over me like streams.
There's still in me the memory
of how young girls sing in church.

But I remember a prophetic image,
a foreshadowing of all ages.
Above the whole universe, above eternity
hands stretch out to hands.

An artist who feels the torment
brings them together as much as he can.
But still the invisible gap remains
between the woman's fingers and the man's.

And it all repeats itself in us,
as with someone many years ago.
Hands stretch to each other,
and the fingertips scream out.

And stretched out over the abyss,
where there is the same, the same muteness,
our poor hands cannot
join together ever.

1960

TRANSLATED BY ALBERT C. TODD AND JAMES RAGAN

Pasternak's Grave

Grave, you're robbed by the railing.
Railing, you've cut him off
from the growling trucks, the green pear trees,
the hail of agate-like currants.

From everything,

. . .

that in him brimmed over, rushed brashly, spurted,
like sparks beneath frenzied hooves.
Always boisterous being—not bland existence.
And battles, too, were common life.

There were creaking carriage springs and bursts of horses' snorting,
the peace of ponds and the crunch of crashing ice floes,
the hazardous fervor of bazaars,
the conserving contemplativeness of temples,
the breaking surf of gardens and layers of cities.

A gift—created to bestow more gifts,
now subdued by stones and roots,
he, like a pilgrim, stepped over the crush
for provender and petty crowns.

He went his way, leaving all the fuss to others.
Firm and springy was the stride
of this silver-headed artist
with a sailor's swarthy cheeks.

In a way Pushkin's double, willingly and greatly,
even though penned in by grievous griefs,
he was a large, childlike smile
upon the face of the age's martyr.

And this I know—that tranquil grave
affords no haven for some mourning faces.
For ages it will be a raging magnet
for boys, flowers, seeds, and birds.

Grave, you're robbed by the railing,
but in the autumn silence I have seen
two pines, like sisters, growing side by side—
one within, the other outside the railing.

And with irrepressible thrusts,
accusing the railing of robbery,
the imprisoned pine holds out her arms
to her unimprisoned sister.

No pruning can hinder it!

Hew them off—branches will grow again.
Those are his arms—it seems to me—
reaching out to embrace both pines and people.

From this earth's griefs, this earth's delights,
no railing will isolate any man
who has lived, as he, a reward to others.
On this earth there are still no such railings.

1960

TRANSLATED BY GEORGE REAVEY (REVISED)

Our Mothers Depart

To R. Pospelov

Our mothers depart from us,
gently,
           on tiptoe,
but we sleep soundly,
                          stuffed with food,
and fail to notice this dread hour.
Our mothers do not leave us suddenly,
                                        no—
it only seems
               sudden.
Slowly they depart, and strangely,
with short steps down
                    the stairs of years.

One year, remembering nervously,
we make a fuss to mark their birthday,
but this belated zeal
will save neither their souls,
                          nor ours.

They withdraw farther,
                    ever farther.

Roused from sleep,
                we stretch toward them,
but our hands suddenly beat the air—
a wall of glass has grown up there!

We are too late.
              The dread hour has struck.
Suppressing tears, we watch our mothers,
in columns quiet and austere,
departing from us . . .

1960
TRANSLATED BY GEORGE REAVEY (REVISED)

Honey

In that terrible year, in '41,
                in Christopol,
where everything was starved and frozen,
a barrel was put out
              in the market snow—
twenty bucketsful—
              of honey!
The vendor was that sort of creep
who makes a profit out of grief,
and grief queued up in a long line,
simple, bitter, and bare.
He took no cash,
              but bartered for blouses,
watches,
        or cuts of cloth.
His trader's hand with many rings
spurned the obvious rags.
He raised each object to the light . . .
An aged artist with one hand
unlaced his boots,
and, in the other,
              held out a bottle.

He watched the honey thickly dripping,
watched it, stooping, uncomplaining,
and then with his honey—

                        that eternal value—
trudged through the snow in his darned socks.
And in her transparent hand

                      a young girl
in a strange and drowsy state
held out a small wineglass
with her mother's little ring at the bottom.
But—

        a sleigh drew up with mighty creaking.
Roses were painted

              on its back.
And wrinkling an imposing official brow,
a man descended,

           tall and heavy,

                  from the sleigh.
Large

    and solemn

           as a portrait in a frame,
without the least shade of pity he commanded:
"The whole barrel!

           I'll settle with carpets.
Hoist it up here, my good fellow!"
The line of people stood there sullenly
as if not involved at all.
The little ring,

           dropping from the wineglass,
fell in the wake of the scudding sleigh . . .
That year of '41 is now far off,
the year of misfortunes and retreats,
but he's still alive—

         that honey-sucker,
and lives on sweetly to this day.
When staidly before him he carries
his bumptious belly,
when he glances at his watch
and strokes his satiate mustache,
I remember that year,
I remember that honey.
That honey seemed

           as though by itself
to flow

over,

and over his mustache.
He cannot ever

wipe away
honey

that's stuck to him

forever!

1960

TRANSLATED BY GEORGE REAVEY (REVISED)

The American Nightingale

In the land of nylon and Dacron,
and science that's become a fetish,
I suddenly heard an oh so kindred
quite inimitable pure sound.

A bird is no burden to a branch,
and on one such branch,
perched an American nightingale,
singing just like a Russian.

He sang mournfully, and happily,
and, ebulliently, someone threw out
bursts of lilac in reply—
earth's awakened joy.

It was at Harvard in the springtime.
Everything was topsy-turvy
in the laughing merry-go-round
of after-exam inebriation.

The students sang, and caroused,
and everything seemed mixed
top to bottom in a rainbow cocktail
of students, birds, and flowers.

Proudly, immutably he rang out,

that so kindred nightingale,
above the half-truths and the lies,
above all the bustling chatter,

above all the black deeds,
the millions of questionnaires,
and the shark-like bodies
of rockets ready for action.

And somewhere in the heart of Russia
the same small sort of scamp,
his little Russian brother,
festively opened his tiny beak and sang.

In Tambov, Cambridge, and Miami,
to the delight of villages and cities,
the branches in all gardens bend
beneath the nubile nightingales.

The music, like a blizzard, lashed
one continent and then another.
All nightingales understand each other—
everywhere they speak one language.

In their tremulous unity,
they sing ever higher, ever more tenderly.
But what of us, we people, shall we never
understand each other this way?!

1960

TRANSLATED BY ALBERT C. TODD

Encounter

In the airport café in Copenhagen
we sat around
         applying ourselves to beer.
There everything was elegant
             and comfortable

and stylish to the point of tedium.
 And suddenly he appeared—
                              that old man
in an ordinary green jacket with a hood,
his face
            scorched by salty wind.
He didn't so much appear
                              as he happened.
He walked,
              plowing a furrow through the crowded room
like a sailor straight from a ship's helm,
and his beard
                like sea foam
outlined
          his face
                    in white.
His gruff, winner's
                    certainty
sent out a wave around him
                              as he walked
through old fashions
                      aping modern fashions,
and modern fashions
                      aping old fashions.
And with the rough collar of his shirt turned up,
stepping aside from vermouth and Pernod,
he demanded a glass of Russian vodka at the bar
and waved away soda with:
                          "No."
With weather-beaten arms in scars
                                  and scratches,
in shoes
          that produced a heavy thud,
in trousers
            that were indescribably soiled,
he was more elegant
                    than all around.
The ground seemed to sink beneath
the heavy authority of his tread.
And one of us smiled and said to me:
"Look at that,
                exactly like Hemingway!"
He walked,
            in each curt gesture was expressed

the difficult gait of a fisherman,
all crudely hewn out of a granite crag,
he walked
       as men walk
            through bullets
                  and centuries.

He walked
       hunched over
            as if in a trench,
pushing aside
       people and furniture.
It was the very image of Hemingway . . .
And later I learned
       that it was he.

1960

TRANSLATED BY ALBERT C. TODD

Talk

You're a brave man
       they tell me.
It's not true.
       I've never been courageous.
I only thought it an unworthy act
to degrade myself to cowardice as others did.

I didn't shake any foundations.
I no more than laughed at the pompous
           and the false.
I wrote verses.
       Never denunciations.
I tried to say what I had thought.

Yes,
    I defended people with talent.
I branded mediocrity,
        those pretending to be writers.

But that is something that has to be done,
and yet they go on about bravery.

Oh, with what a feeling of bitter shame
our descendants will remember,
when they settle
                    with the abomination,
that time
            so strange,
                          when
simple honesty
                looked like courage!

1960

TRANSLATED BY ALBERT C. TODD

Babii Yar*

No monument stands over Babii Yar.†
A drop sheer as a crude gravestone.
I am afraid.
            Today I am as old in years
as all the Jewish people.
Now I seem to be
            a Jew.
Here I plod through ancient Egypt.
Here I perish crucified, on the cross,
and to this day I bear the scars of nails.
I seem to be
            Dreyfus.
The Philistine
            is both informer and judge.
I am behind bars.
                    Beset on every side.
Hounded,
        spat on,
                  slandered.
Squealing, dainty ladies in flounced Brussels lace

stick their parasols into my face.
I seem to be then
                     a young boy in Byelostok.
Blood runs, spilling over the floors.
The barroom rabble-rousers
give off a stench of vodka and onion.
A boot kicks me aside, helpless.
In vain I plead with these pogrom bullies.
While they jeer and shout,
                          "Beat the Yids. Save Russia!"
some grain-marketeer beats up my mother.
O my Russian people!
                     I know
                     you
are international to the core.
But those with unclean hands
have often made a jingle of your purest name.
I know the goodness of my land.
How vile these anti-Semites—
                          without a qualm
they pompously called themselves
the Union of the Russian People!
I seem to be
          Anne Frank
transparent
          as a branch in April.
And I love.
          And have no need of phrases.
My need
     is that we gaze into each other.
How little we can see
                or smell!
We are denied the leaves,
                     we are denied the sky.
Yet we can do so much—
                     tenderly
embrace each other in a darkened room.
They're coming here?
                     Be not afraid. Those are the booming
sounds of spring:
               spring is coming here.
Come then to me.
          Quick, give me your lips.

Are they smashing down the door?

No, it's the ice breaking . . .

The wild grasses rustle over Babii Yar.

The trees look ominous,

like judges.

Here all things scream silently,

and, baring my head,

slowly I feel myself

turning gray.

And I myself

am one massive, soundless scream

above the thousand thousand buried here.

I am

each old man

here shot dead.

I am

every child

here shot dead.

Nothing in me

shall ever forget!

The "Internationale," let it

thunder

when the last anti-Semite on earth

is buried forever.

In my blood there is no Jewish blood.

In their callous rage, all anti-Semites

must hate me now as a Jew.

For that reason

I am a true Russian!

1961

TRANSLATED BY GEORGE REAVEY

*One of five Yevtushenko poems on which Dmitri Shostakovich based his Thirteenth Symphony. See the Introduction for comments about the poem's often misrepresented history of publication.
†Babii Yar: Ravine in the suburbs of Kiev where Nazi forces murdered tens of thousands of Soviet Jews and others during World War II. For a long time there was no monument at the site of the atrocity.

Irpen

Irpen *is the memory of*
the south and summer...
    —B. Pasternak

I once promised so much to you,
and I can give you nothing—
                    I made you poor.
I promised you us in the blue, in the foliage,
on green grass,
                head to head,
cool cherries on each cheek,
and tranquillity that smells lazily of hay.
We wanted to come to Irpen,
                    languid and half asleep,
here on that precipice or tree stump,
the exquisite fugitive wrote
of gillyflowers and forest
                    when he fled here...
But today there is no escaping,
as from a tribunal,
                    out of shame for history.
Clouds burst endlessly,
                    ferociously,
washing away all hope of peace and comfort
for you and me,
                in the blue and foliage,
on green grass,
                head to head...
The toadies swill their borscht,
                    their bellies growling.
A prominent critic approaches
                    who barely reaches my shoulders,
but nevertheless he pats me on them:
"Right now you're just how
                    I've always wanted you.
You haven't swallowed the bait of flattery,
and on civic issues you've come out strong..."
In your eyes I see contempt and shame.
By his praise
            I'm destroyed for you.

Don't believe it—
          I'm not that way,
                    I'm not that way,
                              I'm not that way!
I'm simply smashed to splinters,
                    like a raft in a flood.
That critic lies.
          Don't listen to nonsense!
He just likes the chips that fly off me,
                    but not me!
But you say:
          "No,
                    you're just that way.
You're not a raft,
                    but the pampered fruit of the age,
everyone's favorite,
                    a model son . . ."
and your beautiful glance is unbearably cruel.
You say,
          the epoch is a blood mother to me.
Could a mother maim
                    and break?
Like a horse,
          they harnessed me with a collar,
and beat me with a whip,
                    grinning to boot.
But today they lavishly pass me gingerbread.
Every piece scars me
                    like a whip.
The raw autumn mist clings like a sucking swamp.
The toadies gloomily play dominoes.
The countryside hungers,
                    woods become scarce,
yet cosmonauts are flying to the heavens!
I've impoverished you even more terribly—
          I've impoverished you with my soul.
Forgive me, that I promised you so much.

1961

TRANSLATED BY ALBERT C. TODD AND JAMES RAGAN

Irony

The twentieth century has often fooled us.
We've been squeezed in by falsehood as by taxes.
The breath of life has denuded our ideas
as quickly as it strips a dandelion.

As boys fall back on biting sarcasm,
so we rely for safe defense
on an irony not too suppressed,
not too naked either.

It has served as a wall or dam
to shield us against a flood of lies,
and hands have laughed as they applauded,
and feet sniggered as they marched.

They could write about us, and we've allowed
them to make movies of this scribbled trash,
but we have reserved the right
to treat all this with quiet irony.

In our contempt we felt superior.
All this is so, but probing deeper,
irony, instead of acting as our savior,
you have become our murderer.

We're cautious, hypocritical in love.
Our friendships are lukewarm, not brave,
and our present seems no different from
our past, so cunningly disguised.

Through life we scurry. In history,
like any Faust, we've been prejudged.
With Mephistophelian smile, irony,
like a shadow, dogs our every step.

In vain we try to dodge the shadow.
The paths in front, behind, are blocked.
Irony, to you we've sold our soul,
receiving no Margaret in return.

. . .

You have buried us alive.
Bitter knowledge has made us powerless,
and our weary irony ironically
has turned against ourselves.

1961

TRANSLATED BY GEORGE REAVEY (REVISED)

Girl Beatnik

The girl from New York
does not belong.
Along the neon lights, she
runs away from herself.

To her the world seems odious—
a moralist who's been howled down.
It holds no more truths for her.
Now the "twist" alone is true.

With hair mussed and wild,
in spectacles and a coarse sweater,
on spiked heels she dances
the thinnest of negations.

Everything strikes her as false,
everything—from the Bible to the press.
The Montagues exist, and the Capulets,
but there are no Romeos and Juliets.

The trees stoop broodingly,
and rather drunkenly the moon
staggers like a beatnik sulking
along the milky avenue.

Wanders, as if from bar to bar,
wrapped in thought, unsocial,
and the city spreads underneath
in all its hard-hearted beauty.

. . .

All things look hard—the roofs and walls,
and it's no accident that, over the city,
the television antennae rise
like crucifixions without Christ.

1961

TRANSLATED BY GEORGE REAVEY (REVISED)

"No people are..."

To S. Preobrazhenskii

No people are uninteresting.
Their destinies are like histories of planets.
Nothing in them is not particular,
and no planet is like another.

And if someone lives in obscurity,
befriending that obscurity,
he is interesting to people
by his very obscurity.

Everyone has his own secret, private world.
In that world is a finest moment.
In that world is a tragic hour,
but it all is unknown to us.

And if someone dies
there dies with him his first snow,
and first kiss, and first fight.
He takes it all with him.

Yes, books and bridges remain,
and painted canvas and machinery,
yes, much is sentenced to remain,
but something really departs all the same!

Such is the law of the pitiless game.
It's not people who die, but worlds.

We remember people, sinful and earthly.
But what did we know, in essence, about them?

What do we know of brothers, of friends?
What do we know of our one and only?
And about our own fathers,
knowing everything, we know nothing.

They perish. They cannot be brought back.
Their secret worlds are not regenerated.
And every time I want again
to cry out against the unretrievableness.

1961

TRANSLATED BY ALBERT C. TODD

"Professor . . ."

Professor,
             I don't like you at all.
But your wife likes me
and your son—
                a gloomy lad,
who took after,
                obviously,
                         not his Papa.
Everything about you is suspicious to me—
                                    your rosy color,
and your little anecdote about someone's
                                  little affair,
and your skewbald hedgehog
                      with the slicked-down forehead.
I
 don't like
          people too rosy!
And nevertheless,
                Professor,
                        what good luck,
that right next to yours—

was my friend's dacha,
that you invited me over neighbor-like,
that even we ate hot dogs at your place,
and here,
            tensely and gloomily amusing ourselves,
you and I played table tennis.
Professor,
        neither I
                nor you have forgotten,
that in the most difficult time you were
not with those who were beaten,
                        but with those who did the beating,
and betrayed those
                who were more talented.
Professor,
        the issue here is not personal spite.
Take a look,
        how distrustfully she looks at you,
gloomily and deadly tense,
that beautiful woman—
                your wife.
But the boy,
        Professor,
                your gloomy boy,
how nervously he hits
                the little celluloid ball,
how caustically he doesn't believe
                your words
and struggles toward us in despair,
                not toward you!
Professor,
        you and I still haven't settled accounts.
In the realm of Ping-Pong
                we simply met.
Professor,
        I'll rob you and defame you.
Your wife, maybe,
        I'll leave for you.
I'll leave the wife,
                but keep in mind—
at any rate I'll lead your son away from you!

1962

TRANSLATED BY ALBERT C. TODD

The Dead Hand of the Past

Someone is still living as of old,
attempting to knife whatever's new.
Someone still glares in the Stalin manner,
looking at young men askance.

Someone still untamed and restless
fiercely grips the hour hand and,
in striving to drag it down,
hangs on to history's clock.

Someone pines in impotent anger.
That may be, but I for certain know
it's harder to unclench a fist
if the fist is that of a dead hand.

Dead hand of the past,
your grip on us is still strong.
The dead hand of the past
will yield nought without a struggle.

Dead hand of the past,
you will not destroy the living.
Dead hand of the past,
we'll break your fingers' hold.*

Dead hand of the past,
let it be a hard fight between us.
Dead hand of the past,
you're a dead hand to the last.

1962

TRANSLATED BY GEORGE REAVEY

*Translated from manuscript; the fifth stanza was cut and the sixth stanza altered in the published form.

The Heirs of Stalin

Mute was the marble.
                    Mutely glimmered the glass.
Mute stood the sentries,
                    bronzed by the breeze.
But thin wisps of breath
                    seeped from the coffin
when they bore him
                    out of the mausoleum doors.
Slowly the coffin floated by,
                    grazing the fixed bayonets.
He was also mute—
            he also!—
                    but awesome and mute.
Grimly clenching
            his embalmed fists,
he watched through a crack inside,
                    just pretending to be dead.
He wanted to fix each pallbearer
                    in his memory:
young recruits from Ryazan and Kursk,
in order somehow later
                    to collect strength for a sortie,
and rise from the earth
                    and get
                to them,
                        the unthinking.
He has worked out a scheme.
                    He's merely curled up for a nap.
And I appeal
            to our government with a plea:
to double,
            and treble, the guard at this slab,
so that Stalin will not rise again,
                    and with Stalin—the past.
We sowed crops honestly.
                    Honestly we smelted metal,
and honestly we marched,
                    in ranks as soldiers.
But he feared us.

Believing in a great goal, he forgot
that the means must be worthy
                    of the goal's greatness.
He was farsighted.
                    Wily in the ways of combat,
he left behind him
                    many heirs on this globe.
It seems to me
                    a telephone was installed in the coffin.
To someone once again
                    Stalin is sending his instructions.
Where does the cable yet go
                    from that coffin?
No, Stalin did not die.
                    He thinks death can be fixed.
We removed
            him
                    from the mausoleum.
But how do we remove Stalin
                    from Stalin's heirs?
Some of his heirs
                    tend roses in retirement,
but secretly consider
                    their retirement temporary.
Others,
        from platforms rail against Stalin,
but,
    at night,
                    yearn for the old days.
It is no wonder Stalin's heirs,
                    with reason today
visibly suffer heart attacks.
                    They, the former henchmen,
hate a time
                    when prison camps are empty,
and auditoriums, where people listen to poetry,
                    are overfilled.
My motherland commands me not to be calm.
Even if they say to me: "Be assured . . ."—
                    I am unable.
While the heirs of Stalin
                    are still alive on this earth,

it will seem to me
         that Stalin still lives in the mausoleum.

1962
TRANSLATED BY GEORGE REAVEY (REVISED)

Fears*

Fears are dying out in Russia
like the ghosts of bygone years,
and only like old women, here and there,
they still beg for alms on the steps of a church.

But I remember them in their strength and power
at the court of triumphing falsehood.
Like shadows, fears crept in everywhere,
and penetrated to every floor.

Gradually, they made people subservient,
and set their seal upon all things:
they trained us to shout—when we should keep silent—
and to shut our mouths—when we had need to shout.

Today all this has become remote.
It's strange even to recall nowadays
the secret fear of being denounced,
the secret fear of a knock at the door.

And what of the fear of speaking to a foreigner?
A foreigner's one thing, but what about one's wife?
And what of the boundless fear of remaining
alone with silence after the brass bands have stopped?

We were not afraid of building in the blizzard,
or of going into battle while shells exploded,

but at times we were mortally afraid
of even talking to ourselves.

We were not corrupted or led astray;
and Russia, having conquered her fears,
gives rise—not without reason—to even
greater fear among her enemies!

I wish that people were possessed of the fear
of condemning someone without trial,
the fear of debasing ideas by untruths,
the fear of exalting oneself by untruths,

the fear of remaining indifferent to others,
when someone is in trouble or depressed,
the desperate fear of not being fearless
on canvas or drafting board.

But as I write these lines—
and I am in too great a haste at times—
I write with only the single fear
of not writing with all my power . . .

1962

TRANSLATED BY GEORGE REAVEY (REVISED)

*One of five Yevtushenko poems on which Dmitri Shostakovich based his Thirteenth Symphony.

1963⁄1964

The sea was what I breathed,
it was sorrow I exhaled...

People Were Laughing Behind a Wall

To Ye. Laskina

People were laughing behind a wall,
and I stared hard at that very wall,
while my soul was like an ailing girl
in arms that gradually felt emptier.

People were laughing behind a wall.
They seemed to be making fun of me.
I was the butt of all their laughter,
and how dishonestly they laughed!

But, in reality, they were but guests,
who, tired of shuffling round the floor,
were laughing to wile the time away,
and not personally at me or anybody else.

People were laughing behind a wall,
warming themselves with wine,
and, laughing, they did not suspect at all
my presence there with my ailing soul.

People were laughing . . . How many times
have I also laughed like that myself,
while someone lay dying behind a wall,
painfully reconciling himself to this.

And he was thinking, by misfortune tracked,
and almost on the point of giving in,
that it was I who laughed at him,
and even mocked him, it would seem.

Yes, this is how our globe's arranged,
and will be thus arranged forever:
sobs will sound behind a wall
when nonchalantly we begin to laugh.

But also the globe is so arranged,
and thus will never evanesce:

someone will always laugh behind a wall
when we're about to break out sobbing.

Double your kindness, be fulfilled,
and to avoid offending any person,
allow your heart to see right through a wall
when noisily you burst out laughing.

But, feeling broken and depressed,
do not impose, from envy, on your soul
the sin of regarding it as an offense
when someone laughs behind a wall.

Existence is an equilibrium of sorts.
A show of envy is an insult to oneself.
Another's happiness will expiate
for any misfortune you might suffer.

In your last hour when closing eyes
grow glazed, express your final wish:
Let people laugh behind a wall,
let them laugh indeed, laugh if they must!

1963

TRANSLATED BY GEORGE REAVEY

"Early illusions are beautiful..."

Early illusions are beautiful,
Early illusions wound dangerously...
But what does it matter! We are above vanity,
concerned with the highest kind of knowing,
saved by our happy blindness.

We, who are not afraid of taking a false step—
fools, from reality's point of view—
still bear enchantment in our faces
through all the disillusioned crowd.

· · ·

We are driven into the distance
by a glimmering of something,
away from the daily grind, the calculations
of everyday living,
from pale skeptics and pink schemers,
transforming the world with our reflections.

But the inevitability of disappointments
makes us see too clearly. On all sides
everything suddenly takes shape,
all unknown to us till now.

The world appears before us, undawned, unmisted,
no longer made radiant by something,
but it seems that all this truthfulness unmasked
is deceit, and what is gone was no deception.

You see, it is not the ability to be wise as the serpent,
it is not the doubtful honor of experience,
but the ability to be enchanted by the world
that reveals to us the world as it really is.

Suddenly someone with an enchanted face
flashes past, pursuing some distant gleam,
and it doesn't seem to us that he is blind—
we seem ourselves to be the blind ones.

1963

TRANSLATED BY TINA TUPIKINA-GLAESSNER, GEOFFREY DUTTON, AND
IGOR MEZHAKOFF-KORIAKIN (REVISED)

The Third Memory

We all live through an hour like this,
when with viscid anguish,
and in stark nakedness exposed,
all life appears devoid of meaning.

A deadly chill will creep inside
and, to control that stubborn self,

we weakly summon memory
as we might call a nurse for aid.

In us at times there's such deep night,
at times in us such utter ruin,
that no memory of either reason
or heart can help us in our plight.

The gleam of life forsakes our eyes.
Movement and speech—these all are dead.
But a third memory we have,
the body's memory.

Then vividly let feet recall
the heat of dusty roads that scorched,
and fields of grass that used to chill
our soles when barefoot we tramped about.

And fondly let a cheek remember
the friendly understanding dog
that consoled us, bruised and battered
in a fight, with its good rough tongue.

And, feeling guilty, let your brow
remember how a kiss, in blessing,
touched it almost without sound,
a mother's tenderness expressing.

And let your back voluptuously
remember the drowsy languor biding
in earth's deep soul, as you lie there
with eyes devouring all the sky.*

Let fingers feel the rye and conifers,
the almost impalpable rain,
a sparrow's shiver, and the quiver
down the nervous withers of a horse.

Let lips remember other lips.
Their ice and fire. Their gloom and glow.
The whole world in them. A world
all redolent of oranges and snow . . .

. . .

Shame will awake when you remember.
You'll grasp the crime of censuring life.
And body's memory will then restore
the memory of heart and reason.

And you will say to life: "Forgive!
I used to blame you in my blindness.
As from a grievous sin, absolve
me of my raging bluntness.

And if we are obliged to pay
a savage price because this world
is beautiful—all right, I'll say,
I shall consent to pay the price.

But, life, are all the stringencies
of fate, the losses, sudden blows,
so great a price for me to pay
for all the beauty you contain?!"

1963

TRANSLATED BY GEORGE REAVEY (REVISED)

*Though the poem is often reprinted, stanzas eight, ten, and eleven were variously cut after the first publication.

The Sigh

He's withdrawn,
                    my old friend,
                    withdrawn.
He's driven himself inside.
As in a well, he's shut himself in
deep in his nostalgia,
and his thoughts hammer against that lid,
and his fists smash against it.
He will not tell you what he's thinking,
nor sob out these thoughts brokenly,
and sullenly it all piles up within him,

and I fear
            an explosion.
But no explosion comes,
               only a sigh,
and that sigh's
            like a woman weeping in the hay,
like the sea's shuddering gasp
as it drenches the rocks at dusk.
I was like an open book before,
and never held back at all,
and, for this, fate rebuffed me
like a disdainful woman.
And now I'm tired.
                I've become shut in.
I've ceased to trust.
At times, when drinking,
I almost catch myself exploding.
But no explosion comes,
               only a sigh,
and the sigh's
            like a woman weeping in the hay,
like the sea's shuddering gasp
as it drenches the rocks at dusk.
My old, my unsociable
               friend,
let us sit down as we used to do,
let's fill a glass each,
let us sigh—
            this time together.

1963

TRANSLATED BY GEORGE REAVEY

Picture of Childhood

Elbowing our way, we run.
Someone is being beaten up in the market.
You wouldn't want to miss it!
We pick up speed, racing to the uproar,

scooping up water in our felt boots
and forgetting to wipe our sniffles.

And stood stock-still. In our little hearts something tightened,
when we saw how the ring of sheepskin coats,
fur coats, hooded coats, was contracting,
how he stood up near the green vegetable stall
with his head pulled into his shoulders from the hail
of jabs, kicks, spitting, slaps in the face.

Suddenly someone from the right by the handcart
                    pushed his teeth in,
Suddenly someone from the left bashed his forehead with a
                              chunk of ice.
Blood appeared—and then they started in, in earnest.
All piled up in a heap they began to scream together,
pounding with sticks, reins,
and linchpins out of wheels.

In vain he wheezed to them: "Mates,
                you're my mates—what's the matter?"
The mob wanted to settle accounts fully.
The mob was deaf with rage.
The mob grumbled at those who weren't putting their boots in,
and they trampled something that looked like a body
into the spring snow that was turning into mud.

They beat him up with relish. With ingenuity. Juicy.
I saw how skillfully and precisely
one man kept putting the boots in,
boots with greasy flaps on them,
right under the belt of the man who was down,
smothered in mud and dungy water.

Their owner, a guy with an honest enough mug,
very proud of his high principles,
was saying with each kick: "Don't try your tricks with us!"
booting him deliberately, with the utmost conviction,
and, sweat pouring, with a red face, he jovially called to me:
"Come on, youngster, get in it!"

I can't remember—how many there were, making a din,
                              beating him up.
It may have been a hundred, it may have been more,

but I, just a boy, wept for shame.
And if a hundred are beating somebody up,
howling in a frenzy—even if for a good cause—
I will never make one hundred and one!

1963

TRANSLATED BY TINA TUPIKINA-GLAESSNER, GEOFFREY DUTTON, AND
IGOR MEZHAKOFF-KORIAKIN (REVISED)

Nefertiti

Turn as you may,
                    and twist,
Nefertiti
          did exist.
In this world upon a time
with a pharaoh she lived;
but though she shared his couch,
the future ages to her laid claim.
His so manifest possessions
were a source of worry to him.
With dignity
              he wore his vestments,
and pronounced
                his condemnations.
He kept strengthening his foundations,
but, as Avicenna once remarked,
when, in nature, authority comes face to face
with beauty, its value depreciates.
And the pharaoh was tormented by a complex
of self-depreciation . . .
                          Whenever
he thought of this at dinner,
he rumpled his napkin in gloom.
He had an army,
                chariots of war,
but she had—
              eyes,
                    lashes,
and a brow,

resplendent with stars,
and an astounding curvature of the neck.
When on a litter shoulder-high they floated by,
then the gapers turned
their stares,
       intuitively,
not toward the pharaoh,
              but Nefertiti.
The pharaoh was rather grim in his affections,
and even allowed himself some crude gestures,
sensing the fragility of a potentate
when compared with the potency of fragility.
But slowly
     the sphinxes
           crumbled in the breeze,
and beliefs
     in deadly earnest
            shed their faith,
but through ideas and events,
through all those things
           by which time is fooled,
Nefertiti's neck kept stretching out,
till it reached us today.
She figures now
       in some boy's drawing,
and on a working woman's
           brooch.
She acts to purify and liberate,
without palling
     or growing duller,
and again some person feels
his value depreciate when set beside her.
We're often stuck in the daily rut . . .
And Nefertiti?
     Nefertiti,
through the daily grind,
         events, faces, dates,
still keeps on stretching somewhere . . .
Turn as you may,
     and twist,
Nefertiti did exist.

1964

TRANSLATED BY GEORGE REAVEY (REVISED)

The Far Cry

To Iu. Kazakov

A hut is drowsing on the opposite bank.
A horse looms white against the dark meadow.
I call loudly and fire shot after shot
but I cannot wake a soul.

If only the wind would bring them my shots,
if only some dog would hear!
They sleep like the dead ... *The Far Cry*
is the name of the ferry.

My voice has thundered through the halls, like an alarm,
squares shook to its mighty roll,
but it is too weak to reach
out to this hut, and wake it.

As for the peasants who sleep as though plowing,
breathing heavily, they sleep at their leisure,
they don't hear my voice, any more
than the rustle of the pines and the noise of the rushes.

What sort of an orator are you, what sort of a prophet?
You are confused, soaked and chilled.
Your cartridges are finished. Your voice is getting hoarse.
The rain is flooding your campfire.

But don't grieve that it's vexing enough to make you weep.
You can think deeply, about all sorts of things.
There is plenty of time ... *The Far Cry*
is the name of the ferry.

1963

TRANSLATED BY TINA TUPIKINA-GLAESSNER, GEOFFREY DUTTON, AND
IGOR MEZHAKOFF-KORIAKIN

The Hut

And once again a fisherman's hut
opening to me late in the night,
suddenly as much a part of me
as the one along whose floor I used to crawl.

Quietly I lay down in the corner
as if it were my old lost place—
that shaky, chinky floor,
whose every crack and knot I knew.

And I was home again, painfully at home,
amid the smells of fish and tobacco,
children, kittens, borscht,
fumes rising, purifying.*

Already the room rocked with the fisherman's snores;
the children already had climbed into their bunks,
their teeth nibbling
on steamy pancakes.

Nobody but the housewife stirred,
washing, scrubbing.
A poker, a broom, a needle—
there must always be something in her hands.

Outside a storm was brewing on the Pechora:
you could hear the river seethe.
"She's kicking up her heels," she said,
as if speaking of a coffee-colored cow.

A puff, blowing out the smoky lamp,
left the room to its own darkness.
I could hear the slap-slosh sound
of her laundry chores in the kitchen.

An old clock creaked in the night,
dragging the weight of history.
From the freshly laid kindling
a white fire broke and crackled.

．　．　．

And, full of wonder and fear,
untamed, from the shadows,
eight children's eyes gleamed
like eight sprays from your waters, Pechora.

They leaned out over their bunks
from an impossibly distant distance,
four little selves (myself)
watching a grown-up, me.

A silent prayer crossed my lips,
as I lay still, pretending to sleep.
And the kitchen noises stopped:
I heard the door squeak open.

And in the depth of solitude,
through the veil of this slumber,
I felt the touch of something
remembered from my childhood.

A sheepskin coat—that's what it was—
thrown on me snugly, shaggily, warmly;
and a moment later, from the kitchen tub,
the slapping of the clothes again.

I could almost see those hands dancing
through diapers, bed sheets, dungarees,
to the music of all our passions,
to the roar of world events.

Certainly more than one pretentious nonentity
had wormed his rotten way into eternity,
but only this recurring slap-slosh
struck me, in essence, as eternal.

And a teeming sense of fate
overwhelmed me,
like the exhalation of a hut
where life lies heavy on millions of women,

and where—who knows when?—
after the mastery has been won,

a million little selves (myself)
will watch a grown-up, me.

1963

TRANSLATED BY STANLEY KUNITZ WITH ANTHONY KAHN

*This third stanza was cut after the second publication in *Kater Sviazi: Stikhi* (Moscow 1966).

The Mail Cutter

The ice had not even begun to break,
no boat could possibly sail yet,
but the letters lay in a pile at the post office,
with all their requests and instructions.

Among them trying vainly to leave,
in the scrawls of fishermen,
were reproaches, complaints, cries,
awkward confessions of love.

In vain the huskies gazed out to sea,
searching the waves through the fog,
lying like gray hillocks
on the bottoms of overturned boats.

But, like a ghost, dreamed up
from the desperate monotony,
the ice-covered mail boat
showed her gray masts.

She was beaten up and dirty,
but to the fishing village
her chilly, husky voice
sounded like the sweetest music.

And the gloomy sailors, throwing us a line

to the shore, like Vikings,
silently, skillfully
carried canvas sacks full of people's souls.

And again the ship went out, tiredly,
her hull breaking the ice with difficulty,
and I sat in her dank hold
among the piled sacks.

Tormented, I searched for an answer
with all my restless conscience:
"Just what am I, in fact,
and where am I going?

Can it be I am like a frail boat,
and that the passions, like the waves, roll
and toss me about?" But my inner voice
answered me: "You are a mail boat.

Make speed through the angry waves,
heavy with ice, to all those people
who have been separated by the ice,
who are waiting to get in touch again.

And like the first sign of the ship
for which people waited so long,
carry onward the undying light
of the duty that links us together.

And along the foaming arctic sea of life,
through all the ice and against the nor'wester,
carry with you those mailbags
full of hopelessness and hopes.

But remember, as you hang on the whistle,
as soon as the storms die down,
steamers, real ships,
will go through these waters, not afraid anymore.

And the fishermen, standing up in the barges,
will look admiringly at them,
and their sleek, velvety whistles
will make them forget your husky voice.

. . .

But you, with the stink of fish and blubber,
don't lower your rigging gloomily.
You've done the job on schedule.
Be happy then. You are the mail cutter."

Thus the inner voice spoke to me,
impressing upon me the burden of prophecy.
And amid the white night of the Arctic Ocean
somehow it was all morning for me.

I didn't think enviously
of someone else, covered with honors,
I was simply happy that a few things
also depended on me.

And covered in someone's fur coat,
I was dependent on so much,
and like that letter from Vanka Zhukov,*
I dozed on heaps of other letters.

1963

TRANSLATED BY TINA TUPIKINA-GLAESSNER, GEOFFREY DUTTON, AND
IGOR MEZHAKOFF-KORIAKIN (REVISED)

*The heart-breaking nine-year-old hero of Chekhov's short story "Vanka" (1886). Indentured to
a cruel master in Moscow, he writes his grandfather in the country describing the hunger, cold,
and harsh treatment and begging him to rescue him. Told that letters are delivered all over the
world by being dropped in the mailbox, Vanka addresses it simply "To Grandfather in the village."

Perfection

The wind blows gently, fresh and cool.
The porch is fragrant with damp pine.
A duck stretches its wings wide,
having just laid its egg.

And it looks like a faultless girl,
having laid in God's design,
a perfection of white roundness
on an altar of straw.

. . .

And above the muddy, thawing road,
above the moldering roofs of the huts,
the perfection of the disk of fire
rises slowly in the sky.

The perfection of the woods in spring
all shot through by the dawn,
almost disembodied, shimmers in mist
like the breath of the earth, all over the earth.

Not in the frantic shapes of new fashions,
not in shapes borrowed from others—
perfection is simply being natural,
perfection is the breath of the earth.

Don't torment yourself that art is secondary,
destined only to reflect,
that it remains so limited and lean,
compared with nature itself.

Without acting a part
look to yourself for the source of art,
and quietly and uniquely
reproduce yourself just as you are.

Be reflected, as a creation of nature
bending over a well
draws the reflection of its face
up from the ice-ringed depths.

1963

TRANSLATED BY TINA TUPIKINA-GLAESSNER, GEOFFREY DUTTON,
AND IGOR MEZHAKOFF-KORIAKIN

Wounded Bird

To A. Voznesensky

Here to these wild stretches of the north
where the world first quacked and spawned,

I flew, a wounded bird, a drake,
and settled down on the Pechora.

From my covert by the woods
all my nerve ends tingled
at the smell of ice floes and seals,
the majesty, the vibrant breath, of ocean.

The sea was what I breathed,
it was sorrow I exhaled;
and the scattered buckshot in my blood
I gave as keepsake for Pechora,

my gift of leaden pellets
to the cold riverbed. And trembled
and rose again and flapped my wings,
beating the air with a sudden power.

The winds rocked me gently,
adrift over mosses and bushes;
muskrats showed me the way, puffing down trails
behind their wet whiskers.

Through corridors of unplowed lands,
past flowering brakes and stands of hazelnut,
tender-eyed deer bore me
on the velvet buds of their antlers.

When the tussocks received me,
the tundra said, "Taste me,"
proffering its Iceland moss,
its cranberries sweetened through the winter.

And I—turned to the clang of bolts and breechblocks—
knew that my life was precious,
only because you, shining, touched me,
caressed me, Pechora.

Sometime again, a mighty drake,
unrecognized by you, Pechora,
I'll fly over the north country,
flashing the brocade fan of my feathers.

· · ·

And you will scan the arc of sky,
lost in the plumage and the flight,
forgetting that the gift was yours,
the saving gift, Pechora;

and how one spring you harbored me,
when unremittingly
that plumage spilled its tears of blood
into your light blue hem, Pechora.

1963

TRANSLATED BY STANLEY KUNITZ WITH ANTHONY KAHN

"Citizens, Listen to Me..."

To John Updike

I'm on the SS *Friedrich Engels*,
but in my head there's such heresy
of unticketed thoughts crashing the gate.
I don't understand—what am I hearing?
full of confusion and pain:
"Citizens, listen to me..."*

The deck bends and groans,
doing the Charleston to a concertina,
but on the fo'c'sle, quietly supplicating,
the irritating command of the song
barbarously tries to break through:
"Citizens, listen to me..."

There a soldier sits on a deck barrel,
his forelock bending over a guitar
with fingers lost in dismayed abandon.
He drains guitar and self down to the lees,
but from his lips rises in torment:
"Citizens, listen to me..."

. . .

But the citizens don't want to listen.
They would rather go drinking and eating,
and dancing, and all the rest is nonsense.
Nevertheless—they still need some sleep . . .
Why does he drone on to them urgently:
"Citizens, listen to me . . ."

Someone salts a tomato with relish.
Someone mulls over greasy cards.
Someone pounds the deck with his boots.
Someone tears the hide off the concertina.
But how many times has this command
cried and whispered to everyone:
"Citizens, listen to me . . ."

No one listened to them at times either.
Though bursting ribs and writhing,
their essence never was expressed.
With unkind souls citizens hardly
can hear somebody else's:
"Citizens, listen to me . . ."

Hey, soldier, on a background of barrels,
I'm just the same as you, but without a guitar.
Over rivers, high mountains, and seas,
I roam with my arms stretched out
and, already hoarse, repeat on my own:
"Citizens, listen to me . . ."

It's terrifying, if they don't want to listen.
It's terrifying, if they begin to listen.
What if that whole song is petty and vain?
What if it's all insignificant indeed, except
that bloody tormenting refrain:
"Citizens, listen to me . . ."?!

1963

TRANSLATED BY ALBERT C. TODD

*This refrain echos an unpublished song from the Soviet underworld. It is full of unprintable criminal argot and is often sung to the accompaniment of a guitar or concertina. "Citizens" is a formal and official mode of address, used sardonically in that song. Here, in place of the more common "Comrades," it recalls Mayakovsky's usage in poetic sloganeering on propaganda placards. In the first verion the boat was the SS *Mayakovsky*.

"No, I'll not take the half..."

No, I'll not take the half of anything!
Give me the whole sky! The far-flung earth!
Seas and rivers and mountain avalanches—
All these are mine! I'll accept no less!

No, life, you cannot woo me with a part.
Let it be all or nothing! I can shoulder that!
I don't want happiness by halves,
Nor is half of sorrow what I want.

Yet there's a pillow I would share,
Where gently pressed against a cheek,
Like a helpless star, a falling star,
A ring glimmers on a finger of your hand.

1963
TRANSLATED BY GEORGE REAVEY

Love's Maturity?

Love's maturity, you say?
                    Is that so?
Straining,
        I wait.
                You come.
Glances meet!
            No shudder even!
Instead, repose...
                    as though winded by a blow.
Fingers touch!
            No explosion even!!!
Instead, repose...
                    ready to howl, I run.
Is that all
        between you and me?
Are ashes

the maturity of fire then?
Is love's maturity
no more than affinity,
and that only
in the best of cases?
Who's playing the monster over us,
wicked and leering?
Who, with cold efficacy,
dared fabricate a false definition?
Love has its birth and death.
Love has no maturity.
Love roars,
stoking
the menace of extinction for us,
and it breathes
not with equanimity,
but huskily
gasps—
begging for mercy
and no mercy—
as the stifling earth gasps,
abandoned by reason,
half smothered by the world's creation ...

1963
TRANSLATED BY GEORGE REAVEY

And So Piaf Left Us ...

In a hall, in Paris, in front of the crowd
someone was being extra artistic, jumping around,
dropping witticisms and wriggling about,
and it was all only a prologue—to Piaf.

And then she came on, strangely
resembling a crude small idol,
as if, in a risky little play, tragedy
had wearily blundered in through the wrong door.

Above the nonsense and the clowning
she rose, pale, without strength,

awkward, like a small sparrow with aching eyes,
heavy with her battered wings.

Short, heavily made up,
hiding her cough, barely alive,
she stood astride our time,
her thin legs just holding her up.

She glanced at us, as if at the Seine,
about to step off a cliff down into it,
and I felt like throwing myself at the stage
to hold her up and keep her from falling.

A precise wave of her small wrinkled hand,
and the band began to play . . . She stepped
forward to the edge, aware of her doom,
and, trembling, gathered the music into herself.

And then she sang, taking flight, as if her body,
torn to shreds by surgeons,
was falling from the hold of her eyes
and hoarsely twisting itself into us.

Flying, she sobbed, laughed out loud, whispered,
like the delirious lawns of the Bois de Boulogne,
like a carriage rolling through Saint-Germain,
sang a siren's song. That was Piaf.

Alarms and storms and guns merged in her,
pledges, moans and voices of the shadows.
Unwittingly, we had just been kind to her,
like giants to a Lilliputian.

But from her throat rose sorrow, and faith,
and from her throat rose stars, and bells.
And now like a giantess she took us,
pitiful Lilliputians, playfully in her hands.

The greatest thing of all about her, a true artist,
was that in spite of approaching death,
new artists rose from her throat
leaving lumps of tears in our throats.

.   .   .

Piaf left the stage, prophesying
to us in her exaltation . . .
The little sparrow who sang as the *chimere* of Notre Dame
would have sung to us, descending to the stage.

1963

TRANSLATED BY TINA TUPIKINA-GLAESSNER, GEOFFREY DUTTON, AND
IGOR MEZHAKOFF-KORIAKIN (REVISED)

Hand-rolled Cigarettes

If, in a fisherman's hut, you poke
behind the sagging sideboard with a stick,
you'll find his stock for making cigarettes,
a pile of newspapers, many years' thick.

There you'll meet mobs of secret agents
and doctor-poisoners of the age.
Bedbugs and roaches with mustaches
huddle, and crawl along the page.

Returning late, the tired fisherman
enjoys his ladled kvass's tang,
and sifts tobacco at his ease
onto some bureaucrat's harangue.

Cool in practice of his skill.
with fingers confident and strong,
he coils the speech in a narrow tube
and neatly wets it with his tongue.

The contents?—they're not his affair!
That glowing edge of nicotine
advancing, at the end of day,
eats up the newsprint, line by line.

He would have liked a sunny day,
wind in his sails and a lucky catch.

His yellow nail gleams salmon-bright,
flicking dead words reduced to ash.

Old eulogies and exposés
fulfill their destiny and rise,
with trashy articles and poems,
in spiral columns to the skies.

When evening falls in the north country,
cigarette-tips pinpoint the gray,
as, caught in the mood of dirty weather,
fishermen sit and puff away.

Their worn tobacco pouches rustle
till dawn sweeps inland on the tide.
Listen! They roll another cigarette:
and history is on their side.

1963
TRANSLATED BY STANLEY KUNITZ

A Ballad about Seals

Papa seal sleeps like a deadbeat.
Momma seal loves her son,
and in her teeth, like sweets,
she carries fish across
to her brown-eyed pup
nicknamed Little Sprout.

Seals, seals, you are like children—
you should live and go on living,
but long ago you were budgeted for
in the trade estimates,
and momma seals don't know
that radiograms are flying
from Moscow to our schooner.

Somewhere in the city of Boston,
at the fur auction,

a beaming, smart dealer
throws checks around cordially,
exclaiming: "Peace and friendship!
Peace and Russki Little Sprout!"

So that some lady or other,
skinny as a single rib of Adam,
can wrap her joints in furs,
someone with an important expression on his mug
hammers Morse instructions
into our brains.

Seals, seals, we do truly love you,
but we beat you to death with clubs
because our country demands it.
Savagely we bash your eyes in
because you are hard currency,
and we do need hard currency.

Meanwhile the seals are weeping, weeping,
hiding their children under their bellies,
but we can't be sorry for them.
Once more our clubs whistle
and the screaming eyes of the seals
stick to our huge boots.

And no doubt fish don't want
to be preyed on, but to jump
over the waves, along the waves,
but you seals, you catch them . . .
in nature all things are according to the law.
Fish—for seals. Seals—for us.*

All the same, the seals are crying, crying . . .
If only we could change the world
(but it's not our fate to see that).
Seals, we would not have to beat you to death,
we'd drink vodka with you,
we'd play dominoes together.

All things are lawful! Let's double the quota!
All the bigwigs are pleased with us!
Why are you sad, like a salmon rolled in batter?
A man with money doesn't get the blues.

With your pay you can buy
the most perfect of television sets,
let football in the far city of Madrid
fill you with energy.

But suddenly, in a bitter mood
after shouting yourself too many drinks,
when you threaten your wife with the back of your hand,
your nerves without warning give way . . .
you will flinch—her eyes
scream at you like those of a seal.

1964

TRANSLATED BY TINA TUPIKINA-GLAESSNER, GEOFFREY DUTTON, AND
IGOR MEZHAKOFF-KORIAKIN (REVISED)

*This seventh stanza was cut after the first publication.

Why Are You Doing This?

When Sparks on the Morianna, head bent,
was searching for a radio beacon,
by chance the receiver picked up a woman's voice:
"Why are you doing this? Why are you doing this?"

From the port of Amderma she screamed
across the masts, the ice, and barking dogs,
and like a storm it grew louder all around:
"Why are you doing this? Why are you doing this?"

Inhumanly pressed against each other,
shattering every which way,
ice floes wheezed to one another:
"Why are you doing this? Why are you doing this?"

With all its being the white beluga,
tangled in nets, screamed to the hunter
through a fountain of blood:
"Why are you doing this? Why are you doing this?"

. . .

A rippling wave swept him
from the boat, and the poor fellow
whispered as he perished without a trace:
"Why are you doing this? Why are you doing this?"

Like a bastard I betray you
and nothing stops me at all,
and you implore me with your eyes:
"Why are you doing this? Why are you doing this?"

You look at me, estranged and full of hate,
almost like an enemy,
and hopelessly I implore you:
"Why are you doing this? Why are you doing this?"

And every year more alarmed,
heart to heart, nation to nation
through the darkness screams:
"Why are you doing this? Why are you doing this?"

1964
TRANSLATED BY ALBERT C. TODD

Ballad about Drinking

To V. Chernykh

We had slaughtered a hundred white whales,
civilization was quite forgotten,
our lungs were burned out from smoking shag,
but on sighting port we blew out our chests like barrels
and began to speak to one another politely,
and with the noble goal of drinking
we went ashore from the schooner at Amderma.

In Amderma we walked like gods,
swaggering along with our hands on our hips,
and through the port our beards and sidewhiskers

kept their bearings on the pub,
and passing girls and shellbacks
as well as all the local dogs
went along with us as escort.

But, clouding the whole planet,
a notice hung in the shop: "No Spirits!"
We looked at some sparkling wine from the Don
as if it were feeble fruit juice,
and through our agonized yearning
we realized—it wouldn't work.

Now who could have drunk our spirits, our vodka?
It's dreadful the way people drink—simply ruinous.
But skinny as a skeleton, Petka Markovsky from Odessa,
as it always happens with him,
suddenly disappeared somewhere
giving a secretive "Sh-sshh!"

And shortly afterward, with much clinking,
he turned up with a huge cardboard box,
already slightly merry,
and it was a sweet clinking the box made
as we woke up to the fact: "There she is! She's apples!"
and Markovsky gave us the wink: "She's right!"

We made a splash, waving to everyone—
Chartered a deluxe room in the hotel
and sat down as we were on the bed.
Cords flew off the box
and there, in the glittering columns of the bottles,
bulging, stern, cozy,
absolutely hygienic—
triple-distilled eau de cologne stood before us!

And Markovsky rose, lifting his glass,
pulled down his seaman's jacket,
and began: "I'd like to say something . . ."
"Then say it!" everyone began to shout.
But before anything else
they wanted to wet their whistles.

Markovsky said: "Come on—let's have a swig!
The doctor told me eau de cologne

is the best thing to keep the wrinkles away.
Let them judge us!—We don't give a damn!
We used to drink all sorts of wine!
When we were in Germany
we filled the radiators of our tanks
with wine from the Mosel.

We don't need consumer goods!
We need the wind, the sky!
Old mates, listen to this
in our souls, as though in the safe deposit:
We have the sea, our mothers and young brothers—
All the rest . . . is rubbish!"

Bestriding the earth like a giant,
Markovsky stood with a glass in his hand
that held the foaming seas.
The skipper observed: "Everything is shipshape!"
and only the boatswain sobbed like a child:
"But my mother is dead . . ."

And we all began to burst into tears,
quite easily, quite shamelessly,
as if in the midst of our own families,
mourning with bitter tears
at first for the boatswain's mother,
and afterward simply for ourselves.

Already a rueful notice hung in the chemist's shop—
"No Triple Eau de Cologne"—
but eight of us sea wolves
sobbed over almost all of Russia!
And in our sobs we reeked
like eight barbershops.

Tears, like squalls,
swept away heaps of false values,
of puffed-up names,
and quietly remaining inside us
was only the sea, our mothers and young brothers—
even the mother who was dead . . .

I wept as though I was being set free,
I wept as if I was being born anew,

a different person from what I'd been,
and before God and before myself,
like the tears of those drunken whalemen,
my soul was pure.

1964

*TRANSLATED BY TINA TUPIKINA-GLAESSNER, GEOFFREY DUTTON, AND
IGOR MEZHAKOFF-KORIAKIN (REVISED)*

White Nights in Archangel

The white nights—an unbroken mass of maybes.
Something is shimmering, strangely worrying me.
Maybe it's the sun, but maybe it's the moon.
Brand-new ships' officers wander about,
maybe in Archangel, maybe in Marseille,
maybe in sadness, maybe in joy.

Waitresses, with their eyes rolling
like iceboats beneath their brows,
wander along with them arm in arm.
Can it be the roar of the nor'wester
that prompts them to stop kissing?
Maybe they should, maybe they shouldn't.

The seagulls soar crying over the masts,
maybe they're mourning, maybe they're laughing,
and at the jetty a sailor takes his leave
of a woman, with a long-drawn-out kiss:
"What is your name?" "It's not important..."
Maybe so, maybe not.

Now he's going up the gangplank onto his schooner:
"I'll bring you a sealskin!"
But he's forgotten he doesn't know where.
The woman remains standing there in silence.
Who knows—maybe he'll come back.
Maybe no, maybe yes.

. . .

By the jetty the thought comes to me, unbidden,
that the seagulls aren't seagulls, the waves aren't waves,
that he and she—aren't he and she.
All of that is the aurora of the white nights,
all of that is only fancy, fancy,
maybe of insomnia, maybe of a dream.

The schooner gives a drawn-out hoot of farewell...
He doesn't look sad anymore.
Now he is sailing, detached and remote,
telling dirty stories with relish
on what may be a sea, on what may be a schooner.
Maybe it's him, maybe somebody else.

And namelessly by the jetty—
maybe it's an end, maybe a beginning—
stands the woman, in a thin gray coat,
slowly melting away like a patch of mist.
Maybe she is Vera, maybe Tamara,
maybe Zoya, but maybe—no one at all...

1964

TRANSLATED BY TINA TUPIKINA-GLAESSNER, GEOFFREY DUTTON, AND
IGOR MEZHAKOFF-KORIAKIN (REVISED)

Ballad about Mirages

> *...and those far, elusive lights plunged
> the souls of seamen into darkness, offering
> them false hope...*
>
> —*From an ancient pilot's manual*

We've been bewitched by countless lies,
by azure images of ice,
by false promises of open sky and sea,
and rescued by a God we don't believe in.
Like coppers rattling from a beggar's plate
guiding lights have fallen on our days
and burned and died.

We've pressed our ship
a pilgrimage of nights toward such lights
as, always elusive, they lured and tricked
the keel upon the rocks and ripped
the helmhold from the hand and lashed
the beggared palm to scraps.
Ice tightens at the bow and breath.
To dock, to drop the anchor to its rest,
to drift (a dream!) on waters quieted
and calmed. We can't. We're after a mirage.
(The whiskered walrus brays; the salt sea thaws.
Again, we're off!)
Raised on powdered milk, we'll have no faith
in beacons any longer, nor mistake
real for fake, or waking for a dream.
Beacons can't be trusted. Trust instead
the will of your own hand and head.
Again the captain waves his glass,
sights a beacon, turns and cries
"Helmsman! There's a beacon. Are you blind?"
But Helmsman, with the truer eye,
thinks mutiny and grumbles,
                          "A mirage."

1964

TRANSLATED BY ANTHONY KAHN

"We can't stand . . ."

We can't stand sitting still.
We try, no holds barred, to be liked
by ourselves, friends, the opposition, and the authorities
(I no longer even speak about women).

Then we want to be liked by the country,
then the earth's globe and the epoch,

then by our descendants, and, as a result
our own wives don't like us.

1964
TRANSLATED BY ALBERT C. TODD

A Very Special Soul

There were twenty-eight souls on the schooner.
We divide the whole pile by twenty-eight,
and when there is no catch, we keep up our style,
and divide the nothing by twenty-eight.

Only among all of us shipmates
there is one special soul.
A Jew who knows such things told us
that the lad had been a camp guard.

There's no God or judge among us.
He's now a Seaman Second Class.
Just like the rest of us he hunts the beluga.
Just like the rest of us at times he drinks.

Like all of us he has a sea chest,
with socks, underwear, tobacco,
but in Marilyn, a thousand pardons, Monroe
there's a needle in each eye.

The photograph joke is kind of strange,
even a little bit terrifying.
But then she's not alive, only a portrait.
No matter how many pricks, there is no pain.

Maybe the lad is not even guilty.
They simply handed him a machine gun,
and he just stood there in a watchtower
and possibly never fired a shot.

And maybe on the sly
he slipped bread to a fallen con,
and never put his gun butt to work . . .
There were some like that, they say.

Who knows how he served there . . .
It doesn't seem he got any medals,
but by some invisible line
he is separated from our crew.

Once when we were just fooling around,
with his glass on the table
he suddenly caught a poor cockroach,
and smiling wryly said, "Halt, you con!"

He raised the glass off the table.
The happy cockroach started to run on.
But the tenacious glass, ever vigilant,
now would release him, now would catch him.

The lad banged and banged with his glass,
so that a chill suddenly passed through everyone,
and, interrupting the suspicious strange laugh,
the chief mechanic snatched the glass from him.

The lad began to squirm and play innocent:
"Come on, you guys, I was only kidding . . ."
But his mates were sullen and silent.
What can you say? A very special soul . . .

1964

TRANSLATED BY ALBERT C. TODD

Pitching and Rolling

Here we go! We're *re-e-eling!*
          The glass-framed instructions
                    rip off their nails.
A record player bashes you in the head

with Doris Day.

Borscht, lazing in the galley,
           takes off straight up, splashing
                    madly.

A bay leaf from the borscht,
           stuck to the ceiling, steams.

Reel on, buddy!
      Sure, you'd like to catch hold of a bush or some grass
                  with your hands!

The cabin boy staggers.
           The helmsman staggers.
                  The boatswain staggers.
                    I'm staggering—

The waves like wolfhounds—
      You're just the same, Twentieth Century,
right-left
     left-right
          up-down
             down-up—
Reeling!
     All instructions shatter—
              all the portraits smash to hell!
Faces are death-white, drawn, wasted,
             under the stern, a
                rat-like
                  screech—
And all over the place it's dense with kasha,
            with downwind screams,
nothing but pitching and rolling, staggering, curving
with the taste of sick stomach in your mouth.
Reeling . . .
     A barrel jumps down the deck
             throwing itself at people.
Hey, old buddies, we're in for it now
             but keep it cool anyway.
Crawl out of your cabins, otherwise
             it's kaput for us all.

Reeling . . .
But the eyes of the harpooner
          a ring-tailed roarer
are strained,
      and his forelock's standing straight up.
He makes a soundless sign to the sailors
           and steals sideways

with a rope
          to the flipped-out barrel
and pitches himself like a cat
                    splitting open the crowd.
For he knows,
          you bastard pitch and roll,
things can get rough.
He's learned by heart,
               right through his skin,
                         his red head.
He's had it beat down through his skull:
Either you jump on the barrel
or it'll jump
          all over you!
We're reeling!
          But the barrel's still, it's no longer running
                                    wild . . .
We're reeling!
          Clear weather won't run off from us . . .
Reeling!
     We may be seasick, darkness in front of our eyes—
But we'll out-reel you
               bad trip
                    anyway . . .

1964

TRANSLATED BY JAMES DICKEY WITH ANTHONY KAHN

The City of Yes and the City of No

I am like a train
               rushing for many years now
between the city of Yes
                    and the city of No.
My nerves are strained

                    like wires
between the city of No
                    and the city of Yes.
Everything is deadly,
                    everyone frightened,
                              in the city of No.
It's like a study furnished with dejection.
Every morning its parquet floors are polished with bile.
Its sofas are made of falsehood, its walls of misfortune.
Every portrait looks out suspiciously.
Every object is frowning, withholding something.
You'll get lots of good advice in it—like hell you will!—
neither a bunch of flowers nor even a greeting.
Typewriters chatter a carbon-copy answer:
"No-no-no...
              No-no-no...
                        No-no-no..."
And when the lights go out altogether,
the ghosts in it begin their gloomy ballet.
You'll get a ticket to leave—
                        like hell you will!—
to leave
        the black town of No.

But in the town of Yes—life's like the song of a thrush.
This town's without walls—just like a nest.
The sky is asking you to take any star you like in your hand.
Lips ask for yours, without any shame,
softly murmuring: "Ah—all that nonsense..."—
and daisies, teasing, are asking to be picked,
and lowing herds are offering their milk,
and in no one is there even a trace of suspicion,
and wherever you want to be, you are instantly there,
taking any train, or plane, or ship that you like.
And water, faintly murmuring, whispers through the years:
"Yes-yes-yes...
              Yes-yes-yes...
                        Yes-yes-yes..."
Only to tell the truth, it's a bit boring, at times,
to be given so much, almost without any effort,
in that shining multicolored city of Yes...

                    · · ·

Better let me be tossed around
                              to the end of my days,
between the city of Yes
                    and the city of No!
Let my nerves be strained
                        like wires
between the city of No
                    and the city of Yes!

1964

TRANSLATED BY TINA TUPIKINA-GLAESSNER, GEOFFREY DUTTON, AND IGOR
MEZHAKOFF-KORIAKIN (REVISED)

A Ballad about Benkendorf,
Chief of Gendarmerie,
and Lermontov's Poem
"Death of a Poet"*

I can imagine the fear and the stupor
when they found, in the office of the secret police,
"Death of a Poet" . . . I can imagine
how all those vile reptiles began to scuttle,
shedding dandruff on their official uniforms,
stuffing their nostrils with saving snuff.

And the chief of the gendarmerie, the leading ideologist,
scalding all subordinate idiots,
put on his glasses . . . On reaching the lines "But there is,
there is Divine Justice, you intimates of corruption . . ."
he shuddered, looked stealthily about him,
and was afraid to read it again.

The cooked-up report was already long ago written,
and Lermontov was packed off to the Caucasus.
But from that moment Benkendorf lost sleep.
In the midst of the jests of the court,

in receptions, meetings, ceremonies,
"There is Divine Justice . . ." he would hear amid the hubbub.

"There is Divine Justice . . ." the blizzard cried in the windows.
"There is Divine Justice . . ." the Volga moaned hollowly
through the expanses of the suffering steppes.
"There is Divine Justice . . ." clanked the chains.
"There is Divine Justice . . ." silently cried the eyes
of serfs, taking off their caps.

And the chief, shaking sweatily with fear,
stealthily turned into an atheist.
The chief, as always, went to church,
but afterward in his study he was pleased to reflect
that there isn't a God after all, not in the whole wide world.
And that means there is no such thing as Divine Justice.

But forever—over all the phonies,
gendarmes, suckers-up to the court,
who scandalize and falsify—
the alarm bell resounds inexorably:
"There is Divine Justice, you intimates of corruption . . ."
And the justice of the poet—that is Divine Justice.

1964

TRANSLATED BY TINA TUPIKINA-GLAESSNER, GEOFFREY DUTTON, AND IGOR
MEZHAKOFF-KORIAKIN

*Lermontov's elegy "Death of a Poet" (1837) mourns the death of Pushkin, whom he idolized, and puts the blame for this tragedy directly on those close to the throne. It was interpreted as a call to rebellion and resulted in Lermontov's arrest and banishment/assignment to the campaign in the Caucasus. Yevtushenko, in earlier versions, mistakenly refers to Lermontov's poem as "On the Death of a Poet."

Sleep, My Beloved

The salty spray glistens on the fence.
The wicket gate is bolted tight.

               And the sea,
smoking and heaving and scooping the dikes,
has sucked into itself the salty sun.

Sleep, my beloved...
               don't torment my soul.
Already the mountains and the steppes are falling asleep,
and our lame dog,
               shaggy and sleepy,
lies down and licks his salty chain.
And the branches are murmuring
                              and the waves are trampling
and the dog and his day
               are on the chain,
and I say to you, whispering
               and then half whispering
and then quite silently,
               "Sleep, my beloved..."
Sleep, my beloved...
               Forget that we quarreled.
Imagine—
       we are waking.
               Everything is new.
We are lying in the hay,
       we sleepyheads.
                      Part of the dream
is the scent of sour cream, from somewhere below, from
   the cellar.
Oh, how can I make you
               imagine all this,
you, so mistrustful?
               Sleep, my beloved...
Smile in your dream.
               Put away your tears.
Go and gather flowers
               and wonder where to put them,
burying your face in them.
Are you muttering?
               Tired, perhaps, of tossing?
Muffle yourself up in your dream
                      and wrap yourself in it.
In your dream you can do whatever you want to,
all that we mutter about
               if we don't sleep.
It's reckless not to sleep,
               it's even a crime.
All that is latent
       cries out from the depths.

It is difficult for your eyes.

So much crowded in them.

It will be easier for them under closed eyelids.

Sleep, my beloved . . .

What is it that's making you sleepless?

Is it the roaring sea?

The begging of the trees?

Evil forebodings?

Someone's dishonesty?

And maybe, not someone's,

but simply my own?

Sleep, my beloved . . .

Nothing can be done about it.

But no, I am innocent of that accusation.

Forgive me—do you hear!

Love me—do you hear!

Even if in your dream!

Even if in your dream!

Sleep, my beloved . . .

We are on the earth,

flying savagely along,

threatening to explode,

and we have to embrace

so we won't fall down,

and if we do fall—

we shall fall together.

Sleep, my beloved . . .

don't nurse a grudge.

Let dreams settle softly in your eyes.

It's so difficult to fall asleep on this earth!

And yet—

Do you hear, beloved?

Sleep.

And the branches are murmuring

and the waves are trampling

and the dog and his day

are on the chain,

and I say to you, whispering

and then half whispering

and then quite silently,

"Sleep, my beloved . . ."

1964

TRANSLATED BY GEOFFREY DUTTON WITH TINA TUPIKINA-GLAESSNER

Bratsk Hydroelectric Station*
(Selections)

Prayer Before the Poem

A poet in Russia is more than a poet.
There the fate of being born a poet
falls only on those stirred by the pride
                              of belonging,
who have no comfort, and no peace.

The poet in Russia is the image of his own age,
and the visionary symbol of the future.
Without timidity, the poet sums up
the total of all that has happened before him.

Can I do this? I am not a very cultured man . . .
My hoarded prophecies contain no promises . . .
But the spirit of Russia is soaring over me
and boldly challenges me at least to try.

And, falling quietly to my knees,
prepared for both death and victory,
I humbly ask for help, from you
great Russian poets . . .

Give me, Pushkin, your harmony,
your speech, free and unchained,
your captivating fate—
as if in jest, to call down fire with words.

Give me, Lermontov, your bitter gaze,
the venom of your contempt,
and the monk's cell of your unsociable soul,
where hidden in the silence of your harshness
breathes sister-like the lamp of human kindness.

            .   .   .

Give me, Nekrasov, while soothing my exuberance,
the agonies of your lashed muse—
at main entrances, at railways,
and in the open spaces of forests and fields.
Give me the strength of your inelegance.
Give me the measure of your tormented heroism
so that I can go, hauling all of Russia
like the bargemen heaving on a towrope.

Oh, give me, Blok, the mists of prophecy,
and two curved wings,
so that the music, hiding the eternal riddle,
shall flow through all my body.

Give me, Pasternak, the disorder of days,
the confusion of branches,
the fusion of scents and shadows
with the torment of this century,
so that the word like a garden murmuring
shall blossom and ripen,
so that, for centuries, your candle
shall burn in me.

Yesenin, give me for good luck tenderness
to birch trees and meadows, to beasts and to people,
and to all others on the earth
that you and I love so defenselessly.

Give me, Mayakovsky,
     boulder-lumpiness,
        turbulence,
           a deep bass,
a grim refusal to appease scum,
so that even I,
    hacking my way through time,
may tell of it
    to those to come.

Monologue of the Egyptian Pyramid

I am
    an Egyptian pyramid.
I am wrapped around with legends.
And scribbling writers
            scrutinize
                me,
and museums
        loot
           my treasures,
and scientists bustle about with magnifying glasses,
timidly scraping off dust with pincers,
and the tourists,
           sweating,
              crowd around
to be caught in a snapshot against a background of
                    immortality.
Wherefore is the ancient saying
repeated by the fallahin and the birds,
that all people are frightened
           of time,
but time—
        is it afraid of pyramids?
People, curb the age-old fear!
I shall become good,
             only I pray:
Take away,
      take away,
take away my memory!
In the harsh silence I absorb
all the explosive force of centuries.
Like a cosmic ship
            with a roar
I
 take off
      from the sands.
I float like a Martian mystery
over the earth

over insect-people,
only some little tourist is dangling,
attached to me by his suspenders.
I can see through the nylon-neon:
countries are only outwardly new.
The world is all so frightfully old—
the same most ancient Egypt—

                    alas!

The same meanness in her depravities.
The same jails—

             only modern.
The very same oppressions,
only more hypocritical.
The same thieves,

          greedy grabbers,

                  scandalmongers,

shysters . . .

       As to changing them?

                Rubbish!

Not for nothing are pyramids skeptical.
Pyramids—

       they are not so dumb.
I shall move the clouds aside with my angles,
I shall cut

       like an apparition through them.
Now then, sphinx by the name of Russia,
show your secret image!
I can see familiar sights once more—
only snowdrifts instead of sands.
There are peasants,

         there are workers,
and scribes—

       very many scribblers.
There are officials,

          there's even an army.
There is, probably, their own pharaoh.
I can see some kind of banner . . .

             scarlet.
But—

     I have known so many banners!
I can see

     new buildings piling up,
I can see

     mountains rearing up on their haunches.

I can see
              men toiling . . .
                              A wondrous sight—toiling!
In the past slaves were toiling . . .
I can hear—
              the primeval rustling
of their forests
              called taiga.
I can see something . . .
                              No way, a pyramid!
"Hey, who are you?"
                              "I am the Bratsk Station."
"Yes, I have heard:
              You are first in the world
in power production,
                              etc., etc.
You must listen to me,
                              the pyramid.
I have something to tell you.
I am an Egyptian pyramid,
as to a sister
              I shall open my soul to you.
I am washed by the rain of sands,
but I am still not cleansed of blood.
I am immortal
              but I have no faith in my own thoughts,
and inside me everything screams and sobs.
Any immortality has my curse
if death
       is its foundation!
I remember,
              how slaves with moans,
straining under lashes and sticks,
dragged
       a hundred-ton block
along the sand
              on runners made of palms.
The block derailed . . .
                              But by way of a solution
they were ordered without any hesitation
to dig trenches for the runners
and lie down inside the trenches.
And the slaves lay obediently
under the runners:

as God had willed...
At once the block moved along the slipperiness
of their squashed bodies.
The priest appeared...
                              with a dirty smirk on his face,
surveying the slaves' labors.
He pulled from his beard
a thin hair, smelling of ointment.
Personally he flagged them with a lash
and screamed:
                    'Remake it, you lice!'
if the hair could be drawn swiftly
between the blocks of the pyramid.
And—
          swinging his fists,
bashing forehead or temple:
'You want to rest for an hour?
You want just a piece of bread?
Go and gorge yourselves on sand!
Drink bitch's milk!
Remember—not a hair!
Remember—not a hair!'
And the overseers gorged,
                    grew fat,
and whistled their song with whips."

The Execution of Stenka Razin†

In Moscow, the white-walled capital,
a thief runs with a poppy-seed loaf down the street.
He is not afraid of being lynched today.
There isn't time for loaves. .
                              They are bringing Stenka Razin!
The tsar is milking a little bottle of malmsey,
          before the Swedish mirror,
                              he squeezes a pimple,
and tries on an emerald seal ring—
and into the square...
                    They are bringing Stenka Razin!
Like a little barrel

following a fat barrel
a baby boyar rolls along after his mother,
gnawing a bar of toffee with his baby teeth.
Today is a holiday!
                    They are bringing Stenka Razin!
A merchant shoves his way in,
                              flatulent with peas.
Two buffoons come rushing at a gallop.
Drunkard-rogues come mincing . . .
They are bringing Stenka Razin!!
Old men, scabs all over them,
                         hardly alive,
thick cords round their necks,
mumbling something,
                    dodder along . . .
They are bringing Stenka Razin!
And shameless girls also,
jumping up tipsy from their sleeping mats,
with cucumber smeared over their faces,
come trotting up—
                    with an itch in their thighs . . .
They are bringing Stenka Razin!
And with screams from wives of the Royal Guard‡
amid spitting from all sides
on a ramshackle cart
he
   comes sailing
                in a white shirt.
He is silent,
            all covered with the spit of the mob,
                    he does not wipe it away,
only grins wryly,
smiles at himself:
"Stenka, Stenka,
                you are like a branch
that has lost its leaves.
How you wanted to enter Moscow!
And here you are entering Moscow now . . .
All right then,
                spit!
            Spit!
                    Spit!
after all, it's a free show.
Good people,

                you always spit
at those
            who wish you well.
I so much wished you well
on the shores of Persia,
and then again
                when flying
down the Volga on a boat!
What had I known?
                    Somebody's eyes,
a saber,
        a sail,
                and the saddle . . .
I wasn't much of a scholar . . .
Perhaps this was what let me down?
The tsar's scribe beat me deliberately across the teeth,
repeating,
            fervently:
'Decided to go against the people, did you?
You'll find out about against!'
I held my own, without lowering my eyes.
I spat my answer with my blood:
'Against the boyars—
                    true.
Against the people—
                    no!'
I do not renounce myself,
I have chosen my own fate myself.
Before you,
        the people, I repent,
but not for what
                the tsar's scribe wanted.
My head is to blame.
I can see,
        sentencing myself:
I was halfway
            against things,
when I ought to have gone
                        to the very end.
No,
    it is not in this I have sinned, my people,
for hanging boyars from the towers.
I have sinned in my own eyes in this,
that I hanged too few of them.

I have sinned in this,
                    that in a world of evil
I was a good idiot.
I sinned in this,
                    that being an enemy of serfdom
I was something of a serf myself.
I sinned in this,
                    that I thought of doing battle
for a good tsar.
There are no good tsars,
                    fool . . .
Stenka,
        you are perishing for nothing!"
Bells boomed over Moscow.
They are leading Stenka
                    to the place of execution.
In front of Stenka
                    in the rising wind
the leather apron of the headsman is flapping,
and in his hands
                    above the crowd
is a blue ax,
                    blue as the Volga.
And streaming, silvery,
                    along the blade
boats fly,
        boats
                    like seagulls in the morning . . .
And over the snouts,
                    pig faces,
                            and ugly mugs
of tax collectors
                    and money changers,
like light through the fog,
Stenka
        saw
            faces.
Distance and space was in those faces,
and in their eyes,
                    morosely independent,
as if in smaller, secret Volgas
Stenka's boats were sailing.
It's worth bearing it all without a tear,
to be on the rack and wheel of execution,

if sooner or later
faces
    sprout
        threateningly
on the face of the faceless ones ...
And calmly
        (obviously he hadn't lived for nothing)
Stenka laid his head down on the block,
settled his chin in the chopped-out hollow
and with the back of his head gave the order:
                "Strike, ax ..."
The head started rolling,
           burning in its blood,
and hoarsely the head spoke:
             "Not for nothing ..."
And along the ax there were no longer ships—
but little streams,
        little streams ...
Why, good folk, are you standing, not celebrating?
Caps into sky—and dance!
But the Red Square is frozen stiff,
the halberds are scarcely swaying.
Even the buffoons have fallen silent.
Amid the deadly silence
fleas jumped over
from peasants' jackets
        onto women's robes.
The square had understood something.
The square took off their caps,
and the bells
      struck three times
          seething with rage.
But heavy from its bloody forelock
the head was still rocking,
        alive.
From the blood-wet place of execution,
there,
    where the poor were,
the head threw looks about
        like anonymous letters ...
Bustling,
    the poor trembling priest ran up,
wanting to close Stenka's eyelids.
But straining,

frightful as a beast,
the pupils pushed away his hand.
On the tsar's head,
                    chilled by those devilish eyes,
the Cap of Monomakh,§ began to tremble,
and, savagely,
                    not hiding anything of his triumph,
Stenka's head
                    burst out laughing
                                        at the tsar!

Simbirsk" Fair

Fair!
    Simbirsk fair!
Better than Hamburg!
                    Hang on to your pocket!
Street organs are mumbling,
                    and shawls are rustling,
and throats are shouting:
                    "Buy here! Buy here!"
In the hands of the salesmen,
                    telling tall stories,
there are light sables,
                    and heavy brocades,
but the policeman is watching
                    out of the corner of his eye
with his white glove
            on his saber.
But at times he smiles
                    and his little white glove
jumps like a little fish
                    up to his cap,
when in a light cab
                    with a nice chick,
hiccuping, a caviar king
                    drives past.
And the king likes
                    the way the kerchiefs part before him,
and the three-cornered hats

and the caps,
and how a lady's lips,
                    greased with pressed caviar,
glitter beneath her nose.
The bass voices of the market criers are roaring.
They trade in Russia calf,
                    kid,
                            and satin,
spoiled kvass,#
                holy pictures,
rotten meat,
                and old popular romances.

And having sold her bag of spuds,
and grabbed some first-rate stuff,
a woman dances to a concertina,
scarcely dragging her feet.

And she sings,
                very provocatively,
getting tipsy,
holding her shawl by the edges
as if she were still young:

"I have been to the Oka,
eaten a-p-p-le-s,
looking as if gilded,
preserved in tears.

I have tramped to the Kama,
cooked my porridge in a pot.
The gruel was bitter with Kama.
Kama—river of tears.

I set out for Yaik,
with my boyfriend took a skiff.
We sailed up and down the river,
always on tears.

I went to the quiet Don,
I bought myself a home.
Isn't that a woman's comfort?
But tears came pouring through the roof..."

                    .   .   .

In her eyes everything is swaying,
her head is twisting.
She wants to be young again
and it doesn't come off.

And now the concertina plays boisterously,
and now piercingly,
                like burdock burrs . . .
Drink away, Russia,
            as long as you can,
only don't drink away your soul . . .

Fair!
    Simbirsk fair!
Be merry,
           everyone who wants to be merry!
But the woman is drunk
and lies in the mud.

The tsar boasts,
swimming in a fog . . .
But the woman is drunk
and lies in the mud.

Ministers suffer,
sweating over plans . . .
But the woman is drunk
and lies in the mud.

For someone a monument
is being readied . . .
But the woman is drunk
and lies in the mud.

And nice ladies,
           lowering eyelashes,
passing by,
      pass her by:
           "Simply horrid!
                    Such a shame!"
And a grain merchant
passes by,
      but from behind his beard:
"Look at her lying there . . .

But who's to blame?
All those students
                and Yids..."

And a philosopher—poor devil—
lowers his hat over his eyes,
and suffering proudly,
                      passing by:
"There in the dirt, people, is your fate!"

Is then life so base—
you'll just freeze in the mud?!
But someone took her by the elbow
and quietly said to her: "Arise..."

Fair!
    Simbirsk fair!
In the blue are swings
                  and shrieks
                            and whistles,
and the merchants' wives
                    hiss like geese in rage:
"A boy with a tart...
                  A student!"
He guides her carefully by the elbow,
he doesn't even realize that people are looking at him.
"Jesus bless you, honey,
                  my head is clear,
somehow I'll make it on my own."
And he goes away,
                walking by the barges
on the Volga in springtime,
                      and sadly following with her eyes,
the woman quietly blesses him,
as if she were blessing her own child.
He wanders a long time...
                      All around it is getting dark...
A secret policeman runs about
                        like a squirrel in a cage.
But how can he sniff out
                    who is the most dangerous
when in Russia everyone is dangerous!
Poor policeman. Listen, friend:
The most dangerous is always the one

who has to stop,

who simply can't pass by
someone trampled down.
But the Volga is restless,

snoring,

moaning.
Birch trees over the river

light up the shadows,
like timid candles

put up by the earth
for those who have suffered much on earth.

Fair!

Russian fair!
Selling conscience

shame,

and people,
passing off pieces of glass as rubies and sapphires,
and calling people in to buy

by every means.
You, Russia,

they squandered all of you,
and duped you in taverns,
but those who lied and made fools of others
will themselves stay fools!
You, Russia,

were entangled completely,
but you were not born for slavery.
Russia of Razin,

Russia of Pushkin,
Russia of Herzen,

you shall not be trampled in the dirt!
No,

you, Russia,

are not a drunken woman!
You have been given a great destiny,
and even though moaning

as you fall,
you will rise again all by yourself!

Fair!

Russian fair!
The Russian paradise

brims with tears,

but a boy will come—

                  he will appear again—

and with justice he will say

                  "Arise . . ."

1964

TRANSLATED BY TINA TUPIKINA-GLAESSNER, GEOFFREY DUTTON, AND IGOR

MEZHAKOFF-KORIAKIN (REVISED)

*The huge reservoir and hydroelectric plant are located in the small Siberian town of Bratsk, a river station on the Angara River, which flows from Lake Baikal. It is an ancient community that takes its name from the native Buriat people and not from Russian, as often reported erroneously.

†Dmitri Shostakovich's vocal symphonic poem by the same title is based on the text of this poem.

‡Royal Guard (Streltsy): Military corps in the sixteenth and seventeenth centuries instituted by Ivan the Terrible that enjoyed special privileges.

§Cap of Monomakh: The bejeweled fur cap worn only by the tsar, traced back to the Kievan Prince Vladimir Monomakh (1113–1125).

"Simbirsk: City east of Moscow on the Volga River. It is the birthplace of Lenin (Ulianov) and is now named Ulianovsk.

#kvass: Popular fermented drink made from grains.

1965 ⁄ 1967

It acts kind of crazy, flutteringly,
when it chooses us.

"White snow is falling..."

To A. W. Bouis

The white snow is falling,
as though sliding down a thread...
To live on and on in this world
is surely not possible.

Without a trace, some souls
dissolving in the distance,
like the white snow falling,
go to heaven from the earth.

The white snow is falling...
And I likewise will depart.
I don't grieve because of death
and I don't expect immortality.

I don't believe in miracles.
I am not snow, not a star,
and I will be no longer,
never ever, never ever.

And I, a sinner, think:
Well, just who was I,
who in the rush of life
loved life the most?

But I loved Russia
with all my blood, with my spine—
her rivers in flood
and when under ice,

the spirit of her five-wall huts,
the spirit of her pine forests,
her Pushkin, and Stenka,
and her old men.

When things were bad,
I didn't grieve so much.
So what if I lived absurdly—
it was for Russia I lived.

· · ·

I ache with hope
(full of secret alarms),
that just the tiniest bit
I helped Russia.

Let her forget
about me with ease,
only just let her be
forever and forever.

The white snow falls
as at all times,
as during Pushkin and Stenka
and as after me.

A heavy snow is falling,
so bright it pains,
covering both
my tracks and others...

I haven't the strength to be immortal,
but my hope is,
if Russia is,
it means I will be too.

1965

TRANSLATED BY ALBERT C. TODD

Mating Flight of the Woodcock

Shoulder your gun, be steady, sight.
With bill outstretched, needle-sharp,
the woodcock plunges out of the moon
straight toward you, darkening the moon.

He pitches, whistling on the wing,
down through the evening air. Tell me,
why is he drawn to you, as on a string,
why is your muzzle guided by a string?

. . .

Joy is the music of his fall.
Trembling, you hug your weapon tight.
Hunter, he is your unarmed double.
You are his doomed and wingless double.

Can you atone for winglessness
with a blast of wings? Squeeze out your shot—
but that's yourself in careless flight,
yourself you're shooting down in flight.

1965

TRANSLATED BY STANLEY KUNITZ WITH ANTHONY KAHN

A Superfluous Miracle

To T. P.

Everything, truly, would have been simpler,
and probably kinder and wiser,
if I hadn't rushed the request—
that thoughtless request of mine.

And in the darkness, guarded and sensitive,
out of fallen clothes was born
this white superfluous miracle
in a sinful cloud of dark hair.

And when I stepped out into the street,
I did not expect what happened,
above me I heard only the snow,
below me I saw only the snow.

The city was austere, it was a time for skis.
The mud had concealed itself beneath snowdrifts,
and the lowered, inclining cranes
flew motionlessly through the snow.

What for, from where, why,
by what kind of foolish love

had this new superfluous miracle
suddenly fallen on my shoulders?

It would be better, life, to strike me,
to chop me up for firewood,
than to endow me so senselessly,
to burden so heavily with gifts.

You are kind, you can't be faulted,
but your tenderheartedness is wicked.
If you weren't so beautiful,
you wouldn't also be so frightening.

And that god who cries from hidden places
somewhere deep inside me,
is also, perhaps, a superfluous miracle?
Without him would I be more peaceful?

Thus along the white deserted sidewalks,
tormenting both myself and someone else,
I wandered and wandered, crushed by a gift
of beauty that felled me with a single blow . . .

1965
TRANSLATED BY ALBERT C. TODD

Autumn

To A. Simonov

Inside me the season is autumn,
the chill is in me, you can see through me,
and I am sad, but not altogether cheerless,
and filled with humility and goodness.

But if I rage sometimes,
then I am the one who rages, shedding my leaves,
and the simple thought comes sadly to me
that raging isn't really what we need.

.   .   .

The main need is that I should be able
to see myself and the struggling, shocked world
in autumnal nakedness,
when even you, and the world, can be seen right through.

Flashes of insight are the children of silence.
It doesn't matter, if we don't rage aloud.
We must calmly cast off all mere noise
in the name of the new foliage.

Something has apparently happened to me,
and I am relying on nothing but silence,
when the leaves laying themselves one on another
inaudibly become the earth.

And you can see it all, as if from a height,
when you manage to shed your leaves at the right time,
when without passion inner autumn
lays its airy fingers on your forehead.

1965

TRANSLATED BY TINA TUPIKINA-GLAESSNER, GEOFFREY DUTTON, AND
IGOR MEZHAKOFF-KORIAKIN (REVISED)

"The first presentiment..."

The first presentiment of a poem
in a true poet
is the feeling of sin
committed somewhere, sometime.

Even if that sin was not his,
he considers himself guilty,
his navel connects him
to all the tribes of mankind.

And no longer his own master
he runs away from glory and ecstasy,
with his head ready to admit guilt

but nevertheless held high.

The casualties of war and peace,
every broken branch,
build up in him a feeling of guilt,
his guilt, not just that of the age.

And his life is frightful to him,
he feels it as sinful as sin itself.
Every woman is his guilt,
a gift that cannot be returned.

Shame always moves the poet,
thrusting him into boundless space,
and he builds bridges with his bones,
paying what is unpayable.

And there, and there—at the end of the path,
which is there, and cannot be escaped,
he will say: "God forgive me! . . ."—
without even any hope of it.

And his soul will part from his body,
and descend to hell, not enticed by paradise,
forgiven by God, but never
forgiven by himself.

1965

TRANSLATED BY TINA TUPIKINA-GLAESSNER, GEOFFREY DUTTON,
AND IGOR MEZHAKOFF-KORIAKIN (REVISED)

Kamikaze

And I shudder
              and come to my senses— Look!
His elbows dug into the green table,
a former kamikaze pilot—a dead man, Japanese,
truly—is talking about Raskolnikov.
At a "Symposium on the Novel," he's forty-five,

an old man. He's like
polite sobbing . . .
                    he's like a scream
strangled by a necktie. And through us
and somewhere past us,
through Shimoze flak and the shade of Lazo,
like the yellow shrine of Hiroshima,
reeling,
          his face flies past.
But in his throat you can't tell
whether it's a lump of tears
or a cough-lump, or what.
                         The emperor wanted him to grow
                                                      up
humble, his death already assigned . . .
                              a kamikaze.
Sure, it's great to swim along
hands and bouquets, to be slapped on the back by the military
there, at the parade. Sure,
it's fine to be a "hero of the people." But hero
in the name of *what?*
                      With a few buddies,
this one shucked off his hero status
and said he'd just as soon stay
alive.
      That took more guts than exploding
for a goddamned lie!
                    I'm supposed to be hell-for-leather
myself,
        but what of my life and death, really?
What do I think, sinful and mortal,
among sinful, mortal people?
                            We're all assigned our deaths . . .
We're kamikazes. The "divine wind" . . .
the wind of death whistles in our ears:
every footfall on this bomb-cratered planet
is a step toward death.
                       So what if I get busted up and crushed
but not because a dictator says so? I'll pull the control column
up by the roots,
                firewall the throttle,
on collision course, and go out
like the last battering ram.
                           But sons, daughters,

185

descendants,

       though my body sifts down in ashes, I'd like,
from the scraps of my plane, something good to explode
through to you.

       How strange it is, though,
to seem to yourself always dying

              in the sky for nothing,
to turn out to be lied-to!
And still living in the face of your death-assignment,
to be evil as well!
Yes, a living evil
long since supposed to be gone!

1965

TRANSLATED BY JAMES DICKEY WITH ANTHONY KAHN

Coliseum

Coliseum,
       I haven't come to you as to a museum,
I'm no idle gawker.
Our encounter
       is the meeting of two old friends
and two old enemies,
       Coliseum.
You hoped for my death in vain.
I have returned,
       when you've forgotten,
as to a place
       where I've killed thousands of times,
and thousands of times have myself been killed.
Your lions
       have stroked me with their paws—
their caresses were terrible.
To a gladiator
       all is gladiatorial,
Coliseum,
       at all times.
Wearily,
       in your conceit you wished

me to perish handsomely in the arena
for no good reason or cause,
but no one perishes handsomely.
And when,
                    no longer feeling the spears,
I fell,
        dying like a beast,
a turned-down
                    thumb
                        seemed
to replace
            even a turned-up thumb...
I've returned an avenger—
                        no revenge more dread.
You didn't expect it, Coliseum?
                        Tremble, Coliseum!
And I came not by day,
                    but in the deep of night,
when all your guides had beat it—
                        the dodgers,
and when all around
                    was only the stench of dogs' piss,
abandoned cans
            and broken bricks...
But shout your shouts,
                roar your roars—
in my body
            swords
                turn and twist,
and fragments of claws
                    and fragments of passions...
Again I hear
            the crunch of Christian bones,
the crunch of children's teeth
                        biting candy in the stand.
Coliseum,
        are you not used to such pastimes?
What will you show me today, Coliseum?
Unafraid, rats scour
the ruined nocturnal kingdom.
Pederasts with powdered faces
squeeze each other at the gate to the lion's den.*
In Nero's former box
a society lady quivers with lust.

One can hear the rustling of nylon—
a gigolo is pulling off her panties.
Where it smells of murders,
where my white bones lie in the earth,
there a prostitute has squatted down
swiftly, intent on her business.
Where we, the gladiators,
used to perish, poor hapless fellows,
there someone searches our faces:
"Heroin . . . Who wants a little heroin?"
Accept,
      Coliseum,
                without complaint,
this revenge
                and blame not your fate.
Anemia always comes upon
all things founded on blood.
But, Coliseum,
          let me say
                without irony:
At times I freeze with fear.
This world—
          this out-and-out Coliseum—
only seems to have no heroes.
Of course, men smash atoms,
explore starry spaces,
but the world
          to this day
is still split into spectators and gladiators.
I'll not disparage the gladiators:
I pity them with all my hide and innards—
but, well, I hate the spectators:
in each spectator
          a Nero lives.†
Yes, they're terrible,
          these satiated spectators,
who shout from their seats:
          "Slash him!
                Stab him!"

Well, the most terrible spectators
are those who profit by blood.
Instigators,
      loudmouths,
without shame you incite others.

You would like us,
                gladiators,
                            to be always,
                                        killing each other?
Hallooers,
        hounders,
from your safe seats
you squeal
            at us to be fearless,
to split ourselves
                    beautifully on a sword . . .
I curse
        the Nero-like gestures,
and hear me,
                you scoundrels:
in our world there are
                        victims and executioners,
but there's also a third force—
                            the fighters!
I wander about,
                hungering for brotherhood;
stumbling, I wander through the ages
and in my gladiatorial dreams
I see a new Spartacus.
There I stand in the arena
before an audience seething as hell.
I'm done for,
            worn out,
                        covered with wounds,
but I do not fall:
                they will not spare me.
Amid the general roar I expect
                            the lion's growl.
The whole arena crackles beneath the claws.
Questions are hurled at me
                        like javelins,
but, well, my skin's
                    my only shield.
Coliseum,
        applaud,
                gaze your fill!
May you be accursed,
                    Coliseum-the-executioner!
And thanks for teaching me!

Above the screams and squeals
                         I raise
my avenging hand
and, showing no mercy,
                    turn my thumb down ...

1965

TRANSLATED BY GEORGE REAVEY

*The next four lines were cut after the first publication.
†The next seven lines were cut after the first publication.

The Confessional

The little window of the confessional ...
approaching it, in the religious shade
the threadbare face of the ravaged woman,
flickering with hope.

A child of the purlieus of Naples
waits her turn at the side,
an open Bible
on her telltale belly.

Without rifle or service cap
a soldier comes to be judged,
the skin of his back twitching
under the coarse uniform.

Housewives lug from the washtubs
and gamblers from the races
the sins of their imagination
along with their real sins.

Is there no confessional for me?
To whom shall I go, quelling my fears,
with the sinful dust, the foreign dust,
on my errant feet?

                    •   •   •

Enough of idleness and sloth!
What's the address? I'll find the way.
But people are crawling in my path,
begging to confess to me.

How can the confessor teach
those who are lost and sick at heart,
when he himself, among the sinners,
is worst, and most forsaken?

It is only a game we play
with other people's sins.
Besides, everyone knows
that everyone lies confessing.

And the priest lies too,
wanting to be good to them;
for the cozy fib, the double fib,
coddles and does not burn.

But I have no right to have faith in faith,
however I smash my brains on the stones,
when, almost like a truth to a truth,
a lie confesses to a lie.

1965
TRANSLATED BY STANLEY KUNITZ WITH ANTHONY KAHN

Procession with the Madonna

To Ludovico Corrao

In the small, untroubled town of Taormina
a grave procession passed with its Madonna.
Smoke from the candles rose and came to nothing,
as frail as any moment's brief enigma.

There in forefront, all attired in white,
the young girls walked, holding their candles tightly.

Flushed with a timid rapture, on they came,
full of themselves and of the world's delight.

And the girls stared at the candles in their hands,
and in those flames, unstable in the wind,
they saw stupendous meetings, deep communions,
and heard endearments past all understanding.

Oh, it was right that the young girls should be hopeful.
The hour of their deception was not ripe.
But there behind them, like their fates impending,
the women marched along with weary step.

Attired in black, the women marched along,
and they too held their candles tightly, strongly,
heavily shuffling, grave and undeceived,
and full of an accustomed sense of wrong.

And the women stared at the candles in their hands,
and in those flames, unstable in the wind,
they saw the scrawny shoulders of their children
and heard the vacant speeches of their husbands.

Thus, street by street, they all went on together,
declaring that the Madonna was their mother,
and bearing the Madonna like some strange
victim who stands erect upon her stretcher.

The Madonna's heart, or so it appeared, was pained
both for the girls and for the women behind them;
and yet—or so it appeared—she had decreed
that life go on like this, world without end.

I walked beside the Madonna, and my glance
found in the candles no glad radiance,
no weary sorrow, but a muddled vision
full of sweet hope and bitterness at once.

And so I live—still dreaming, still unmarried,
and yet already doomed forevermore—
somewhere between the girls in their white dresses
and the gray women in their black attire.

1965

TRANSLATED BY RICHARD WILBUR WITH ANTHONY KAHN

Letter to Paris

When will we return to Russia?
—G. Adamovich

The cross of solitudes doesn't save us.
The spirit of unfreedom is not victorious.
Georgii Viktorovich Adamovich,*
and are you free
                    when you're alone?
We were chatting together,
                          just two Russians,
about whatever
                in the café "Coupole"
when suddenly
              to this Petersburger
came the pain of serfdom,
                          and it was such pain . . .
Yes, all we Russians
                    are serfs,
remembering with our backs
                          the cudgels
of our master
              in capricious Russia
and more compellingly
                      when on the run.
Gregorii Viktorovich Adamovich,
we were born in such a country
where you can't stop the urge to flee,
but we creep
            if only in our sleep.
And maybe our freedom
                      is just in this
that we are in bondage,
                        no matter how much we grieve,
and no cup
          will pass us
be it a cup of poison
                      in the hand of Rus.†
We have been scattered about,
                            smashed into pieces,

193

as in a sea of ice floe,
>> but not defeated.
Russian culture
>> is always a single whole
and is only being tested
>> for fissures.
And, when he discarded his gypsy tambourine,
Kuprin returned
>> to die,
as Bunin returned under a book jacket,
and you will return
>> in the future,
>> in the future.
Even if you hide yourself in Mecca,
>> or leap into Lethe,
there's Russia in your guts.
>> Nothing can tear it out!
>> Nothing!

There is no never returning to Russia.
Don't run away from your own heart.
Don't part with her,
>> don't loose the bonds.
Though she be damned!
>> A longing for her
grabs, like a Ryazan thistle,
the cloth of a Paris jacket.
But, if in books there is the gloom of the homeland
and the squeal,
.   until it pains of home,
>> in a peasant hut,
such a book is
>> like a Russian passport
that you have ordered for yourself.

1965

TRANSLATED BY ALBERT C. TODD

*Georgii Viktorovich Adamovich: Russian poet and critic (1894–1972) who emigrated to Paris in 1922.
†Rus: Ancient Russia. The name of the eastern Slavonic tribe, it became the name of the early feudal state and nation in the ninth century.

A Hundred Miles

To Georgii Semyonov

A hundred miles from the capital of all hopes,
from the Hotel Ukraine and the Budapest,
from cafés of the young,
from trusty auxiliary police,
from embassy limousines,
from hard currency shops,
from terribly important ministries,
from terribly unimportant, but terribly nice bitches,
from closed film screenings,
from evening paper crosswords,
from the howl "Kill the ump!"
from peace congresses,
from tours of "The Ice Revue"
it's ever so quiet, like in paradise.
The Ugra River runs there,
skipping rocks all by itself,
and everything in the world has its own account.

A hundred miles from the capital of all hopes,
is a village without bridegrooms or brides,
three cottages falling to pieces,
three old women in three cottages,
and one old man, a self-promoting liar,
like a single samovar for all three.
The three old women fish and mow grass
and say to him: "Be careful, don't you ever die . . .
We'll mow the hay for you,
we'll haul the water too,
only just keep on, you old devil, telling us lies,
but tell us beauties, right from the heart."

The old man says: "I've lied myself out."
The old man says: "I've plowed my piece.
War and Moscow took all my children,
and grass grows on my roof,
and in my thoughts there's confusion,
what sort of lying nonsense is here, old gals."
And, fixing his eyes on the ceiling,

he lay there, not as a liar, as a prophet,
and onto the tip of his jutting beard
the roof, heavy with goosefoot, is ready to collapse.

The three old women are not used to living with anguish.
The three old women sharpen their scythes on a whetstone.
The three old women mow furiously in the grove.
Their sarafan smocks grow heavy with dew,
and the soul is easier from the scythe.

A fisherman from the capital of all hopes
makes a quick sally out into nature.
"How charming it is, our Russian mowing..."
he sighs, wiping sweat from his brow.
"Well now, old gals, where is your old tsar?"
"Our tsar these days, dearie, doesn't mow.
He's turned his eyes away from us.
Laid down on a bench. Made up his mind to die.
Only, dearie, here's what I think of it.
I was dying once, but it passed..."

The scythes whistle, cutting easily
wave after wave of grass.
"Well, and where were you dying and when?"
"In captivity, dearie, in captivity."

And with strokes, now of joy, now of pain,
and maybe, both of them together.
"In what captivity, old gal, you mean the Germans?"
"In our own, dearie, in our own..."

The fisherman freezes and brushes thistles off his knees:
"But what sort of our own captivity, old gal?"
"Maybe it's not the right word, my dear,
but they banished us to the sands, the whole family.
We never were kulaks ever,
so that misery seemed like captivity..."

The fisherman from the capital of all hopes
suddenly backed away—awkwardly, to one side.
"Well, I hope that our old man will get better..."
and after him came calmly: "God grant he does."

. . .

The fisherman from the capital of all hopes
started his "Moskvich" in consternation.
It's better to give the soul its airing on asphalt,
better to buy fish in stores,
better to live and let live among the unknowing
who haven't comprehended the price of those hopes.

And there flew by, God help them!
airplanes, Russian born,
raising fastidiously their landing gear
above the grass blossoming on roofs, into the heavens ...

1965

TRANSLATED BY ALBERT C. TODD

Letter to Yesenin

Russian poets,
             we abuse each other.
The Russian Parnassus is rife with squabbles,
but we are all bound to those dear to us—
any one of us is at once a little bit Yesenin.
And I am Yesenin,
                but quite another.
On the kolkhoz my horse was pink from birth.*
Like Russia I am more of steel
and like Russia, less of birches.†
Dear Yesenin,
             Old Russia has changed,
but there's no point, I think, in crying.
I'm afraid to say it's for
                     the better,
and it's dangerous to say it's for
                              the worse.
What great building,
                  what satellites in our land!
But we lost
          along a very rough way
both twenty million in the war,

and twenty million
                   in the war with our people.
Should we forget about this
                     by chopping off our memory?
But where's the ax that can chop off memory altogether?
No one has saved others
                like Russians have,
no one slaughters
                 their own self like Russians do.
But our ship sails on.
                 When the water is shallow,
we drag Russia forward over a dry row.
That there are bastards enough
                    is no calamity.
But that there is no Lenin,
                 that's really tough.
And it's tough that there's no you.
Nor your rival—the great bawler.‡
Of course, I'm not the judge of either of you,
but nonetheless you left us too soon.
When a red-faced Komsomol leader
roars
      at us poets
              with his fist,
and wants to knead our souls
                  like wax,
to sculpt out his own likeness,
his words, Yesenin, aren't frightening,
but it's difficult to be happy about it,
and I've no desire,
            believe me,
                 to pull on my pants
and chase after this Komsomol type.
Sometimes it hurts and all is bitter,
and there isn't the strength to oppose nonsense,
and death drags you under a wheel
the way a scarf once dragged Isadora.§
But you have to live.
            Neither vodka,
                nor a noose,
nor women—
          none of them are salvation.
You are salvation—
           land of Old Russia.

Salvation is

        your truthfulness, Yesenin.

And Russian poetry goes

forward through suspicions and assaults,

and with Yesenin's skillful hold throws

Europe, like Poddubny," to the mat.

1965

TRANSLATED BY ALBERT C. TODD

*pink horse: Yesenin speaks of riding a pink horse in his well-known poem "I don't regret..."
†birches: A well-known symbol of Russia itself, the birch is a particularly frequent image in Yesenin's verse.
‡great bawler: Vladimir Vladimirovich Mayakovsky (1893–1930) was noted for his flamboyant manner and declamatory verse. An active revolutionary, he greeted the October Revolution with enthusiasm and devised propaganda verses, slogans, and posters. Disillusioned, he committed suicide by shooting himself; but personal, not political, factors may have been most significant.
§Isadora: Isadora Duncan, the American dancer, was married to Yesenin and then divorced. She was killed when her scarf became entangled in a car wheel.
"Poddubny: Ivan Poddubny. Renowned Russian strongman wrestler at the beginning of the twentieth century.

Italian Tears

In the village of Anzeba, close to Bratsk,
a red-haired storekeeper was weeping drunkenly.
A terrible thing, it always gives me the shivers,
to see a man, not a woman, sobbing.

Inhumanly straining his face,
the man tried to look composed,
but his meager shoulders were shaking,
and from his eyes tears poured and poured.

To the last drop he was spilling it out;
how he had been captured near Smolensk,
and had then been packed off by long-
distance rail to Italy far away.

"You'll understand," he said, "my spade would not dig
in the sector fenced off from all,
and on the highway we could see the dew rise,

you understand, the dew on the highway!

"And with a basket one day a child,
an Italian girl, was passing by,
and, as if she were Russian, she grasped at once
there were hungry men behind that fence.

"She was beak-nosed like a young rook,
and she held out an Italian fruit to us,
in her seven-year-old little hands
that were like the hands of a compassionate woman.

"But, as for those damned fascists—
what did they care for children or people!
A guard struck her with a rifle butt,
and booted her hard into the bargain.

"And she fell with arms flung out,
and lay sprawling on the highway,
and bitterly she began to sob in Russian,
and we understood it all at once.

"Though our band of brothers had gone through much,
and suffered many trials so far from home,
yet we could stand it no longer
to hear that little girl sobbing.

"And with spades we attacked the dogs and the guards,
splitting their bastard cartilages,
and then we took to the automatics:
they did their work well.

"And freedom gushed to our throats,
and as elusive as a spinning top,
that little girl led us into the mountains
to join the Italian partisans there.

"Among them were also working lads,
and peasants too—and I took courage.
Likewise there was a priest—'padre,' they called him . . .
and thus it was, brother, I came nearer to God.

"We shared the delays and the bullets,
all of our innermost secrets,

and at times, I swear, I couldn't tell
a Russian from an Italian in that detachment.

"Olive tree or birch tree, brother,
it was almost all the same.
Italian tears or Russian tears
or other tears—it is all the same . . ."

"And then?"—"And then, bearing arms,
we entered Rome to the sound of music.
Gladioli showered down into the puddles
and we trampled them as we marched.

"The partisan flag was also fluttering,
and endearingly the Union Jack was there,
and also the Stars and Stripes—
but Rome had forgotten all about our flag.

"But next to a church an elderly man
came up to us and said in Russian:
'I'm a chauffeur at the embassy of Siam,
and our fascist ambassador took to his heels.

" 'Though an emigrant, I remembered my land . . .
It's close by, the house I abandoned.
Just look at that flag—a field of crimson,
but somehow a lion has intruded upon it.'

"And then, in no way embarrassed,
with our knives we ripped off the lion,
but something was still missing—
we didn't quite get it at first.

"And Maria, that black little rook,
(may the Siamese Ambassador forgive her!)
snatched a pair of scissors from a barber's,
and snipped off the hem of her skirt.

"And chirping out some words,
with a sly smile on her face,
she kept cutting bits and pieces,
and then sewing them onto the flag.

"And then it flew high—bringing tears
to the eyes of that rough fighting band—

that flag with a hammer and sickle upon it,
fashioned from the skirt of the little girl."

"What then?" He frowned and stammered, and took
a swig of crude liquor and a mouthful of plum jam,
while his face was all freckled like a child's,
with wrinkles that weren't a child's at all.

"And then we were crossing the Caspian.
We hugged each other and danced on board!
We were some kind of heroes,
but heroes only until we reached Baku.

"We were not greeted with gladioli,
but were met with fixed bayonets, brother.
And sullenly the police dogs growled
as we were carried away.

"The clean-shaven faces of our convoy guards
stared with suspicion at us,
and small boys yelled out: 'Down with the Fritzes!'
And this made tears well up in our eyes.

"A pimply lieutenant, who hadn't seen fire,
all decked out in a new uniform—may he rot!—
addressed us calmly: 'No hysterics now!'
and he added: 'Give up your arms!'

"Proud of our weapons,
we spat on that command:
'We never have and never will
surrender them without a fight.'

"But like shepherds, the guards
counted us like sheep and then drove us along
to the 'barbed-wire retreat' we knew so well,
all burgeoning with familiar iron flowers.

"And where had you, partisan valor
of former days, so inexplicably vanished
in the land of our own flesh and blood?
Or, perhaps, it had been only a dream?

"We hung our heads low,
and easily surrendered our arms.

Now Italy was not at all near,
and freedom was truly far.

"Throwing down my arms and ragged belongings,
I tucked that flag under my shirt;
but they took it away when they frisked me.
'You're unworthy,' they said. 'You're an enemy.'

"And there it lay on speechless weapons,
that red flag swinishly taken down by scoundrels,*
the hammer and sickle on it
made from the little girl's skirt . . ."

"And what then?" He gave a jaundiced smile,
took another gulp of crude liquor
and, grimacing, followed it up
with a spoonful of chunky plum jam.

Again he made an effort to look composed,
not knowing where to hide his face:
"Ah, it's not worth it . . . What's done is done,
but may it never happen again.

"I must get up early tomorrow—there's work to do.
But if you ever find yourself in Italy:
somewhere in the town of Monte Rotondo
you'll come across our brother-partisans living there.

"And Maria—with all her black ringlets,
and even gray ones, maybe—many years have passed.
Give her my greetings, if she remembers of course,
greetings from red-haired Vanya.

"Don't tell her about the camp, you understand.
As I said, what's done is done.
But tell them—they'll be glad to hear it—
that Vanya's living well, on the whole . . ."

Vanya, all the same, I did go to Monte
Rotondo, as you had asked me to do.
The peasant, the chauffeur, and the repairmen,
embraced me like a brother there.

I did not see Signora Maria,

but simply paid a call to her house,
and there I saw your blue eyes looking down
from a photograph beside the image of Christ.

I was asked by the peasants and
by the priest—all white as snow:
"How's Vanya?" "How's Vanya?" How's Vanya?"
and they said with a sigh, "What a man!"

The partisans stood in ranks—
so many had come to ask questions,
and I kept affirming, restraining my sobs:
"Your Vanya's living fairly well, on the whole..."

We were neither too drunk, nor too sober—
all we did was to sing and drink wine.
Italian tears or Russian tears
or any other tears—are very much the same.

Why are you weeping, gulping liquor again,
Why do you mutter: "Ah, it's only a fancy!"?
Italy still remembers you, Vanya,
and Russia will recall you too—so don't weep!

1966

TRANSLATED BY GEORGE REAVEY (REVISED)

*This line, censored in earlier published editions, was inadvertently forgotten and uncorrected in
the *Sob. soch.*, 1987.

The Stage

The curse upon me,
                    the waste of my soul in rage,
is the stage.
I was young.
            Wanted to climb a pedestal,
wanted the showers of applause and flowers
when I came forward
                    and stood, feeling laughable,

on the talcum powder left from the ballet shoes.
As yet I had absolutely nothing to say,
there was only this ringing inside me,
                              in my throat,
but something was trying so powerfully to come out
that no stage fright could frighten it away.
And as my breaking voice began to cry,
time, breaking itself, began to shout
and I was that moment of time,
                              and it was I.
And on the stage,
                in the fiery line of the footlights
it was as if all those things still unexpressed,
hiding their tiny glow within the darkness,
were suddenly in me and I was one great light.
The mystique of the stage was set in motion
and fame stood separate beside us, as the third.
As in the Bible,
                in the beginning was the word,
and then—well then,
                in the word was the explosion.
You fools—
                of course I'm no Severianin!
My bones had no strength in them yet, I know,
but on my face, hacking
                away the pimples,
the features of Mayakovsky began to glow.
And the golden head of Yesenin,
of all poets the most reckless, the craziest,
with the scent of the wise wheat fields of his origin,
rose above my head, and I was possessed.
My teachers,
                I have not disgraced you, I swear,
and secretly I have given my laurels back to you.
The whole world was applauding us together,
Paris and Hamburg,
                and Melbourne and London.
But what have you done to me,
                O Stage—

is your hunger assuaged?
My verse did not soften
                or disintegrate,
but became cruder and cruder
                in style and theme.

Stage,

  you gave me the light in which to scintillate
but took away the soft shadow and the subtle gleam.
I was turning purple from the intolerable strain.
I was painting great placards,

     rationalizing slyly
that a watercolor can hardly be seen
in a large hall,

   especially from the gallery.
I began to cherish not quietness—

     but thunder,
and when you do this it is easy to go wrong.
I could throw the bright colors around,

      make people wonder,
but forgot the intimate shades are just as strong.
And then there was something even more terrible:
when the audience were slipping into their coats
bits of me were scattered among thousands of people,
and I was leaving the hall myself,

    becoming remote.
And my double,

   pockmarked with perspiration,
would sit in the makeup room,

    a finished magician,
thousand-faced

   with all the accumulation
of other faces inside him,

    beyond recognition.
O Stage—

   why pay such a horrible wage?
"Good-bye, Stage . . ."—

    I will whisper quietly,
although I have forgotten the art of whispering.
I will abandon noise and listen for a rustling,
leaning on the slender shoulder of a birch tree.
But, demanding my help, as the moment before the storm
demands the coming explosion

    and the scatter of birds,
everything unexpressed in distant fields and farms
tightens in my throat

   and fuses into words.
The degradation of the living and the dead,
in this world

   still so far from paradise,

still demands my help,

              dragging the shreds

of my voice from the chords I vulgarized.

I am not jealous, other poets are my friends.

I don't need anything—

              I'll give away all,

my fame,

        yes, even my crazy head,

in order that you may have what you deserve!

Of course, it will be quite obvious to posterity,

that I—alas!—represent no ideal,

and yet—

         whether crude or with some dexterity—

from the stage I did waken some kind of feelings.

And I will mutter hoarsely

              when there is left

not even a whisper of my voice's pride:

"Forgive me,

       I was what I was, only myself,

and whether I lived as I should have—

                let God decide."

And I will leave you for the dark without fear,

O Stage . . .

1966

TRANSLATED BY GEOFFREY DUTTON WITH IGOR MEZHAKOFF-KORIAKIN
(REVISED)

"Poetry gives off smoke . . ."

But only the divine word . . .
—A. Pushkin

Poetry gives off smoke

but it doesn't die out.

It acts kind of crazy, flutteringly,

when it chooses us.

          This fellow's no fool,

sucking tranquilizers,

toting in a little briefcase
a boiled beetroot.

        Right now he'd like a mousse
or baba au rhum,

          but the Muse—

               some kind of Muse!—
grabs him

      by the scruff of the neck!
Thoughts drill a hole in his forehead,
and he's mislaid the spoon—
and he's a giant! Socrates, for the Lord's sake . . .
in an Oblomov dust jacket. OK . . .
he's no Apollo—

           he's puny and ugly,
skinny: he's like a golden mushroom,
unsteady . . .

     transparent.
But suddenly some sort of whistling
is in his ears, and then . . .

        a period!
And like a slugger's hook

         across the chops of the ages,
a lime!

    And there

       an insane little bird
falls off its feet,

     a crazy ragpicker,

         drunk,
a kind of society clown. But something gives her the word
and—

    like branches in winter,
God rings from within, and her eyelids turn
to marble.

    And here's a bum—

        a shaman,
really—

    from among the lunatics!
Pour him champagne,

      bring him
women, not rum cakes!

       Suddenly an order from within
will come through sternly, and he's the instant
voice of the people, damned near
Savonarola!

Poetry acts kind of strange, it flutters
when it chooses us.
And it has no mercy, either,
afterward. It stamps "Pure Souls"
on us ... but who's the judge?
                                    Yes,
for the horse-blinkered multitudes we're "decadent,"
but for ourselves, we ourselves are ... are ...
well, yes! Redemption!

1966

TRANSLATED BY JAMES DICKEY WITH ANTHONY KAHN

Dwarf Birches

We are dwarf birches.
We sit firmly, like splinters,
under the nails of frosts

and the Khanate of Eternal Freeze
engages in many shenanigans
to bend us down lower and lower.
Are you astonished, Parisian chestnuts?

Are you pained, haughty palms,
that we seem to have fallen low?
Are you embittered, pacesetters of fashion,
that we are all such Quasimodos?

While safe and warm, though,
you are pleased with our courage,
and you send us, pompous and mournful,
your moral support.

You figure, dear colleagues of ours,
that we are not trees but cripples.
Yet our leaves—though ugly—
seem progressive to you, for the frost.

Thanks a million. Alone, if you please,

we shall weather it under the sky,
even if savagely bent and twisted.
Without your moral support.

Of course, you command more freedom.
But, for all that, our roots are more strong.
Of course, we don't dwell in Paris,
but we are valued more in the tundra.

We are dwarf birches.
We have cleverly made up our poses.
But all this is largely pretense.
Constraint bears the form of rebellion.

We believe, bent down forever,
eternal frost can't last.
Its horror will yield.
Our right to stand upright will come.

Should the climate change, won't
our branches at once grow
into shapes that are free?
Yet we're now used to being maimed.

And this worries and worries us,
and the frost twists and twists us,
but we dig in, like splinters,
we—dwarf birches!

1966
TRANSLATED BY VERA DUNHAM

The Torments of Conscience

To D. Shostakovich

We live, dying is not our business,
shame is another lost episode,
but like an unseen madonna, conscience
is standing at every crossroad.

. . .

And her children and her grandchildren,
the torments of conscience—strange torments—
with a tramp's walking stick and bag wander
the world that is shameless to so many.

From one gate once more to the next gate,
once again from doorstep to doorstep,
they journey like pilgrims
who have in their bosoms—a god.

Surely it was they who always haunted
the serfs, tapping with one finger
secretly on their mica windows, and who pounded
with their fists on the mansions of the tsars?

Surely they hurried off dead Pushkin
on a sleigh in the snow from a black sky,
it was they who drove Dostoyevsky to prison,
it was they who whispered to Tolstoy: "Run!"

The executioners understood it thus:
"He who torments himself is a troublemaker.
Torments of conscience—this is dangerous!
Let's liquidate conscience so there'll be no torments."

But like the clanging of an alarm bell
rattling their roofs at nighttime,
torments of conscience—terrible torments—
seeped through to the executioners themselves.

For even the guardians of injustice,
who abandoned all honor long ago,
may no longer know the meaning of conscience,
but the torments of conscience they do know.

And if in this wide world where no one,
no one is guiltless, someone has heard
within himself the cry "What have I done?"
then something can be done with this world.

I do not believe in the prophets construing
the coming of the Second or the Thousandth Rome,
I believe in a quiet "What are you doing?"
I believe in a bitter "What are *we* doing?"

• • •

And on the slippery edge of lost faith
I am kissing your dark hands,
for you alone are my last faith,
torments of conscience—fierce torments!

1966

TRANSLATED BY GEOFFREY DUTTON WITH IGOR MEZHAKOFF-KORIAKIN
(REVISED)

Old Women

On the day I was admitted to bagels and tea
by a high society of old women,
there reigned, saved from all ruination,
a natural spirit of refinement,
the kind I rarely notice nowadays.

Their subtly cultivated mischievousness,
their subtly concealed curiosity
revealed more than any chronicler
about the best people of the age.

And for me, whose speech was impoverished,
like a burglared house,
forgotten, pure Russian turns of speech
were almost foreign.

The old women were famous because
they were loved by those who were famous.
An invisible Masonic sign of the elite
bestowed on these mortal remains of bird figures
the lofty shadow of involvement.

Not intruding in the conversation,
from their stares from time to time I felt
awkward, like a cheap dessert wine
in the company of Cliquot and Montillado.

But to accuse them somehow of snobbishness,

I warrant would be, truly, monstrous.
In their superiority there was nothing
of the plebeian consciousness of superiority.

And how many wars passed through them,
without burning their souls in angry fires:
two world wars, and one that was their own,
and thousands of daily wars without blazes.

To what distances punishment drove them!
And in barbed-wire gnashing and snarling
Inta and Karaganda* appeared to me
above the prim little cups of tea.

No criminal patina adhered to the old women,
while in the prison quilted jackets that served them without sentence,
they silenced someone's capricious cursing
with the haughty look of Blok's unknown lady.

And, digging the frozen earth until dark,
when terrible blizzards caused them to reel,
they whispered some glorified names
with rightful familiarity.

A country of superspeed and superscience,
superphysicists, superlyricists, and superconstruction,
Russia, you are still a country of old women,
perhaps superforgiving, but severe.

In unfashionable turned-up collars,
almost fleshless, the old women drank tea,
but nevertheless in them, not in any slogans,†
the traits of Russia were personified.

I listened to them with all my power to hear.
But what will they yet hear from us?
Let others write for young girls,
I want to write for such old women.

1966

TRANSLATED BY ALBERT C. TODD

*Inta and Karaganda: Infamous labor camps of the Stalin era.
†This line was printed in a censored version only until *Stikhotvoreniia* (Moscow 1987), pp. 127–28.

In Memory of Akhmatova

Two ages ours—and gone. How could we weep?
The very thought was dry. Alive,
she was beyond belief.
How could she die?

Gone like a nightsong, feathers
dipped through garden air
to a dim branch, as if forever
gone to Petersburg from Leningrad.

The parted times, the scattered days
regroup within her hazy light.
If Pushkin is our sun, surely she
is our White Night.

Beyond the give-and-take of breath,
the struggle in the mind of death
and immortality, between
the future and the past, she lies.

The past streamed softly by her grave:
proud gray ladies, lifting faces
shocked in silver, wearing bonnets
of another age.

Yes, time had dimmed that beauty, prized
highly by a Russia that had been,
but, lamps of kindliness, their eyes
still danced against the wind.

And, shoulders still too weak for worlds,
the future comes with molten eyes:
schoolboys, with their hands in fists,
pressing notebooks tight.

And schoolgirls, bearing in their satchels,
surely, notes and diaries,
all of them in this alike:
blissful, Russian, and naive.

. . .

And oh, worldwide decay, pass on and never
cut this tie of times—we need its aid.
For, certainly, two Russias cannot ever
exist or two Akhmatovas be made.

2.

In another grave, not far away,
like a folk song by the Bible's side
a woman near Akhmatova in age
lay simply dressed, in white.

She lay as if awaiting a marriage
with nothing left to darn or wipe or sweep:
a peasant, said her face, her hands, her carriage,
a domestic, it would seem.

To be no more—how heavenly a state.
The people of the house were kind enough,
and like a child before a holiday
they washed and neatly dressed her up.

True, they didn't smother her with lilies,
but the coffin fit, and, oh,
such fancy slippers on her, new ones nearly
with the repairman's stamp still on the soles.

And there she lay, absolvingly serene,
her dry hands folded on her breast,
reverentially, it seemed,
as if they had a candle there to press.

Alive, those hands (so skilled at this) had scurried,
(writing, true, mere turns and twists)
dark and stern and strong as bronze,
and never known a kiss.

Then I thought: Perhaps, just suppose
two different Russias do exist:
a Russia of the hands and of the soul,
two different lands that never mixed.

. . .

No one ever mourned that woman. Night
dropped upon her with no dawn to come.
And above her, high, aloofly white
Akhmatova's patrician profile hung.

Akhmatova, above mere honor
reposed in state: disdainful, droll.
Acknowledging the high rank placed upon her
above the low impostures of the soul.

Aristocrat? Fair denizen, conveyed
on roadways ringing to the prancing trotters?
Yet her hands, afloat on a bouquet
seemed to rock and, rocking, something betrayed.

They labored to their limit, but at times
they reached beyond their strength, and then,
so light in Pushkin's hold, the pen
with sudden weight would grin and break her fingers.

Done with the swift chill of Aix wine
and kisses caught in Petersburg and Nice,
these fingers met upon her breast, resigned
and fragrant with a peasant girl's fatigue.

Without a staff, without a crown a queen
among the tarnished gifts of state and man,
she lay absolvingly serene,
like that woman dressed in secondhand.

And in that other grave the woman lay
who never looked on Nice, and on her brow
appeared Akhmatova's stern grace.
And between them there is no frontier.

1966

TRANSLATED BY ANTHONY KAHN (REVISED)

"I fell out of love with you ..."

I fell out of love with you—what a banal denouement,
just as banal as life, just as banal as death is.
Let me snap the sting of this intolerable love song,
smash the guitar in two—why force a comedy!

Only the pup, shaggy little monster, cannot understand
why you and I make complex every simple thing.
As soon as I let him in, he runs to your door and scratches,
but he scratches at my door every time you let him in.

Really, you could go mad, dashing about like this.
Sentimental dog, I know you're immature,
but I refuse to become a sentimentalist.
To drag out the last act is to prolong the torture.

To be sentimental is not a weakness but a crime—
when you soften again, again promise reconciliation,
and groaning attempt to stage a show, yet another time,
under the insipid name of "Love's Salvation."

You should start saving love right at the beginning
from those passionate "Forevers!," those childish "Nevers!"
"Do not make promises!"—the trains were bellowing.
"Do not make promises!"—mumbled the telephone wires.

Half-cracked branches of trees and the smoke-smudged sky
were warning us, so ignorant in our conceit,
that optimism is merely untaught simplicity,
that hopes are always safer when they are not too great.

It is kinder to stay quite sober and soberly weigh the worth
of the links before putting them on—that's the creed of the chain,
not to promise heaven but at least to give the earth,
not to promise until death do part but at least give life again.

When you are in love it is kinder not to keep on saying "I love you."
How hard it is later, from the same mouth, to hear it destroyed
in words that are void of truth, in sneers, gibes that mock you,
making the world we had thought perfect seem false and void.

. . .

It is better not to promise. Love is something one can't realize,
why then lead someone into deceit as to the altar?
Of course the vision is wonderful, until it flies.
It is kinder not to love when you know love has no future.

Our poor dog keeps on whining, enough to drive us to madness,
with his paws scratching now on your door, now on my door.
I no longer love you; for that I do not ask forgiveness.
I did love you; that is what I ask forgiveness for.

1966

TRANSLATED BY GEOFFREY DUTTON WITH IGOR MEZHAKOFF-KORIAKIN

The Ballad of the Big Stamp

On the Lena's laid-back shore,
enthralled by women's singing eyes
in the end just plain fatigued
from rural adventures no doubt,
Cupid's lucky spoiled boy,
to be on the safe side I picked up sadly
the lingo the castrates tout.

When from your business here with dolls
they cut off just your *nails*,
then, no matter how much your protest calls,
it's just a little stamp, that's clear.
After that there's the big play
with nothing to get in the way
resurrecting both flesh and soul today
and in your pants space and grace so dear.

And so I'll begin my little ballad:
Just to keep tradition valid
I'll tell you from the start,
there lived a sluggard, Samson.
Generally backward in thought.
Leisurely lazy at work,
but something dangled in his pants,
and with that he was satisfied.

His range was mighty:
he loved the fat ones, the medium, and the thin,
he loved them in straw, in hay, in groves,
in cow sheds, in ditches, in tractors.
The sowing was diverted, the milking disrupted,
Lizka sobbed, Zoika wailed,
and our sleepless Samson bold
like a butter churn flailed
the vodka still when cold.
But next to this kolkhoz mediocrity,
as a supra-historical curiosity,
labored earnest fall to fall
private farmers—castrates all.
Senile faces everywhere,
a need for clothing did not nurture,
but for a youth who had a future,
from whom their hopes could grow—
who'd fight for their right to sow.

And the tip-top castrate squeaked:
"Samson, forget your sinful world so weak
by loving our world without sin.
I'll cut that thing off in a min,
and how much free livin'
you'll suddenly be given!
We'll give you, my poor dear friend,
a hut with a metal roof,
a horse, cows, chickens, doe rabbits,
a thousand new bills—just grab it?
Only a tiny detail, without a bit of strife
I'll snip-snap it with a sterile little knife!"

Samson hadn't yet drowned his mind with drink.
He was acquainted with a security fink
and like a proper Soviet who'd never defect,
Samson said: "Comrade-organ* not so small,
I'm harassed by an enemy sect—
they should be exposed one and all!"

The fink rose up, squeezing his rod,
what do the castrates want to prove to God?
That a bungled world to them will hearken?
And maybe—the thought was alarming—
they think it's possible to live without the organ?

And his answer was severe—
"Not here in Soviet land, never fear!"
He made a decision: "Agree to their calls!
Be afraid for your conscience—not for your *nails*,
let their gang gather in,
you sing out, we'll save your skin..."
And, feeling that a burden so worn
could be useful like an ear of corn,
"I serve the Soviet Union! For that I was born!"
Samson exclaimed with pride.
In a hut concealed in a pine wood
the castrates gathered for the secret forum bravura,
the choir sang coloratura,
when, for the good of the whole land,
Samson, the simple-hearted informer,
with someone's cordial helping hand
solemnly took down his pants.

Following with lively interest
the size, the weight, the zest,
as though in a stereo movie park
the castrates watched from the dark
a phenomenon of colorful detail,
which they hadn't seen for so long.

They brought in Samson tenderly,
the choir singing serenely,
to where, in thick incense
stood a modest, reassuring little bench,
plain and simple without decor
and without a seat anymore
(we'll remember that later on).
And then appeared the old bird
emaciated like a dried-up turd.
He gave Samson half a glass without a word,
said through his nose: "Be brave, dear boy..."
placed a whetstone on the floor
and sharpened his sterile knife,
with such a touching smile,
the way children's dentists beguile.
Samson decided, sensing the moment,
when he'll step toward me, I'll jump up
and start yelling, with all my strength,
but someone, after creeping outside the walls

from underground shouting: "Repentance calls!"
suddenly grabbed him by the *nails*
and in general snipped everything off.
And our Samson like someone half asleep
felt with a shaking hand carefully
where once was that
which he wore as a medal like a cat
and with which he had labored so artfully,
there was a completely smooth nothing.
And Samson screamed so frightfully,
but everything now was in vain—
on him there lay without a strain
the big stamp—the mark of fate's devices
and the fink who had exposed the sect
slapped him on the shoulder and neck:
"All struggles require sacrifices!"

So justice like Delilah
cut something off from Samson.
The ballad's probably worn you out?
I hope these lines never refer
even as a hint to anyone here,
but tell us—didn't they castrate you with fear,
and yet perhaps to you that never did occur?

1966

TRANSLATED BY ALBERT C. TODD

*organ: The KGB is commonly referred to as "the organ."

"The old house..."

The old house was swaying, composing a chorale with its creaking,
and the creaking of the chorale was a funeral service sung for us.
This house of many creaks could sense that secretly
you and I were slowly mingling with its dust.

"Do not die yet"—the words were in the neighing from the meadows,
in the long howl of the dogs, the incantation of the pines,

but side by side, each to the other, we were dying already,
and it's no different than dying anywhere, anytime.

And yet what a yearning to live! The woodpecker tapping the pine log,
a tame hedgehog running about in the mushrooms near the house,
and the night floating like a shaggy-coated, wet, black dog,
holding a star like a water lily in its mouth.

Through the window the darkness was breathing the scent of wet raspberries,
and behind my back—my back had eyes that never missed!—
my beloved was sleeping with Platonov's Fro,* worn out with worries,
as peacefully as with a newly discovered sister.

I lay thinking of the dull imperfection of marriages,
of the dishonorableness of us all—traitors, dissemblers.
For I loved you as much as forty thousand brothers,
and was destroying you as if you were that many enemies.

Yes, you're a different person now. The tightening of your eyelids
is angry and merciless. Bitter your ridicule of other people.
And yet, who but we ourselves make those we love
into such creatures, beyond our power to love?†

What good thing then has all my fiery declaiming stirred,
if, scattering myself from the stage, making the clichés roll,
I wanted to give happiness to the whole world
and found I could not give it to one living soul?

Yes, we were dying. But there was something that would not let me
be completely convinced that you and I did not exist.
Love still existed there. Love could still draw breath
and mist the mirror held in front of her weak lips.

Swaying and creaking among the nettles, the old house survived,
volunteering to lend us its endurance.
We were dying in it, but we were still alive.
We loved each other, this was the proof of our existence.

Some time in the future—God, do not let me, do not let me!—
when I will fall out of love with you, and really die,
my flesh will stir in the darkness and secretly laugh at me:
"You're alive"—it will whisper in the deceptive fever of the night.

But in the drive of passion, wiser, though sadly mortified,
suddenly I will understand that the voice of the flesh tells lies,

and I will say to myself: "I fell out of love. I died.
But once upon a time I loved and was alive."

1966

TRANSLATED BY GEOFFREY DUTTON WITH IGOR MEZHAKOFF-KORIAKIN (REVISED)

*Fro: Title character in a short story by Andrei Platonov (1899-1951) about a woman who lived
only for her love.
†This sixth stanza and the present seventh stanza were reversed when first published.

"The snow will begin again..."

To. K. Shulzhenko

The snow will begin again, falling, falling,
and in its canvas I will read
the image of my youth again, calling
me wherever it may lead.

And it will lead me by the hand to the mystery
of someone's shadow, the tap of feet,
drawing me into the old, old conspiracy
of the lights, the trees, the blizzard in the street.

And those Moscow streets, the Mokhovaias,
the Stretenkas, it will seem to me,
it will seem to me I still have not been young yet
but am touching the possibility.

And the vortex of night will start whirling, whirling,
and I will be funneled into wrong,
and my youth I have been following will be curtained
off by snow, nothing will belong.

But suddenly under the impartial sunstream
all her makeup is there to see,
like a gypsy bitch who has rubbed her orgasm against me
my youth will clear off and abandon me.

I will start over again, and change my life's pattern,
will put my naiveté to shame,

223

and gloomily will hold out my neck and attach
myself, like a stray dog, to a chain.

But the snow will begin again, falling, falling,
everything turning round like a spindle,
and my youth like a gypsy girl will be calling
again to me outside my window.

And the snow will begin again, falling, falling,
and I will gnaw my way through the chain,
and my life like a snowball will be rolling
toward a girl's fur boots again.

1966

TRANSLATED BY GEOFFREY DUTTON WITH IGOR MEZHAKOFF-KORIAKIN

Yelabuga Nail

Do you remember, geranium Yelabuga,*
that city girl, who, as she wept
an eternity ago, smoked long and hard
your corrosive home-grown tobacco?

Prayerful and wounded, she begged God
that they would give her laundry to wash.
You will allow me, Marina Ivanovna,
to stand a while there, where you lived.

A granny opened the rickety wicket-gate
"It's agony gittin' old—don'no how come.
They keep a comin' and a comin,' jus' wear me out.
House should be sold, but nobody'll buy it.

"I remember—she was strict, big-boned.
Not one to be doin' laundry.
Had trouble rollin' her own.
I rolled 'em. Didn't do the rope."

Dank entrance hall. No windows. A place

where hemp felt right at home,
where afterward from the chilling Kama
I chanced to wet my lips from a bucket.

A nail, and not a hook.
                              Square, heavy duty—
for harnesses, for fishing gear.
It's too low here
                    to decide to hang yourself.
Just strangle yourself—it's easier.

And the old woman, who had survived half-starved,
said to me, as though to an important guest:
"What should I do with this here nail?
Everyone stares and touches.
Maybe you could take the nail with you?"

Granny, I beg of you, as a kindness—
just don't ask that again.
"But why did she suicide herself?
You're a scholar aren't you. You understand better."

Granny, the hall and room terrify me.
I could weep on your shoulder.
In this world there's only killing, remember.
There's no suicide at all.

1966

TRANSLATED BY ALBERT C. TODD

*Yelabuga: Small town near the Kama River just east of Kazan on the Volga. Notorious as the place of evacuation and suicide of the great Russian poet Marina Tsvetayeva (1892–1941).

Belly Dance

By the dispassionate pyramids
under the clicking of tongues,
there rose her belly—
the pitiful yolk of a yellow moon.
It rose in front of sucking eyes,

lewd and coarse winks.
It hung over pilaf
               and bottles,
over the howling men,
                     their thick necks,
over fat,
          over greasy mouths,
                       over bellies . . .
And the pharaoh belly-power
spilled over from the fullness
of feeling and filth.
Howling and growling
with pleasure,
they looked on
as if she were a slave.
They watched
the sweaty belly of a worker
devour itself.

Squinting a frightened eye,
the belly spun like a top,
spilling the woman on the floor,
now flat on her back,
now facedown.

The belly drew itself in like a moan.
A fish flailing with its tail
against the net of derision,
the crazed belly
flung against the floor
its woman's head.

The belly enacted fever.
It staged birth. It trembled
as if a stuck dagger were being forced
deeper and deeper.

The belly was seized and twisted
as if hunger held it in its grip.
The artist had grown up in hunger.
And life is the yardstick of craft.

                ·   ·   ·

Well, later in the sad hotel room,
in the dusk of numb dawn,
her small slipper was crushed
by a shoe made in New York.

Work was leaving her body
while the soul came in slowly.
She liked him. There was something to him.
She would not have said yes just like that.

A restless spirit, half the world
he had crisscrossed time and again.
With the drug of excitement
he hoped to still his pain.

He had known the all-knowing woman.
He possessed, one might say, largesse.
And it's only by accident he had not slept
with a dancer like this.

But in vain, morose lecher,
did he wait for the sweets of the East,
for sighs new and quite special,
for the ancient Egyptian style.

Her body turned peaceful and quiet.
All of its surface had died.
Only inside there raced, otherworldly,
the hidden tremor of stars.

As if dreaming, she touched her own belly
with the hand of a child.
A tomb it was, her belly,
for the children killed by the dance.

She was too worn out to make love.
Her lips barely moved.
She felt pure joy from her belly,
which had come to rest.

1967

TRANSLATED BY VERA DUNHAM

The Mark of Cain

In memory of R. Kennedy

The poor pilgrims dragged themselves wearily
along to Mecca through gray Syria,
huddled
   and doubled up
the pilgrims stumbled along—
away from delusion and ferment
to repent,
   repent,
     repent...
And I was standing like an impenitent sinner
on the summit of the mountain
where once upon a time
      (don't stir!)
Abel was killed by Cain.
And—of all communiqués of blood
   the most unforgettable—
the elemental voice was heard:
"Cain,
   where is your brother, Abel?"
But once again the Pharisees,
   with their vile-sweet voices:
"Why do you worry about visions that are fake?
Yes,
  with Abel maybe we should have held back.
Admittedly, there was a little mistake,
but generally speaking we were on the right track..."
And I was standing on the summit
between those ahead and the hosts behind,
above a world
    where people could commit
every corruption of their own kind.
There was no lightning
     and no thunder,
but the stones were crying with mouths opened wide:
"The corruption of the soul may be bloodless
but it is also fratricide!"
And I imagined a gloomy, dead
brick orphanage,

where as with henbane
the children of Abel are spoonfed
with lies by the children of Cain.
And in the faces of Abel's children,
doing what they know that they must do,
which is always to stay silent,
the red mark of Cain shows through . . .

And I, no one's murderer,
was standing
           on the sticky summit,
but my conscience murmured
like the Bible:
           "You won't be able to quit!
You're corrupting your spirit with lies,
and your spirit is crumbling,
              cracking inside.
And to kill yourself—
           you cannot disguise
that that is also fratricide!
And how many women, you twister,
lie like crucifixions along your way—
but women, they are your sisters,
worth more than brothers can repay.
And the Hussars' toasts 'To the ladies,'
what are they worth?
           Bravado,
              empty form.
To kill love—
           you cannot evade it,
that is also fratricide.
And someone's gray
           brown eyes
staring at you with disdain,
on your forehead cicatrize
you with the eternal mark of Cain . . ."
I shuddered:
           "Quiet, O conscience . . .
You know this is not comparable,
it is like comparing a children's circus
with a bloody Roman shambles."

But the shadow of bony Cain
jutted out from the rocks near at hand,

and the blood of the brother he had slain
was endlessly dripping from my hand.

"Look—
        my bloody hands shake.
As a child it was fun to improvise,
out of curiosity to break
the velvet wings of butterflies
and then—
           fratricide."

My conscience—
          the protectress
of the mark of Cain,
the prophetess-seer
            said again
with prophetically bitter sadness:
"What will you say
           to the eternal skies
and the court of stars
            when you cannot run back—
To say I am sinless would be telling lies,
but generally speaking I'm on the right track!
You know, all those whom you hate
set this up as the true state,
while the cigarettes take on
the smell of burning flesh, the Winstons
             and the Kents,
and the bullet
         that passed through John
kills Robert Kennedy.
And the bombs charge the earth, turn
brown villages bloodred, fire black.
Admittedly they fall on children,
but generally speaking they're on the right track ...
Everything begins with the butterflies,
later it comes round to bombs ...
No amount of washing purifies—
the blood on your hands will be your doom.
The only murder that is fit—
is to kill
        the Cain inside!"

. . .

And losing my footing on the sticky summit,
face to face with the infinite,
I tore the flesh open in my side
and the strangled
                    embryo Cain
                              died.
I strangled everything mean and evil,
all that you would later despise,
but it was far too late to heal
the broken wings of the butterflies.
And the wind, blood-soaked, invisible,
lashed at me from the fury of space
as if the pages of the Bible
were lashing
            me
                  on the face . . .

1967

TRANSLATED BY GEOFFREY DUTTON WITH IGOR MEZHAKOFF-KORIAKIN
(REVISED)

Love in Portuguese

Night licked the fires like wounds.
The stars stare with the eyes of a prison,
but we are beneath the Bridge of Salazar—
in its blacker than black shadow.

The dictator has done us a service,
and, unseen by him under the bridge,
we emigrate into each other's lips
from this unhappy land.

Under the bridge made of concrete and fear,
under the bridge of this doltish regime
our lips are beautiful countries,
where we are free together.

                    • • •

I steal freedom, I steal,
and in the sacred stolen instant
I'm happy that at least in a kiss
my sinful tongue is uncensored.

Even in the world where fascists rule,
where people's rights are so meager,
downy eyelashes remain,
and beneath them are other worlds.

But, dressed in a thin raincoat,
making a gift of a ring to me,
woman of Portugal, why do you weep?
I don't cry. I've cried it all out.

Give me your lips. Press close and don't think. .
You and I, little sister, are helpless,
beneath the bridge, like two tears
beneath a sullen brow, unseen by the world . . .

1967
Lisbon
TRANSLATED BY ALBERT C. TODD

When They Murdered Lorca

When they murdered Lorca—
and indeed they murdered him!—
a gendarme was teasing a young girl,
showing off on a mare.

When they murdered Lorca—
and indeed they murdered him!—
neither a spoon nor a bowl
could fellow citizens forget.

Grieving a moment,
Carmen in fashionable dress
embraced the living—
you don't bed down with the dead.

· · ·

A well-known fortune-teller
loitered about the peasant huts.
She felt sorry for Lorca,
but you can't tell fortunes to a corpse.

Life remained life—
both the wine-bibber's mug,
and swine in yellow swill,
and a rose in the bodice.

Youth and old age remained,
and the lowly and the lords.
Though everything remained on earth—
Lorca did not remain.

And only in a dusty shop,
like companies of soldiers,
not believing in the death of Lorca,
toy Don Quixotes stood.

Let the ignorant reign
and lying fortune-tellers,
and you, toy hidalgo,
live on through hope.

Among the rubbish of souvenirs,
sighing bitterly, they,
the absurd little swords,
screamed: "Where are you, Lorca?

Neither an elm nor a willow of you
did they knock from the ledger,
after all, you're immortal—nor
from us, from the Don Quixotes!"

And the grasses sang haltingly,
and the cranes trumpeted
that Lorca wasn't murdered,
when they did murder him.

1967
Madrid—Moscow

TRANSLATED BY ALBERT C. TODD AND JAMES RAGAN

Barcelona's Little Streets

In Barcelona the streets are narrow,
like cat's-pupils in anguish.

Some are busy with love, some with punishment—
everything contrary is heard through the window.
If someone slices onions on the right,
all on the left side are in tears.

Women in black-eyed folly
now splash out a tub on a woman neighbor,
now tumble out of windows, disemboweling
each other's coiffures in the air.

And, rejoicing on the windowsills,
knocking down flowerpots,
children crisscross streams
with their pink water cannons.

A fight! Husbands of all are cuckolded!
Abysses will swallow all profligates!
And over their heads like rockets,
fish, snouts extended, go flying.

I walk down the center of the street,
only the center is uncertain because,
in the furor the right and the left cheeks
are just asking for sardines.

I would sing praise for life's prose
for a single unexpected rose
if (even with a mocking thorn)
it should lash my cheeks.

One wants, of course, kindness,
but on my jacket, tailored to fashion,
from the right—slops crash down,
from the left—tomcats gloomily tumble.

Somewhere near, searches, interrogations,
in prisons unknown voices are moaning,

well, but here, there are threats to burn out
a rival's eyes with vitriol.

And while the fascist censor
drowns thoughts, like cats in a bag,
someone screams to a woman: "Stupid tit!"
of course, in the Spanish language.

People, tired and pinched,
all, venting their fury at trifles,
have become executioners to one another,
forgetting about the main executioners.

Peace is threatened by brooms and knives.
I would embrace peace, but here, my God!—
there's no way to spread your arms! Walls
clutch from the right and the left.

In Barcelona the streets are narrow,
like cat's-pupils in anguish.

1967

TRANSLATED BY ALBERT C. TODD

Happiness Andalusian Style

The Andaluzka
                is cloistered
                                deftly in her corset.
Two earthly orbs
                endeavor to burst the strings,
and underskirts,
                like layers of a cake,
crackle
        during impulsive movements.
And by her side
                a pomaded lad walks
soldered
        into a black suit with jacket.

In a raised hand,
                    like a leather idol,
a lamb wineskin
                    bounces sideways,
and with arduous effort
                    two white cloth teeth
proudly stick out
                    of his breast pocket.
I know,
          standing quietly nearby,
that the little cloth teeth
                    are sewn on cardboard.
To buy a handkerchief
                    is too impractical.
The cardboard isn't seen outside,
                              and is thus acceptable.
What is happiness?
                    Two earthly orbs on a slip of a girl,
two white teeth-like protrusions
                              sewn on cardboard,
and a bit of wine
                    in a former lamb.

1967

TRANSLATED BY ALBERT C. TODD AND JAMES RAGAN

The Revue of Old People

In that famous Barcelona cabaret
the hall stood on its end like hair on a boar,
and with a grin the lighting technician stabbed
two rays, like two fangs, into the old man.

Rouged all over, the old man could barely stand,
and like a black kite a wig covered his bald patch.
He wheezed, a grandfather, tightly corseted:
"We—the Corps of Corpses—begin our concert!"

· · ·

But the hall guffawed, expecting a verbal trick,
since the word *corpse* is very funny
when you are sitting and drinking, full of health and life,
with your hands on the knees of a trollop.

The emcee, big-nosed à la Mephistopheles,
presented to us the human zoo:
"Announcing the first number!
A singer who died,
probably, twenty five years ago . . ."

And out came a second decrepit grandfather,
wretchedly clicking his feeble feet,
praying to his youthful, unreliable dentures
not to fall out when he hits a "la" note.

The old man, artificially, drags an old tango,
but the hall roars with all its might: "Go, go!"
Wrenching himself, the old man squeaks like a rooster,
and the hall in response lets out a "Ha-ha-ha!"

Again the emcee wheezes, barely alive:
"Our dance number—is a fiery number!
Legs—that are peaches in syrup!
Legs—the best in Europe,
but, I make no secret, only before World War I."

And with plaster on her cheeks here comes
a great-grandmother in netted naughty stockings.
On red slippers in false sparkles of tinsel
I see the terrible lumps of old age.

But the hall snaps its fingers like a trap.
But the hall grows weary salivating: "Cancan! Cancan!"
A young man pimply and green as spinach
feverishly hisses to her: "The splits. The splits!"

Here a creaking leg does a *grand battement,*
but like a scabrous wild herd the hall gives a "Ha-ha-ha . . ."
I don't raise my head from shame,
and all around me nothing but "Hee-hee-hee . . ."

O Hall, who are you? What sort of cruel beast?
You know it's impossible to be more base and wicked.

Have pity on the old ones, come to love them
with a love of sadness as though for your future selves.

Oh, you howling whimperers, snivelers
after all, you are the coming old women and old men,
and someday a future young reptile
will force you, dear people, to do the splits.

And I wander about Barcelona as though plague-stricken.
And the specter of my old age goes after me.
So far we still travel separately, but
where, on what corner, will we come together as one?

Yes, I pity the old ones. I'm a throwback.
I grab the arms of those passing by the fence:
"I announce a new number!
I am a poet who died,
but I don't remember how many years ago..."

1967
Barcelona — Moscow
TRANSLATED BY ALBERT C. TODD

Black Banderilla

By the rules of the corrida, in place of
the usual pink, as a sign of contempt, black
banderillas are thrust into a cowardly bull.

The flower of a fighting toro
                    is mourning, affixed since birth.
The path of a fighting toro
                    is the arena, and later the scales.
If condemned by nature
                    to death by the sword,
remember—the shrewd cowardice of the fox
                            for the bull is not ceremony.
No way out, old chap.
            One must die properly.
One must die excellently

to intimidate enemies.

After the fight all the same

someone by custom

will mark a sign with chalk:

"Such and such number of kilograms."

A carcass goes by kilograms.

Courage is measured in grams.

A carcass goes for meat.

Courage goes against the pricks.

It's foolish to be daring, if

it's immaturity of the mind.

It's foolish to be a coward, if

you're surrounded anyway.

Why fuss in the arena?

You're a fine little bull.

Why pretend to be lame?

Your legs are still strong.

Hey, you clumsy malingerer . . .

Some were stronger than you—

in the end they divide up everyone

on hooks in the meat shop.

Fling yourself shabbily to meet

the hungering band—or else

for the crowd's pleasure

the slippery banderilleros will thrust

black banderillas,

black banderillas

like flares of shame,

into the nape of your neck.

Fool, what's there for you to win

in a miserable game with rogues?!

Those afraid of the fight

are not suited for the corrida.

Scraggy, streetwalker-cows

will lure you from the arena

with delicate little bells,

well, and then under the knife.

Since it all ends anyway,

let it end in a sweat.

Let the butchers' ballet dancers

huff and puff and dance.

Be a real toro!

Don't lower yourself to the level

of this crowd made up of

nothing but cowardly bulls.
Have they given many grams
                              of courage to the world?
And the black banderillas,
                        the black banderillas
graze the walls,
                  blinds, and door frames,
plunged into jackets
                    like trembling skin.

1967
Seville—Moscow
TRANSLATED BY ALBERT C. TODD

"I dreamed I already..."

I dreamed I already loved you.
I dreamed I already killed you.

But you rose again; another form, but you,
a girl on the little ball of the earth,
naive simplicity, curve-necked
on that early canvas of Picasso,
and prayed to me with your ribs:
"Love me," as though you said, "Don't push me
    off."

I'm that played-out, grown-up acrobat,
hunchbacked with senseless muscles,
who knows that advice is a lie,
that sooner or later there's falling.

I'm too scared to say: "I love you,"
because I'd be saying: "I'll kill you."

For in the depths of a face I can see through
I see the faces—can't count them—
that, right on the spot, or maybe
not right away, I tortured to death.

· · ·

You're pale from the mortal balance. You say:
"I know everything; I was all of them.
I know you've already loved me.
I know you've already killed me.
But I won't spin the globe backwards:
Love again, and then kill again."

Lord, you're young. Stop your globe.
I'm tired of killing. I'm not a damn thing but old.

You move the earth beneath your little feet,
you fall, "Love me."
It's only in those eyes, so similar, you say:
"This time don't kill me!"

1967

TRANSLATED BY JAMES DICKEY WITH ANTHONY KAHN (REVISED)

Stolen Apples

Fences careened in the storm;
we stole through the bitter shadows
like thieving children warmed
by shirtfuls of stolen apples.

The apples wanted to spill;
to bite them was scandalous.
But we loved one another
and that fact redeemed us.

Secluding the criminal twins
in a cosmos of dirty waves,
the snug cottage whispered,
"Be brave and love...be brave..."

And the yield of lunar light
whispered through dusty leaves:
"In stealing that which might
be stolen by life—you're not thieves..."

. . .

The cottage's owner, an ex–
soccer hero, from his photo
dim on the glimmering mantel,
urged, "Be bold . . . plunge through . . ."

So, pivoting and twisting,
we burst through the penalty zone,
slipped past the last defender,
and billowed the nets of the goal!

Rest period. Above us, dust
flickered; we seemed to dream,
small soccer shoes vibrated
on an invisible field.

"Play," each mote insisted,
"Play, but play earnestly.
The earth's heavy globe is a speck,
like us, essentially."

We played again; we kicked.
The game perhaps was stupid
but we did love one another
and that felt splendid.

Drugged by its roaring, the sea
mumbled of something profound
but then a golden fish, your bang,
splashed upon your brow,

and I was unconcerned to know
that once on the storm's other side,
for all my bravura folly,
I'd sink back with the tide.

Let slander pursue me;
love isn't for the feeble.
The odor of love is the scent
not of bought but of stolen apples.

Will we be happy? Not hardly . . .
But we'd curse the world's events,

if we'd stolen from ourselves
the chance to steal these moments.

What matters the watchman's shout
when, wrapped in the sea's far hiss,
I can cushion my head between
two salty apples I've filched.

1967
TRANSLATED BY JOHN UPDIKE WITH ANTHONY KAHN
(REVISED)

An Attempt at Blasphemy

Turning to the eternal magnet
in the pitch-dark night of my soul
I whisper my only prayer:
"O Lord, forgive me, help me."

And the Lord forgives and helps,
however helplessly he shrugs
at man's prolonged ingratitude
for his many mercies.

Clearly his people frighten God.
Call him by any name you choose—
Jehovah, Buddha, Allah—
he's one, and tired of being God.

If he could dematerialize,
or shrink in scale to a pocket idol,
he'd gladly slip away and hide
from our slobber in a private corner.

But it's not right for him to hide,
or stoop, like an African slave.
God also wants to believe in god,
but there's no god in the world for God.

And when, neglectful of our obligations,
we stick him with rotten little petitions,

to whom shall he address his prayer:
"O Lord, forgive me, help me"?

1967

TRANSLATED BY STANLEY KUNITZ WITH ANTHONY KAHN

In a Steelworker's Home

I love America,
    the America who swam
the Maytime Elbe
    holding aloft whiskey
with a tired right arm,
    paddling with the left;
yes, and Russia swam to meet her in
the Maytime Elbe,
    holding aloft vodka
with a tired left arm,
    paddling with the right,
as vodka and whiskey—
    neat!—without translation
understood
    each other perfectly,
        goddammit,
on the waters where victories met!

I love America,
    the America who now
sits with me in the prefab ranch house
of a steelworker.
On the worker's arms
blue veins bulge and fork,
like secret tributaries of our Elbe.
There are no governments between us now.
Our invisible government
    has been chosen by us wordlessly—
those same tired soldiers,
    boys from Irkutsk and Kentucky,

who invisibly swim to each other
    until today on the Maytime Elbe.

Murmuring, murmuring,
invisible waves surge
across the plain fraternal table,
and wineglasses of cheap Chianti,
cradled by us on these waves,
redden like guiding buoys.
We talk
    as if we were swimming
to embrace each other like brothers,
    but
for twenty years they have polluted the Elbe.
They've dumped so much sewage in her—
the backwaters of falsehood,
    our era's super-cesspools:
Newspapers soaked in poison,
    dregs of inflammatory speeches,
the spit of scoundrels,
    Kleenexes soggy with snot,
and greasy sweat fastidiously wiped
from the hypocrite faces of long-winded orators.
Beneath the surface of our Elbe are hiding
moss-covered mines of distrust
and sleek new submarines
pregnant with torpedoes,
offspring of a marriage of fear
    and science.
Oh, when
    will we understand each other
as vodka and whiskey—
    straight!—without translation
understood
    each other perfectly,
      goddammit,
on the waters where victory met victory!
Really, do we need a new Hitler
to unite us
    again?
A price
    like maybe
      much too high . . .
Russia and America,

your path
to each other is tortuous,
    but I believe,
        do believe
that through all the refuse and the mossy mines,
    we will swim to one another,
        we will swim,
we will embrace
    as in the Maytime of '45,
and this time,
    I dare believe,
        for keeps!
True, there are oceans of malice between us.
True, the Great Ocean, the Pacific, is between us.
But we will swim it;
    no ocean is so great
it cannot become an Elbe!
I love America,
    the America who now,
snuggled in her crib, wiggles her delicate toes;
her slender feet shine for us, the disenchanted,
like candles radiating hope.
What is her name—
    Jan?
        Or, perhaps, Lara?
Her eyes
    are huge
        and blue,
two trusting drops
of that same Elbe,
    our common Elbe
we must not betray.
Russia and America,
    swim closer!

1967

TRANSLATED BY JOHN UPDIKE WITH ALBERT C. TODD

My Handwriting

My handwriting is not calligraphic.
Not following the rules of beauty,
words stagger about,
reeling,
        as if clobbered on the jaw.

But you, the descendant, my textual critic,
following on the heels of the past,
take stock of those gales
your ancestor got caught in.

He walked on a pugnacious coastal freighter,
a bit arrogant,
        but you
should see beyond the pitched handwriting
not only the author's traits.

Your ancestor wrote while tossed about,
not kept too warm by squalls,
habitually,
        like having a pack
of his usual cigarettes.

Of course, far off we made our way courageously,
but it's hard to write a line,
when your head is smashed with relish
against the bulkhead.

Risking skin and bones,
it's tough to sing acclaim,
when what you see compels you
not to praise, but only to throw up.

When churning water strangles motors
and a wave's curl is aimed at your forehead,
then smudges are better than flourishes.
They're black—but true.

Here—
        fingers simply grew numb.

Here—
the swell slyly tormented.
Here—
the pen jerked with uncertainty
away from some mean shoal.

But if through all the clumsiness,
through the clutches of awkwardness,
an idea breaks through the way a freighter on
the Lena
breaks through to the arctic shore—

then, descendant, be slow to curse the style,
don't judge an ancestor severely,
and even in the handwriting of the poet
find a solution to the enigma of time.

1967
TRANSLATED BY ALBERT C. TODD

Ballad of the Running Start

For P. Demidov

Aoo, little swan, lagging behind the flock!
I understand you—we're both tired.
Of course, your delicate curve is divine,
and your wings flash like bright snow,
but so what—they're not grown,
and you, little swan, are not for the sky.

Nevertheless on the ground they all pet you—
flirt with you, wear you ragged.
Yes, there are shortages in the store's flour department,
and shortages in the morality department,
but in our village—it's high time to celebrate—
we have a swan, and a tame one at that.

Trying to seize the sky as its own property,
the blizzard rips apart wires like nerves.

Barrels and posts hurtle through the air,
and even an uprooted mailbox
turns somersaults flying above the clouds—
only your wings were still too feeble.

No one even knew, amid the howling snow,
the unbridled drinking and swinishness,
that at night, when it's pitch-black above the village,
in an apartment smelling of herring and insect poison,
under a stand with a porcelain figure of someone,
your wings grow with an excruciating crackle,
knocking over the master's boots.

Yes, your wings were changing,
already taut with new strength,
they made you seem wild and prankish,
and when you wanted—with a threatening gesture,
like an iceberg—you wrecked the manager's apartment,
whom you hated, though pitied.

And only once, rebelling against the rules,
you spread your foamy white wings,
like a bird cherry bush that had blossomed,
and the owner sighed—not from joy,
but from indignation—that the pride of the store—
the knocked-over bust, was shattered by your wings.

The owner understood that now you're dangerous.
Put you in the chicken house? You're too beautiful
for the company of chickens, and people won't understand.
Roast you for dinner? You're too well known.
Leave you in the apartment? You don't fit there.
Today it's porcelain, tomorrow a dresser.

Hundreds of people gathered on the embankment.
Hiding a smile, the manager brought you out—
like a gift on a tray, stunned and numbed.
They all came closer, and everyone endeavored
to touch your nose and pull your wings
to the popping of camera flashes and the fury of dogs.

Picturesquely placed on the ground by the manager,
you stand unmoving, fragile as crystal,
like a white vase on the dirty ground,

but the people keep coming, coming, coming,
and the greasy fingers of lisping flattery
soil the feathers on each wing.

Already shrugging their shoulders, they reproach you:
"Why don't you take off? Aren't your wings grown?"
"Maybe you're putting on airs, just look at you!"
Just for fun a little boy chimes in:
"Are you a weakling? We studied about Sparta in class.
In Sparta they had a law—finish off the weak ones."

And suddenly—round-faced like a cheesecake,
an old woman came up to help you,
sharp as a tack, a hundred years old if a day, .
and, closing your wings, declared:
"You don't give him room for a running start!
Comrades, are you people or what?"

Having shown everyone her quarrelsome nature,
in a moment she shoved aside the idle gawkers and reporters,
pushed back the crowd so it would be easier to breathe,
and said: "Son, fly away as quickly as you can!"
and on the takeoff runway she had cleared,
you suddenly ran, and ran, and ran . . .

You ran from the store manager, from the furious crowd,
from the baying of a bedraggled little dog,
and shot upward into the sky, to your native kingdom.
From below, from the mountains and valleys, could be heard only:
"Good luck, son . . . Fly away wherever you want,
only, son, fly as far away as you can . . ."

1967

TRANSLATED BY ALBERT C. TODD

"Hurry is the curse . . ."

Hurry is the curse of our century
and man, mopping the sweat from his forehead,

zigzags through life like a pawn in a fury
of being trapped on the board with his time expired.

Hurriedly we drink, hurriedly we love,
our souls eroding go to waste.
Hurriedly we push and shove
and later we repent, at haste.

But at least once, whether your home
in the world is sleeping or boiling with untruths,
stop, like a horse smothered in foam
sensing the abyss before its hooves.

For God's sake stop, even halfway,
trust heaven, as you would your fate,
think—even if you do not pray
to God—at least of your own taste.

When the collapsing leaves flutter,
when the locomotive gives its hoarse cry,
know this: The tired runner is pitiful,
the one who has stopped stands high.

Sweep off the dust of vanity of vanities,
at last remember eternity,
and holy indecision will freeze
your feet in immobility.

There is strength in indecision
when you hesitate to follow
the path leading to perdition
at the end of which false beacons glow.

As you trample on people's faces like leaves,
stop! Like Vii,* you are blind.
Don't forgo this last reprieve
by rushing on with a mad wind.

When you stride so confidently toward your goal
over bodies as though they were steps,
stop—you who have forgotten God—
you are really stepping on yourself!

. . .

When spite is shoving you forward,
making your own soul a hypocrite,
toward the disgrace of a shot or a word—
don't hurry, don't do it!

Stop, O people of the earth, as you run
so blindly to the next assault!
Bullet, freeze as you fly from the gun,
and you, bomb in midair, halt!

O man, whose very name is sacred,
lifting the prayer of your eyes like a periscope
over disintegration and hatred,
for God's sake stop, for God's sake stop!

1967

TRANSLATED BY GEOFFREY DUTTON WITH IGOR MEZHAKOFF-
KORIAKIN

*Vii: Blind monster-gnome of Ukrainian folklore whose eyelids touch the ground; if his eyes are opened nothing can be hidden from them. It is portrayed in Gogol's story by the same name.

Monologue of a Poet

To Robert Lowell

A loved one leaves
    like air from the lungs—
vapor amid the final dry snowflakes,
the black branches clicking and sagging
    with ice.
She can't be breathed back in.
A mere gesture, I abrade my cheek
    on the rust-scaled trunk
of a drainpipe.
    To no purpose, I weep.
        She departs.
Friends depart,
    fellow sufferers,

peers,
    as from the field of the young
    we are led toward separate pens
    away from the once-shared milk.
    In vain, like an unweaned whelp,
        I whine for friends;
they don't come back.
Hopes depart—
      such darling ladies,
whom I use on such useless occasions!
Only their petticoats stay in my hands;
hopes are meant to be held for a moment.
Certitude departs.
      I remember, I swore a sacred oath
to break my stupid head against the wall
    or the wall with my stupid head.
My head is scratched, true,
      but unbroken.
And what of the wall?
      The bastard smirks;
on its blankness they are blandly changing
the posters,
      the portraits of heroes . . .
Certitude,
      where are you?
New York,
      your dark sky circles above me
         like a hawk.
America, believe me,
    I'm finished,
        I'm finished,
            finished.
I am a ship
    where all the cabins smell of doom
and rats leap in terror from the clammy deck.
Hey, seagulls—don't weep!
    Don't,
        don't pity me!
My lovely leggy guests abandon me.
They take their places, as prescribed,
    the first in the lifeboat—
Farewell, my mistresses!
My apple-cheeked cadets abandon me.
They want to live.

Fair enough,
    they are still young.
Farewell, lads!
   Row ahead.
     You are men.
Now the inane rumble of the engine shuts down.
Only talent
   like a drunken, unshaven captain
stands somberly on the bridge.
    The captain is the captain.
But he too, tears smearing his windburned skin,
he too abandons me,
   he too . . .
      he too . . .
Hey, lifeboats—stand away!
A ship, when it sinks,
   makes a maelstrom around it.
To be totally alone
   hurts worse than a knife,
but I won't suck anyone down with me.
I forgive you all.
   Robed in death's foam,
I bequeath it to you to demolish that bastardly wall.
   My trumpet juts from the marble swirls:
     brothers, battle on.

1967
TRANSLATED BY JOHN UPDIKE WITH ALBERT C. TODD

Monologue of an Actress

Said an actress from Broadway
   time had pillaged like Troy:
"There are simply no more roles.
No role
   to extract from me all my tears,
no role
   to turn me inside out.
From this life, really,

one must flee to the desert.
There are simply no roles anymore!
Broadway blazes
like a hot computer
but, believe me, there's no role—
    not one role
amid hundreds of parts.
Honestly, we are drowning in rolelessness...
    Where are the great writers! Where?
The poor classics have broken out in sweat,
    like a team of tumblers whose act is too long,
but what do they know
    about Hiroshima,
about the murder of the Six Million,
    about all our pain?!
Is it really *all* so inexpressible?
Not one role!
It's like being without a compass.
You know how dreadful the world is
when it builds up inside you,
    builds up and builds up,
and there's absolutely no way out for it.
Oh yes,
    there are road companies.
For that matter,
    there are TV serials.
But the *roles* have been removed.
They put you off with bit parts.
I drink. Oh, I know it's weak of me,
but what can you *do*, when there are no more people,
no more roles?
Somewhere a worker is drinking,
    from a glass opaque with greasy fingerprints.
He has no role!
And a farmer is drinking,
    bellowing like a mule because he's impotent:
he has no role!
A sixteen-year old *child*
    is stabbed with a switchblade by his friends
        because they have *nothing* better to do ...
There are no roles!
Without *some* sort of role, life
    is simply slow rot.
In the womb, we are all geniuses.

But potential geniuses become idiots
without a role to play.
Without demanding anyone's blood,
I
    do demand
       a *role*!"

1967

TRANSLATED BY JOHN UPDIKE WITH ALBERT C. TODD

A Ballad about Nuggets

To A. Todd

Night. The town of Fairbanks sleeps,
                exhausted. But invisible
squeakings walk the snowy streets
                cloaked in hides and wool.
Wearing the face of an adolescent
                and a painted caribou parka,
an Eskimo striptease *artiste*
                hurries to work in a bar.
Drunken fliers from the air base,
                aching for a shack-up,
ruttish louts, brave buddies,
                throw snowballs at her back.
But she in darkness carries
                her frozen breath
through the leers like a pure
                white rose in her teeth.
In out of the cold
                as hoary as owls,
in through the saloon doors
                come clamorous clouds
with people inside them!—
                a miner, a hunter, a trapper.
They all toss their caps
                on the walrus-tusk hat rack.
Who comes from where?

What nation? Who cares!
Among these Alaskans
                    I'm one of the bears;
        for us holy vodka
                    will answer all prayers.
    Pal Bob, fellow sourdough, have a drink,
                                down the hatch.
    Your big mitts have hugged me,
                        your stiff whiskers scratch.
    Your grin gleams with gold.
                        You look worn out, man.
    "Listen, Rooshian, I've been prospecting
                            all my life, understand?
    No ruddier bastard than me swung a pick.
                            Now I'm trash.
    My bald head's a runway
                    for mosquitoes and gnats.
    Now I'm set to cash in,
                    to add it up proper:
    a mouthful of gold
                    and a fistful of copper.
    Ah, when I buried my old lady, Viv,
    I recall how the sled dogs gave
    a howl at the edge of the hole,
                        at the edge of her grave.
    Viv was a knockout once, just like
                    those Playgirls you unfold.
    Her body white as quartz all over,
                        with little flecks of gold.
    I had a good eye then, as young as you,
                        as lucky and game.
    I said to her: 'I've staked you out.
                        Viv, you're my claim.'
    I tortured her for forty years,
                    I was crazy,
    lifelong crazy, to find my strike,
                    to find nuggets.
    She didn't ask for fancy clothes
                    but shyly,
    for a son. She dreamt of a son like me,
                        and I, of nuggets.
    I drank. Like yellow fish
                    alive in a muddy sea,
    they came at me, teased me,

      nuggets.
So I closed my shop,
     a bankrupt boss.
My pick and shovel
      made Viv a cross.
I ain't forgot how I dragged that box
         on the hard-froze earth.
I never dug up my nugget,
      I buried her."
Bob counts the coppers in his paw.
        He is drunk, disconsolate.
"Without gold, I . . . 'Scuse me, Rooshian,
        lend me a stake."

Having forgotten his cap,
     he shakily seeks the way out
and jabs the swinging doors
      and plunges into his cloud.
Then I too wander in the dark,
     a child of the saloon.
Nothingness pulls on my pockets
as I walk along.
I still haven't shut up shop,
     I'm too timid;
but perhaps my nugget
     is already buried.
Boy-faced beside me,
     a silent companion,
the Eskimo stripper,
     exhausted, hurries home.
Zero. Icicles
   beard my chin,
and birds frozen in flight fall
     like nuggets, with a clink.

1967

TRANSLATED BY JOHN UPDIKE WITH EDWARD KEENAN

New York Elegy

To S. Mitman

At night, in New York's Central Park,
chilled to the bone and belonging to no one,
I talked quietly with America:
both of us were weary of speeches.

I talked with my footsteps—
unlike words, they do not lie—
and I was answered with circles
dead leaves uttered, falling onto a pond.

Snow was falling, sliding embarrassed
past bars where noisiness never ceases,
settling tinted on the swollen neon veins
on the city's sleepless brow;
on the incessant smile of a candidate
who was trying, not without difficulty, to get in
somewhere, I don't remember just where,
and to the snow it didn't matter where.

But in the park it fell undisturbed:
the snowflakes descended cautiously
onto the softly sinking leaves,
soggy multicolored floats;
onto a pink and tremulous balloon
childishly fastened with chewing gum
to the trunk of an evergreen
and sleepily rubbing its cheek against the sky;
onto someone's forgotten glove;
onto the zoo, which had shown its guests out;
onto the bench with its wistful legend:
"Place for Lost Children."

Dogs licked the snow in a puzzled way,
and squirrels with eyes like lost beads
flickered between cast-iron baskets,
amid trees lost in the woods of themselves.
Great juttings of granite stood about
morosely, preserving in mineral calm

a silent question, a reproach—
lost children of former mountains.

Behind a wire fence, zebras munching hay
peered, at a loss, into a striped darkness.
Seals, poking their noses from the pool,
caught snow in mid-flight on their whiskers;
they gazed around them, quizzical, confused,
forsaken children of Mother Ocean
taking pity, in their slippery style,
on people—lost children of the earth.

I walked alone. Now and then, in the thicket,
the crimson firefly of a cigarette
floated before an unseen face—
the staring pupil of night's wide eye.

And I felt some stranger's feeling of being lost
was searching embarrassed
for a feeling of being lost like my own,
not knowing that this was what I longed for.

At night, beneath this snowfall,
its whispered secret having made us one,
America and I sat down together
in the place for lost children.

1967

TRANSLATED BY JOHN UPDIKE WITH ALBERT C. TODD

Monologue of a Blue Fox

I am a blue fox on a gray farm.
Condemned to slaughter by my color
behind this gnawproof wire screen,
I find no comfort in being blue.

Lord, but I want to molt! I burn
to strip myself of myself in my frenzy;

but the luxuriant, bristling blue
seeps through the skin—scintillant traitor.

How I howl—feverishly I howl
like a furry trumpet of the Last Judgment,
beseeching the stars for either freedom forever,
or at least forever to be molting.

A passing visitor captured my howl
on a tape recorder. What a fool!
He didn't howl himself, but he might
begin to, if he were caught in here!

I fall to the floor, dying.
Yet somehow, I fail to die.
I stare in depression at my own Dachau
and I know: I'll never escape.

Once, after dining on a rotten fish,
I saw that the door was unhooked;
toward the starry abyss of flight I leaped
with a pup's perennial recklessness.

Lunar gems cascaded across my eyes.
The moon was a circle! I understood
that the sky is not broken into squares,
as it had been from within the cage.

Alaska's snowdrifts towered all around,
and I desperately capered, diseased,
and freedom did a "twist" inside my lungs
with the stars I had swallowed.

I played pranks, I barked nonsense
at the trees. I was my own pure self.
And the iridescent snow was unafraid
that it was also very blue.

My mother and father didn't love each other,
but they mated. How I'd like
to find a girl-fox so that I could
tumble and fly with her in this sumptuous powder!

. . .

But then I'm tired. The snow is too much.
I cannot lift my sticking paws.
I have found no friend, no girlfriend.
A child of captivity is too weak for freedom.

He who's conceived in a cage will weep for a cage.
Horrified, I understood how much I love
that cage, where they hide me behind a screen,
and the fur farm—my motherland.

And so I returned, frazzled and beaten.
No sooner did the cage clang shut
than my sense of guilt became resentment
and love was alchemized again to hate.*

True, there are changes on the fur farm.
They used to suffocate us in sacks.
Now they kill us in the modern mode—
electrocution. It's wonderfully tidy.

I contemplate my Eskimo-girl keeper.
Her hand rustles endearingly over me.
Her fingers scratch the back of my neck.
But a Judas sadness floods her angel eyes.

She saves me from all diseases
and won't let me die of hunger,
but I know that when the time, set firm as iron,
arrives, she will betray me, as is her duty.

Brushing a touch of moisture from her eyes,
she will ease a wire down my throat, crooning.
"Be Humane to the Employees! On Fur Farms
Institute the Office of Executioner!†

I would like to be naive, like my father,
but I was born in captivity: I am not him.
The one who feeds me will betray me.
The one who pets me will kill me.

1967

TRANSLATED BY JOHN UPDIKE WITH ALBERT C. TODD

*The fourteenth stanza, locating the scene specifically in Alaska, was cut after the first publication.
†The slogans echo the absurd propaganda signs typical on a collective farm.

The Restaurant for Two

Honolulu,
you loll dreamily on your back in a silver-black nowhere.
The breeze moves moons
across the waves and along your mermaidenly thighs.
Ubiquitous scintillation.
Like a savage, you adore glinting trinkets in shopwindows.
Like brooches
great ships ride pinned in your watery hair.
In heedless brown hands
you shuffle Yanks, Japs, and cards from Down Under.
You dance,
and tiny gilded fish tinkle in your heels.
A Scots laird
in a multicolored kilt reels with you, drooling,
and lubriciously
slips his hand under somebody's skirt, not his own.
But a modest hut,
a "Restaurant à deux," on its pilings of palm
like a gnome on stilts
has attained to the stars, a unique toy temple.
No aerial
tops its conical cap of green leaves.
Within, the walls
are woven of bamboo and mystery, and what takes place
is *hush-hush*.
A "boy," Malayan, smirking, fetches up the stairway
baked shark's fin
steeped in pineapple, golden through and through.
Two places set.
Two candles. Two conspirators. Two fugitives.
Into each other's eyes
as if into cathedrals they have fled the world's bedlam.
It's shaky in here,
that is to say, it's substanceless—and still, so pleasant!
The samba's throb,
the stars' murmuring, the thunder from the breakwater—
all for these two.
Gladly I would beat it to that Restaurant à deux.
I would crush
my glass of flat champagne and shout to the sourpussed mob:

"I am dying,
you bore me so. I yearn for the Restaurant à deux."
　　Oh no, you say?
One must do this, do that, but never, never the other?
　　I am fed up.
I am tired of death. I want *in* to the Restaurant à deux.
　　Reconsider?
Struggle on, be committed? Oh, I gave it a whack—so what?
　　That little hut
has shown me the answer, the exit, the Restaurant à deux.
　　Let them judge me!
I'm off! And yet, running away . . . is cowardly stuff.
　　What would happen
If everybody were to hide in a restaurant à deux?!
　　That's no way out,
in an epoch of open wounds—to seek shelter from ennui
　　in a gnome-home,
in the trees and lips of another, in her knees and brow.
　　A demon's whisper
impels us to flee; we cannot comprehend
　　that after flight
it is even worse than before to be a galley-slave.
　　. . . Amid the stars,
they sit as in a dainty boat, having had their fun, at peace,
　　two fugitives:
while below them, life with its dogs like a sheriff waits.
　　The Malayan
daydreams at the foot of the sacrosanct stairway
　　and scornfully
entertains a stir of pity for innocence so hollow.
　　He observes
a half hour remains to closing time (then, scram!)
　　and switches on
the bird song tape-recorded to lend the illusion of paradise.

1967

TRANSLATED BY JOHN UPDIKE WITH EDWARD KEENAN

Cemetery of Whales

To V. Naumov

A cemetery of whales:
    in a snowy graveyard
instead of crosses
    their own bones stand.
They couldn't be gnawed by teeth;
    teeth are too soft.
They couldn't be used for soup;
    pots are too shallow.
The straining wind bends them,
    but they keep their position,
rooted in ice,
    arching like black rainbows.
Thirsty for a snort,
    an Eskimo hunchback,
shaped like a question mark,
    huddles in them as in parentheses.
Who playfully clicked a camera?
    Restrain your photophilia.
Let's leave the whales in peace,
    if only after death.
They lived, these whales,
    without offense to people,
in infantile simplicity,
    reveling in their own fountains,
while the crimson ball of the sun
    danced in a torrent of rays . . .
Thar she blows!
    Come on, lads, let's get 'em!
Where can we hide?
    But you're broader than space!
The world doesn't hold enough water
    for you to dive under.
You think you're God?
    A risky bit of impudence.
One harpoon, smack in the flank,
    rewards enormity.
Enormity commands everyone
    to hunt for it.

Whoever is big is stupid.
　　Who's smaller is wiser.
Sardines, like vermicelli,
　　are an impossible target,
lost in the generic—
　　but greatness is helpless.
On board, binoculars tremble
　　as the crew takes aim;
streaming harpoon in his side,
　　huge Tolstoy runs from the Zeiss.
A baby cetacean, not full-fledged,
　　though certainly a whale,
Yesenin flutters and kicks,
　　hoisted high on a harpoon shaft.
The title of "whale" is a bloody dignity.
　　Greatness kills greatness.
Mayakovsky himself
　　pounds in the lance.
The shallows are also a menace:
　　dashed on the shoals by the chase,
Gorky hawks and disgorges
　　fragments of steel and hickory.
Without even moaning,
　　gliding along the path of blood,
Pasternak with a snatch of lime
　　sinks into Lethe.
Hemingway is silent;
　　but from his grave a threatening shaft
shoots out of the grass,
　　growing up from the coffin.
And hidden behind the mob,
　　murder in his eye,
the Dallas whaler
　　with a telescopic sight.
A big drive is on;
　　we cherish their names posthumously.
Your law is more honest,
　　cruel Alaska.
In the cemetery of whales
　　by the hummocks of ice
there are no sanctimonious flowers:
　　the Eskimos have tact.
Hey, Eskimo hunchback,
　　white men have a funny custom:

after planting the harpoon,
    they weep over the corpse.
Murderers mourn like maidens,
    and tearfully suck tranquilizers,
and parade in crepe,
    and stand honor guard.
The professional hunters,
    who would look out of place,
send wreaths to the whales
    from the State Bureau of Harpoonery.
But the flowers are twisted together
    with steel cables and barbs.
Enough of such goodness!
    Let me live among Eskimos!

1967

TRANSLATED BY JOHN UPDIKE WITH ALBERT C. TODD

Smog

I awake in the Chelsea Hotel.
Am I dreaming?
   Is it the heat?
      I seem to see
black streams,
   cloudy black worms,
slithering into the cracks across the floor.
Galia's* nightgown has become a shroud:
soot is sprinkled
   on the pale cotton
like coal on sugar.
   Cruel as a rasp,
a cough tears her chest.
   "Zhenia,† I'm frightened!"
In our cell of a room,
   the odor Dachau.
"Zhenia, sweet Zhenia,
   I'm suffocating!"
Her face becomes a martyr's,

imitated in wax.
"Air,
    air ..."
The window opens wide and—
    I know I'm not dreaming—
a shaggy faceless beast is in the room,
    opaque as a nimbus cloud,
        surging ...
"Zhenia, I cannot breathe!"
Galia, my love,
    I am already half dead.
The air I gulp
    is airless.
There's no vent!
Shall we perish on one another's lips?
Give respiration each to each?
Equally we're prisoners of the smog;
it's too late.
    Both of us are poisoned,
        both of us,
and a kiss in this stench
would be mutual poisoning.
There are framed instructions
    on maples and elms:
"How to Kiss in Gas Masks."
In bars, they hang the brand-new slogan:
"You Can Breathe Best
    Through Vodka."
And the uptown radio
doesn't give a damn,
blaring out joyously:
"And the smog rolls on ..."
Who comes here,
    shambling along the sidewalks
with the childlike sadness of
Marcello Mastroianni?
Miller?
    Arthur?
        Slowly he whispers to me:
"It smells of fires,
    of a witch hunt ..."
Miller coughs,
    emaciated,
        his face a handsome hatchet.

Harshly he speaks in a spirit of prophecy:
"More inquisitions will set further fires.
Smog—
    This is the smoke of burnings to come."
Awkwardly shielding himself with his wing,
thirsting for secrets
    and weary of secrets,
gaunt as a stork
    on a house of his own books,
anxiously stands Updike with his noble beak.
"Zhenia,
    men have been cruelly duped;
the earth has been set on
the backs of nonexistent whales.
Mankind, all of it,
    is overstrained
with tension,
    like a centaur.
Biune, it neighs and brays,
chafed by its own duality.
Possibly smog
    is the furious steam
from the centaur's distended nostrils!"
Wiping the smog from his glasses,
standing amid books as if among gravestones,
Lowell spoke to me, clearing his throat,
in a lofty professional style:
"Only ghosts and books have a sense of honor.
Of what are we ashamed?
Only of ghosts am I ashamed.
And I am a product of ghosts. I am
Aliosha Karamazov‡ and Saint-Just together.
I believe in the vengeance of history,
in the vengeance of heaven for depravity.
Possibly smog is an ectoplasm
sent down for vengeance upon the world's baseness."
Allen Ginsberg—
    cagey prophet-baboon—
thumps his hairy chest
    as a shaman thumps a tambourine:
"Darkness is coming,
    darkness!
It reeks of deepest hell.
Those who can breathe this stench

are not worth keeping alive!
When the world is a cadaver,
a cesspool of fog and chaos,
it is a sign of excellence
to sink and drown.
False ideas,
    false morality,
fuming so many years,
    have soiled
        the sky.
Brahma lets fall this slime—
you can't suck it in."
But above the smog,
above today's exhausted vapors,
Whitman's basso thunders
    like the roar of Sabaoth:
"Listen!
    It is easy to lose your breath on a precipice.
But breathe deeply,
    breathe deeply!
        Give it a try!
Inhale all together!
    You will see—
        only inhale,
and the phantom smog
    by your breathing will be swept from the sky!"
And I felt the epoch
    standing still awaiting,
like a revolution of the universe,
    our common deep breath.

1967
New York

TRANSLATED BY JOHN UPDIKE WITH ALBERT C. TODD

*Galia: Galina Semionovna Yevtushenko, the author's wife.
†Zhenia: Affectionate familiar form of Yevgeny.
‡Aliosha Karamazov: The spiritual youngest brother in Dostoyevsky's novel *The Brothers Karamazov*.

On the Question of Freedom

Dachau's ashes burn my feet
The asphalt smokes under me
Warheads & bayonets stuck
under my nails

I'll stroke a stray strand of my beloved's hair
And I myself shall smoke
crucified Christ-like on wings of bombers
flying through this night to kill Christ's kids

My skin trembles with explosions
as if it were Vietnam
and breaking my back and ribs
the Berlin Wall runs through me

You talk to me of freedom? Empty question
under umbrellas of bombs in the sky
It's a disgrace to be free of your own age
A hundred times more shameful than to be its slave

Yes I'm enslaved to Tashkent women
and to Dallas bullets and Peking slogans
and Vietnam widows and Russian women
with picks beside the tracks and kerchiefs over their eyes

Yes I'm not free of Pushkin and Blok
Not free of the state of Maryland and Zima Station
Not free of the Devil and God
Not free of earth's beauty and its shit

Yes I'm enslaved to a thirst for taking a wet mop
to the heads of all the bickerers & butchers of the world
Yes I'm enslaved to the honor of busting the mugs
of all the bastards on earth

And maybe I'll be loved by the people for this
For spending my life
(not without precedent in this iron age)
glorifying unfreedom from
the true struggle for freedom

1967

TRANSLATED BY LAWRENCE FERLINGHETTI WITH ANTHONY KAHN

1968-1972

... I'll come seeping through
those rainy bits of slipperiness
between the toes of barefoot urchins.

Monologue of a Restorer

My love is a demolished church
above the turbid river of memories
near a cemetery with tin crosses
and plywood stars above the dust
of untimely deceased hopes.
I restore frescoes with trepidation
that I begin too late—
only ruins make us more humane,
and only time reveals the value
of that destroyed by willful ignorance.

The angels in flight become raw and damp,
and their wings fall down in a scrap heap.
Little hearts are crudely drawn in exchange.
Will a "Misha and Masha were here" really
prevail as the symbol of our life, scrawled
over a picture of the Day of Judgment?
Will a potato and a dry sausage,
our smug pitiful litter,
supplant God for people forevermore?

I say again and again: I am God, but I think art.
You know, just such art at one time
elevated us, hairy and shaggy, off four legs
and won't let us cover ourselves over and over with hair
and gallop anew on all fours,
and it is bitter for me to see, I tell you honestly,
how my hirsute contemporary in church,
completely unabashed by his shagginess,
daubs crudely: "No God here. Everything sucks."

Hey, simpleton, a church is here,
and in that there's God.
It floats with serene beauty
not quite made from cottage cheese,
not quite from snow,
nonvindictive, like the Princess-Swan,
radiating, forgetting boorishness.
Well, and when the weather is good,
the river, as though my secret colleague,

makes a copy of the church and there shine
two churches, like a snow-white folding icon—
one in the water, another on the hill.

Oblivion is no better than insult.
They jump around today, like fleas,
not icon painters but icon graffitists.
More than a windbag-orator,
preaching about protection for antiquity,
we need today a tender and intrepid restorer,
who will wash away the ephemera of wretched scrawls
and who, understanding redemption in it,
will give back to the nation the nation's treasure.

I change yawns into radiance,
and I restore a horse and spear to St. George
so that he will finish stamping out the dragon.
I won't paint over my own eyes,
but I cleanse the Lord's eyes,
so that he will see the traitor Judas,
whom—forgive me, wicked people!—
I made a contemporary, and now to inform
on me the cemetery watchman's tomboy,
after seeing my work, is already on the run.

When I drink, I become shaggy,
but don't judge too strictly—
in church the hair immediately falls off me,
only part of my shagginess quivers
on my brush, reminding me of my sins.
One cleanses eternity—as one cleanses oneself—
and my mix washes away all dirt from the soul,
and my brush returns God to you,
and my little boy—not just anyone's—
at the top of his voice
bawls in the arms of the Mother of God . . .

1968

TRANSLATED BY ALBERT C. TODD

Ballad about Sausage

Like a signal flare, nineteen forty-one
was fading in the mud underfoot.
Like the boards of great tragedies,
Russia's platforms shook.

And on that musty stage
among ragged youths
representing Russia's destitute,
I played my first part.

My poor, cracked voice
sang to the guitar strings of rain.
My skitterish childish hunger
sang for equally hungry people.

I was lean, dressed in rags
at the instant when in my sky,
like the moon, a sausage rose up
through the holes of a "perhaps" net bag.*

Breaking off my hoarse solo,
I saw in my febrile heat
white headlights of fat
showing through the burnished skin.

More lush than a French roll,
its owner in a hat with a doltish feather
sat on her stuffed suitcases, like a Buddha,
regarding the platform anxiously.

Yes, war demeans a child—
in wartime he's full only of hunger,
and the gypsy boy's eyes glowed
like the coal he had stolen.

But as I was a blond gypsy boy,
a representative of artistic forces,
I approached the lady
and sang "Little Bricks" for her.

· · ·

Simplifying the goals of art
and convinced of its magic,
I sang, filled with great admiration
for that amazing sausage.

Rummaging in her shopping bag,
like a mountain that had been moved,
the lady handed me a caramel,
a sticky square of kindness.

But a peasant woman sitting nearby
could not help herself,
and over a clean sheet of notepaper
broke her bread in half.

The bread, damp and full of holes,
its crust completely gone,
sighed, guiltily,
that I wouldn't eat it all.

The old woman also sighed guiltily
and hiding the sigh deep inside
handed me with some relief
half of her half.

And then she cried a bit
and only said, "Oh, you boys..."
and licked off the bitter crumb
that stuck in the wrinkles of her hand.

...Life goes on. As in a fog, countries
float by—they're not about us,
and meridians sway,
like links of sausage with bites taken out.

I no longer dream of sausage,
I wear an imported jacket,
and I carelessly knock off crumbs,
if they sadly stick to my hand.

In my kitchen a refrigerator
crouches like a polar bear,
and when hunger makes me want to cry
I begin to sing.

. . .

And it's not a powerful voice
that can overwhelm the din of crowds,
but my hunger, my orphan's hunger,
my fierce hunger for human kindness.

But, really, there's no need to cry.
It's a sin to think the earth's not generous
if someone with affliction offers you
a too sticky square of kindness.

Parasites scurry over the planet,
crutches hobble across as well,
but kindness is not in transit
on the shaking platform of the earth.

I love my platform with my umbilical gut,
and until I stop loving it,
they'll break off half of their half
for me, and I'll break off mine.

1968
TRANSLATED BY ANTONINA W. BOUIS

*A string or plastic net bag, *avos'ka*, which means "perhaps," is traditionally carried by Russians.

Knowing and Not-Knowing

Knowing gloomily says: "Aha . . ."
Not-knowing screams its "Aho!"
From knowing to rosy not-knowing
I flee as though from the enemy.

Knowing sniggers like a snake.
Not-knowing laughs like a brook.
It's easy for not-knowing to imagine
that there's no poison, but only milk.

Knowing walks on two legs,
but cautiously—sparing them.

Not-knowing charges on all its feet,
enthusiastically breaking gait.

Not-knowing says: "Take any seat!"—
and a raised finger means: "Stop!"
Not-knowing shoots us down
with the heavenliness of its intrepid eyes.

Knowing, after wearing holes in books,
doesn't rush at once to blow up the whole world,
but the tempting example of not-knowing
immediately demands urgent measures.

So not-knowing with cries breaks away
out of the hands of knowing, makes its way ahead.
Wisely, knowing doesn't hurry:
you see, it once was not-knowing.

1968

TRANSLATED BY ALBERT C. TODD

"Light died in the hall . . ."

Light died in the hall . . . Yet while, upon the boards,
darkness arose and played the only role,
there poured through all my veins, in icy chords,
the chill of an inaudible chorale.

I knew that there, prepared for the prologue, seen
by none, perhaps, but the wide eye of God.
Like a sliver of the darkness, like a lean
shade among shadows, slim and alive, you stood.

I had not God's high vision, yet within,
like the voice of God, I felt the music rise,
and I saw, not with my sight but with my skin,
as with a thousand small, concerted eyes,

. . .

And there, in the dark, in the intermittencies
of someone's breathing, the dense transparencies
of the incorporeal shadows, I discovered
with a wild guess, and could in rapture tell
that point, apart from paradise or hell,
where, waiting for its flame, a candle hovered.

And you were kindled, and the light re-uttered,
and the chaos of strange blackness was no more,
and only a little golden forelock fluttered
before me, like a wind-whipped tongue of fire.

1968

TRANSLATED BY RICHARD WILBUR WITH ANTHONY KAHN

The Streetcar of Poetry

The streetcar of poetry,
                    like social security,
is stuffed full of people and letters.
I didn't get on by the front platform—
I dangled on the bumper.
Later, on the step, I held on cunningly
by a hand
              in the slammed door,
and I can't believe myself,
how I finally shoved my way inside.
I always gave a seat to my elders.
I never hid from the ticket inspector.
I didn't step on people's feet.
When they stepped on me I didn't cry.
People read
              newspapers in the corners.
People sat
              on menacing bundles.
People forced their way into the streetcar,
                              as if it were paradise,
full of the most desperate enemies.

The logic of insurrection quickly changed
to the logic of those who ride.
They grumbled gloomily, examining the press,
clucking little chickens over their product:
"The streetcar is not made of rubber ...

                                        Stop pounding on the doors!

Don't open up, Conductor!"
I'm for those
            who get off to knead and build,
not for those
            who forbid entrance.
I'm for those
            who want to get on the streetcar
when they aren't permitted.
This world is cruel, like Moscow in the winter,
when blown by a blizzard.
Streetcars are made of rubber.
                              There is room!

Open the doors, Conductor!

1968

TRANSLATED BY ALBERT C. TODD

Gratitude

To M.B.

She whispered: "Yes, he's sleeping now I'm sure."
To screen her young son's crib she drew the curtain
and put the light out; fumbling and uncertain,
she shivered, dropped her bathrobe to the floor.

We did not talk of love; instead, beneath
the sheets she whispered softly to me, burring
the letter *r* as though a cat lay purring
behind the bright, white curtain of her teeth:

                    •   •   •

"I'd written off my chances in this life;
I was a drudge, a workhorse . . . Am I dreaming?
All that has changed; you gave me back the feeling
that I'm a woman—it's beyond belief!"

Yet I'm the one who should show gratitude.
Although I played the hunter, I was hunted;
and in its yielding, grateful attitude
her gentle body gave the peace I wanted.

She wet my cheeks with tears, she spoke my name
and lay, exhausted, as her soft limbs flanked me;
it burned me with a wave of ice-cold shame,
because this woman felt the need to thank me.

For I should serenade her with my verse,
and, blushing and confused, surrender to her.
But that a woman thanked me! It's perverse;
and just because a man was tender to her!

How has this happened in the world today—
to so forget a woman's primal meaning
and cast her from her rightful place? I say
to make her be man's equal is demeaning.

Absurd the difference between our "now" and "then":
The day's already come (at least it's coming),
when women will almost resemble men
and men take on the character of women.

How hard beneath my fingers in that bout
her naked shoulder thrust with all its fullness,
and how her eyes, once dim with neuter dullness,
became a woman's eyes as she cried out!

And then in twilight dark her eyes were veiled,
two distant candle-flames, elusive, glowing . . .
My God—how little does a woman need
for her to feel herself once more a woman!

1968

TRANSLATED BY MICHAEL GLENNY

Russian Tanks in Prague

Tanks are rolling across Prague
in the sunset blood of dawn.
Tanks are rolling across truth,
not a newspaper named *Pravda*.*

Tanks are rolling across the temptation
to live free from the power of clichés.
Tanks are rolling across the soldiers
who sit inside those tanks.

My God, how vile this is,
God, what degradation!
Tanks across Jan Hus,
Pushkin, and Petőfi.

Tanks are rolling across crypts,
across those not yet born.
Rosaries of bureaucracy's paper clips
mutate into tank tracks.

You trampled on conscience and honor.
Like a fat-bellied monster,
fear, armored by loutishness,
rides in tank bodies across Prague.

Could I be an enemy to Russia?
Didn't I, as a happy kid,
once rub my snotty nose
on other tanks that defended my motherland?

How can I live as before,
if, like a carpenter's plane,
tanks roll across the hope
that they defend my motherland?

Before I bite the dust,
no matter what they call me,
I turn to my descendants
with only one request:

. . .

Above me without sobbing
let them write, in truth:
"A Russian writer crushed
by Russian tanks in Prague."

23 August 1968

TRANSLATED BY ALBERT C. TODD

Pravda in Russian means "truth" and in earlier historical usage it meant "justice" or "truth as justice." As the name of the ideologically tedious and censorship-controlled Communist Party's official newspaper it has long been the butt of sarcastic humor.

The Art of Flower Arranging

*Dedicated to the oldest Georgian flower
specialist, Mikhail Mamulashvili*

An art of arranging sunsets?
An art of arranging dawns?
But there was a Swiss who
was the best at arranging flowers.

Fat, dressed in suede shorts,
a drunkard, always hung over,
he prepared bouquets like cakes
with candied fruits and creams.

He grew narcissi, cyclamens,
preferring for parties, nonetheless,
chrysanthemum as foam
dripping from a beer mug.

Did the king of rubber have a son?
Fine. Orchids. Two baskets.
Shots fired in Sarajevo?
Fine . . . Send immortelles.

The dairymaid's son died?
Well, let's have a modest wreath.
Gas creeping across Europe?

A nightmare, of course,
            but business will improve.

A cynic, he knows that amid
            all wars and rebellions
no one will suffer who knows
the secret of flower arranging.

Nevertheless, he had drunk away
                    the secrets long ago,
busy with business, not art.
Imagination loses money;
sucking up to tastes means profits.

He tormented his pupils, tricked them,
not trusting them to make bouquets,
and the secret of his teaching lay
in the ability to hide his secrets.

Of those who puttered in the greenhouses
with hoses and clever fertilizers,
only Mishiko—a boy from Tiflis—
did not approve of his master.

He performed his work honestly,
but laughed privately and bitterly
as he poured tkemali, that rebel plum sauce,
on pallid Swiss cutlets.

And the master shuddered, his flesh jiggling,
when the boy made a face at him
and took beet leaves—with purple veins—
to wrap a golden rose.

The bouquet was crude, absurdly wild,
but, clutching his garden knife,
the Swiss sensed that he was a confectioner
and the boy a true artist.

There is no forgiveness for businessmen in art.
For them the client's taste is stimulation,
while art is the daring juxtaposition
of what everyone thought incompatible.

                ·   ·   ·

The master drank, mixing beer and vodka.
"What would you like to eat?" the waiter asked
with caution.
                    Angrily he answered: "Beet leaves!"
"What?" The waiter paled.
                              "And—a rose, a rose."

1969
TRANSLATED BY ANTONINA W. BOUIS

Thanks

To I. Lyubimov

Say thanks to your tears.
Don't hurry to wipe them.
Better to weep and to be.
Not to be is to die.

To be alive—bent and beaten.
Not to vanish in the dark of the plasm.
To catch the lizard-green minute
from creation's cart.

Bite into joy like you bite
                              a radish.
Laugh as you catch the knife's blade.
Not to be born, that's what's
                                    frightening
even if it's frightening that you
                                          live.

He who is—is already lucky.
Life is a risky card.
To be drawn—that's a cocky occasion.
It's to draw a straight flush.

In the sway of wild cherry blossoms,
drunk on all, drunk on nothing,

don't shake off the large wonder
of your entrance upon the scene.

Don't count on pie in the sky.
Don't offend the earth by bitching.
For a second life cannot be
as the first did not have to be.

Don't trust decay. Trust the flare-up.
Sink into milkwood and feathery grass.
Pile the universe on your back
without cajoling too much.

Don't be a show-off in grief.
Even on the ruins of your soul,
dirty and tethered, like Zorba,
celebrate shame. And dance!

Thanks to the blackest cats
whom you hated askance.
Thanks to all the melon peels
on which you slipped.

Thanks to the fiercest of pains
for it kept giving.
And thanks to the shabbiest fate.
After all, it has come.

1969
TRANSLATED BY VERA DUNHAM

Marektinsky Shoals

V. Chernykh

The moment *Apollo* landed on the moon,
we landed on a rock.

We gave up,
            and raised the huge oars of *Chaldon*.
It was punishment
for brazenly barging ahead.
The soles of our boots crunched
on caramels that slipped from underfoot.
To those who believe the world is limitlessly deep,
the punishment is
            the shoals.
But crawling along the sandbar
is still possible at a cockroach gait . . .
To those who believe they can pass over all rocks,
the punishment is
            a rock.
It hit us with a brutal blow.
Bonged the bell that was
                stolen twice,
from the church for the port
and from the port by us.
The bosun got lightly baptized.
Clearly we need very little:
a prick against a boulder,
to remember God.
Howling and bellowing
the water twisted and screwed us
into that rock
in the middle of the Vitim.
The shoal wailed like a witch.
We magnificently pretend not to give up:
the winch squirmed pathetically,
the pump slushily grunted.
Night wrapped around us.
Hey, brother, time to fetch the juice
if neither courage
                nor sapling levers
can help.
We're alive,
           and thanks for that.
Ladle the borscht even thicker,
and vodka
           is better than fish:
it's forever without bones.
Fully balanced,
the world has dual destinies.

You take off, *Apollo.*
We sit here,
                stuck quite fundamentally.
And the process of getting used to it
takes place 'cause we're sloshed,
the process of getting used to the rock
on which
            it all winds down.
We're grounded on a rock,
but what the hell:
                    "Come on, make some tea!"
We're grounded on a rock,
but what the hell, there's dames,
                                politics.
We're jerks, but gradually
to ourselves seem to be great guys, heroes.
We're grounded on a rock
and we think
            we're on a pedestal.
We rejected
forewarnings, bragging:
                    "We are our own bosses!"
We're grounded on a rock,
which we ourselves shoved in our path.
He who finds pleasure in being grounded on a rock
will disappear,
                sink away,
vanish, just like that, from ridicule and laughter.
The current ripples like a horse's mane,
and we sit crosswise,
                    inimitable,
like Don Quixote on Rosinante romancing Dulcinea,
always in the same position
                        grounded on a rock.
We forget,
        giving way to merriment,
elegantly arranging our seats,
that on a rock,
                where we've planted our behinds,
we will not cultivate Candide's garden.
And from the salty jokes of a storyteller,
who's forgotten what's ahead,
so comfortable on a busted boat,
just try to grow even ivy.

And with mildewed kasha
we drink—already vomiting—
for our beloved motherland rock
(for the damned thing to blow itself up!).

1969

TRANSLATED BY ALBERT C. TODD

A Special Vantage Point

The garden's yellows and pinks
witnessed our parting rite;
the bread on the plate imbibed
the tender drops of the grape.

She barely said a word
while, from the branch above,
one flower from the fig tree
trailed its lilac bud.

I felt her subtle touch
and heard, as if inside:
"There's a special vantage point . . .
Here . . . Open your eyes."

I tossed my head. The tree,
decked in persimmon fruit,
wrinkled like an early widow,
listed, creaked, stood firm.

It seemed the tree would speak
to forgive me, or find fault,
when suddenly it rushed at me
and, through me, sprouted out.

A kilometer or two
from the mountaintop
the sea below broke into view
upon our straining eyes.

. . .

Obliterating distance
somehow, league on league,
a tiny boat now trembled
on the rusty edge of a leaf.

Suddenly I knew
what had found us out;
love is just a point of view
and nothing more, perhaps.

She was beautiful;
her majesty in this:
there was nothing that she wished,
not even an address.

Resolving everything for me,
she left beyond recall;
but what greater request could there be
than the one not asked at all?

1969

TRANSLATED BY ANTHONY KAHN

Russianness

There's a Russianness higher than blood,
when before a moral tribunal,
one who was born a Russian, during a pogrom
will feel himself a Jew.

But in a Rus* searching for a Vendée,†
spitting bullets into icons,
Jews became Chekists,‡
like Black Hundreds§ scum.

The brotherhood of peoples was fierce.
At the leader's command,
now a Russian, now a Georgian became Maliutas,"
sparing neither Georgian nor Russian.

· · ·

And the Orthodox Church crushed
itself with a twisted chuckle
with a Russophile's new "lapta"# play stick,
with a Caucasian-Roman boot.

And someone who used to be beaten takes root
like the disease of goosestepping parades.
The evil of gendarmerie and playing general
is not Russian, but Prussian in spirit.

Whither, the path not discerning,
have you drifted through pools of blood,
Rus, bird, troika extraordinary,
listing under the weight of dead souls?**

And in spite of laurels in battles,
carrying on larceny in our own land,
we have defeated ourselves
as Rome was devastated by itself.

And even from Russian rockets
comes the menacing spirit
of the smashing to pieces,
of the last Roman chariots.

Will Russians really flaccidly
sleep through their own decline,
and in a new Russian-Prussian Rome
will there be all-around disintegration?

But there still is faith in Russia,
when Russians know how
to look on Russian bayonets
with the eyes of a Czech or Hungarian!

The inner worth of Russia
is not in restoring churches,
but in our leading our children
to morality as if it were a church.

Immorality already is not Russianness,
but if morality is alive,
Russia will remain standing, will not collapse,
Moscow will reject the Roman way.

. . .

But the new Rome—let it
inevitably collapse in filth!
Where in Rus is the fall of Rome
there is the rebirth of Rus.

1969

TRANSLATED BY ALBERT C. TODD

*Rus: Ancient Russia. The name of the eastern Slavonic tribe, it became the name of the emerging
nation and the early feudal state in the ninth century.
†Vendée: La Vendée province in western France gave its name to the reaction there among the
peasants against the liberal reforms of the French Revolution.
‡Chekists: Members of the Cheka, organized under Lenin to protect the Revolution of 1917. It
became the parent of the Soviet system of state security and secret police.
§Black Hundreds: Extreme right-wing opponents of liberalism and revolution at the beginning of
the twentieth century. Notoriously anti-Semitic mobs recruited unofficially by the tsarist police
from among minor tradesmen or non-factory workers as "patriots" to conduct brutal pogroms.
"Maliutas: Maliuta Skuriatov was a leader and executioner among Ivan the Terrible's oppressive
inner circle of guards called the oprichniks.
#lapta: Ancient Russian game played with stick and ball.
**dead souls: Nikolai Gogol's novel *Dead Souls* ends with Russia being addressed as a troika that
is dashing off at breakneck speed. It does not answer the question, Where is it flying?

The Singing Dam

Along the dam over the Volga,
                    the dam over sleeping Kazan,
the dam over life,
                where death punishes for some unknown crime,
along the dam spanning the cries of gulls,
                            adopted by nature,
the graduates walk—all in white dresses
                            ripe as wild cherries.
Along the dam,
            the dam
they sing,
        a pure vision reflected in a squalid wave...
Give,
    give
a little youth to me!
You walk on this June night,
when the nightingales of ships' horns
                            sing with you,

along the dam—
        still between childhood and youth—
while I am
      between maturity and . . .
          —you understand it—
             and . . .
Yes, weariness is layered early in my soul,
and must be called old age,
        I suppose.
It's neither death that I fear
        nor the body's aging, believe me,
but the slow living death
      of my spirit.
I'm not whimpering
      nor howling in despair,
but what lies inside me weighs like a sheet of iron.
I'm aging,
    I'm aging,
a warehouse filled with junk.
I'm hardening,
      hardening—
you cannot pierce me with a missile.
But it's frightening and painful,
inexpressibly so,
to be
   impenetrable
even to love.
Judge of the era,
first be ruthless
in judgment
     of yourself,
and only then
     of the era.
Acting up a storm,
have you turned into a villain?
Faces tried on,
have you become the face?
We came out onto the dam
       from the restaurant's chatter,
you and I
    both inexplicably sober.
Forgive my silence.
      Believe me, I'm not acting—now.
But being near you,

I'm beyond a line.
And your sobbing
                doesn't bother me in the least.
How lucky you are:
            You suffer.
                    You love.
                        You can.
The dam is like a church portico
where I kneel and pray
for the ability to weep,
or merely to understand that I love.
Along the dam over the Volga,
                        the dam over sleeping Kazan,
the touch of the girls' dresses
is a touch from another world.
Two lag behind.
                They won't be found till morning,
and boys' lips
            are pushing the girls' lips.
The girls' lips, shut tight,
                    try to veer to one side,
and their flaxen tresses
                are caught with simple rubber bands.
And I hear with envy—
                    alas, not without reason:
"Get away with your kisses!
                    What a pervert you are!"
And I feel a loss
you won't understand.
Ah, I should be so "perverted,"
but it's too late to adopt it now.
And yet, perhaps, it's not too late
when stars light the earth
and faces fall from my face,
and there is the unconquerable stirring
of wild cherry,
            of swan,
which has no end?!

1970

TRANSLATED BY ANTONINA W. BOUIS AND JAMES RAGAN

The Grave of a Child

We sailed down the Lena at evening.
The river, fast-flowing but calm,
with daughterly love and affection
caressed the Siberian shore.

The bow wave that flared out before us
thrilled our eyes with pure, driven foam,
like the surge of a chorus, insistent,
an age-old familiar song.

The thrill of illicit adventure
set our teeth very slightly on edge,
like the taste of fresh snow on the palate,
like a taste of the secret of life.

The chart that the captain was holding
was tattered and torn half across;
as it rustled he seemed to be seeing
a portent of dangers to come.

And gruffly but quietly he told us,
a frown passing over his face:
"The name of this headland we're passing
is grim: it's 'The Grave of a Child.' "

Far older than telephone networks
is something that links all mankind;
the long-drawn-out bond of that moment
was snapped by a bell's urgent peal.

This world deals us no second chances;
escapes never meet with success.
That link joining us is misfortune,
a chain that can never be cut.

I felt a sensation of choking
at the thought better not said aloud:
To link the word "child" with a gravestone
is cruel and intolerably sad.

.   .   .

I thought of all those who lay buried,
of all that lies buried in us;
love, too, in its way, is our offspring,
and to bury that child is a sin.

Yet twice I have shoveled the earth on,
dispatching my love to its doom.
Which one of us hasn't done likewise
and buried his love in a grave?

Without even tears of contrition—
it's become such a habit, you see—
we bury our hopes under tombstones
like digging a grave for a child.

We are aged by accursed ambition,
by pursuit of our vain, empty goals;
there's a child that has perished within us:
each of us is the grave of a child.

We sailed past that menacing headland,
past grim and precipitous cliffs,
as though past a cold, naked symbol
of loss, of unrealized hopes.

We all have been bitterly punished
for that which lies buried within;
in each one a bell is heard tolling
for ourselves and for all of mankind...

1970
TRANSLATED BY MICHAEL GLENNY

Come to My Merry Grave

Come to my graveside,
come sober or drunk.
Both sandals and boots
I'll hear above me.

· · ·

Bring pine and rowan branches
or any that you wish,
bring the ones you love,
bring along the kids.

Sit down on the grass and bench,
open some wine if it's there,
don't be embarrassed before me,
render the dead its due.

Speak of the pain that is hidden
which tortures you from below,
speak, if only of football—
I fear losing touch with the crowd.

Neither granite nor colored marble,
exalted tears or speeches brave,
but just more sweet nonsense
over my merry grave.

Give honor to what's not been quoted!
Forget the authors of books.
Recall the liar, the friend. Let out
a kindergarten-cannibal shout.

Cook up lies and tales about me,
but keep the fibs
of Siberia and Tahiti
a little like my own.

For in my boastful, willful life
between the hawks and doves,
one bit was really true—
that is, I really was.

Fables turn out to be true
and facts wound round with legend,
but scandal didn't kill me
and legend cannot now.

I will remain not only by my verse.
My golden charm is this:
I loved unmeasured this whole earth
and she fell in love with me.

. . .

And the earth wanted me,
so that people could not tell
where is my end-of-summer body
where earth's fun-loving last.

'Tis sweet with bone-chilled edge
to understand, when all is done,
that I'll come seeping through
those rainy bits of slipperiness
between the toes of barefoot urchins.

I don't have the strength to die completely.
Obituaries and mourning are a bunch of rot.
Only come to my graveside,
to the grave where I am not.

1970

TRANSLATED BY ALBERT C. TODD

Unrequited Love

To. I. Kvasha

Love unrequited is a crushing yoke;
but if you see love as a game,

                a trophy,
then unrequited love's absurd, a joke—
like Cyrano de Bergerac's odd profile.
One day a hard-boiled Russian in the theater
said to his wife, in words that clearly hurt her:
"Why does this Cyrano upset you all?
The fool!

        Now I, for instance, I would never
allow some bitch to get me in a fever . . .
I'd simply find another one—

                that's all."
Behind his wife's reproachful eyes there gleamed

a beaten, widowed look of desperation.
From every pore her husband oozed,

                        it seemed,

the lethal sweat of crude self-satisfaction.
How many are like him—

                 great healthy men,

who, lacking the capacity to suffer,
call women "chicks" or "broads";

                   it sounds much tougher.

Yet am I not myself a bit like them?
We yawn

         and play at shabby little passions,

discarding hearts as though they're last year's fashions,
afraid of tragedy,

             afraid to pay.

And you and I, no doubt, are being weaklings
whenever we so often force our feelings
to take the easier,

            less binding way.

I often hear the inner coward whining,
from murky depths my impulse undermining:
"Hey, careful now;

            don't get involved ..."

I weakly take the line of least resistance,
and lose, who knows, from sheer lack of persistence,
a priceless chance of unrequited love.
A man who's clever and can use his head
can always count on a response from women,
for poor Cyrano's chivalry's not dead:
it is not men who show it now, but women.
In love you're either chivalrous

            or you

don't love.

       All men of one law stand indicted:

if you can't love with love that's unrequited,
you cannot love—no matter what you do.
God grant us grace that we may know the pain
of fruitless longing,

           unreturned emotion,

delightful torment as we wait in vain:
the hapless happiness of vain devotion.
For secretly I'm longing to be brave,
to warm my ice-cold heart with passion's burning;

in lukewarm love affairs enmeshed,
                                    I rave
of unrequited love and hopeless yearning.

1971

TRANSLATED BY MICHAEL GLENNY

The Salty Hammock

To Ye. Rein

Like time's clever sand,
tobacco rustles in the pouch...
And just as wood of a whaleboat decays,
so also people and nets.

And happy as old men,
those transparent fences
of moldered netting
listen to the hubbub of children.

They've done their catching,
but out of habit still seine
for scraps and rain
and spent matches.

Now a star gets entrapped in them,
now the babble of young love,
now somebody's curse
or an accidental sigh.

They snare everything—a gust of wind,
someone's song and phrase—
and, hooking a button,
return it, but not right away.

And an old fisherman
(of the sturdy kind who put off death)

makes himself a hammock
from old nets that have served their time.

And hiding his pain inside,
recognized in lonely fragments,
from the gray, tangled knots
he tastes salt on his teeth.

Sway, salty hammock,
in the measured rustle of firs.
Every retired fisherman
in turn becomes a catch.

In old age we are in a lane
from which we answer for the past,
and where we all writhe
in our forgotten nets.

You were a prattler, a wastrel.
No time for fights now. You have scabs.
Sway, salty hammock,
create an illusion of the sea.

But the sea won't splash your sides,
and the sky remains treacherously clear.
Intentional swaying isn't the same—
it's much too wise.

And he wants squalls and storms—
the hell with all this coziness!
If only his youth could come back!
He'd give up his excess wisdom!

But it's a lie that you're unhappy.
He who has not known storms is luckless.
And you are so different
from any cottage hammock rider.

You've known every storm's punch;
you took on hurricanes.
Let every freshwater hammock envy
this salty one.

There is a special taste to swaying—
even if it brings misfortune.

Sway on, salty hammock,
sway,
       sway,
              sway ...

1971

TRANSLATED BY ANTONINA W. BOUIS AND JAMES RAGAN

A Moment Half-Winter, Half-Fall

The moment half-winter, half-fall,
what fortune did your little shoe divine?
It stirred the dead leaves up,
trying to work answers from the earth,
answers the earth wouldn't give at all.

Like a defenseless, little animal,
your shoe nuzzled its mouth against my shoe,
but, embarrassed and a little dead,
it, too, kept itself from a reply.
All about, the rustling rakes
gathered up the dead leaves at our feet.

The dead leaves hadn't yet been burned to ash.
I was consumed. Our song was sung
if to the chaos of a shattered soul
we find no answer breaking in our own.
Looking for advice? What better words than these:
Don't stir up dead leaves.

Nearby your child played in the sand.
Across the way, at home, so limitless his trust,
your husband, moving his fanatic brush,
did a landscape with a setting sun.
I felt like a knave. A two-face
doing off with someone else's colors.
As usual, the dead leaves burned and sank,
issuing their smoke in mute chorales.

.   .   .

A chorus of crows darkened the landscape
and branches, bearing mist in their pale arms,
the same dead leaves, same you, same empty bench
and child. Good God, like a phantom of betrayal,
will I, too, rise, uncovered by the brush?

Life had no use for my amusements.
I was greedy. This childlike hunger, unappeased,
at times transformed itself to ruthlessness
that dismissed the longed-for apple with one bite.
Omnivore, you're more than criminal
if you work another family's grief.

A crime before a brother is a crime
before mankind. It's just as much a sin
to do a single family in
as to wrong entire nations
and just as base, if you can't build another,
to bring a passing life down on the fly.

The trolley bell is a prophetic bell.
I'm on the footboard, roadways flashing by.
Alone again. No matter, it'll pass;
it's not the first time. Or the last.
Still, better isolation than, for warmth,
a bonfire of live souls, like dead leaves at my feet.
What else could I do? The tale's complete.

1971
TRANSLATED BY ANTHONY KAHN (REVISED)

Keys of the Comandante

Our horses pad their way to the village
                    where they killed you,
                            Comandante.

Near the precipice go, as in politics,
            neither too far to the left,
                  nor too wide to the right.

Let go the reins, muchachos,
                              give the horses lead
to direct our destinations,
                              otherwise we'll vanish in vain.
There is in the sullen cheekbones of the rock face
                              a partisan look
the wind
          has sculpted with longing and pain.
The clouds are heavy, unmoving
                              above the forests and swamps,
like exhausted thoughts
                              of the scowling Bolivian mountains.
We struggle upward,
                    as though evading pursuit.
Better to confront phantoms in the mountains
                              than adjust to the marsh's slime
The clip-clop of horseshoes dictates
                              the rhythm of these lines,
stumbling on the stones
                    of this deadly serpentine trail.
But fear makes bad reins.
                    And while not particularly fearful,
I detect with every nerve
                    the putrid smell of immortality.
Remembering you, Comandante—
                              overwinds the soul,
and the quiet inside
                    pulsates like an earthquake.
Comandante, in trading you,
                              bidding the price ever higher,
they sell your precious name
                    too cheaply.
With my own eyes, Comandante,
                    in Paris I saw
your portrait, your beret with a star,
                              on modern "hot pants."
Your beard, Comandante,
                    on bracelet charms, brooches, and saucers.
In life you were once pure flame,
                    they turn you into smoke.
But you fell, Comandante,
                    in the name of justice, of revolution—

not in order to become an ad
                              for the commerce of the "left"-minded.
You were shot in this school,
              where my horse suddenly grows still:
                        "Where are the keys to the school?"
The campesinos are unfriendly and silent
                            with guilt in their eyes.
A rusty padlock crowns the door.
                    A glance through the window—it's dark and bare,
    and the wall is white like the sail of a ship
                                with no captain.
The ancient village bell slumbers.
                        A drunkard drags on a can of beer.
Horse manure by the doors
                    leaves an odor of posthumous chrysanthemums.
I repeat: "Where are the keys to the school?"
            "The keys! Do you understand?!"—I yell in Spanish.
"We don't know, señor, we don't know ..."
                The campesinos stand like a wall.
All the same, where are the keys to the school,
                    and to your soul, Comandante?
Time to go back, muchachos.
                    The clouds are pregnant with a storm.
This key is held by a mystery,
                    and just try and get
the real key—not a picklock!
                    You see, breaking in would settle nothing.
I understand
        how through the pain in your hearts, muchachos,
your hands itch for rifles
                    or machine guns.
If they pull you to the right, muchachos—
                to the left, boys, always to the left,
but not more left than your hearts,
                        otherwise the precipice awaits.
They hacked off your hands, Che,
                    there, in the square of Valle Grande,
in order to remove your fingerprints.
                    (Perhaps, "sewed on" others, in haste.)
But the rebellious hands of the muchachos—
                    are your hands, Comandante,
and no one can chop them off

—they'd grow back anew.
Trust your horses, muchachos,
                    and not simply youthful impulse.
The horses have a peasant wisdom—
                    no matter what their age.
A vulture circles in the sky above us,
                    led on by his rapacious beak,
his talons drawn in,
            but, while waiting for victims,
                            takes aim.

1971
La Paz
TRANSLATED BY ALBERT C. TODD AND JAMES RAGAN

My Peruvian Girl

In the hour when newspapers die,
they change into the rubbish of night,
and a dog with the remains of a biscuit,
grows still as he holds me in his sight;

in the hour when instincts are resurrected,
the ones that sanctimoniously hide by day,
taxi drivers cry: "Hey, Gringo!
Una chica Peruana—lez go, oke!";

in the hour when the post office is closed,
and the telegraph chatters sleeplessly,
and a muchacho, wrapped in a poncho,
slumbers, pressed against someone's statue;

in the hour when prostitutes and muses
smear their faces with makeup
and the next day's rubbish is being prepared
in huge-type headlines across the top;

in the hour when everything is unseen and seen,
neither going to or coming from an invitation,

I wander through the Avenue de Lima,
as though it were a cemetery of news.

All covered with spittle and grapefruit rinds,
the street smells like a latrine,
but look over there—a human contour
appears through a pile of newspaper.

This old woman, contorted in deafness,
blaming no one for anything,
has made herself a poncho
from the events of yesterday.

She'd wrapped herself up to the eyebrows,
right and left, to hide from the cold.
It doesn't matter to her what's left and what's right,
if she could only get a tiny bit warmer.

She is wrapped in scandals, intrigues,
and football games—down to her heels.
From under Twiggy's model legs
her own bare feet stick out.

Limousines, submarines, rockets
stick to the asphalt when dumped.
Horse races, yachts, stripteases, and banquets
lay always on her peasant shoulders.

And a white store-window llama
in sorrow sees from behind the glass:
the still warm blood of Vietnam showing
through a photo on her shoulder blades.

From beneath the litter of the world's marketplace,
not knowing how to understand any of it,
like a hunted llama, the Inca woman stares—
humanity's Mother of Sorrows.

The era's injustice has bent her,
whole stories weigh her down,
and, like a living sculpture, she is
the truth of the world beneath a pile of lies.

. . .

Oh, you store-window white llama,
nestle up to her hollow chest,
set her free from the rubbish,
lead her away to the Sierra Blanca!

A representative of a Great Power,
I bow to her like a son without words,
before this tormented face—
a face of sorrows with canyons of wrinkles.

Barely breathing beneath the rags,
the greatest power in the world
has crazily taken refuge inside,
you know, it's the human soul.

"Una chica Peruana, gringo!" they cry
with a hiss, but I remain silent.
I don't want to explain to the taxi drivers
that I have found my Peruvian girl.

1971
Lima
TRANSLATED BY ALBERT C. TODD

Satchmo

Great Satchmo plays all bathed in sweat.
A salty Niagara pours from his brow,
but when the trumpet rises to the clouds,
it growls,
           it roars.
He played to the whole world
                        the way he loved.
He is stolen from us now by the grave,
but even before his birth
he was stolen
              from his sweet Africa.
In secret revenge for the chains of his ancestors

310

he enslaves us all
                    like helpless babes.
The whites of his great eyes flicker in sorrow
as he howls and horns about the globe—
this kid from an orphanage
in the town of New Orleans.
Great Satchmo plays all bathed in sweat,
his nostrils smoke
                    like two black muzzles,
and teeth dazzle in his mouth
like thirty white projectors.
And the sparkling sweat pours off
as if a beautiful mighty hippo
has risen
            snorting,
                    from an African river.
Stamping on fan notes with his heel,
and wiping the downpour from his brow,
he throws handkerchief after handkerchief
into the piano's open womb.
Again back to the microphone he goes,
pressing the stage till it cracks,
and each wet handkerchief is as heavy
as the crown of art.
Art is very far
from the lady whose name is Pose,
and when it labors
it's not ashamed of sweat.
Art is
        not the charm of prattlers,
but, full of movement of heavy things,
the tragic labor of a trumpet player
whose music is tatters of lung.
Though art is bartered and sold,
that's not what it's all about.
The poet
            and the great jazzman
are like brothers
                    in their rasping delivery.
Great Satchmo, will you make it to heaven?
Who knows!
                But if you do—play!
Let the good times roll once more!
Shake up

that boring state of little angels.
But so there'll be no remorse in hell,
so death will cheer us sinners up,
Archangel Gabriel,
pass your horn
                        to the better player,
to Louis!

1971
TRANSLATED BY ALBERT C. TODD

Son and Father

Child, be father of the man—
after all, your father is also a child.
He'd *like* to show more authority,
but it's hard—you can tell from his face.

He's reading to you from a book
about Mowgli and Shere Khan,
but deep in himself—wound on festering wound,
he can scarcely stifle a groan.

Child, rather than turning on tears,
cheer him up with a nice noisy game
on his way back from the jungle,
when he can't believe he's really alive.

But with your childish willfulness
and smiling insensitivity,
don't fool about with your inheritance—
your father's pain!

1972
TRANSLATED BY ARTHUR BOYARS AND SIMON FRANKLIN

The Family

And she, the woman whom you loved,
                    whose life you've made a hell,
now looks at you with hate and fear
                    instead of love and warmth,
as reeling home at night again
                    you lean upon the bell,
and, lurching in, defile the house
                    which never did you harm.
In fear, your dog will turn away,
                    you kick at him and miss;
he smells the trouble that you bring
                    and crawls beneath the bed.
Your little son won't come to you
                    tomorrow for a kiss—
the innocence that once shone out
                    from his young eyes is dead.
You wanted to assert yourself
                    as prizing "freedom" more
than ties of family and home;
                    well, now that aim is won.
If you despise the family,
                    it's you who deserve the scorn,
if, marrying, you then reject
                    your wife, your home, your son.
The thought of your unhappiness
                    is terrible; and yet
perversely, it's a pleasure too,
                    to justify your life
by whining to the world at large
                    that you're "misunderstood"...
Just tell me: Have you ever tried
                    to understand your wife?
Attack's the best defense? For shame!
                    when she who bears your name
is so defenseless, and whose life
                    you've helped to stunt and maim;
and when remorse is just a ruse,
                    a ticket you can use
to prove repentance—and then go
                    back out and start again.

And still your son will see in you

                         the idol of his heart;

in his blue eyes the blue's so clear

                        it almost makes you stay,

yet you forget to muss his hair

                    this time as you depart,

and loudly slamming all the doors

                      to "freedom" rush away.

Oh, bless the family, dear Lord,

                  the crown of all mankind,

the very world is borne upon

                  our children's little heads;

the Holy Trinity of life

              is Father, Mother, Child.

The human race itself must be

                a family—or dead.

It's time to stop this game, you fool,

                  before it is too late,

before your wife despises you

                before you've gone too far;

before you are too numb to feel

                the warning hand of fate,

and still can sense the hope within

                the glimmer of a star.

1972

TRANSLATED BY MICHAEL GLENNY

Tips of Hair

There was a meeting by the pond,
short and hope-destroying.
There was understanding of a kind,
limited, because there was so much
between the poles of the earth,
here, on the two ends of the bench
where the man and woman sat silently,
their shoulders shielding two different families,
as if they were two foreign lands.

. . .

And she said, not seriously,
half-guiltily, half-joking:
"Only the tips of my hair still remember
your stroking."
And warding off closeness, as a sorrow,
she somehow suppressed the crying within.
"I'm going to the hairdresser tomorrow
to cut off even this memory."

The man said not a word.
Quietly he kissed her hand
and returned to the dark station,
a drunken, filthy place, but still a friend.
Once more they parted for many years,
bearing a crying wound that smarted
more than any other on earth:
eternal belonging to one another.

1972

TRANSLATED BY ELEANOR JACKA AND GEOFFREY DUTTON (REVISED)

Pompeii

Man falls apart,
                sheds his wits,
if his strength
            of mind
                grows feeble.
Man perishes
            like Pompeii,
bringing down
            Vesuvius
                upon himself.
Eagerness for power
                or vulgar glory
has turned his head,
                has led him by the nose,
but in the underground cauldron
                the lava's already simmering,

the lava
      that
          people themselves have cooked up.
Lava doesn't spare
         temples
           or pedestals,
and it rushes in,
         without ringing the bell,
making molds out of people,
           as it finds them,
burning their flesh,
         preserving their postures.
What will the bankrupt spirit bequeath?
             Molds of indolence,
molds of slavery,
        molds of shameless conceit,
molds of orgies,
       of businesslike copulations,
and inside all these molds—
         nothing!
Man has an urge to buck himself up with blarney,
he bathes in the bootlicking, burbles buckets,
revels in luxury,
       like a Roman swell in a marble bathhouse,
while the volcano
      is already smoking over his shoulder.
He sits there
      pissed as a newt,
he's forgotten
      he gave up being human long ago;
he's forgotten
      why Pompeii was punished—
and amnesia is always
        the start of the trouble.
How the bubbles play inside the goblet!
But in the Pompeii of the tavern
        the black dust
of vexed volcano
      has already settled
on the crucified barbecued chicken . . .

1972

TRANSLATED BY ARTHUR BOYARS AND SIMON FRANKLIN

A Childish Scream

An exasperating childish scream,
loud enough to set off a nervous spasm
among the lovers of a peaceful hour,
forced its rebellious way into Parnassus,
and the cup of patience, so to speak,
of makers of books really ran over.

Shields won't protect you in the least.
There's something crawling, something squealing
under the very feet of Socialist Realism.
The childish slogan screams: "War on the creators!"
How unlike your cold, efficient fathers,
children, it seems you've really broken from your chains!

That snub-nosed youngster is quite vicious.
He keeps on blowing a policeman's whistle
so that his daddy's novel won't work out.
And artistically hopping on one leg,
the daughter of the critic G. is throwing
cherrystones into his "Great Inspiration."

Children keep whistling, make gargling noises,
just to put their fathers off their meter,
suddenly shove a frog onto their desks,
then shout, preventing them from rhyming
such words as *frantic—romantic, winning—sinning,
tractor—tractate, insidiously—deciduously.*

Every now and then, even in poetry,
there comes an hour for relaxation—
for laziness, short wind, belching, a little yawn—
but this blackout of the spirit doesn't last for ever—
a childish scream will burst out from somewhere,
piercing the "peaceful hour," and then explode.

A childish scream is primitively savage,
but only fools and madwomen won't recognize
the greatness of the truth it utters.
Life screams, perched on the carrion it tramples.

A childish scream exasperates you? And rightly so.
Literature does the same.

1972

TRANSLATED BY ARTHUR BOYARS AND SIMON FRANKLIN (REVISED)

A Few Tender Days

A few tender days:
pebbles trembling away
at the touch of our feet
toeing the waves.
On the bloom of your cheek,
in the flow of your hand,
little islands of moles,
sweet with your scent.

We had only one night:
the surf rushed the dam,
the gale-maddened shades
tried to leap from their frames
to the deep as it raged.
Looting the shores,
the gale ripped in two
the starry world formed
by storm-scented lips.

Entangled forever
like brother and sister
or ruin and rise,
passion and fear
fuel the flames;
your arms round my back,
your teeth set in pain,
you frightened yourself
and I am to blame.

One drink is enough,
the cormorant shrieks,

the glum derrick moans,
lugging sand from the beach.
Your pillow is bare:
in that desert of sheets,
meaningfully stuck:
one fine strand of your hair.

There's a strange children's home
where love's minutes and days
like lost children cry
all day and all night.
There, ever more sad,
roaming the shades,
are a few tender days:
your children and mine.

1972

TRANSLATED BY ANTHONY KAHN

Kompromise Kompromisovich

Kompromise Kompromisovich
whispers to me from within:
"Come on, no need to be temperamental,
alter the line just a little!"
Kompromise Kompromisovich
is no fanatical hangman.
In the guise of a friend,
                        thinking grand thoughts,
he pushes us nearer the top.
He encourages drinking (in moderation),
even a little debauchery,
sinners are worth his while:
a bit of sin makes a man
                        a bit of a coward.
Counting it all up on the abacus,
Kompromise, the recruiter,
buys
     us like big

babies, with trinkets.
He buys us with apartments,
bits of furniture,

        togs,

and we drop our hectoring tone,
but we get fairly rowdy—

               if we drink.

Something—

      listen carefully—

           clicks

in the "ZIL"* fridge.
Kompromise, with his little rosy cheeks,
has just sunk his white teeth in the salmon.
Hardly as

      large as a gnome,

that little tramp Kompromise
sometimes

      sticks out his

tongue at us from the TV.
The "Zhiguli"† has just been bought,
and there's that cunning rogue Kompromise
swinging from a string
like a free baby doll!
Kompromise Kompromisovich
is superb as a writer—
the author

      of heartrending

savings books.
Kompromise Kompromisovich,
"our friend,"

      weighed down by his duties,

who, because he's a

        soft and polite little rat,

bit by bit eats us up . . .

1972

TRANSLATED BY ARTHUR BOYARS AND SIMON FRANKLIN (REVISED)

Zavod imeni Lenina (the Lenin Factory).
†Zhiguli is the name of a popular Soviet automobile.

Vietnam Classic

The Vietnam classic
                     was a seventy-year-old child,
with the face of a tired, wise turtle.
Not from his own extraordinary fame
did he suffer,
              but from the fact
                    that he was in fear
of the behavior of a red-haired tomcat
that followed after us with an ulterior motive.
The cat reclined on a bookshelf,
choosing a volume of Saint-John Perse as his mat.
The Vietnam classic kept a wary eye
when he tossed three pepper pods on a saucer,
though cats—
            when sitting half-starved—
won't eat, perhaps, only peppers.
A prose writer,
           but, in essence, a poet,
though afraid of not entertaining,
              as one should—
the classic never once fell to complaining
that
    there wasn't a spare crust in the house.
He poured a drop of whiskey in a glass of water,
and over an alcohol-lamp,
                with a rolling laugh,
heated small pieces of cuttlefish—
a dried delicacy of war.
In him was the striking,
            deeply moving,
spiritual staying power of a Buddhist,
and on a bicyclist's trouser leg
was a forgotten clothespin.
Dismissing with a hand the flames of battle,
he spoke of Bo Tzu-i,
           Baudelaire,
and I thought:
        "What could be meaner—
than to destroy such a man!"
And fear

pierced through,
                broke through,
                                burned through me:
the tomcat
        made a jump
                from the bookshelf.
Burning hunger had flared up in him.
The cat landed near a bottle
and snatched a piece of cuttlefish in his teeth
right from my fork.
The host in Vietnamese screamed:
                                "Scat!"
and, dismayed by the tactless act,
spread his hands,
                visibly afraid,
that I will consider it all unseemly.
I took the cat joylessly in my arms.
The cat himself was none too joyful about the theft,
and I froze with numbness,
                        when
suddenly I sensed:
                he weighed nothing.
A red-haired bit of nature and a warm grain of sand,
trying to arch his back like a wheel,
he was weightless in my palms,
like the fluff of a poplar.
"Forgive me . . ."—
                sadly glimmered in his pupils.
And nothing—
                I say in all conscience—
did I ever hold in my hands heavier
than the weight of that terrifying weightlessness.

1972
Hanoi
TRANSLATED BY ALBERT C. TODD

Who Are You, Grand Canyon?

A thing
      laminating,
            ever bifurcating,
a thing
      melting away
            from itself,
frightened
      by its own terrible weight,
like a lizard
      hiding its soul from the tourists
beneath the rocks.
A thing
      unimaginably old,
something of the very beginning,
            something of the end,
something
      of Cain and Abel.
Womb of the ages,
      turned inside out,
a sphinx
      whose enigma,
            aired out by time,
unsolved by us,
drips away into oblivion.
The body of history,
      not split into chapters,
but ripped asunder by a tomahawk,
both guts and dung.
Granite sandwiches
      of red icebergs,
as if, like sunflower seeds,
      they had pressed into oil cakes
all the blood of the murdered, drop by drop.
Creases,
      like all the wrinkles of mankind
gathered together by eternity.
... Who are you,
      Grand Canyon?
Who are you, Grand Canyon?
      What is it you want?

You
    are the circles of Dante's hell.
Noah's Ark,
      Babylon.
          Hellas.
Roman circuses—
          luxuria of tyrants
on the Arizona sand.
In each of your scorching grains
hide Huns,
      Aztecs,
          Incas,
like fire in tiny pieces of coal.
These precipices
        are redskin chiefs
lodging their wary thoughts
in the caldron
      with spears.
You
    are the partition in all the pyramids,
the walls of the Kremlin
         with the ghost
of Ivan the Terrible in his cowl.
Who are you,
      Grand Canyon?
The answer strains.
The rocks struggle.
        Each one is a clever devil.
They want to press each other down,
but there are no victors:
all are injured
      by the struggle,
all are defeated,
      all are pinned down
by the weight of years.
The rocks languish from the senseless combat.
Afterward
     they huddle together,
and embrace,
and break apart,
hoarsely wheezing at the end.
Those who ruled in grandeur,
all Macedonians,
      Xerxes and Dariuses,

the planters of fear in souls—
fleas
    who only seemed to be giants—
what have they become today
                    in the Grand Canyon?
Red dust
      in the nostrils of mules.
Wretched,
      like Napoleon in Egypt,
I could almost cry out:
           "Help me!"
standing before the face of immortality.
Where is the emperor's cocked hat?
In layers of red,
like a needle in a haystack.
I see—
      jutting out in basalt thickness
the gaunt brush of Hitler's mustache—
hey mule,
      chew it up—it's a trifle!
Into the Grand Canyon
          with all who are sick
                    with megalomania!
As a guest in the abyss,
        the dwarf will quickly understand
that he is a dwarf.
Who are you, Grand Canyon?
               The stratification
of inexplicable existence—
like volumes upon volumes.
Here is no mountainette
        from Disney World.
Like the complete works of Dostoyevsky,
mountains of suffering,
mountains of wisdom!
Nearby newspapers turned to stone,
but unfortunately,
        grown no wiser—
mountains of dung.
Who are you, Grand Canyon?
              You are like the Revolution.
Your roaring waterfalls are uncontrollable,
like the rebellion of Spartacus.
Above the shoals of the Colorado

cliffs—
       like barricades in Paris—
make you young,
           old man.
You
   sail proudly
above the raging torrents
           like the battleship *Potemkin**
which immortalized a princeling's name.
Sputnik there in shadows,
           blacker than pitch,
is like the flashlight of Che Guevara,
somewhere hiding till today.
Who are you, Grand Canyon?
           The image of America.
There are trails like workers'
           and farmers' veins—
they almost could elect you president!
The air of Whitman,
        Robert Frost,
but look around,
         there are chasms beyond chasms.
Hawks in the sky,
        black ravens,
clans of trees,
        grown out above the abyss,
are the descendants of emigrant
          families
who have not forgotten their own land.
The wind—
      a prayerful Mormon chorus.
Cactuses—
      the unshaven hippies of the incline.
As if they were students,
          sudden avalanches.
Like the silent majority,
        the cliffs
have a hard icy crust
        on their foreheads.
You were made, Grand Canyon,
          not by the rules.
You are a skyscraper
        only turned inward.
A stone apple pie.

You,
    Grand Canyon,
             are filled with chimeras,
like a Notre Dame de Paris of America,
and are cluttered with things,
             like a barn.
You,
    like America,
          are restless and not in place,
you,
    like her,
          are uncoordinated and dissonant.
But even though split asunder,
            you are whole—
that's how God made you,
          with a Frank Lloyd Wright
devil's daring.
Who are you, Grand Canyon?
           You are the people's reward.

A young girl descends to the Colorado River.
About sixteen.
        She is so delighted,
sleeping gear juts out of her rucksack.
She looks about unearthly,
          heavenly.
A dog on a safety leash
pulls her
        along the edge of the abyss.
This tourist is a little different:
she has no fear of the deadly risk,
she has no desire to cling to the shadows.
She moves strangely,
         stepping cautiously.
Shudder, Grand Canyon:
        she is blind.
Let not a tiny stone strike her.
Quietly she moves on the leash above the river,
touching the sky with her free hand,
caressing tenderly the clouds with her cheeks
in the morning hour.
There is something of an old woman in her step,
but on her face so many freckles—
childlike all-seeing eyes!

Greedily gulping the air
her skin sees
                    the Grand Canyon,
the miracle of its beauty.
And wounded by its healing beauty,
a blind girl
                    down in the Grand Canyon
is,
    Grand Canyon,
                    above you.

1972
Grand Canyon, Arizona
TRANSLATED BY ALBERT C. TODD

Potemkin: Famed warship of revolutionary action in 1905 (celebrated in Eisenstein's film), named after Catherine the Great's lover and chief minister, Grigorii Aleksandrovich Potiomkin.

Wolf House

I.

Jack London
            named it
                    Wolf House,
bitterly seeing in it a last lair,
fleeing from fame,
as a wolf flees the hounding.
And Jack London might have hoarsely whispered,
                                        sobbing,
from a secret fear that permeated to the very bone:
"The age of the wolfhound has fallen on my shoulders,
but I'm not a wolf by blood."
Fear designed the bedrooms,
                    the dining room, and shelves for books.
Fear projected the swimming pool
                    and reared the chimneys of stone,
but the one who entered without a knock,
                    fear tightly buttoned in black,
was your undying emissary,

human destruction.
But who did the master fear?

He feared false passions,
because at one time

he knew genuine passion,
and he feared guests,

because he loved guests,
but not those

who came

to steal his destiny crumb by crumb,
and also he feared bad news,
though he didn't expect good news,

these cards were not the same suit

as his forebodings.
If the sea would someday come to visit,
then, likely,

it wouldn't be so difficult,
only the sea doesn't come as a guest,
but plays bones with sailors ...
It's more frightening than obscurity,

Martin Eden,
if for someone you are

a pagan idol.
It's more frightening than all washhouses,

Martin Eden,
if by the curious you're seen

right down to the blemishes.
It's more frightening than all knife fights,

Martin Eden,
if your unenviable success

becomes envied.

2.

In that society, where glory

is poison,
literature

is a strange hell,
where amid the hubbub

and screams
brother

roasts brother
in the Lenten butter

of humanism.

In this strange hell
someone
            put the problem thus:
Help—
            only those who've fallen on hard times,
worry to death—
                        all those who've fallen into success.
The mean look of a bastard
                        doesn't offend.
The envy of a friend is terrible,
                        Martin Eden.
There's an urge to scream out,
                        on the verge of tears:
Is it possible fame
            is a matter of luck?!

                        3.

Sullenly you torment the cue with chalk,
drunk over the table.
You're surrounded, dear boy,
on four sides.

If you want to hide your tracks,
there's the old saying
of escaped convicts:
"Lay down on the bottom."

But like someone close,
a flattering devil whispers:
"It's going to be,
            my Jack-Faust,
comfortable
            even on the bottom."

And you built your bottom,
like a demon's work,
so that it would tower
to heaven itself.

And the plans for a bottom-palace,
the cost estimates, the excavation pit
destroyed their creator.
The Devil is a clever devil.

The house burned down—let it vanish,
but the ashes whisper hoarsely:
the genius was burned up
by his own house, and burned totally.

4.

There is in the old film
                    Citizen Kane
a castle,
            whose servants had servants.
Sevrige vases,
                    Saxony porcelain,
and this citizen,
                    a high-class thief,
defrauded
            his own country:
her honor
            he put in his pocket,
and he was caught by no one
                        but a fire:
snarling,
        he ran
                    across tapestries,
and all,
        which was ageless,
went up in clouds
                    of black smoke,
                        stupefying smoke . . .
Thus
    ends
        every cheat:
a lie
    goes up
        in spontaneous combustion.

5.

But you, Jack London,
                    were not
                        a thief—
you amazed everyone with your unselfishness.
Why did the fire condemn you
to such a sentence?
You brought in

honesty
                    like a slap in the face
to the thieving, cowardly riffraff,
but in that exchange,
                         where thieves steal from thieves,
destroying themselves,
you stole from yourself the obscurity,
which meant freedom,
you stole from yourself the sea,
which meant you.
And the fire,
            like a sword of Damocles,
hung over your head.
And it consumed first of all
                         Wolf House,
and then
        it consumed even the master.
There is in fire itself
                    a thief-like something.
It will devour
            even an innocent shelter,
but sometimes I'm astonished
                         what a flair
a fire
    has
        for thieves.

                                6.

Welcome to Wolf House!
Don't try
        to knock.
An omission is concealed in the wreckage.
Life
    will fill it in.
As a justification for passing glory,
grasses long ago
grew over the whole study.
The green flower cluster of mare's tail,
a sheep's mustache . . .
Welcome to Wolf House,
lost sheep!
The latch will not click gaily,
the house will not creak,

and Jack London will not shake in his hands
a cocktail with ice.
Looking like the Kennedy brothers,
he will not set his sharp crew cut
on a northwest course again.
The past is lost.
In the fogs on dry land
his helm
strayed from his tack.
Jack simply let himself go too much
and—(burned out).
Like Johnny dozed off in the train,
he took refuge
in the corner of his own grave,
(laying down on the bottom).
But even in death there's no sense,
when there's no way
even after dying, you can get away
from the hordes of idle gapers.
Tourists
           are glad for your ruins,
glad
      is the dead wolf.
Aim your cameras
and click—all at once!
Welcome to the ashes
of another's hopes!
Here are neither doors nor even hinges,
but the walls
                are the same.
I warn you:
             Be careful,
slipping in sideways,
but you can still touch them
with your little finger.
Oh, how you love to touch trifles,
the dust of greatness,
as if you will change yourself
after setting him straight.
And, frightening carefree people,
from far away
above the ash heap is heard
                    only White Fang's

eternal
    howl.

1972
Valley of the Moon, California — Moscow
TRANSLATED BY ALBERT C. TODD

Two Blacks

An enormous black man
                    lies near the ocean in Florida.
He throws pebbles in the sky,
                catches them,
and the disturbing question:
                "What are you doing?"—
does not dawn
          on his violet lips.
Blacks now do not lionize
              Harriet Beecher Stowe—
and if a black,
        an anguished black,
                groans—
he prefers to do it at night,
          at home.
But here, on the beach,
           he spreads out a newspaper,
and in truth
      is proud
        of his blackness,
and exposes to the sun
          his white heels
so they will turn a little dark
            beneath the sun.
And next to the black—
         are another's faded jeans.
An odd kind of white man
          with gooseflesh.
He's running away

as if from the jailer
                    of life.
He's completely overwrought,
                    knowing
                              that he's a fugitive.
They catch him, they return him . . .
                         No, they won't hang him,
but once again chain him to the job
                         that's killing him.
And the black—could
                    give him useful advice,
how to get away.
                   But the white is afraid to ask questions.
And he envies
          the black sprawled out,
when he sees his body,
                    all taut,
his blissful devil-may-care languor,
the loftiness
          of a slave, now free.
And in coming to this shore
                    the white thinks,
to rest his nerves in nature
                    at least a little:
In all the world
          there's neither black nor white,
in all the world
          there are only jailers
                         and victims.
Two Negroes lie here.
                    Where is he—their common John Brown?
Two Negroes lie here,
               not consulting,
                         not quarreling,
and the all-understanding,
               arching sea
licks the wounds
          of mankind.

1972

Florida

TRANSLATED BY ALBERT C. TODD

335

Saints of Jazz

The Saints of Jazz are playing.
Gray hair shakes to the beat,
and oldness, of course, is terrible,
but like youth, it comes just once.

Senile quick movement is sad,
yet age is younger than youth,
when a youngster grown wiser
pounds the keys within.

Looking like a kitchen cook,
the mulattress cross-handed
bangs jauntily on a baby grand,
and, fat and black, it dances away.

Without envy for green youngsters,
an old codger clowns on a trumpet,
and his unbuttoned collar
plunges into a mug of beer.

His neighbor lists decrepitly,
but with a cagey wanton in his eyes,
he plucks the double bass
like a gorgeous giggling girl.

The drummer's hands are a ballet.
Where's old age in a gray-haired tomboy?
Like a white lady, a smile
dances on the black face.

Their throats and thoughts are hoarse,
but the sounds are refreshing and youthful—
now slack, like the Mississippi,
now, like Niagara, stormy and wild.

Ah, how much the jazz artists
of all countries have stolen from here,
but nevertheless New Orleans
was not taken from New Orleans.

The Saints of Jazz are playing—
magnificent old people.

You, our blasphemer-age, be compassionate—
safeguard at least these Saints!

Earth's not crowded with saints,
and if it's up to us,
then let there be art—
jazz, at least, as last resort.

The harsh slave market of the stage
wrings dry its slaves,
and if the slaves are a trifle old,
they will be hidden in a grand piano of graves.

Life goes skidding downhill,
and if there is no way out,
then to the blues let it roll on,
ringing twilight in the end.

Sunset is not the end for a poet,
nor is death for you, musician.
The eternal strength of dawn
is in you, O noblest sunset.

1972
New Orleans
TRANSLATED BY ALBERT C. TODD

From Desire to Desire

To H. Sard

I.

My honeymoon was strange,
                both a joy and a wound.
The sweetness of honey,
            the heaviness of honey,
                    in my exhausted body.
My honeymoon was bitter,
              a crazy chase
from desire to desire,
                with desire behind the wheel.
The fulfillment of desire

is often the death of desire,
and then—a desert in the body,
if it really doesn't matter
whose body, next to yours,
has also become a desert.
And two sweating cadavers lie together . . .
How many times it has been this way, but . . .

2.

For all my offenses, life
has fully paid me out with the stars of Florida,
with the childish shamelessness of your Lolita hands,
and the purity of your Cinderella eyes.
When in one's soul
there is calculating sobriety,
then even a kiss
is lewd and loathsome.
In love all impertinence is permitted,
shamelessness unvarnished is permitted.
Sex alone
is no more than reciprocal masturbation.
The bed is pure
when an angel is at your side.
The one who loves,
God has saved from the dirt.
And we loved, however best we could.
Desire never adorned itself in words.
After fulfillment
desire did not end.
Desire pitched and rolled in our eyes.
Desire radiated from our skin.
Desire itself desired us.

3.

The love of two moving cadavers
dressed in naked words,
even with all the tricks refined,
is dead,
dead,
dead.
Love is alive,
the love of people, that is,
and not brute animals—
when with desire,

the one you desire
gazes into your eyes.

                                        4.

Hobos in a car,
we stopped,
            and stopped,
                        and stopped,
and never stopped loving
with love's own permission.
Love is
        the master license
to kill dark instincts,
                    the religion
of all the unfortunate,
                    the party
of all the oppressed.
Through all the chewing of chewing gum,
over all America,
flew our unquenchable desire,
pure like the Virgin's body.
Deadly curves screamed,
neon hissed,
            docks creaked.
Motel Bibles whispered,
their pages turning over with our breathing.
Elegant ladies looked askance
as we embraced,
            but nonetheless,
the alligators understood us
with their kind,
            fatherly eyes.
Primary campaigns were in full swing:
hustling,
        wheeling,
                dealing,
but we had such good luck
we simply elected each other.

                                        5.

And in the starry, dragonfly twilight
a tiny fire on the pointed little end
of a dry twig of jasmine
smoldered like a firefly

through the horror of the world.
And we are fragrant
like jasmine,
                    sweet Hanna.
The honey was bitter
                    from the immutability
that you will slip away,
                    melt,
or break like a twig
and cease to scent the air about you.
But the honey roams through me
                              in syrupy leisure,
rewarding everything,
and blinding and scalding within
a star is born again.
And at the earliest early each morning,
when the blue honey of desire is rocking,
the roar of the Gulf of Mexico
impatiently awakens us.
All problems of laundry and repair
are flooded by the honey.
                    Your freckles
move in the foreground
                    like grains of sand
fastened by the ocean,
or like spray from that honey
whose pseudonym for us is nature.
A whole day was too little for the honey.
Desire smoldered through our eyelashes
and on your breast arose
two cranberries from St. Louis.

6.

Where there is no love,
                    how foul
                              and disgusting
to copulate—
                    even though you sob with tears.
When we love,
          nothing is base or tasteless.
When we love,
          nothing is shameful.
When we love,
          there is freedom within.

The honey liberates us
                    from bondage,
and the smell of honey,
                    and the smell of honey
forgives everything,
                    permits everything.
When we love,
                    it is not our fault
that the thirst for honey dances in our throats,
and all who love
                    are Huckleberry Finns
with mustaches of honey
                    they've snitched.

                    7.
They are unhappy whose
body and soul are parted.
To make love, as one makes something,
is all that they have been given.

How boring to be a playboy.
Who was Don Juan? A castrate.
It's no purer to be a monk.
A kind of debauchery.

But we sinned boldly,
sinned without sinning.
The soul was as the body
and the body as the soul.

Eyelashes to eyelashes,
thick honey moving through them,
and there was no boundary
between the body and the soul.

                    8.
The slow death of desire,
both mine and yours.
The resurrection of desire,
both yours and mine.
Slow, ductile honey,
                    mighty honey,
give not satisfaction—
                    give thirst,

torment me with the ebbing of the tide,
reward me with its flood.

9.

Setting the body above the soul,
                  life deserves a monster.
Setting the soul above the body
                  is a false kind of freedom.
Help me, Mother Nature,
              not to be among the crippled.
Help me, so that the sweetness,
                  so that the heaviness,
                          so that even the bitter taste
                                of honey
will glue my soul and my body
                together forever!

1972
Florida
TRANSLATED BY ALBERT C. TODD

I Would Like

I would like
        to be born
                in every country,
have a passport
         for them all
to throw
        all foreign offices
                into panic,
be every fish
        in every ocean
and every dog
         in the streets of the world.
I don't want to bow down
             before any idols
or play at being
         an Orthodox church hippie,

but I would like to plunge
                    deep into Lake Baikal
and surface snorting
                somewhere,
                            why not in the Mississippi?
In my damned beloved universe
                            I would like
to be a lonely weed,
                but not a delicate Narcissus
kissing his own mug
                    in the mirror.
I would like to be
                any of God's creatures
right down to the last mangy hyena—
but never a tyrant
                or even the cat of a tyrant.
I would like to be
                reincarnated as a man
                            in any circumstance:
a victim of Paraguayan prison tortures,
a homeless child in the slums of Hong Kong,
a living skeleton in Bangladesh,
a holy beggar in Tibet,
a black in Cape Town,
but never
        in the image of Rambo.
The only people whom I hate
                    are the hypocrites—
pickled hyenas
            in heavy syrup.
I would like to lie
        .   under the knives of all the surgeons in the world,
be hunchbacked, blind,
                suffer all kinds of diseases,
                                wounds and scars,
be a victim of war,
                or a sweeper of cigarette butts,
just so a filthy microbe of superiority
                                doesn't creep inside.
I would not like to be in the elite,
nor, of course,
            in the cowardly herd,
nor be a guard dog of that herd,
nor a shepherd,

343

sheltered by that herd.
And I would like happiness,
                    but not at the expense of the unhappy,
and I would like freedom,
                    but not at the expense of the unfree.
I would like to love
                all the women in the world,
and I would like to be a woman, too—
                                just once . . .
Men have been diminished
                        by Mother Nature.
Suppose she'd given motherhood
                        to men?
If an innocent child
                stirred
                    below his heart,
man would probably
                    not be so cruel.
I would like to be man's daily bread—
say,
    a cup of rice
                for a Vietnamese woman in mourning,
cheap wine
            in a Neapolitan workers' trattoria,
or a tiny tube of cheese
                    in orbit round the moon.
Let them eat me,
                let them drink me,
only let my death
                be of some use.
I would like to belong to all times,
                            shock all history so much
that it would be amazed
                what a smart aleck I was.
I would like to bring Nefertiti
                    to Pushkin in a troika.
I would like to increase
                the space of a moment
                                a hundredfold,
so that in the same moment
            I could drink vodka with fishermen in Siberia
and sit together with Homer,
                    Dante,
                        Shakespeare,

and Tolstoy,
drinking anything,
except, of course,
Coca-Cola,
—dance to the tom-toms in the Congo,
—strike at Renault,
—chase a ball with Brazilian boys
at Copacabana Beach.
I would like to know every language,
the secret waters under the earth,
and do all kinds of work at once.
I would make sure
that one Yevtushenko was merely a poet,
the second—an underground fighter
somewhere,
I couldn't say where
for security reasons,
the third—a student at Berkeley,
the fourth—a jolly Georgian drinker,
and the fifth—
maybe a teacher of Eskimo children in Alaska,
the sixth—
a young president,
somewhere, say even in Sierra Leone,
the seventh—
would still be shaking a rattle in his stroller,
and the tenth . . .
the hundredth . . .
the millionth . . .
For me it's not enough to be myself,
let me be everyone!
Every creature
usually has a double,
but God was stingy
with the carbon paper,
and in his Paradise Publishing Company
made a unique copy of me.
But I shall muddle up
all God's cards—
I shall confound God!
I shall be in a thousand copies to the end of my days,
so that the earth buzzes with me,
and computers go berserk
in the world census of me.

I would like to fight on all your barricades,

humanity,

dying each night

an exhausted moon,

and being resurrected each morning

like a newborn sun,

with an immortal soft spot

on my skull.

And when I die,

a smart-aleck Siberian François Villon,

do not lay me in the earth

of France

or Italy,

but in our Russian, Siberian earth,

on a still-green hill,

where I first felt

that I was

everyone.

1972

TRANSLATED BY THE AUTHOR

Kazan University: A Poem (Excerpts)

Lesgaft

... A person who has allowed himself to act in such a manner ... should not be tolerated in Education Service ...

—A note inserted in the report of the Minister for Enlightenment, D. A. Tolstoy, in connection with an article by P. Lesgaft in the St. Petersburg Gazette *that revealed the state of affairs in the University of Kazan*

The Tsar's Resolution: It goes without saying that he must be discharged, must not be allowed to continue.

Every arbitrary act is very sad, but it is still sadder, and more distressing, when there is no defense against arbitrary admininstration and unlawful action, when people refuse, not only to understand, but even to listen to what is going on . . .

—*P. F. Lesgaft**

"Why have you,
                    dearest Piotr Franzevich,
got involved in seditious affairs?
Your love for liberal phrases
has led you into foolishness.
It is unprofitable to get involved in politics.
You'll get eaten up with whatever kind of sauce,
only the buttons will be spat out . . ."
"They won't spit them out . . .
                    they bear the coat of arms, after all."
"When you have such talent for anatomy,
to spoil a career in one moment!
Why, explain to me?"
                    "Is that necessary?
After all, your conscience
                    is only rudimentary."
"That means I am a scoundrel?"
                    "Not completely.
That you are a complete coward
                    is true,
and cowardice has long been
a nourishing medium for infamy."
"But subtle strategy also exists.
Sometimes it is wiser
                    to retreat.
Posterity glorifies
only the one
          who knows how to retreat.
Stubborn rashness is senseless . . ."
"But often,
          when we rationalize,
the beautiful word *strategy*
is only a pseudonym for cowardice . . ."
"Aren't you tired of writing protests?"
"A bit . . ."
          "You'll soon be completely sick of it.
No social protest is worth a scientific discovery.

The wall will not crumble,
                    because you shout..."
"If it only totters,
                    that is enough.
Social protest
                    is the discovery
of oneself
                    for oneself.
It is time to get rid of this wall.
There is water under the still stone..."
"It does flow, rest assured, Piotr Franzevich,
but it is less trouble for the stone..."
"No,
        this progress by small degrees
is just as ridiculous, forgive me,
as putting iodine on the legs of the bed
where the ill man
                    lies groaning.
An idiot would make a better doctor.
What is all this rotten regime?
A malignant growth!
But we treasure it so!
To what purpose these magical exorcisms?
The spirits will not descend from above.
Only surgical intervention
can possibly save Russia!"
"To slash living tissue?
                    Can't you see
the danger?"
                    "Of course I can, I'm sober.
But one should make a decisive cut
with the scalpel of publicity..."
"But where are you living,
                    Piotr Franzevich?
You must have completely forgotten
                            where.
To talk in Russia
                about equality and fraternity?!
That's asking for the whip!
Should censorship soften even slightly
what will be printed?
                    Smut?
Shall we disband the police force?
                            Just wonderful!

All shops will be looted in a second.
And your downtrodden brother,
                          barking at you furiously—
because your spectacles aren't the right kind—
will knock you down
                      with an axle,
as a symbol for 'fraternity.'
All this
          is my cold reasoning,
the fruits of my mediations,
                          there you are!
But tell me,
          Piotr Franzevich,
how do you see
              our future?"
"I see a different Russia:
a Russia ruled neither by the whip
nor by axles used as clubs,
both are alien to me.
She will be ruled, not by a pack of mongrels
but by the best people of the nation."
"You are naive ...
              Neither now, nor in the future,
can power be in the hands of the people.
The people are beasts of burden,
                          Piotr Franzevich,
and if, at times, the people,
disgruntled shake their yoke,
it's not at all because they thirst for freedom.
It's better fodder
              they would like
It's cleaner sties
              they're after ...
The educated need freedom,
but the illiterate: fodder.
What need has he of your call to protest?"
"The struggle for freedom is a great education
in itself ..."
"Or perhaps only a change of yoke?"
"Are you trying to scare me?"
                      "I side with the optimists.
Wide vistas will yet be flung open,
and the real Truth, as queen, will yet ascend
the Russian throne.

Of course, we are somewhat barbaric,
a little brutish, too, of course,
and we have been torn out of history,
but we will thrust ourselves back in.
We are Pushkin's heirs,
                              and Herzen's.
We are the seed.
                    We will yet bear fruit.
The meaning of 'intelligentsia'
will be the same as 'the people,' yet."
"Would you permit me
                    an indiscreet question?
It seems you have been expelled from the faculty,
but are still carrying on
                              regardless?
Forgive this ticklish question,
but I am curious,
                    it's one of my faults."
"I am
    a citizen.
        From this faculty
one can never be expelled."

Saturday

A provincial newspaper presents an interesting list of expenses incurred by an official who was sent to the provinces in the course of duty. "Two glasses of vodka— 20 kopeks, one glass—10k., one carafe of vodka—40k., one herring—30k., two servings salad—60k., one serving stew—30k., four servings suckling pig—1 ruble 20k., six servings ice cream—1r. 80k., one bottle wine—2r., one bottle bicarbonate of soda—25k., one bottle tokay—5r., two bottles lemonade—60k., one glass vintage vodka—15k., one serving suckling pig—30k., one serving beefsteak—40k., one serving cake—25k., nuts—30k., one bottle beer—30k., one wax candle—10k., samovar—10k. 1 serving whiting—40k., one bottle beer—30k., necessary relaxation after work (?!)—10r.

Total, no more and no less than 28r. 10k.

—From the Kazan newspaper
The Volga Herald,
2 April 1877

A harsh avenger will arise, and his strength will be greater than ours.

—From a revolutionary song

"Watchman,

what's all the noise in the street?
Do they have to be flogged again?"
"But it's Saturday...

Russia's on a spree...
A booze-up,

your hiccellence..."
People,

blue with cold,
hug lampposts.
Outside it's forty degrees below,
inside it's forty proof.
Who is hounding Russia?
Who is running Russia?
A mistress in glass—
accursed vodka.
Horses gallop over the drunk.
God,

what's going on!
Vodka nowadays in Russia
is like an empress!
A crown of sealing wax
is on the imperial locks,
a salted cucumber,
is the empire's scepter.
Your eyes,

Russia,

are bleak,
and your weakened hands

shake.
You won't swim far away
along the Mother Vodka.
If you are seeing double,
Russia,

you are doubly feeble.
A drunkard when drunk isn't scared,
but when sober, a drunk

is a coward.
Hey, muzhik,†

are you reaching again for the glass?
But when hands are shaking
you can't hold a paling,
you can't ring alarm bells.

Or weren't you beaten well enough,
or was that less useless—
in the tsar's own monopoly
you're not all dangerous.
When you're drunk,
                        tsar and priest
                                    are your kin,
you could kiss them on the chin.
You and the powers
                        are like blood brothers, today
you down your vodka
                        and so do they.
And through the town of Kazan,
flattening the peasantry,
stately sleighs speed on
with gilded tassels dangling.
"Jews and ragged rabble,
get out of the way,
                        into the ditch!"
Here comes the drunken chief of gendarmes
with Aza
                        daughter of the gypsy tents.
And jingling her earrings
Azotchka hangs
a garter rose,
still warm from her thigh,
on Colonel Gangardt's
military cockade.
Meanwhile in Shchetinkin's rooms
                                    such a racket!
Champagne in volleys
                        shoots up to the ceilings.
To hell with the pretext—
                        celebrate, Russia—Asia,
and a touch of obscenity
                        is a sauce for good measure.
The merchants are so drunk
                        they'd turn their pockets inside out.
Money was got by cunning,
                        and to spend it—
                                    d'you think it's hard?
Bring on the chicken giblets
                        and the blackberry pies,
but if they're offered horsemeat—

they never know the difference.
Croaking like a guildmaster,
                jingling his belly chain,
a merchant, his legs sagging,
                just makes it to the wall.
He shouts in a drunken rage,
                his bloated belly bursting:
"I want to walk out right here to piss,
                cut out a door to let me!"
Meanwhile the Russian mob below
has poked its nose into the snow,
glowering.
Whipping itself with air.
Like false liberty,
that filthy whore,
                Saturday,‡
is stripping herself bare!
But in Lyssy's beer shop
where even pigeon's milk's on tap,
the waiter, like a fox,
is hopping and eavesdropping.
Watching you,
                boys,
Pop, as they call him,
scoops up news
worth reporting.
Saturday:
                is a cow of a day,
there is a harvest of drunks,
and if swearing
                were sedition,
all Russia would be behind bars.
But the waiter's ear
is twitching,
                twitching,
                        twitching,
toward the hanged boy's brother
who sits silently, as yet.
As yet he's a young adolescent,
with an unruly head of hair,
but his general stern appearance
is much older
                than his years.
And let them holler recklessly,

to the ringing of their glasses,
rebellious silence
speaks louder than any blustering.
A tipsy, well-off, reactionary student
lurched up with a half-pint glass:
"Hey, you seem a decent fellow,
let's drink to progress!"
Waiter,

      twist all this on your mustache!
He is silent.

        Any minute he'll explode.
Bloody circles widen
in front of boyish eyes.
He stands up awkwardly,
crookedly, as if impaled,
and whispers to no one, yet to all:
"I shall avenge my brother!"
No, it is not meant for tipsy elegance,
but directed somewhere much farther:
"I shall avenge,

      I shall avenge,
I shall avenge my brother!"
Did you note that, waiter,

        did you write it down?
Now whistle for a gendarme.
A genius is always the informer
on his very thoughts.
As yet he is young and easily broken,
and he makes one feel frightened.
As yet his understanding of "brother"
is limited only to "Sasha."§
But the pain of a closer kinship
will pierce him very soon:
for a man's brother

      is anyone
whom injustice has slain.
And a brother is anyone

      whose groan is heard
in fields or factories,
and a brother is anyone

      who's oppressed
but strives for freedom.
And the vision of the Day of Judgment
catches every executioner's breath,

and revolution is always, in the end,
the avenging of a brother's death.

A Tartar Song

When peoples, all quarrels forgotten . . .
—A. Pushkin

Whomever you may talk to, do not think about
his religion, but concentrate on his mind.
—Kayum Nasyri"

Even the watchman's wife Parashka
shouts at the Armenian:
                    "Hey, Armyashka!"
Even some slovenly slut
shrieks at a gray-haired Jew:
                    "You Yid!"
Even some lousy peasant makes a crack
at a harmless Pole:
                    "Polack!"
Even a drunk,
            in the gutter thinks
he can turn on a Tartar:
                    "Hey you, prince!"
The poor beggars,
            driven to bestiality,
are taught by the pub
            and by authority
concepts of personal superiority:
"I may be off the bottom
                    but I've a Russian soul!"

But Volodia# remembers Kokushkino,**
and burrs stuck to a whip's tail
and the gentle swaying of bluebells
and Bakhavy, the Tartar shepherd boy.
And tossing a hot baked potato

from the palm of one hand to the other,
Bakhavy starts
                        his song,
his sad song,
                    taken up by sighing willows:
"Sarý, sarý sap-sary!
Sarý, chechék, saplary.
Sagynyrsyn, sargairsyn,
kil'se sugysh, cheklary.
Yellow, yellow, yellow,
are the flowers. Out of sorrow?
Times of war and times of trouble
make you yellow, make you feeble . . ."

Twigs are crackling in the fire
and it aches
                    with a familiar pain.
It's so very Russian, this song,
could it be because
                        it is a Tartar song?
And the empire,
                    mother of many monsters,
personified by a double-headed eagle,
has become a terrible prison of peoples,
including even the Russians themselves.
But not only Russian devils have tails,
so also has the Tartar *shaitan* . . .
The minaret, like an old man's pale finger,
is raised above the mosque of Kazan.
Here, hidden from the rest of the kingdom,
is a kingdom of sorrows and wounds,
and on Tartar faces the wrinkles
are to Russians a well-known Koran.

Volodia wanders into the mosque
where, on the dusty stone floor,
whisper among themselves the lost
and ragged
                    by Allah ignored.
And not far off, in Christ's temple,
dropping a thousand tears on the floor,
the candles whisper among themselves
of all those

whom Christ ignored.
Shadows sway, each one solitary,
lifting their hands to a common heaven.
All have the same enemy—
                    oppression,
only the gods of each vary.
The rabbi prophesies a Jewish heaven,
the most Orthodox bliss is promised by the priest,
but, not believing in such heavenly salvation,
Tukai†† would smile and bitterly insist!
"Sacred truth, faith, and honor
                        are valued less than gold,
gold is more mighty than the Gospels,
                        the Koran, and the Talmud."
But (God's children),
                    will anything unite you,
you Tartar,
        you Russian,
                you Jew?
Can it be that money,
            only money,
is the common creed of men?
And you, mullah,
            mumble dully,
through your gross folds of fat,
that there is no god, save Allah,
and his prophet—
            Muhammad?!
But no, salvation
            is not in icons,
not in invocations of the gods,
and not in Muhammad or Jehovah;
mankind will have to save itself.
And this belief will be shared by all men,
and a time will come when someone will say:
"There is not god, there is only man,
and his prophet—
            is he, himself."
And let there sound above the idols
a song, which deifies mankind,
that simple song of yours,
            Bakhavy,
that pure and simple song:

"Sarý, sarý, sap-sary!
Sarý, chechék, saplary.
Sagynyrsyn, sargairsyn,
kil'se sugysh, cheklary."

1970
Kazan—Moscow

TRANSLATED BY ELEANOR JACKA AND GEOFFREY DUTTON (REVISED)

*Lesgaft: Piotr Franzevich Lesgaft (1837–1909). Russian teacher, physician, and important theoretician and researcher in anatomy and psychology.
†muzhik: Russian for "peasant," "lout," or "bumpkin" also used colloquially for "man" or "fellow."
‡Saturday (*Subbota*): The Russian word *Subbotnik* derived from "Saturday" is the euphemistic name given to a Soviet officially organized day of "voluntary" labor levied on students and workers.
§Sasha: The familiar form of Aleksandr, the name of Lenin's brother whose execution by the tsarist regime spurred his revolutionary life. The full poem treats many famous persons who studied at Kazan University.
"Kayum Nasyri: Tartar educator, writer, and scholar of great eminence (1825–1913).
#Volodia: Diminutive of Vladimir, Lenin's first name.
**Kokushkino: Now the town of Lenina, not far from the Kazan, where the Ulianovs, Lenin's family, spent a month in the summer of 1887.
††Tukai: Abdullah Tukaev (1886–1913). Tartar poet and editor of the satirical journal *Lightning*, published in Kazan in the first decade of this century.

Under the Skin of the Statue of Liberty: A Poem (Excerpts)

"I'm Raskolnikov. Yes, the very same,
in shoes worn thin,
prodigal son, beloved by Mamma,
even with blood on my pale hands.

From miserable staircases spattered with spittle,
apartments permeated with the stench of kero-
    sene,
the consumptive Petersburg moon
directed me to the old woman.

With an ax under my coat flap I thought:
Humanity is one thing, but an old woman,

like a mere artifact, is something else,
and it's all the same whether alive or not.

And I didn't pity the old woman,
only she trembled and trembles still now,
but the pregnant housemaid
turned up under that same ax.

And with eyes still blind the child
pounded in her murdered belly.
He who slays something bygone—
instantly slays someone's future.

But, tottering with torment,
climbing to that floor,
I didn't think then that I would serve
as someone's justification for murder.

On a billboard in neon radiance
I am an exciting movie hero,
and the Raskolnikovs of New York
walk beneath me somewhere below.

The past repeats itself as farce,
and in the darkness of alleys and courtyards
"baloneys" bulge out
from optical axes.

Here it is, the root of the world's woe:
Humanity is one thing, but a victim,
like a mere artifact, is something else,
and it's all the same, whether alive or not.

—————

Senator Robert Kennedy had unusual eyes.
They were alway tense.
Like pale blue razor blades they pierced through anyone in conversation with him as if someone dangerous were lurking behind the person's back.
Even when the senator smiled and his golden forelock leaped on a mountain skier's peeling, sunburned forehead, and blinding white teeth capered in his mouth like children on the grass, his eyes lived a separate guarded life. For his birthday today he wore a bright green jacket, raspberry bow tie, gay plaid trousers, and light suede shoes. However, all of this bright multicolored

clothing was planned to distract the guests from the main thing—the host's eyes.

The senator's energetic hands assisted his guests in removing their over-coats and tousled the clipped heads of numerous little Kennedys who had composed some domestic jazz and were rapturously banging on metal plates. The senator's thin lips smile, knowing full well how enchantingly they do it, and at the same time they manage to say something particularly pleasant to each guest.

But the senator's eyes—two blue clots of will and anxiety—caressed no one on the head, smiled at no one. They inhabited his face like two beings uninvolved in the general gaiety. Within these eyes an exhausting hidden work transpired.

"Remember my words—this man will be president of the United States," Averell Harriman said bending toward me.

The table was dominated by the celebrated columnist Art Buchwald, who looked like a kindhearted, well-fed tomcat that nonetheless, from time to time, loved to dig his claws into those who pet him.

Buchwald artfully demonstrated his independence by deftly and casually ridiculing everything and everybody, including the master of the house. Wise kings always invited mercilessly venomous jesters to their festivities. Jesters have always ridiculed kings in their presence, which made them appear even wiser. A tamed accuser is not frightening, but rather useful. However, only wise kings have understood this.

And Robert Kennedy, laughing loudly in delight at Buchwald's talented mockery of him, embraced the columnist, and they clicked their glasses to-gether.

But the senator's eyes continued to work.

Meanwhile, a game of blindman's buff was organized.

A long-legged artist, who had put a black band over her eyes, wandered about the room in uncertainty, her arms, draped in red chiffon, stretched out searchingly.

Her fingers, manicured the color of the moon, were barely stirring as they approached the tongue of flame flickering above a candle.

"Watch out, you'll burn yourself on the candle . . ." said the senator standing nearby.

"And that's you, Bobby." The woman burst out laughing and rushed in the direction of his voice.

Bobby adroitly dodged her and leaped away toward a wall. But the woman with the black band over her eyes went straight toward him, preventing an escape route by her outstretched arms.

Bobby pressed himself against the wall as though he were trying to squeeze himself into it, but the wall would not let him in.

When the evening had reached its end, Robert Kennedy and I stood alone in the corridor. In our hands were antique crystal goblets in which tiny green sparks of champagne were dancing.

"Tell me, do you really want to become president?" I asked. "It seems to me that it's a rather thankless job."

"I know." He grinned. Then he became serious. "But I would like to continue my brother's work."

"Then let's drink to that," I said. "But in order for it to come true, according to an old Russian custom, we must drain the goblets right to the bottom and then smash them against the floor . . ."

Glancing at the goblets, Robert Kennedy suddenly became embarrassed.

"All right, only I must ask Ethel's permission. These are heirlooms from her dowry . . ."

He disappeared with the crystal goblets and appeared later still more embarrassed: "Wives will be wives . . . I got some other glasses that were on hand in the kitchen . . ."

It surprised me somewhat that one could think about some insignificant glasses when such a toast was being proposed, but, of course, wives will be wives. We drank in one gulp and simultaneously threw down the emptied goblets. But they didn't break and, bouncing softly, rolled over the red shag of the rug.

I have always been superstitious and a terrible foreboding passed through me. I looked at Robert Kennedy. He had turned pale. Probably he too was superstitious. In this respect politicians aren't very different from poets.

The work in the senator's eyes came to a halt. They grew still, staring at the unbroken goblets.

Robert Kennedy picked up one of them and tapped it with his finger. The sound was muted and dull.

The goblets were made of transparent plastic.

Since then I never ask others to break their glasses and I try never to do it myself.

"I, Robert Kennedy, Bobby,
                          was shot by the age,
            nominated to the gods
                          in the absence of a god.
Money was good to me.
                          People loved me
            for my name—or
                          for my blue eyes.
But there is a special something
                          on the brow of the favored,
            like the cross of murder
                          on the doors of the Huguenots.
And I was slain,
                          not as an example to hypocrites—
but because a forelock too eagerly

distinguished itself against the gray.
It's easy to aim at a lamp,
                    it's difficult at something not concrete.
Brightness is talent's weakness,
                    grayness the strength of the ungifted.
With a vengeance I have hated
                    grayness—the curse of the age—
from the time when at my brother's side
                    I became the attorney general.
With no satisfaction
                    and a heavy heart,
I climbed into skyscrapers of denunciations.
                            Their architect is grayness!
Grayness chokes zealously,
                    grayness chokes duplicitously
all attempts not to be
                    gray, at least in part.
Grayness is a whore, an ignoramus,
                            but passions are not alien to her.
Grayness leaped from calumny as though from a trampoline
                                        and is in power!
Like a millrace for washing ore
                    grayness sifts through souls.
Whole nuggets are coming down from the ravine!
                            Our gold is grayness!
Throughout the land
                    talent is put into storage
like merchandise that has lost its value.
                    The demand is for grayness, for grayness!
You who inhabit this place, look around you
                            at how freely sprawled
and growing into the seat
                    is the grayness with the chair-like behind.
You who inhabit this place, don't listen
                            to the persuasion of the swamp:
"After all, gray is better
                    than something bloody . . ."
You ought to tremble with a ghastly shudder
                            at a cozy dinner—
for the brown horror
                    is shoving its way behind the grayness.
Instead of idylls, you ought to remember,
                            when slicing your pudding,

how they sank into my forelock

a clot of grayness—a bullet..."

ـنـــــــب

I was not a miracle-maker—the apostles lie.
Popes embellished me, vulgarized me,
but I abide always one and the same,
no friend of death or money changers,
without halos that rub the neck too much,
son of a carpenter, and a carpenter, Jesus.

I grew up amid Galilee's myrtle bushes,
where blue thrushes landing did not bend
the peaceful morning grasses,
and for me, a free urchin, foals wetted
whirlwinds with watery lips
that knew not the bridle's taste.

Both clouds and sheep rubbed themselves
tenderly on my hands in fish scales
by that lake of Tiberius,
when in the warm softened twilight I
stretched out wet nets on stakes
with the moon half stuck in the netting.

But if I drew out the world with a sweep net,
inside me goodness and hatred struggled.
Expending myself now on one, now on the other,
growing conscious of the world's duality,
I both summoned all to turn a peaceful cheek to an enemy,
and with a whip I drove money changers from the temple.

No, I was not a kindly person—that's a fabrication.
I despised you, tyrants and miscreants,
progeny of the viper's family.
I became dangerous—that is, too knowing,
and my snow-white garments
became a banner for all people.

But more frightening than all Roman procurators
is the tidy rote learning of truth,

the flattery of calculating disciples.
Esteeming paradise a lucrative establishment,
the sons of Zebedee already desired
to sit in higher places through influence.

I, a former simple-hearted man of the common people,
am guilty in the crime of Judas.
I educated him and I'm responsible.
And, punishing myself to the utmost,
asking Cain: "Where is your brother, Abel?"
I say to Abel: "Where is your brother, Cain?"

And at supper on my last free day
I felt the imminent betrayal,
hovering above the fraternal fireplace.
A serpent, sometimes, hides even in the falcon,
but is the teaching true, if after all,
the teacher is betrayed by the disciple?!

Shrouded in cowls, the hawk-faced
Inquisition made the sign of the crucifix
over its fires—don't pray for mercy!
And I tore myself down from crucifixes
in the fingers of degenerates
and asked, sobbing out my cry for centuries:
"So this is you—my disciples?"

Throwing brushwood into the flame,
crusaders marched as Christ's army,
with a swastika in embryo on their shield,
and a pious murderer from Auschwitz
sent out Christmas cards, having been informed
that he is burning brothers in Christ.

Now neon hisses. Snow scatters through headlights,
but I see the same Pharisee faces
and the Sadducees' vindictive calculation,
and money changers, driven by me from the temple,
want to expel all those who in the temple of truth
are not sold and do not sell.

And above the planet, burning with rage,
bullets fly, like still-scorching
hot coals of those same Inquisitions,

and feeling myself in the hands of constables,
I shake on crosses with terrible laughter:
"So that's what you are, disciples!"

To be sung of daily by you
and to be crucified daily by you,
I can no longer endure, but weakened
by spittle and lashes, how can I save myself,
crucified on a cross—the creation of a carpenter,
son of a carpenter, and a carpenter—Jesus?!

1968

TRANSLATED BY ALBERT C. TODD

1973/1975

*A poet is always in danger
when he lives too safely*

An Old Friend

I dream of an old friend,
                  who has become an enemy,
but in my dream he's not an enemy,
                        but still the same old friend.
He's not *with* me,
                but he's there wherever I am,
and my head goes
                spinning around with the dreams.
I dream of an old friend,
                  a confessional cry by the walls
on a staircase so steep
                that the Devil would break a leg,
and his hatred,
            not of me, but of those
who had been our enemies
                  and will remain so, thank God!
I dream of an old friend,
                as I would of an old love
that is already
            forever beyond recovery.
We gambled on risk,
                we gambled on conflict,
and now we're enemies,
                  who had been two blood brothers.
I dream of an old friend,
                  like the splashing of banners
is dreamed of by soldiers
                  whose war has ended in wretchedness.
Without him, I'm not "I,"
                without me, he's not "He,"
and if we're enemies,
                it's already a different age.
I dream of an old friend.
                  Like me, he's a fool.
Who's right, who's wrong,
                  I'll not begin to inquire.
What are new friends?
            Better an old enemy.

An enemy can be new,
                              but the only friend is an old friend.

1973

TRANSLATED BY ARTHUR BOYARS AND SIMON FRANKLIN

The Drunken Cow

The cow
              was drinking
                              beer—
spitting with disgust,
                              but drinking.
One thing was clear to the cow:
things were going badly for her.
The cow
              drank
                     out of fright.
The watchman,
                     small, puppet-like,
forced her mouth open
with a sticky bottle of Asakhi.
In the town of Matsusalla,
behind the walls of the abattoir,
they've a cunning ritual for killing:
beer,
       massage,
                     ax.
Tremble, old man,
                     how low can you get!
The cow's destiny is terrible.
She, you realize, is just as Japanese
as you are.
give her some plain mash,
give her some plain grass . . .
Let cows, at least,
be sober in a besotted world!
The cow
              lamented,

sobbing violently,
swaying like a drunkard.
Her coat was black
like the black smoke of Hiroshima.
Her groans shook
the gloomy cow temple.
Her seven hundred kilos
made the earth
                    sag.
People are sensitive,
however,
            only
before the warm beef
has reached the plate.
After the cow had been dispatched to paradise
we ate by the sweat of our brow,
grabbing the delicate morsels
of meat with our chopsticks.
The hostess surveyed the scene proudly.
To this day she remembers
how the actor who played Bond
praised the sukiyaki.
And, sitting at the table,
a drunk with a purple face
                            shouted:
"Friends,
        let's drink to the cow,
who was also a drinker!
For how do we differ from cows
if, simply with a shout of
                            'Cheers!'
somebody pours
sake and beer down our throats?
Munching hay is a dull way to live.
Our own experience is like the cows'—
being served before slaughter
a drink and a massage.
And wherever they treat people
like cattle who drink,
if you don't kick and fight
you're sure to go under.
If a live cow groans,
she's not worth very much.
But after she's been turned into meat,

the price immediately soars.
Let us rise gravely from our mats.
Brothers,
            let's finish drinking in silence
whatever sister cow
has left us in our glasses.
In this joyful paradise,
sodden with the smell of drunkenness,
we ever weep beer—
the beer of bleary eyes—
over the cheapness of our lives,
over drunkenness in the hour of death,
over how expensive we are
when they've slaughtered us."

1973

TRANSLATED BY ARTHUR BOYARS AND SIMON FRANKLIN (REVISED)

Love Is Always in Danger

"Love is always in danger,"
a Japanese girl said to me,
and all at once the era ground to a halt,
the era of strippers and atomic mushrooms;
and with his trousers half off, a tourist
ground to a halt on top of a half-geisha,
and on a sakura a tiny leaf ground to a halt in its growth,
trembling over the fate of the country.
A youth still half a child froze
as he was rushing to the film *Sex Among Animals*,
and so many fingers, bloated, sweaty,
froze in the act of crinkling yen.
Millions of lips froze
a millimeter from a kiss.
On death's naked thighs the equator
froze like a Hula-Hoop.
The world, all around the globe, is ringed

with one and the same fearful risk.
Chopsticks froze over rice,
and, somewhere, spoons over borscht.
In Cambodia snakes froze and sniffed around
at bombs in the grass,
and, a second before betrayal,
you, wincing, ground to a halt in Moscow.
And I ground to a halt in mid-stride
in the ancient city of Kyoto,
where, once again, I was looking for someone,
having forgotten to find myself in myself.
And so, all around, everything *ground to a halt*.
But, just as if their time had now come,
Buddhas stepped down from their pedestals,
shaking the dust from their rusty hands.
Almost unrecognizable,
they set off in columns
through markets, bars, and restaurants,
like demonstrators made of bronze.
They walked past the plastic dishes,
past the beads of the gamblers
and potbellied TVs,
the latest Buddha-substitutes.
Through the gilt of weighty foreheads
the Buddhas' wrinkles could be distinguished.
In the Buddhas' hands floated placards:
"Love is always in danger."

The whole world is always in danger
where wooden shoes step over bones,
where they even bathe children in tubs
among unexploded mines.
A poet is always in danger
when he lives too safely,
when everything is deceptively clear to him,
and he is not afraid for people.
The globe is strapped onto me.
Like an exhausted Japanese girl,
I carry the whole world around, like a sobbing
child, on my back.

1973

TRANSLATED BY ARTHUR BOYARS AND SIMON FRANKLIN

Wisdom and Folly

Wisdom has certainly increased
                                    but folly has not deserted me.
Folly has a most amiable soul.
Folly, a very rabbit,
                        with unabating ardor,
tries to find friends
                        in the slimy society of boa constrictors.
Wisdom gives a wry smile:
                            "Oh, folly, get wise!
Don't look for friends in the scaly family.
You won't find any warmth in cold-snakiness.
A cold snake's
                    forever a cold snake."
Folly stays cheerful:
                        "But under the scales,
I hope,
        there's something human."
Answers wisdom:
                        "Folly, I really don't know whose wife
you can be—
                    except, perhaps, an idiot's!
Now you'll tell me
                    that Myshkin was an idiot
in the reptiles' eyes,
but naive enthusiasm even in folly is no bad quality
if there's the tiniest spark of wit in it.
Give up hoping,
                    folly,
for the balm of somebody's charity,
and change the noble fire of indignation
into lofty disdain."
I listened very closely to the argument,
torn sometimes by pride,
                            sometimes by cowardice,
that I am master of my wisdom,
but not the master of my folly.
There's the folly of the good-for-nothing, and cattle,
there's reckless feats on precipices,
and a man is hardly a man
                            when

he's dead to the blissful folly of yielding to impulse.
What does "getting wise" really mean
when the soul sips the poison of unbelief?
Better that memory should betray me
as long as I've still got my credulity.
Wisdom,
            don't be mockingly morose;
holy Folly, don't get wise
                        and worldly!
I've no respect for wisdom grown foolish,
and folly grown wise gets only my pity.

1973

TRANSLATED BY ARTHUR BOYARS AND SIMON FRANKLIN

A Father's Ear

To M. & I. Kolokoltsev

The footcloths had already dried over the bonfire
and two fishermen were listening to the waters of the Vilyui;
one was,
            I imagine, over fifty,
while the other was
                        still too young to own a passport.
The father brushed the bread crumbs
from his stubble into his palm,
then washed them down with fish soup,
                                    thick as honey.
A tooth—
            gold, as it happened—
clapped against the blackened aluminum of the spoon.
The father was leaden-faced with fatigue.
On his forehead, as if in layers, receded
war,
    work,
            employment without end,
and apprehension for his son—
                        the father's secret cross.
Rummaging for a tear in the net,

the father said,

             thrusting his hand toward the sun:
"Mishka, just you take a look,

                   the mist
is clearing after all . . .

               It's beautiful!"
The son went on eating with a show of scorn.
A white-gold forelock hid his eyes
with such a haughty overhang of hair
as if to say why should I raise my head

                       for such a trifle.
Then he flicked a fish-eye from his sailor's shirt
and pulled his fishing boots right on,
with their billowing turn-downs, proof of the luxury
of this life

           where people know their way around.
The father stamped out the smoking bonfire
and muttered as if completely by the by:
"I can hear from your boots, Mishka,
you've left your footcloths off again . . ."
The son ceased gulping soup from a jar
as if betraying his humiliation.
He pulled off his fishing boots,

                wrapped his feet with footcloths,
and angrily rammed them back into his boots.
But even *he* will understand—

               too late, it's true,
the isolation of our spirit and our flesh
when there is nobody on earth who hears
the things

        heard by a father's ear . . . .

1973
TRANSLATED BY ARTHUR BOYARS AND SIMON FRANKLIN (REVISED)

The Face Behind the Face

Where does it live, the face behind the face?
Everyone ought

to know all that there is
about the face that is his.

People often haven't a clue
about their very own "I."
Each of us makes his own
best defense counsel.

Nero, apparently, thought
he was a poet,
Hitler thought that he
would redeem the world from woe!

The mean man thinks: "I'm so generous."
The shallow man: "I'm profound."
Sometimes God will sigh: "I'm a worm."
The worm hisses: "I'm God!"

Worms climb arrogantly upward.
The coward screams: "I'm brave!"
Only the free man
thinks: "I am a slave."

1973

TRANSLATED BY ARTHUR BOYARS AND SIMON FRANKLIN (REVISED)

For Your Attention

I wish to bring to your attention,
passengers on this rattling train of years,
that on the map there's no sign of
                              the destination
for which you have reserved your tickets.
It has been established with precision in the course of inquiry
that there's no
              station
                      called Second Youth.
I wish to bring to your attention
that you dribbled away your first youth in vain,

babies to the last,
and, regrettably, in you
                    I recognize myself.
I wish to bring to your attention
the fact that farther on are the stations Old Age and Death,
but professing an unconfirmed immortality
you do not care to think of this in advance.
I wish to bring to your attention
the fact that if, gentlemen,
                    your luggage
                              contains
stale goods
          and only the anecdotes are fresh—
why then, you've already arrived
                              at Death station.
I wish to bring to your attention
the fact that the years,
               without further ado,
                              will swallow you all—
only those pale little chickens,
                    which you've gobbled up,
will flutter like phantoms
                    pursuing the train . . .

1973

TRANSLATED BY ARTHUR BOYARS AND SIMON FRANKLIN

Epistle to Neruda

Superb,
          like a seasoned lion,
Neruda buys bread in the shop.
He asks for it to be wrapped in paper
and solemnly puts it under his arm:
"Let *someone* at least think
that at *some* time
                    I bought a book . . ."
Waving his hand in farewell,

like a Roman
        rather dreamily royal,
in the air scented with mollusks,

                oysters,

                    rice,

he walks with the bread through Valparaiso.
He says:
        "Eugenio, look!
You see—
        over there, among the puddles and garbage,
standing up under the red lamps
stands Bilbao—with the soul
            of a poet—in bronze.
Bilbao was a tramp and a rebel.
Originally
        they set up the monument, fenced off
by a chain, with due pomp, right in the center,
although the poet had lived in the slums.
Then there was some minor overthrow or other,
and the poet was thrown out, beyond the gates.
Sweating,
        they removed
            the pedestal
to a filthy little red-light district.
And the poet stood,
        as the sailor's adopted brother,
against a background
        you might call native to him.
Our Bilbao loved cracking jokes.
He would say:
        'On this best of possible planets
there are prostitutes and politutes—
as I'm a poet,
        I prefer the former.' "
And Neruda comments, with a hint of slyness:
"A poet is
        beyond the rise and fall of values.
It's not hard to remove us from the center,
but the spot where they set us down
            becomes the center!"
I remember that noon,
        Pablo,
as I tune my transistor at night, by the window,

now,
      when a wicked war with the people of Chile
brings back the smell of Spain.
Playing about at a new overthrow,
politutes in generals' uniforms
wanted, whichever way they could,
to hustle your poetry out of sight.
But today I see Neruda—
he's always right in the center
                      and, not faltering,
he carries his poetry to the people
as simply and calmly
              as a loaf of bread.
Many poets follow false paths,
but if the poet is with the people to the bitter end,
like a conscience—
           then nothing
can possibly overthrow poetry.

1973

TRANSLATED BY ARTHUR BOYARS AND SIMON FRANKLIN

Wounds

To D.G.

I have been wounded so often and so painfully,
dragging my way home at the merest crawl,
impaled not only by malicious tongues—
one can be wounded even by a petal.

And I myself have wounded—quite unwittingly—
with casual tenderness while passing by,
and later someone felt the pain,
it was like walking barefoot over the ice.

So why do I step upon the ruins
of those most near and dear to me,

I, who can be so simply and so sharply wounded
and can wound others with such deadly ease?

1973

TRANSLATED BY ARTHUR BOYARS AND SIMON FRANKLIN

Memento

Like a reminder of this life
of trams, sun, sparrows,
and the flighty uncontrolledness
of streams leaping like thermometers,
and because ducks are quacking somewhere
above the crackling of the last, paper-thin ice,
and because children are crying bitterly
(remember children's lives are so sweet!)
and because in the drunken, shimmering starlight
the new moon whoops it up,
and a stocking crackles a bit at the knee,
gold in itself and tinged by the sun,
like a reminder of life,
and because there is resin on tree trunks,
and because I was madly mistaken
in thinking that my life was over,
like a reminder of my life—
you entered into me on stockinged feet.
You entered—neither too late nor too early—
at exactly the right time, as my very own,
and with a smile, uprooted me
from memories, as from a grave.
And I, once again whirling among
the painted horses, gladly exchange,
for one reminder of life,
all its memories.

1974

TRANSLATED BY ARTHUR BOYARS AND SIMON FRANKLIN

Mother

Between mother and son
                         there's a fatal lack of equality,
especially if he's grown-up
                         and the only one.
The last man
                  whose eyes a woman tries to attract,
for whom she tries to look smart—is her son.
When my mother
                  sits gently down on the edge
of my bed,
              after pulling off her soaking shoes,
there rises to her lips,
                  not happy, but not reproachful either,
the question, murderously tender:
                         "Son, what's troubling you?"
You can't land an answer from a son
                        even with tenderness as bait.
Ready for
            the ground to swallow me up,
I mumble feebly:
                "Everything's all right . . .
                and by the way, you're looking well . . ."—
using the false rules
              of the cowardly son's game.
Have I really and truly nothing
                  to say to my mother,
who's brought me up,
              only to be ground down so helplessly?
I hide in words:
                "Calm down . . . don't worry about anything . . ."
I do have things to say,
              but I'm sorry for her—
                              I can't speak.
The gulf between us
              is gradually filled with tears,
but one can't bridge the gulf that makes us strangers.
Surely it's unthinkable to load
                  onto my mother's shoulders
burdens I can hardly bear myself.

Fathers can be accidental.
                    Only mothers are always
                                        real.
No power on earth can truly replace them,
and a mother,
            coming on a visit,
                            and then going away—
is already the transgression
                    of her brutal son.
When we grow old,
                then with delayed penance
we come to our mothers,
                        to mounds of moist earth;
then, holding nothing back,
                        we pour out to them
everything that,
            during their lifetimes, we could not say.

1974

TRANSLATED BY ARTHUR BOYARS AND SIMON FRANKLIN

"When I cast off for . . ."

When I cast off for the canopy of ages
I should like to rest in the open air,
not in a rainbowed Garden of Eden,
but in a plain vegetable patch!

So that all around my face
life might guiltily grow green
with pimples of a cucumber,
with its faintly bluish bloom.

And that against my teeth might scrape,
springing nimbly into my lips,
a beautiful delicate carrot,
with earth in its youthful wrinkles.

                    .   .   .

And that a cheeky little shoot,
alarmingly precocious,
might spike me in the side, indecently:
"Move up! You're stunting my growth!"
and I would ask him:

     "Comrade,

Who are you—
   an onion or a garlic?"

1974

TRANSLATED BY ARTHUR BOYARS AND SIMON FRANKLIN

Lament for a Brother

To V. Shchukin

With blood still dripping from its
       warm and sticky beak,
its neck dangling over a bucket's edge,
a goose lies rocking in a boat,
      like an ingot
of slightly tarnished silver.
There had been two of them flying above the Vilyui.
The first had been brought down in flight
       while the other,
gliding low,
   risking his neck,
hovers over the lake,
     cries over the forest:
"My dove-gray brother,
      we came into the world
clamorously breaking through our shells,
but every morning
     Mother and Father
fed you first,
   when it might have been me.
My dove-gray brother,

                        you had this blue
                                        tinge,
teasing the sky with a bold similarity.
I was darker,
                    and the females desired
you more,
                when it might have been me.
My dove-gray brother,
                            without fear for the return,
you and I flew away, over the seas,
but obnoxious geese from other lands surrounded
you first,
                when it might have been me.
My dove-gray brother,
                            we were beaten and bowed.
Together we were lashed by the tempests,
but for some reason the water slid
more easily off *your* goose's back
                            when it might have been mine.
My dove-gray brother,
                        we frayed our feathers.
People will eat both of us by the fireside—
perhaps because the struggle to be first
devoured you,
                consumed me.
My dove-gray brother,
                            half our lives was a pecking match,
not treasuring our brotherhood, our wings, and our souls.
Was reliance really impossible—
I on you,
            and you on me?
My dove-gray brother,
                    I beg at least for a pellet,
curbing my envy too late;
but for my punishment people killed
you first,
            when it might have been me..."

1974

TRANSLATED BY ARTHUR BOYARS AND SIMON FRANKLIN

Russia

So who, in hell's name, are you,
what's so special about *your* fate,
that you fall over, lapping up vodka,
and still give yourself such airs?

So who, in hell's name, are you,
when, like absolute riffraff
glinting with plastic ear-clips,
you've started playing the Golden Girl?

So who, in hell's name, are you,
acting the slave to dubious praise,
you coward, stopping up the mouths
of those who still had any faith in you?

So who, in hell's name, are you,
and who, in hell's name, am I,
that I can howl, reproaching you,
still bound to you with chains of longing?

1974
TRANSLATED BY ARTHUR BOYARS AND SIMON FRANKLIN

Malachite Frog

Salutations from the birch logs, small and time-worn,
that showed us such tenderness in the darkening wood
when we pressed against each other,

                                  as we sat down on them
under the gaze of a gentle malachite frog.
Ever curling,
            the white bark of the birch
opened slightly under my hand, so easily,
and the pulp, still pink, came seeping through

and started, so bitterly, to weep onto my hand.
Softly I stood up, rather numbed,
and went over to
                          a birch, not yet cut down,
and I pressed against its body with my own,
rubbing my fingers
                          with chalk, like a happy schoolboy,
and the tips of my fingers
                               wiped your tears all away
with warm, powdery moth-dust
                               from that birch.
In that forest's glistening dusk
there was a constant flowing together: you into the birch, the birch into you . . .
And the dusk,
               smelling of burdock and mushrooms,
would squeeze us again,
                          autumnal,
                               damp.
Don't treat the benevolent dusk
                               harshly.
Don't be afraid of it
                    when it drops in at the apartment,
and give it some yogurt to eat when it's tired,
and put it up for the night on an old camp bed,
and ask about that malachite frog.
Salutations from the skier
                          on the strangest of practice-rollers,
there on the highway,
                         in the quietest and shadiest shade,
where, sorrowing over the August asphalt,
ski-sticks would knock
                         with the lightest of sparks.
Salutations from the menacing motorcar,
                                   which loomed up
beating its way from afar with its lights through the pines,
and moved in its clumsy,
                         ponderous, oversized way,
making all suburban Moscow resound with its terrible roar,
revolving furiously over enfeebled life
its lightning-faced blue and white
                         rotator.
And we, as if glued to the spot,
                    kept racking our brains with the question:

What kind of monster is that?

       What distant parts is it making for?

And the car splattered us lightly with water,

and suddenly turned out to be wearing an army star

and suddenly seemed a hope—

      not a disaster,

and the soldiers' lean boyish faces

wanted so much to share something with us . . .

And salutations from me,

      who am slightly ill,

slightly old,

   a little ridiculous,

and drunk often,

    and sober rarely,

and foolish, luckily,

     and wise, unluckily,

but love you very much,

     like this August,

like the heaviness of the air,

      which is no burden,

like this forest,

    where everything birch-milkily

flows perfectly pure into everything else,

like this car

   smelling of young life,

with a wet army star,

like a freckle dropped into the dirt by a skier,

like the gentle malachite frog.

1974

TRANSLATED BY ARTHUR BOYARS AND SIMON FRANKLIN (REVISED)

Interconnection of Phenomena

A rocky crag sleeps like a tired elephant,
so tiny in the starry cosmos.

Tired of hunting to live,
a boa sleeps in a crag in a cave.

    . . .

Inside the boa a rabbit sleeps peacefully
and softly snores away.

Awkwardly turning about,
a carrot sleeps inside the rabbit.

And inside the carrot a silent worm
has settled down on its side.

1974
TRANSLATED BY ALBERT C. TODD

Metamorphoses

Childhood is the village of Rosycheekly,
Little Silly, Clamberingoverham,
Leapfrogmorton, going toward Cruelidge,
through Unmaliciousness and Clearvisiondon.*

Youth is the village of Hopeworth,
Expansiongrove, Seducehall,
and, well, if it's a bit like Foolmouth,
all the same it is Promising.

Maturity is the village of Divideways,
either Involvementhaven or Hidewell,
either Cowardsbridge or Bravewater,
either Crookedwood or Justfield.

Old age is the village of Tiredhead,
Understandmore, Little Reproach,
Forgetfast, Overgrownend,
and, God keep us from it, Lonelybury.

1974
TRANSLATED BY ARTHUR BOYARS AND SIMON FRANKLIN

*For the unusual names of Russian villages in the original the translators found authentic English
historical villages.

Verbosity

To. V. Solovyov

I am verbose both in my daily life
and in my verse—that's your bad luck—
but I am cunning: I realize
that there's no lack of will
behind this endless drivel,
rather my strong ill will!

A superfluity of words conceals
camouflaged existence's pure essence—
the thread of gold lost in the yarn.
And Vinokurov, many years ago,
speaking of the superfluous, said
it was even indispensable.

Cutting the cackle, you can't avoid dramas.
Just think, if I should stick to the point,
how crudely the message would emerge—
when, like a muzhik,* not a weakling,
I blurt it all out at once, laconic,
in good old four-letter words.

I am, thank heaven, a graphomaniac,
and one day I'll bring crashing down
onto your heads, heavy as thunder,
a novel, seven hundred pages long, and more!
That's what the bard gets driven to,
that's where he'll unload his soul!

Eternal verities rest on the precise;
precision, though, consists in sacrifice.
Not for nothing does the bard get scared—
the price of brevity is blood.
Like fear of prophecies contained in dreams,
the fear of writing down eternal words
is the real reason for verbosity.

1974

TRANSLATED BY ARTHUR BOYARS AND SIMON FRANKLIN

---

*muzhik: Russian for "peasant," "clod," "bumpkin," and, colloquially, "man" or "fellow."

"A drop fell..."

A drop fell
      and vanished
on that gray temple
as if it had silently buried
itself in sand.
Are not friendship and love likewise
interred,
just like the body of a drop melting
on that gray hair?
Where there's a friend, then love's absence
does not frighten us,
(although we get the itch
from time to time).
Absence of friends won't seem such an abyss
when love
places its palm
as a bulwark before the precipice.
More frightening, by far, when fully armed,
uniting,
both absence of love
           and absence of friends
encircle us.
Then we betray ourselves in mock
depravity.
We attribute
      features of loved ones
to those not loved.
Wandering painfully,
         as in a field,
during a blizzard,
against our will we look for a friend
in an enemy's face.
Naive to expect a comforting word
from a dead mouth.
To demand feelings
      is repugnant
to the very nature of feelings,
and a cold stranger
will shrink with fear
at the frantic shriek of

"Comrade,
          friend..."
And a woman will sigh under her breath
from the warm shadows,
when our confessions are superfluous,
though pretty enough.
But stuck in the glutinous morass,
and amid the losses,
one so wants to embrace somebody:
"Comrade, believe!"
And is it really a sin
                    when, amid the tormented
                                        gloom,
the backbiting,
          the abuse,
one so wants to say to somebody:
"I love you..."?

1974

TRANSLATED BY ARTHUR BOYARS AND SIMON FRANKLIN

Potato Flower

To I. Shkliarevskii

Impertinent,
          but no blasphemer,
I love, as god's gift, asphodel
and lily-of-the-valley,
                    and the cornflower,
but I detest any catspiss-guttery,
flowery-scented eau de cologne,
corrupting chaste scent
like chemical verses.
And better than any—
                    joking aside—
I love the flower of the simple potato,
as I love my brother,
for its smell of earth untainted with caramel,

for the fact that no one could possibly devise
a deception
at least out of *it*!

1974

TRANSLATED BY ARTHUR BOYARS AND SIMON FRANKLIN (REVISED)

Hope

It is terrible to replace dead feelings
with memories of feelings,
but still more terrible if even
the memories are dead,
and like the spittle of black blood
you slaver onto a sheet of paper:
"Life has no meaning when it consists
of moments made meaningless."

And with its inaudible key
despair will enter the apartment,
like a woman, no stranger,
but somehow near and familiar.
She'll lie down beside you,
and with her cold frame will erase you,
and you'll start to feed her desire,
yourself dwindling into a slave.

Despair is more cunning than hope
and wears the face of the wise;
but her wisdom is depraved, grasping—
she's cold and calculating.
Instead of children, warm and alive,
she'll bear you only phantoms,
and imprison time
like a drowsy fly in amber.

As hope's wicked stepmother
she'll mock at her,

rearrange everything—thoughts, things,
like your legally wedded wife,
and, wiping her tears with her tiny fist,
hope will leave the house like an orphan
with a dirty bundle—
leave the house where she is needed no longer.

She'll go out into the wide world,
she'll travel through forests and fields,
and late at night you'll wake up
in your icy lover's embrace,
transfixed by hope's childish screams
as ruffians ravish her
in those blind alleys, where despair
drove her into their clutches.

Search for hope, the innocent,
like a drop of heaven in a sieve!
Search for her on every station platform,
by every precipice and bonfire!
Kill despair, the old hag!
Rescue hope in the end!
For, as Pushkin once said:
"Hope is a faithful sister."

1975

TRANSLATED BY ARTHUR BOYARS AND SIMON FRANKLIN

A Tear

A tear surges up,
surges up to be shed,
for life is complex precisely because
it is cut short.
A tear surges up,
surges up to be shed,
but why—

        the tongue
              cannot bring
itself to say.
A tear surges up,
surges up to be shed,
not from insult,
            not from malice,
not from stupidity.
A tear surges up,
surges up to be shed,
and stops on the eyelashes
like the tear of a fever.
A tear surges up,
surges up to be shed,
and don't be afraid
            that words
are lost.
A tear surges up,
surges up to be shed,
and toward where—
            your course
lies there concealed . . .

1975

TRANSLATED BY ARTHUR BOYARS AND SIMON FRANKLIN
(REVISED)

The Ringing of the Earth

The kind of ringing once dinned through my head
and right round the city of Moscow everything
doubled, then trebled and resounded:
tramcars, sparrows, lampposts—
and something, summoned up within me,
a pure uncoiling, went completely wild.

The ringing crashed careering down on me
as if onto a savage stallion,

and striking at my ribs with its sharp heels
the ringing called me to the sky-blue gap,
right where the town glutted itself on pasties,
tore everything to shreds, but in a kindly way.

The ringing knew things I didn't know myself.
It was as much at home in the pure sky
as in the trash of out-of-town ravines.
The ringing was colored music without words,
blending the egg yolks of church cupolas
with red-clothed slurping splashing out of flags.

The ringing imagined verses for me
out of rough husks of sunflower seeds
crunched underfoot on station platforms;
and answering I rang out to the earth's ringing,
and lines rushed from the tunnel of my throat
like railway carriages, crammed with the ringing.

And there was no more time—only the ringing.
It chose me as its incarnation,
but dropped me—started to look for someone younger.
And, as you loved me for that borrowed ringing,
you ceased to be. The ringing created you,
and you died in the ringing when it ended.

1975

TRANSLATED BY ARTHUR BOYARS AND SIMON FRANKLIN

But Before . . .

Beloved,
        can this really be you and me,
worn out, like after illness,
by such long years of struggle,
not with mere outsiders,
                        but with each other?
But before . . .

Our son is crying in his sleep!
we separate . . .
              The wind is almost ripping down the house!
Come, at least once, where my eyes can follow,
come with your former eyes.
But before we separate, as you propose,
don't go looking for advice out there
where the void,
              mimicking dense shrub land,
pretends to act as wet nurse to the moon.
But before we separate, as you propose,
hear how the ice drones in the night,
while the bluish light transforms to green,
and that green light cuts through the dark.
But before . . .
              we lived on cruelty!
For this we deserve to be buried alive!
When did we learn to be such strangers?
When did we unlearn our way of speaking?
Her answer:
              "Don't call me 'Beloved.' "
It serves me right.
              I deserved it.
                    I can say nothing.
But, by all our twisted
              broken
                 life,
I beg you:
        Before
you look at me,
           unseeing,
I ask you,
           and on my knees,
calling you no longer "Beloved":
"My old friend,
           don't leave me . . ."

1975

TRANSLATED BY ARTHUR BOYARS AND SIMON FRANKLIN

Iron Staircase

In the entrance to your place on the Petrovka*
there's an iron staircase.
Its pre-revolutionary pattern
is worn to a gun-metal blue.
The boots of the swells in gaiters
used to scuff the steps,
and tattered vixens, baring their teeth,
used to leer from the shoulders of whores.

Here combed boots, leggings,
and felt overshoes used to compete
with initialed galoshes
and boots of the secret police.
Also such gutter talk as:
"Gimme the dough, mister!"
Then the more ladylike: "Really, kitten!"
And the totally proletarian:
"Bugger off!"

On this very staircase, perhaps,
Rasputin† threw up
and Savinkov‡ offered a cold Browning
automatic to a girl student;
And I will visit you at midnight,
and my ringing will wake
you—who have as many secrets
as Moscow itself.

And you won't be surprised to see me, as if
we'd arranged a secret rendezvous,
and you'll understand everything, without my explaining,
without any need to be taught;
you, there, warm as a raisin roll in the morning
straight from the baker's,
with raisin moles on your neck,
with gleaming raisins for eyes.

You, like Moscow, are all hidden in Moscow.
You, a number in the street directory,

hide, like a house that
has not yet been completely gutted—
only sometimes does your gaze glitter
icily, like a Maximalist,§
whose chances today of being herself
would be minimal!

In the entrance to your place on the Petrovka
there's an iron staircase
that we tread at different times,
but in one and the same crowd
as all of you, precious
and repellent ghosts,
where, gradually, we ourselves will
turn into ghosts . . .

1975

TRANSLATED BY ARTHUR BOYARS AND SIMON FRANKLIN (REVISED)

*Petrovka: Street in central Moscow.
†Rasputin: Notorious lecher priest, debauched confidential adviser to Tsarina Aleksandra and thus Tsar Nikolai II by pretending to heal their hemophiliac son and heir in the fatal years just before the Revolution of 1917.
‡Savinkov: Boris Viktorovich Savinkov (Ropshin) (1879–1925). Revolutionary and writer. Arrested in 1924 and perished in the Lubianka prison headquarters of the secret police.
§Maximalist: Member of the left wing of the Socialist Revolutionary Party, which was the major competitor of the Bolsheviks in 1917.

The Easter Procession

There was a procession at the church in the suburbs:
the priest swinging his Vesuvius-on-a-chain,
and a crowd of old women with candles in their hands.
The old age pensioners, hardly able to stand,
lifted their banners with a hymn of faith,
and Christ's Image swayed unsteady in the clouds.

In Volgas, Zhigulis, and Zaporozhetses*
the crowds rolled up—congestion on the route to Christ!
They belched and shoved their neighbors black and blue.

Then the pawing started, an extra bit of fun,
like at a match where, just for a lark,
they play football with the head of Christ.

Midget Man's essence was revealed again:
to get himself a better inch of space.
What's gained in scrapping is the Lord's own gift!
And so the vespers was their battlefield—
for these lads, mini-Beatles, it's all the same,
Jesus Christ or Adamo.

Two rather quiet and clearly highbrow girls
attached themselves to the old women in the crowd,
sidling along like proper democrats.
Hiding behind a wall of Part-Time Constables,
with faces of repulsive bureaucrats,
the mob of priests stepped out with pomp.

There was a whiff of port and incense mixed with sweat,
the kind of smell you get in sour, stale marshland
where the snipe won't even try to whistle.
Forgive me, Christ, for my hard-hearted question:
But was it ever worth your sacrifice
to stick your image in such vulgar shows?

But how is that old woman guilty of vulgarity,
terrorized by all the flurrying
and turmoil of the drunk, rampaging crowd?
Her hand, so overworked with upraised candle,
like a grandmother straining toward her kidnapped
        grandson,
she, Christ, so stretches out to you.

When the flock went back into the church,
the door squeezed out the overflow like toothpaste,
and there rang out a cry, shrill through a hundred yards!
The door so pressed on the old woman's hand
that only the first joint of her poor fingers
entered the building, reaching out to Christ.

Crucifix—you are like a crossroads:
one end in fire, the other in depravity.
But you, Christ, also accept *this* world.

Do not permit that for the simple souls
all should begin in a mirage of miracles,
and end with bolted doors.

1975

TRANSLATED BY ARTHUR BOYARS AND SIMON FRANKLIN

*Volga, Zhiguli, and Zaporozhets are Soviet automobiles.

Memory's Revenge

It would appear, then,
                that it's impossible
for me ever to be reconciled with my memory.
It and I have long been at daggers drawn.
Having jostled me onto a dark track,
knocking me over,
                then sticking its knee in my chest,
it holds a knife to my throat:
"So you loved someone, did you?
                      And what did you do
to love,
        stabbing it like that below the heart?"—
"I didn't mean..."
                Then, to me, out of the dark:
"Accidentally?
        Ha ha...
                How very kind!
I'll spare you,
           you won't die,
But I'll pierce you,
              pay you a knife for a knife!
As a knife
        in your body I'll remain
                    living with you
all your life—
           that's how your memory takes its revenge!"
I've no need to remember you—

for under my shirt, straining at the nylon
as it sticks out of my ribs,

                      a knife handle breathes
bandaged with adhesive tape ...

1975
TRANSLATED BY ARTHUR BOYARS AND SIMON FRANKLIN

To Beginners

A distressingly businesslike spirit
glimmers
            in certain beginners.
A depressingly "smooth" look
to lines
        that haven't known the torture
                          of rough drafts.
In ever-so-neat verse making,
where the happy ending comes with a flourish,
having no character
            has become its character,
and having no face
           is the face!
I implore
        as desperate daring,
the skill to be clumsy!
I implore,
        as an act of courage,
just one genuine word!
How to write
        and what about—save your inquiries.
Ask life,
       and leave it at that!
Poetic fearlessness
is fear when the page stares back at you, empty.
How to define the creative mood
I couldn't care less.
          I'll tell you a small secret:

It's in bridging the gap
between the word
                and our hearts.
Don't expect an apotheosis,
but a mixed blessing is
the state
        of not being in a state
to betray
        by your words
                the truths that lie under them.
Whose side are you on, turbulent youth:
                        the snow-swept night
or the essential recommendation
for the long-hoped-for writers' paradise?
Whose side are you on:
                the Master
                        or Woland?*

Whose side are you on:
                hunger
                        or the fat of the land?

Choose!

1975

TRANSLATED BY ARTHUR BOYARS AND SIMON FRANKLIN

*Master or Woland: Characters embodying the forces of good and evil (in the Faustian sense) in
Mikhail Bulgakov's novel *The Master and Margarita*.

Alder Catkin

Whenever the wind
                drops an alder catkin into my palm,
or a cuckoo calls merrily,
                with trains screaming by,
I fall to reflecting,
                and struggle to grasp life's meaning,
and, as usual, arrive
                at the place where it slips from my grasp.

Reducing oneself
                    to a speck of dust in a starry nebula
is an old way out,
                    but wiser than trumped-up grandeur,
and it's no degradation
                    to realize one's own insignificance,
for in it we realize sadly
                    the implicit grandeur of life.
Alder catkin,
                    weightless as down,
only blow it away
                    and all changes utterly,
and life, it appears,
                    is not such a trifling matter,
when nothing about it
                    seems merely a trifle.
Alder catkin,
                    loftier than any prophecy!
The person who silently
                    pulls it to pieces is changed.
So what, if we can't
                    change the world in a flash, as we'd like—
when we change,
                    the world changes too!
We're then transported
                    into a kind of new quality.
as we sail into the distance
                    to a new unknown land,
and we don't even notice
                    the rocking's strange rhythm
on new waters,
                    and a completely different ship.
When there suddenly wakes
                    the starless feeling of being a castaway
from those shores
                    where you greeted the dawn with such hope,
my dear companion,
                    there's no need, take it from me, to despair—
Trust in the unknown
                    alarmingly black anchorage!
What often alarms from afar
                    seems hardly perturbing in close-up.
There too are eyes, voices,

                          the minute glow of cigarettes.
But as you grow used to it,
                          the creak of what seems like a haven
will murmur to you
                          that no single haven exists.
Translucent the soul
                          that can't be embittered by change!
Forgive the friends who've misunderstood
                                    or even betrayed you.
Forgive, understand,
                          even if your lover stops loving you!
Set her free from your palm
                          like an alder catkin.
And don't trust a new haven
                          that starts to enfold you;
your vocation is
                    the havenless far-off distance.
Break away from the morning
                          if you become moored by habit,
and cast off again
                    and set sail for a different sorrow.
Let people say:
                "Really, when will he get some sense!"
Don't worry!
                You can't please them all at one time.
What base common sense:
                    "It'll all blow over, it'll all come right in the end ..."
When it all comes right in the end,
                          there's no point in living.
And what can't be explained
                    is in no way nonsensical.
All reassessments should not worry one in the least—
since the value of life
                    won't be lowered
                          or raised:
the worth of what's beyond value
                    isn't subject to change.
... Why am I saying all this?
                          Because one stupid
chatterbox of a cuckoo
                    predicts a long life for me.
Why am I saying all this?
                          Because an alder catkin

lies in my palm,
and quivers, as if it were living...

1975

TRANSLATED BY ARTHUR BOYARS AND SIMON FRANKLIN

"In moments of ..."

In moments of sudden confusion,
so as to regain your bearings
don't demean yourself
by feeling bitter.

Don't submit
to a hateful mob.
Don't fall prey
to a lust for revenge.

"An eye for an eye,
and a tooth for a tooth ..."
How utterly shallow!
How brainless the author!

What's all right for a cretin
in *you* is cause for reproach.
"Holy malice"
was Blok's invention.

Be poor with dignity,
feel calm and refreshed!
Don't gnaw at yourself!
Don't gnaw at others!

But utter forgiveness
of all grovelers
is dire revenge
on your friends.

And compassion
toward all who are brutal and boorish

is madness,
though with a crazy logic.

Oh, how repulsive,
when one defeated
by scum
proceeds to suck up to it.

Don't puff yourself up
into terrible turbulence,
don't drop down
to kiss all the arses!

1975

TRANSLATED BY ARTHUR BOYARS AND SIMON FRANKLIN

The Wild Ass's Skin

Fear sidled into me, soft, slippery;
I feel my time is really running out.

My days were golden but my life was poor,
time was of no particular account.

I've known restraint and freedom from restraint,
but there are still too many nuts to crack.

Quite feverishly I still scratch around,
no longer able to improve my fate.

To speak my heart comes harder all the time—
I find my nights and days are all too few.

Now I collapse exhausted on the bed—
I feel I've started more than I can finish.

I feel that as my soul strips off its rust
my words will peter out before the end.

. . .

The rustling of the wild ass's skin
must be an omen that my soul is shriveling.

Or is it just the thought that frightens me,
that it will shrink and disappear?

And fear dins into me: "Write, write,
before your very soul has vanished."

1975

TRANSLATED BY ARTHUR BOYARS AND SIMON FRANKLIN

"Once people..."

Once people
       get under
             my skin,
they never find the exit.
They romp around,
           fill my insides with their song and dance,
make lots of noise, using my dumbness as their cover-up.
I'm full to bursting
       with wise men
and fools—
       they've utterly exhausted me!
So much so that my skin's
           quite worn through
by their heels, rubbing from inside!
Give me a chance to breathe!
It's all impossible!
       I'm stuffed to the gills
with those who've brought me so much joy
as well as those who've given most offense.
What has come over me?
What can I do with this great throng
stuck in my own small heart—
police are needed to keep order there!
I've gone a little cracked,
for there, in that secluded shade,

I've dropped none of the women
and none of them's dropped me!
It's awkward to revive dead friendships
however much you tire yourself with trying.
The only friends I've lost
                           were on the outside,
but of those inside I've lost nobody.
All the people in my life I've quarreled with,
                           or made friends with,
or only shaken hands with,
have merged in a new life under the old one's skin—
a secret conflagration without flame.
The repossession of the unpossessable
is like a waterfall that rushes upward.
Those who have died
                have been born again in me,
those who have not been born as yet
                           cry out.
My population is too large,
beyond the strength of just one man—
but then, a person would be incomplete
if he contained no others.

1975

TRANSLATED BY ARTHUR BOYARS AND SIMON FRANKLIN

Safari in Ulster

*The gates of the Safari are invitingly open to car tourists. You are strongly advised
not to open your car windows, slow down, or stop. The management cannot be held
responsible if these rules are not observed.*

                                        —*From a guidebook*

                    I.

Lions' fates
            are thorny
                        like people's fates.
On the deceptive couch
                    of Irish grass
lions
      recline

like the most peaceful terrorists
                              of our time.
And the lions nonchalantly
                    munch their breakfasts,
each one
          like a mute sandy dune,
and they wait
              for the cry of Africa
to summon
              them home.
Brother lion,
              behind the wire fence
you have not
              ceased to be real.
but each of your claws
                    testing the wire
realized long ago
                  that you are a prisoner.
Sister lioness,
              by nature you are easily appeased.
Tourists don't anger you
                    for long,
but how will you teach
                  your cubs,
born captive,
            to hunt freely?
She gets up,
            apparently offended.
Quivering,
          aroused,
                    she lashes her tail
and suddenly leaps at the car,
                              arching her body,
becoming steel
              in the air.
Driver, did you tremble?
                    Are you afraid?
Blue-eyed girl,
              you are only twenty-three.
Your forebears
            were Irish rebels.
But now you've decided to drive—
                          drive on!

You, too, are inside
                this wire cage.
The only difference is—
                you're at the wheel.
Is the windscreen
                really that strong?
The car has stalled . . .
                We're alone with the lioness.
Suddenly
        her reddish paw was lowered on the glass
with longing,
                and without haste
the lioness pressed herself
                lamentingly to the glass,
and I felt
        she was even
                whispering.
Of course, these were not sobs or whispers,
but only the persecuted face
                of a woman,
only the terrible grief of animal knowledge,
and her cry
        became, through nature,
                            a roar.
Sister lioness,
        how I wanted to share
our one secret moment
                with you—
for you are a woman
                and you won't betray.

                        2.

I, too, have a growing cub.
How shall I watch over him?
What will they put into his little head?
What shall I
        put into it?
Here I am far away from Russia,
my snowy Africa,
but again I am tortured
                by the thought of my son,

and the future of all children.
Here,
  both renowned
     and slandered,
enraged by the crackling fire,
in fenced-in glory
     I feel like
a lion
  in a mousetrap.
But someone is trying to make me yelp
so that I may prove my right to roar,
but that is just like making
the lions
   in Ireland
     yelp at Africa.
Photographers
    and clinging ladies
ask me,
  like a rare lion from the taiga
to bare my fangs,
     just to smile a little,
but *never*, of course,
    to roar at them!
Fame
  brings unemployment to lions' fangs.
Believe my words
    like a roar:
The poet
  is a hunter who is hunted,
but you understand this,
     lions,
only too well.

3.

Sister lioness,
   I was in Londonderry
where they would even shoot
     at your tails
where hands froze
    on the wheel at night

from uncertainty

        and the void.

And headlights

        wrenched a boy's face out of the darkness,

dotted with freckles

        and drops of rain.

A soldier in a camouflage jacket

        dived out,

poking a machine gun at us:

"Turn out yer lights"—

        he yelled.

        "Quick!"

He grabbed our documents,

        shaking with fear.

"Sorry,

        I thought you were terrorists.

They blind us

        with headlights.

So you're from Russia."

        "Yes, from Russia."

"Why are you here?"

        "I've been invited to read poetry."

"Poetry?

        In Londonderry?

        You must be crazy.

This is a place for gravediggers,

        not poets."

"Where're the hotels here?"

        "What hotels?

All of 'em went up in smoke

        long ago."

"What about restaurants?"

        "Same thing. All blown up,

There's a Chinese one, though,

        but the food's horrible.

Toads, worms,

        snakes and all that.

Can you use chopsticks?"

        "Yes, I can."

Then I heard him whisper

        after us sadly:

"Yes, the Russians

        are a crazy people."

And in the restaurant
                    "Chinese Garden"
we squeezed in somewhere against the wall,
like travelers
enjoying a feast
                    in a time of plague.
And we were frightened
not by the scorpion or shark's fin,
but by the wind
                    flapping the curtain
in the window,
                    smashed by a blast.
At the rickety table,
around which the war went on invisibly,
I became drunker.
Now I felt like a Catholic,
now like a Protestant.
Fame was no longer worth anything.
For the first time in my life
I wanted to shout:
"I belong to the Russian Orthodox Church."
But we didn't stay long,
we felt uneasy,
                    although we had gone to a place
where the shots sounded
                    or seemed far away.
O Londonderry streets
in the night,
                    like depots of darkness,
where a human fear of people
lurks in every tree,
where the apertures of houses
                            are bricked up
against bullets in the night,
and all these bricks
                    have been stolen
from the rubble
                    of other houses.
Everything had been blown up:
the town hall, law courts, honor, the flag, the cross,
the rampant shameful lies

that freedom and progress exist.
We walked through the debris.
In the dark desert even an old man with a little dog,
cocking its leg against the remains of a Ford Capri,
looked fresh.
And bombs, ticking,
had no objection to blowing up somewhere nearby.
It was a beautiful silent night,
St. Bartholomew's Night.

5.

And the old man with the dog approached us,
striding as if through Dante's Inferno,
and he recited an Irish ballad for us,
which I shall retell you now:
"A Protestant's Great Dane
only vaguely understood
           the meaning of God,
and a Catholic's mangy mongrel bitch
was, poor thing, not a Catholic.
The Dane was not proud of his bloodline,
the mongrel not ashamed of her own,
and both,
      tugging at the leash,
pulled toward each other,
           as though toward freedom,
and the Romeo and Juliet of Londonderry
stared at each other from afar.
The Catholic was killed on some wasteland,
while walking his dog in the evening.
And it howled until dawn,
appealing to everyone,
          even to layabouts,
but its dead master's hand
stiffened
      and would not let go of the leash.
And, having polished his gold medals,
the Protestant took his Great Dane out in the morning.
And the good,
        simple-hearted dog
broke the leash

and tore'toward that howling mongrel,
and, forgetting it was a Protestant,
licked it
            and howled together with it."
The old man finished his story with a sigh:
"Atheist dogs are cleaner than us believers.
God has many faces,
                and if that is so,
then God was born not among men,
                        but among dogs."

6.

So this is Safari in Ulster!
Sister lioness,
            you're better off
on your reserve,
            like an island
that rocks in the blood.
So this is civilization,
when, shut indoors for months on end,
Irish children have to save themselves,
nestling against
            your stony tits.
Damned atomic Middle Ages
where it's harder for people to survive
than it is for lions,
when crosses are drawn not with chalk
but in blood.
"His faith isn't right—so button him up!"
I'm not a Protestant, nor am I a Catholic,
but I fear the void of the future,
when all the doors will have been
                        blown out
where crosses cannot even be drawn.
And what indifference?
                It only drinks and chews ...
Will the age really lead to this—
man exterminated by man—
suddenly a rare species?
And the old man whispers—
                this Londonderry leprechaun

with the little dog,
                    for the time being, still alive:
"Where are we heading?
                    What do we believe in
amid so many senseless losses?
When humans
          become
               animals,
animals
     seem human."
And, squeezing their jaws politely
when someone
          throws them tidbits,
the lions
     turn
          their noses away
from foul-smelling mankind.

1975
Belfast — Londonderry
TRANSLATED BY TED HUGHES (REVISED)

Snow in Tokyo: A Japanese Poem

Her husband was, it seems, one of those very
cultured Japanese. That didn't stop him
slightly despising her because she was,
when all was said and done, a woman.
Every morning he'd sit immersed in books
bound in thick leather, whose gilt titles
were almost rubbed away, and diligently try
to become even more cultured.
She would bring his tea into the library,
and the black lacquered tray that she set down
had pheasants painted on it,

and on it lay slices of raw tuna,
wooden chopsticks,
and a saucer filled with soy sauce.
He would partly notice her, busy as he was
reflecting on the universal spirit,
and she would go outside to prune the roses.
This she did with heavy silver scissors
handed down from her Samurai grandfather
who, as well as being a good gardener,
had been a general, ending his life by hara-kiri
after his dust-caked soldier's boots
had stepped aboard the U.S. battleship *Missouri*,
and his hands had trembled under the onus
of the surrender note that had been rustling
in the grasp of his immediate superior.
For quite a while the woman didn't rinse her fingers
smelling of the garden, and later made a start
on dinner preparations; and while the food was eaten
she'd be presented with the silence of
her spouse, whose thoughts were of eternity.
Then she would wash the plates,
and a tiny delicate pink petal,
perched like a butterfly upon her wrist,
would be washed away, mingling with the water in the kitchen sink.
About the same time, the time for meditations
on life and death would terminate, regulated
by her husband's Swiss wristwatch, and his thoughts,
having switched off ideas of death, already pointed
only in life's direction. He'd then slip out
of his workaday kimono into a clean, crackling shirt,
breasted with a frost of finest lace,
and his wife would help insert into the cuffs
his golden cufflinks showing the rising sun.
Then he would get into his French Tergal suit
tapered a little at the waist, tastefully glossy,
and instead of homely geta he'd put on
Italian moccasins made from the skins
of completely innocent Nile crocodiles.
There was no formal leave-taking or
any indication of when he might return;
his "good-bye" was the deliberately festive roar
of the car speeding off into the dusk—
a Toyota van or, more often, a Jaguar two-seater.

And she'd sit down at the old Chinese mirror
and with her fingertips would try to smooth out
the wrinkles on her forehead, round her eyes,
which, nonetheless, still sparkled youthfully
like moist dark cherries on the white porcelain
of her face.
          The car would return at dawn,
worn out like a dog that had run itself to a standstill,
and if its hide had not been polished, thorns
from night-life's thicket would have stuck to it.
Her husband would ask for tea, then Alka-Seltzer,
a great invention of the former enemies
who'd dropped the A-bomb on Hiroshima,
but also, just the same, suffered from hangovers—
and this drew them closer, spiritually, to the drinking
scions of the Land of the Rising Sun.
Her husband would collapse straight onto the blanket
in his suit, and fall asleep immediately,
and she'd pull off his moccasins—
a flattened cigarette was sticking to one sole,
its tip, bloodstained with lipstick, she also noted,
as well as a hair from a natural wig of South Korea
that was now clinging to the Tergal,
and also, on the left cuff of his shirt,
one of the rising suns was missing.
Then she would fall asleep;
following her grandmother's advice, she'd
conjure up an autumn thicket, and a pond with emerald film,
and a blackboard on the still water.
She'd use her gaze to draw, as with chalk, upon the blackboard,
6:30—the hour of morning awakening,
and, with her gaze, softly sink the board right to the bottom,
in such a way, however, that the vital figures shone
from there, through the yellow leaves, rocked by the pond.
One day she was returning from the temple where
Buddha had patiently heard her prayer but hadn't
given any advice. She suddenly turned her head
toward the cool columns of the university
of Vaseda, where she had once studied.
The reason why she turned was partly nostalgia
for her youth, drowned in the still water
like a leaf filched by the wind from a sakura tree,
a leaf just yellowing on the branches, just in flight,

but at the kiss forced on it by the slime,
now drenched completely in the slime's own color;
and partly because a summoning voice
was stalking through the columns.
A youth was standing on the steps
wearing an orange helmet,
covered in scars and scratches,
the current headgear of student demonstrators
in Japan, protecting—albeit relatively—their heads
from assault by the police-force rubber truncheons
that fairly often would rain down upon them.
From underneath the helmet, like a small waterfall,
seethed some tousled oil-black hair,
and little childish slanting eyes
glowed, unchildishly embittered,
opposed in meaning but identical in expression
to the ferocity of warlike Samurai
brandishing their sabers on the screen.
His hand clasping a microphone, as though it were an apple
from the tree of knowledge, which in politics
had turned into a new bone of contention,
convulsively dissatisfied he shouted something
against the background of a poster with a beard
resembling Bakunin's, and called for world revolution.
This small and clearly hungry orator was so alone
she felt the urge to feed him, taking from her bag
delicious dried cuttlefish wrapped in cellophane,
but all the same couldn't quite decide to do it.
And so he went on shouting, waxing furious
at the general apathy of students who rushed shamefully
to the canteen or library, and two of them—
reactionaries, most likely—started playing
with badminton rackets and a small shuttlecock
over the helmet of the orator scarred in the global struggle.
And still he kept on shouting, the lone orator,
shouting out both truths and untruths,
but at least shouting out *something* . . .
And she sensed in that moment
the supremacy of even an impotent shout
over the slavery of her own dumbness,
late in the evening, just after the Jaguar
had glided out of the gates,
she put the children to bed—

and there were three of them: eleven, nine, and seven
very lovely years old, when they don't understand much,
but still, vaguely guess
at the relations between the grown-ups,
and prefer not to interfere.
And so she put the children to bed
and went out into the autumn night.
This was the birth of the rebellion—
a rebellion without slogans and tanks,
without any program, but a rebellion nonetheless,
one of those that flare up imperceptibly
but are not publicized
by the mass media.

First she went to a café
and started thinking about suicide,
perhaps because, once,
Akutagava used to sit there
also thinking about it as he swallowed
warm sake out of an earthenware cup.
Then the thought passed.
Sadly she reflected on the fact
that suicide was a form of egoism,
and that her children would suffer all their lives,
also her mother in Nagasaki,
who bowed to the waist before the emperor
staring impassively from a dish hung on the wall,
so that he might pray for her daughter.
And besides, she imagined very vividly
how her husband would order a dress jacket for his bereavement,
and cheerfully posing in front of the pier glass
would hiss at the tailor: "It's tight under the arm,"
and ask him to flare the trousers a tiny bit,
as much as would look decent at a funeral.
Damnable life,
where even dying can't solve anything!

She paid her bill and she left.
Then suddenly she saw Tokyo under early snow, unexpected,
like a hangover hitting you not as you wake up in the

morning,

but before you've plunged into sleep.
Like crumbs of white bread
aimlessly revolving in a fish tank,
the snowflakes swirled whitening the backs of passing cars,
and even the autumn dirt under the twentieth century's feet.
She laughed, like a worn-out geisha
who suddenly feels that she is unemployed.
A geisha's free only to be cold and hungry,
but the joy of a rebellion of the soul
lies in bringing as little as possible of the so-called useful
to our so-called society.
She caught the light white flakes of freedom
and licked them from her palm, before they melted.
Accompanied by the snow she wandered
right through the night along the Tokyo streets,
and the snow showed her many districts
she'd never visited before. The snow led her
by the hand toward an entertainment booth
where a woman in a ragged golden leotard,
wriggling just like a snake, ate a *real* snake,
sinking her wide-gapped crooked teeth,
which lived a separate life, one from another,
into the body of the snake whose head,
torn off only a moment earlier was lying,
incidentally, on the wooden rostrum,
with its beady eyes still quite alive,
while living quivering bits of body convulsed inside the gullet
of the unfortunate snake-swallower.
Damnable life,
in which you swallow sorrows like bits of snake,
while life
imperceptibly swallows you also, bit by bit.

The woman hurried out of the entertainment booth,
tucked herself up in the snow's wet snout,
and it led her into the distance, as if it were a dog
waving its dirty white tail.
Then she began to feel cold. Her coat
was far too light,
her flimsy lacquered shoes
with their blunt cutout toes
cheeped, like ducklings,
gulping the dirt with the snow

through their black open beaks. By a marble fountain
still gushing water, foolish against the snow,
she sat down on a soaking bench,
on somebody's decomposing newspapers
which had portraits of the leaders of the ruling party,
and also leaders of the opposition,
and fell asleep at once; clumsily the snow
tried to protect her from itself,
wrapping her all up from head to toe
inside a blanket sometimes gentle and fluffy,
but sometimes meltingly wet.
She awoke from somebody's gaze.
Someone unknown was standing there before her
wearing an unfashionable hat with large spots
on its shiny worn ribbon.
In a hand densely covered with gray,
he held a tattered umbrella, which covered his head.
He was in jeans unseemly for his years,
and all over them—this was the strange thing!—
happy flecks of paint seemed to be leaping
like a rainbow in the midst of a snowstorm.
"Come with me . . ." said the unknown man
and took her freezing hand;
then they dived into a basement,
stepping over the rats that poked about on the stairs,
and, thrusting his umbrella somewhere into the murk,
with the words "This umbrella is my key,"
the unknown man
either opened the door, or something resembling a door,
and they entered what looked like a house.
The host didn't switch on the overhead light,
but only a strange standard lamp,
on whose colored shade, once it was plugged in,
tints, which then came to life, began writhing enigmatically.
The host placed a coffeepot on the electric stove
and gave her some hot coffee in a plastic mug.
He didn't ask about anything.
Out of the lumber he produced a shepherd's simple reed pipe,
just like the one she had seen
in her childhood at Hokkaido
in the hands of a drunken barefoot peasant.
As he led cows doomed from birth to the slaughterhouse,
and tried to bring a little color to their

last steps on the grass,
the host drew from the pipe the pure trembling sounds
of a half-forgotten folk song,
and began a shuffling dance around his guest,
seated on an old stool cracked by the heat,
and she, having removed her shoes, was pointing her feet
in sodden stockings in the blissful direction
of the electric stove. The host's eyes were those
of one who, while knowing nothing about her,
had known her even in childhood, had known her in youth,
had delivered her children,
and had helped her to pull off her husband's moccasins
and he sat somewhere close to her in the café,
having noticed her suicidal thoughts
drifting in a light cloudlet of smoke
above the tiny cup of coffee in her hand.
But he, playing on the reed pipe,
expressed no condescending pity,
but with a whirling turn of melody
and his sad but smiling eyes,
he said to his guest:
"All passes away.
Of course, life too will pass away—that can't be helped!
But if we *are* alive, why die before our time?
We're all of us doomed, like cows from birth,
but there's also the joy of playing a reed pipe
or listening to one played by someone else.
And very likely there are in each of us
some notes that seem impossible to reach,
but all one needs to do is quietly close one's eyes,
stretch out expectant hands, palms upward,
and suddenly there appears in them, as if
by magic, the wooden body of a pipe,
and all one needs to do is press one's lips
to the round holes bored into this mystery,
and mingling with our breath there flows from us
our only melody—
then life will never pass away
but death *will* pass away, having glutted its ears with life."
And the guest, hearing these words
uttered only by his eyes,
and by his lightly dancing reed pipe,
started not exactly to cry, but to liberate herself with tears,

giving birth to tears like thousands of little children,
and, without being aware of it, she fell asleep
on the aluminum camp bed,
wrapped in a soldier's old greatcoat,
which smelled of peace, not war.

When she awoke,
first of all she saw pictures.
Pictures hung on the walls, stood, or simply lay around.
They were quite different from the pictures
she used to choose with her husband
when buying decorations for the house
in the Ginza galleries.
There the pictures resembled extensions to furniture.
The pictures of Ginza—a lavish luxury-market—
didn't make conversation, didn't shout,
but only mildly massaged the mood
like masseurs whose tongues had been cut out.
But these pictures shouted, conversed,
and even sang songs on a reed pipe;
and if they were silent, then even the silence
resembled a shout or a whisper.
But dominating all these pictures was War,
not the parade-ground, bemedaled war of generals,
but the filthy, bloody, typhoid-ridden war of soldiers,
war not pretending to be grand!
She was struck by one picture in particular:
the artist had called it *Rebellion*.
It showed the well-tended hands of someone or something invisible,
with shirt-cuffs, on one of which,
she seemed to notice,
one rising sun remained,
and next to it another had fallen out
and lay neglected in the dust.
The well-tended hands presented a soldier with a small medal
made from atomic mushroom cloud.
The soldier, swollen and frightful to behold,
like a drowned man with a dead face the color of khaki,
and eyes like swamps,
pointed his rifle butt, covered in blood still moist,
toward that bit of metal, the image of the fallen cufflink,
in a gesture of scornful rage and eternal rejection.

· · ·

The guest looked around, hoping to find the artist,
but he had evaporated and it seemed as if
all these pictures had in fact painted themselves.
Only on the homemade trestle
that served the host as bed and table
lay a note:
"I won't be back before evening. Make yourself at home,"
and beside it there rocked, as if living,
as if molded out of yesterday's snow, two eggs.
She cracked them very carefully,
as if afraid to cause them pain,
made scrambled eggs, boiled coffee,
then taking a brush from its repose
and dipping it into the paint, started
moving it across an untouched canvas,
and this was like liberating herself with tears,
except that the tears now had a different color.
Of course, she had learned painting while at school,
or rather had copied from things, not painted—
like an apple, perhaps, or a jug.
But now she yearned for something different:
to copy from what was inside her,
and to copy from what was not—
from the air, which smelled of the reed pipe.
Something was being born, through the paint's tears:
and this was her face,
and this was not *her* face,
but the face that lay within:
the face behind the face.

She left that basement
before her host returned,
took a taxi and went home
through the town that had foolishly trampled
the snow that fell to earth as foolishly.
Her husband rushed at her in fury.
She
made a sign in his direction:
not one of scornful rage,
but irrefutably rejecting him, as reality,
which, if you think about it,
is only real if you submit to it,
and her husband turned tail, terrified, feeling

that here was a different woman, whom he did not know.
She went toward the nursery, kissed
three small dark heads smelling of soap and sleep,
and, asked where she had vanished to for so long,
replied:
"I was listening to a reed pipe in a field."
Next morning
she drove the Toyota van to a shop
and carried home a multitude of paints:
cadmium lilac, yellow, purple,
light red and dark red;
ochres—muffled and golden,
brown mars, orange mars;
whites: lead, zinc, titanic;
greens: emerald green, bright "Paolo Veronese" green;
and browns: "Van Dyke," natural umber,
archangel brown,
bluish brown "caput mortuum,"
blacks: peach black,
burnt ivory,
grape black
(actually, as it happens, made from grape seeds);
and also ultramarine,
Berlin azure and Turkish blue;
oils, nut oil and linseed oil;
varnishes: mastic and pistachio;
brushes: bristle, squirrel, badger, Siberian mink,
as well as palette knives and spatulas
of various sizes and pliancies,
colored pencils, stylographs,
easels, sketching-pads, underframes,
canvases, primed and unprimed,
paper in rolls, sheets of Whatman,
and also hammers and pliers,
and nails both large and small
for every purpose, except for one: hammering
into her fellow humans' palms.

Now the rebellion was becoming armed.

Quite calmly she demanded of her husband
that he clear the flowers immediately
out of the winter greenhouse.

On hearing this he shook his head slightly,
but quite alarmed gave in to the request
made by his wife, now quite out of her mind!
This was the first building taken in the rebellion.
And then she started painting, and would admit
only children to the rebellion's headquarters.
And, at first, only her own.
And they, dazzled by such a quantity
of pencils and clean paper, switched themselves on
to the rebellion's wavelength,
and, filled with cheerful malice, depicted
Father resembling an octopus,
as well as an octopus resembling Father.
She did not favor that direct approach
in her attack upon the "status quo,"
but delegated it to her civic-minded children.
She combated ugliness not by direct exposé
but by the essential beauty of mixing colors—
for the strongest opponent of ugliness
is the human spirit, stripped to its purest form,
and not basely framed indignation
at the supremacy of baseness.

She painted cows she remembered from Hokkaido
with the oppressed eyes of the women of Japan.
She painted the women of Japan
with the oppressed eyes of the Hokkaido cows.
Her husband took her away to Africa, hoping this way
to dissipate her sudden urge.
They traveled luxury class
and even had a license to shoot elephants.
But the jungle didn't in the least attract her
with its toilets punctuating every path.
What really appealed to her was the tumbledown huts
made of palm leaves and bamboo
where women, using wooden pestles,
pounded batatas into flour;
and so she painted African women
with the oppressed eyes of the women of Japan,
and she painted the women of Japan
with the oppressed eyes of African women.

And one day *Experts* visited the converted greenhouse:
not the kind that does the rounds at private shows

so as to hold, in one hand a daiquiri in a frosted glass,
and, in the other, free, or rather *ostensibly* free,
hand, to wave majestically
to the talents of this world,
and obsequiously, following the mighty of this world,
not even guessing that they're wrong in their assessments,
since the world's main motive force
is talent, and not force itself.

The two Japanese experts who arrived at the greenhouse
were two old men *in no way* of this world,
but envoys from the great world of the great Hokusai,
Rublev, Bosch, El Greco,
who spoke of Pablo Picasso
as being competent, but frivolous nonetheless.
There was something childlike about these two old men,
and perhaps this was the reason why
the not-so-young woman, but very young artist,
let them enter the studio where
before only children had been admitted.

The first old man, despite the heat,
wore a severe black suit, and round his neck
wrinkled by the passage of governments,
a garish Parisian foulard,
given to him in the twenties in Montparnasse
by a girlfriend he had snatched
from Eluard, who was only starting out.

The second old man, whose mouth showed specimens
of prime Krupp steel produced even before
Hitler came on the scene (unfortunately, even then
it didn't lose its quality), appeared in tennis shorts,
holding a Dunlop racket, but all the same
he wore a pair of simple geta.

The artist was very frightened that the Experts
wouldn't confer on her the rank of artist.
And, feeling a failure, she hardly looked at them
while shifting canvases around, just like a cart-horse,
and asking: "Is it catching the light too much d'you think?"

The first old man asked her: "Have you been painting long?"
He had a stony, otherworldy look.

She hurriedly answered: "Yes."
The second old man asked her, without concern:
"Have you exhibited before?"
And she dejectedly admitted "No."
"Who taught you?" asked the first.
"A man," she answered edgily.
"Aha . . ." and he took back his tactless question.
The second, tapping for some reason with his racket
against the frame of the picture under inspection,
as if testing its solidity,
remarked with an unexpected smile:
"I think *this* one's more like it . . ."
"Like what, like whom?" she uttered, twitching nervously.
"Like painting . . ." He smiled faintly;
the first, a little piqued at not having got in first,
added: "I feel the same about it
as my distinguished colleague,
but I don't advise you to hurry to exhibit."
The second, twirling his racket on the floor,
said, and here he giggled slyly,
"And I *do* advise you to hurry,
although there is a grain of sense
in what my colleague said.
Of course, one loses by hurrying too much,
but one gains nothing by not hurrying at all.
To conceal works of art from the people
is just the same as robbing them.
But if a person who conceals them is
not just anybody, but the artist himself,
then it is, forgive me, nothing but egoism.
And, by the way, don't you have a glass
so that I and my colleague might join you
in a toast to your first exhibition?
My colleague and I will undertake
all the arrangements, isn't that right, colleague?"
"Of course, of course . . ." mumbled the other.
"When I advised you not to hurry,
I was advising like a father,
but sometimes childish wisdom is superior
to the wise unhurriedness of fathers . . ."

Oh, how great is every artist's need
to be *called* an artist,

not by ignorant illiterates,
and not by empty-headed groupies,
wetting themselves in ecstasy,
but by two old men who have gorged themselves on paint—
by imperturbable *Experts*!

And so three glasses placed in the middle
of the perkily rocking racket,
right in the very middle,
a bit discolored by play,
decided the whole thing, and the exhibition took place.

It took place, alas, in Ginza,
for which the artist felt no love at all,
and, by one of fate's little ironies,
in that giant new department store
where her husband used to buy his braces,
cufflinks, neckties, and other personal trifles.
He too, incidentally, came on the opening day,
and in spite of being so immensely cultured,
secretly felt no pride at all,
but a wild, almost animal, feeling of terror:
his wife was finally slipping beyond his reach.
The department store building became
the second one taken during the rebellion,
although, unfortunately, not completely.

An old man wearing colorful jeans went up to her,
and she knew him at once, not by his jeans,
but by his strong gray hands
in which a reed pipe danced invisibly.
Her first word to him was "Teacher . . ."
But he waved it away with a gentle gesture,
saying: "Teacher? In art, I don't know what that means.
Teacher—that word's an empty kind of medal,
even if one receives it from the kindest hand.
In art, what can be more unnatural
than so-called relationships
between so-called teachers
and their so-called pupils!
We're both artists, and so we're friends and enemies
and our tender hostility will help protect
each of us, but mutual reverence will destroy us.

I can respect you as a forceful enemy,
and if things ever should go wrong for you,
remember, find your way to that old basement—
that's where you'll find a cup of coffee,
and I'll gladly play to you again on the reed pipe..."
The exhibition had one rather strange feature:
while men, of course, dropped in to see it,
the women literally flocked there, as to a shop
where they handed out freedom from husbands and the daily grind,
and even women from the embassies—
white women all the way from Europe
and also some from the United States,
stood there for hours examining the canvases,
recognizing their own sufferings painted
in the eyes of Japanese and African women
and of the doomed cows from Hokkaido,
and seeing in the turbulence of rebellious colors
their own repressed desire for rebellion.
One enterprising manufacturer
placed in the miscellaneous leather goods
department of this selfsame store
thousands of leather handbags,
with white characters on a black background
spelling out a short but eloquent "No."
And after visiting the exhibition,
and walking down only a single flight,
women would acquire these handbags
bearing the slogan of moral rebellion
against men—the disparaging "No."

One day the artist had a visitor:
it was a Japanese woman in her early forties
wearing a cheap kimono, not made of silk;
her eyes were the oppressed eyes of the Hokkaido cows,
in which, however, there clearly glimmered
the bonfires at the outbreak of rebellion.
"I'm from the Sony factory," she said, "of course
"I'm nothing like as educated as you.
I've never done any painting in my life,
but now, I beg you, teach me how to paint!"
The artist started giving her lessons,
and something came to light in that woman
who, in her watercolors, would depict

other Japanese women assembling transistors—
dustbins for the world's lies and music.
The factory women seemed to resemble
lotuses buckling under the burden
of heavy snow, but the woman painting
them stood straighter with each successive painting.
Then the woman from the Sony factory
brought a friend with her—a box-office attendant
from the kabuki theater, and *she*, in turn,
brought *her* friend—an actress from a rival
theater, and *she* brought a friend—
a boxer's wife, whose husband sometimes
used her face for sparring practice.

In a short time the greenhouse witnessed the birth
of a kind of underground organization,
struggling, if not to procure men's downfall,
then at least for something like democracy.
Certain women only stayed a certain time,
coquettishly wishing to intimidate
their husbands with art, which they then deserted
for doubtful peace within the family's bosom.
But other women stayed very much longer
and formed some sort of executive committee.
And, as in most committees, there were plots and intrigues,
which soon had no connection with the purity
of the original idea. And the artist sometimes
would regret that she had got mixed up
in all this business, where art quite unavoidably
had started smelling of politics—extremist politics
at that! Women's liberation from men?
That kind of program was one-sided:
for men, as well, are far from being free,
let's say, at least, in their own jobs, from bosses.
And often, though it's dreadful to admit,
in their own homes, from domineering wives.
The mutual liberation of men and women—
that was the program she accepted;
and, having in mind this noble, ultimate aim,
perhaps forever unattainable,
and for this reason still more noble,
she hadn't the heart to close the fragile doors
of the revolutionary headquarters

(that is, the greenhouse) in the faces
of new legions of aspiring women.
The greenhouse was shaken by contradictions,
since people's championing their individual styles
was deemed by their opponents as betrayal
of the revolution's ideology.
Here one could find little realists,
little surrealists, little abstractionists,
pop artists, as well as op artists,
and each of these directions made the claim
that it alone was worthy of first place.
The artist tried to reconcile them all,
using the principle of the carrot and the stick.
But all the same they'd scratch each other's pictures
with their palette knives, and use the turps,
reserved for final touches to their chefs d'oeuvre,
for splashing, irreconcilably, each other's faces.
Besides, despite their stated hatred for the male sex,
when any man appeared inside the greenhouse,
quite unobtrusively, they'd preen themselves,
ready to bite out each other's throats.
But, nonetheless, with all these listed drawbacks,
this was indeed a rebellion,
and what rebellion
ever got going without victims and other losses?
And the artist, worn out in the struggle,
continued, not only painting pictures,
but also standing at the head of the rebellion
which it was now impossible to abandon;
for deprived of wisdom in its leadership
it could turn into a rebellion against its own.

And the artist steadfastly led the rebellion,
conscious that she had also made mistakes,
but convinced at the same time of her own rightness,
and that of the rebellion, as such,
for life is a rebellion against death,
and art is a rebellion against life,
if life and death become too much alike.

... But sometimes, if snow appeared outside the window,
the artist felt an urge to go out into it
away from all the meetings and the voting.
And, filled with relief, she would remember

that somewhere out there was a dingy basement,
and living in that basement was an artist,
and in his strong gray hands, a healing reed pipe.

1974
Tokyo — Moscow
TRANSLATED BY ARTHUR BOYARS AND SIMON FRANKLIN (REVISED)

1976⁄1978

Hunger has the speed of sound,
when beginning as a moan, it becomes a scream.

Good-for-nothing Places

For the artist Tselkov*
life makes sense in its own way:
From fear he can't make friends with Aeroflot,
and pays duty to two gods, that is,
he knows as much about drinking as working,
and he works the way he drinks.
A convinced believer in hopelessness,
he is afraid even of the Caucasus,
and in Siberia the gnats,
but, with hangman's humanity,
I said: "The tickets are in my pocket . . .
It's time to do Siberia . . ."

Onto the marshes of Yakutsk he fell
out of a helicopter onto the moss,
bandying his way in the clouds,
together with gloomy giggles
and with transparent peccadilloes,
and what is more with two bags
under his eyes, not on his arms.

The artist Tselkov has
tenacious views and obstinate words,
and probably not without purpose,
sullenly huddling himself up,
grumbled about the Vilyui taiga:
"Brothers, this place is good for nothing . . ."

We weren't about to pick on him:
"You know, we're not your brothers,
and, anyway, you're a modernist . . ."
We were crestfallen,
and looked about at nature,
but we didn't want to pick on it either.

The region really was dismal.
The scraggly, gnarled, and twisted
forest scrambled sideways.
Moss hung on the crags like oakum

and for hundreds of miles not a whiff
either of a campfire or tobacco.

But there was such splendor
in the poverty-stricken, gloomy beauty
scattered with cloudberries.
This reign of misfitism
dislodges arrogance from a visitor
and holds him in fear.

All artists are misfits,
but the artist was not intimidated
by the taiga along the way:
he simply saw in the flesh,
in the doomed proud branches,
his own essence clearly.

And the artist got used to the taiga,
wrung the Vilyui out of his jeans,
gobbled bilberries from the bushes,
devoured ducks along with shot,
but an alarm rumbled in his belly:
"Brothers, this place is good for nothing . . ."

Listen, if your painting
is a swamp for someone,
it doesn't matter if he is an expert.
Art is a good-for-nothing place,
but from bootlicking as from destruction
there's salvation only in art.

I've been in such palaces
on those triumphal banisters,
now there's ruin for you, for sure!
You've got ghosts of lackeys,
"Very good!" and "Molto bene!"—
everything, only no salmon trout,
no rapids in intoxicated foam,
no wooden skiff *Ekonda,*
called by us *Giaconda.*

And in some son-of-a-bitch's office
where the green sucking swamp
is under glass on the table

in moldy telephone hummocks
a good-for-nothing smell lingers—
that cadaverous stench of a bastard.

And in someone's bedroom accidentally,
in the lying-crying, liberal-playing world,
where in real matters there is cowardice,
where there are quagmire looks and lips,
I whispered: "Clear out of here to the taiga!
The place is good for nothing."

There is no insurance for genius
other than its own fear of
becoming the likes of a petty tradesman.
Genius perishes as does the untalented,
if the dried-up soul becomes
a good-for-nothing abyss.

God grant to you, Tselkov
to find a lucky horseshoe
in the mountain streams,
so that you won't give up, and swim on,
so the most "good-for-nothing" place
in your destiny will be the Vilyui.

Anyone who is a true artist
is at heart a man of the taiga.
The whole wide world is like the taiga.
Amid the rot, the ashes, the dried-out places
are souls that have perished—
there are no good-for-nothing places in the world.

1976

TRANSLATED BY ALBERT C. TODD

*Tselkov: Oleg Tselkov. Russian painter now living in Paris.

Long Life

I
  have lived longer than
        Pushkin,
            Lermontov,
                Yesenin,
                    Mayakovsky,
a good fortune, undeserved,
        apparently sucked in with the milk.
I've been in sixty-four countries
        more than all the poets before me.
The civilized have applauded me
          as well as the primitive.
What's there to say, no doubt—
      a lucky kid with a double gold spoon—
after all they didn't let Pushkin
         go abroad at all.
I've spoken with presidents,
        with cabinet secretaries—
but due to historical circumstances
         never with tsars.
After the fate of Koltsov,*
        or of Polezhaev,†
my fate is supernatural,
        my destiny astonishing.
Kolya Otrada‡ was killed at the front,
         twenty years old,
and to this day I am amazed at the miracle
        of my own survival.
I have recited in the Sports Palace,
    sometimes been elected to the presidium.
A Russian poet with such a fate
      is morally already under suspicion.
But, my honest word as poet,
   I haven't rocked myself to sleep with fame,
having unprecedentedly in poetry
      made a precedent of good fortune.
I ask you to relate to me
      critically, but respectfully.
Forty-year-old poets
      in Russia are long-livers.

But how can I pay in full
                    for fame given in abundance,
          for living long,
                    for being older than Pushkin?!

1976

TRANSLATED BY ALBERT C. TODD

*Koltsov: Mikhail Efimovich Koltsov (real name: Fridliand) (1898–1942). Prolific journalist, editor, political activist, and academician, recognized for his literary quality. Arrested in 1938, perished in prison.
†Polezhaev: Aleksandr Ivanovich Polezhaev (1805–38). Russian poet sentenced by Tsar Nikolai I to serve in the army for revolutionary protest poetry after repression of the Decembrist Rebellion (1825). Died from harsh treatment, physical punishment, and consumption.
‡Otrada: Nikolai Karpovich Otrada (real name: Turochkin) (1918–40). Soviet poet, unpublished in his lifetime, full of romantic faith in Communism, killed (age twenty-one) as a volunteer in the war against Finland.

Woman Midget

At the Little Eagle children's theater
beneath posters for the cartoon
                    "Just Wait!"
a woman midget moved
                    like a broken-off stem,
clutching a bag of oranges
                    to her chest.
She was both
          humpbacked
                    and lame,
with arms
          of different length,
and everyone looked away,
                    understanding
how one is drawn to horrible sights.
So bent,
          twisted,
                    and gnarled,
with limbs cross warped
                    and distorted,

443

even the ghoulish woman janitor
handed her
                two fallen oranges.
She bunched them in the bag
                            and tucked the corners
so nothing more could spill out,
and sighing,
            flailed her stick
to break the ice
                from the rainspout.
Everyone loves to seem pathetic;
it's a weakness no one can resist.
Even as an angry cabdriver called out:
                        "To Kazansky Station!"
he suddenly choked,
                    spying the crawling lump.
And thought, perhaps:
                "Who cares about my quota
                            or my boss . . . ?
Here is real misfortune . . ."
And when a hung-over drunkard
                        with a cretin's face
gradually turning more human,
forgot his mug,
                you could hear
snow fall onto the beer foam.
A girl and boy
                pressing close together,
on seeing the midget cross their path,
turned their fear,
later of course, to greater
                        love.
And I,
        mustering all my will,
whispered:
            "I'll remember this,
and will never allow myself
an ounce
        of self-pity.
But how to keep from turning pleasure
                            into indifference,
so that every fortunate person
                        saves someone else,

the way another's misery

                always

saves us from our own.

1976

TRANSLATED BY ANTONINA W. BOUIS

Tomorrow's Wind

Why am I without joy,

               achieving everything,

but grasping

         nothing at all?

I dream of the wind

             that has overtaken me,

the wind

         that has leaped over me.

It shreds

         all the telephone lines that sag

from unending chatter,

and all that's wasted,

              all that's turned sour

it catapults

         into oblivion.

All sorts of butwhatifers,

shaking,

        like jelly in jackets,

whirled up in a vortex,

            like fallen leaves,

shout down indignantly:

          "How come?"

Where there's no wind,

          there's no faith.

Let clammy red pencils

         be strewn

among the reeds,

        scattered madly

by tomorrow's wind.

Wind
      does not crawl
           before idols,
it swirls scraps
          of newspapers and posters,
yesterday's glories,
          turning somersaults
over warped roofs.
As if it had swilled
          the Decembrists' hot punch,
tipsy,
      the wind flings upward
all the important little papers
that press us down
          to the ground.
The wind
      showers
          under constellations
the garbage
        in which the world is bogged down:
automobiles,
        which have ridden over people,
furniture,
        which has sprawled on us.
The wind
      pulls away from sticky screens
all the bewitched
        simpletons and fools,
and without thinking
          plants them
             like shashlik
on the spike of their beloved TV tower . . .
Timid youth,
        I am preaching to you:
Charge forward,
        headlong into the epoch,
without wasting
        the wind of history
either on fads
      or the flimsy.
Each
   new generation
must create
      a special wind.

If it doesn't shake
           bits of dust,
young people
        should send
           an SOS.
Youth
    is the age for a fresh airing.
In old age
        it's harder to be precocious,
if you put off
        being young
in your youth.
Is it possible for you
          all to be unfit?
Suck in the time
        with a feverous mouth.
The calm will be
        inhaled by you,
by the wind
     exhaled
        afterward.
And the wind,
      making a gift of itself
             to the universe,
is born,
    sprawling
      in a burst,
and structures
      built on sand
rightfully will crumble.
And I, having reared
        these structures not a little,
will look on happily,
      blaming no one,
as it withdraws,
     arching its mane,
the wind
    that has leaped over me.

1977

TRANSLATED BY ALBERT C. TODD

Gogol's Mistake

Once when Gogol shuddered
before a vision of the end,
as if before a barren steppe
where there was neither fire
nor sleigh bell—
his weakened will
dragged itself away from all passions,
like a tumbleweed,
under the wheel of the authorities' love.
What crushed him? The paddy wagon?
The tsar's mighty carriage?
Does it matter?
                    Such tenderness
for genius is not in vain.
Even in weakness he dared
to seek sympathy from those
you have mocked—
what daring!
                    It's comic and sad.
To whom did he, a miserable wretch, repent?
Where did his feet take him?
Could some policeman have been
transformed by love?
But, seeing chaos even in love,
and relishing their blue pencil marks,
the authorities, chuckling,
censored his confession of love for them.
How delirious he was, how rushed.
how tormented,
using scraps of correspondence
to sew his own shroud.
How shattered he was, how beleaguered,
when to the jangle of chains
he bore the idea of a special lyricism—

in praise of tsars.
He addressed himself to rusty odes.
He gilded Derzhavin's
shackled rank . . .
                    But why Derzhavin!
Let him speak for himself:
"They caught a songbird,
and squeeze it in their hands.
The poor thing squeaks instead of whistling,
and they keep saying, sing, birdie, sing."

Such crushed lyricism
did have a special sound.
At death's door, can't an old man tell a lie?
There are those who lie even in the grave.
O Derzhavin's ode,
I greet and bow to you,
but one that elevates fresh air and freedom
and not Felitsa's* sweaty throne.
They lied out of oppression, misery,
squeezed like the lowest vermin,
out of desire to enlighten the authorities
for whom enlightenment meant death.
Damnation, and not rebuke,
for the hand choking the soul's voice
when the "special aspect of lyricism"
leads geniuses to lie.

But Belinsky with his harsh young truth
did not shy
before the mammoth grim shadow
of the tiny emaciated figure.
For even had the genius fallen
into darkness and renunciation,
the immortal exposés of his
innocent books were not lost.

O genius, you live in illusion,
when being so naive
you expect kindness and understanding
from your executioner.
And Gogol hunched up, bristling,
turned his face to the ages,
when Nozdrev's reins lashed out

449

in answer
to his extended arms.

1977

TRANSLATED BY ANTONINA W. BOUIS

*Felitsa's: A sobriquet (from the Latin *felicitas*) often applied to Catherine II, used by Derzhavin in his ode.

Across Eight Thousand Kilometers

In Kolyma's* crags, like a death prisoner,
alone and concealed in the taiga,
across eight thousand kilometers
I am starving for you.

Across eight thousand kilometers
I want to sprout arms.
Across eight thousand kilometers
I want to embrace, to save you.

Across eight thousand kilometers,
all teeth are broken on the ice,
my hunger waits, my hunger believes,
doesn't wait, doesn't believe, once again waits.

And driving, driving, driving me,
sinking in the treacherous mosses,
my hunger starves itself,
even farther, and farther from you.

I have only your phantom to gnaw on
and I become like a phantom myself.
I hunger for a voice
and I hunger for eyes.

And, transformed into a body, which waits
for a mere drop from a bucket,
my soul trembles and staggers.
like an illusory Kolyma ghost.

. . .

And trespassing rudely by your door,
escaping from watchtowers and roundups,
my over-parched lips
thrust out through the telegram blank.

The expanse of space is not parting.
In parting one can be near.
Hunger has the speed of sound,
when beginning as a moan, it becomes a scream.

And on the wing of any Iliushin,†
having clawed its way into a cell like a beast,
my soul, which in setting up a howl
has become hunger, will fly to you.

Across eight thousand kilometers
resurrect love through the expanse.
Send me your answering hunger
and with its pangs save me.

Send it, don't wait, don't hesitate—
know that eyelashes can wound
across eight thousand kilometers
the soul or the flesh unto death.

1977

TRANSLATED BY ALBERT C. TODD

*Kolyma: Site of notorious labor camps in northeastern Siberia.
†Iliushin: Type of series of Soviet passenger jet aircraft.

"When the clover field stirs..."

When the clover field stirs,
when pine trees creak and sigh,
my heart freezes, listens, remembers
that someday I will die.

On the roof by the rainspout cool,
a boy will stand up with a plump dove

and I'll grasp that dying is cruel
to one's self, and to others we love.

No feeling of life without a feeling of death.
We depart not like water into sand so clever.
But the living, those, who relieve the dead,
will never take the place of the dead ever.

Something of this I understood in life—
which means, I wasn't knocked about in vain.
I forgot, it seems, everything that I remembered,
but I remembered everything that I forgot.

I understood that in childhood snow is fluffier,
that the hills are greener in youth.
I understood that in life there are so many lives,
and how many times we love in truth.

I understood that I was secretly connected
to so many people from all times all at once.
I understood that man is not happy
because he searches for happiness.

In happiness there's such stupidity sometimes.
Happiness stares emptily and easily will sleep.
Misery stares, sadly lowering its eyes,
because it sees so deep.

Happiness is like a glimpse from an airplane.
Misery sees the earth without adornments.
In happiness there is something treacherous—
misery never betrays man.

I was imprudently lucky,
thank God—happiness didn't happen.
I wanted that which is impossible.
It's good that I didn't succeed.

I love you, human people,
and I forgive the striving for happiness.
I have now become happy forever,
because I don't search for it.

· · ·

I need only to keep safe
the sweetness of clover on hardened lips.
I need only a little weakness
after all, not to die at all.

1977

TRANSLATED BY ALBERT C. TODD

Insurance Agent

The car drove under a snowfall
that softened nothing in the world,
and a woman wept next to
the stonily silent driver.

For Women's Day she held in her hands
bedraggled and crushed mimosa,
trembling beneath her sobs
so chick-like and defenseless.

Her sobbing exhaustion seemed
to smash dishes to pieces:
"Well, all right—I'll be with you.
But when you leave—I'll stay . . ."

Already from tomorrow's injury,
already from yesterday's grief,
nearly out of their orbit,
her eyes dangled by threads.

And somewhere around Preobrazhenka,
in a shower of tears like an avalanche,
there suddenly burst out so womanly:
"What must I do to be loved?

I'm obviously bad at love.
They avoid me the morning after.
It's not tears men want, but laughter.
I cry too easily—that scares them off.

. . .

I ruined things with you again.
What the hell, here I am,
an insurance agent, pouring
uninsured tears on my mimosa!

I like going from apartment to apartment,
even though it's awkward.
But insurance, like solace,
ties so many people to the world.

Sometimes there's an ancient granny,
breathing incense, sick and dying,
but a paper plaything flatters
that nevertheless she is insured.

Piotr Stepanych was here before me,
and out of yesterday's inertia
I'm offered a little glass
of homemade wine.

Along with greetings to my son,
at the door I'm furtively handed
forty kopecks 'for chocolates,'
as Piotr Stepanych was 'for beer.' "

The car moved inexorably.
Snow flew toward them howling.
The driver seemed frantic
but just gripped the wheel tighter.

It was March, cold and empty,
and far from April.
All around uninsured feelings
burned invisibly.

And blue sparks struck
against the windshield,
as the cry rose in the snowy howl:
"What must I do to be loved!"

1977

TRANSLATED BY ANTONINA W. BOUIS

Don't Disappear

Don't disappear . . . By disappearing from me,
you will disappear from yourself,
betraying your own self forever,
and that will be the basest dishonesty.

Don't disappear . . . To disappear is so easy.
It's impossible to resurrect one another.
Death drags one down too deep.
To become dead even for a moment is not prudent.

Don't disappear . . . Forget the third shadow.
In love there are only two. There are no thirds.
We both will be pure on Judgment Day,
when the trumpets call us to account.

Don't disappear . . . We have redeemed sin.
We both are free of the law, we are sinless.
We are worthy together of the forgiveness of those
whom we have unintentionally wounded.

Don't disappear . . . One can disappear in an instant,
but how could we meet later in the centuries ahead?
Is your double possible in the world,
and my double? Only just in our children.

Don't disappear . . . Give me your palm.
I am written on it—this I believe.
What makes one's last love terrible
is that it is not love, but fear of loss.

1977
TRANSLATED BY ALBERT C. TODD

Nice People

"There'll be nice people..."—
                                        buzzes in my ear,
inviting me to dinner;
                        like a hedgehog,
my needles
                restrained ahead of time,
giving me to understand
                        the undesirability of insurrection.
I'm tired of the tyranny of "nice people"
without sharp nails
                        sticking out of them.
In this cottony
                private
                        empty twaddle
there's no one
                who could even scratch me
                                        with a needle!
I go in.
        I try to be a nice hedgehog.
They don't saw off my needles with a knife,
but they stick pieces of shish kebob on them,
so they would prick
                only slightly.
Where are these people's needles?
                        Where are their sharp corners?
How nauseatingly nice they are
                        and round!
There progressivism
                amounts to a joke,
and what progressivism is it—
                hostingism,
                        invitingism!
The only thing they can stab is a mushroom
                        with a fork.
They used to be hedgehogs,
                but now they're small round loafs.
They ran from the wolf,
                and they ran from the fox,
and they put on airs,
                that anyway they're not scoundrels.

But, like a powerful
                    clinging magnet,
daily life pulled out
                    all their former needles.
Is a villain frightening
                    when he's obviously a villain?
How to save ourselves from not so obvious
                                        "beautiful people"?
I depart, abandoning their little world,
and after me comes:
                    "Well, isn't it true darling,
                                        he's a darling."
And, as though it were a banner,
                                        the midnight dark
I impale
        in solitude
                    on a needle.

1977
TRANSLATED BY ALBERT C. TODD

Moscow-Ivanovo

Riding the train to Ivanovo
unable to sleep all night,
I was like a half-welcome
and almost uninvited guest.

I was on the slow train
where they clutched like a vise
microporous oranges—
the fruits of Mother Moscow.

Together with wheezes and snores,
through the forests swept
the imported laundry soap powder,
and the synthetics, and the baloney.

People slept as though they were dead
in the moon's reflected blue light,

their hard-won booty
rocking them to sleep.

But what kinds of dreams nursed them
along the singing wires,
are known only to the pillowcases
of the night Russian train.

And beyond all price in value,
like cars filled with stillness,
straightaway were coupled to that train
the dreams of all Russia.

Four of us dozed in one compartment.
How are we to live now?
What has been destined for us—
who can even imagine? . . .

Our train moved through a rain shower,
its rays burning through the night,
and snoring, each pressed firmly
something to his breast.

Granny pressed to her heart
a precious parcel with only
a jar of instant coffee.
Granny barely slept.

Tormenting his bed for that night,
a traveler on assignment
pressed close the important garbage
locked in his overworked briefcase.

The big-bosomed worsted-goods lady,
whistling softly through her nose,
squeezed, like the government,
her very own child.

And all this that's most precious,
though fallen with exhaustion,
the heartland of Russia,
I want to press to my breast.

· · ·

With her revolutions and wars,
with her ashes of villages and towns,
with the never-ceasing wailing
of Russian blizzards and Russian widows.

I ask myself to the whistling
of the train and the wires:
"We've known so much of horror—
maybe, it's enough to last forever?"

On and on the questions renew:
"After so many bitter years,
haven't we earned the good life?
Do we deserve it or not?"

Distorted, battered
by all of our Russian trials,
our wagon car muttered,
whispered, and squeaked on:

"Not all we imagine will come true
by crossing the first bridge.
What doesn't happen—will be forgotten
beneath a birch tree cross."

1978

TRANSLATED BY ALBERT C. TODD

The Unexpressed

The unexpressed,
                    the unarticulated
are frightening,
                    when as fragments
they burn
          beneath the skin,
with no way at all

to be scratched out,
plucked out,
                or brought to reason.
Events
        bricked up inside
cry out in despair:
                    "We've been forgotten.
We'll be eliminated
                    from history:
let us out!
            let us out!"
Suffering rises up
                like a lump in the throat:
"We are
        like stifled sobs.
We long so
            for our liberation:
express us!
                express us!"
Smashing through ribs,
                        new ideas call out their appeal:
"We are crowded inside.
                        We are torn to pieces there."
Words that are beautiful
                    but unuttered
scream:
        "We have been buried alive."
And all mistakes,
                sins that have been secreted,
pound themselves
                like epileptics saying:
"That which is not expressed
                        will be forgotten,
and what is forgotten
                will happen again."
Repentance gnaws out:
                    "I need to break loose.
I was a tiny thing.
                Now I am full grown!"
Grief,
        not expressed in time,
howls in twilight:
                "I want to be free!"
And joy weeps

quite joylessly:
"All your feelings—
                    they are what is robbed,
when you think
                    that you show your wit
by
    not expressing even your joy."
And gentleness whispers:
                        "They are ashamed of me,
they talk to each other
                    with rudeness.
Why do you conceal,
                    tormenting one another,
not only the worst
                    but even the best?
Hidden pain
            is terrifying
and inevitably
                will kill,
but even gentleness is deadly,
                                if
it is concealed . . ."
Start the confession,
                    even slowly, bit by bit.
Make an attempt
                to begin,
                            to try.
When a confession
                is whole and done,
then what obtains
                is admonition.
But we are shy,
                like wrongful accusations,
not only of what is terrible,
                            but even of what is beautiful.
We are shy about love,
                    acting as if we were too young,
and conceal even
                love of country.
But I don't believe
                in that kind of sincerity:
there is in it something obviously
                                unsubstantiated—
when the simplest cowardice

plays

at subtle understatement.

1978

TRANSLATED BY ALBERT C. TODD

Psychotherapy

Pain gnaws into man,
lacerating with its claws.
It's deposited like salt
somewhere between the vertebrae.

Shout something to the crowd?
That's a lot of respect for cattle.
Confess to a priest?
Man doesn't believe in God.

Confess to the wife?
A pain inscrutable for her.
Confess to the country?
That's so immense it terrifies.

And the psychiatrist arrives
with a musketeer beard,
warmly phlegmatic,
faintly smelling of vodka.

And though you tear your hair—
he will listen for two hours
to your woes and vexations,
and all for two bills.

Afterward he goes on foot
through grimy lanes,
and under his tongue lays
a tranquilizer.

. . .

There's a trick to attentiveness:
not the least merit in it,
and he himself longs for a fellow
psychiatrist—a friend for hire.

1978

TRANSLATED BY ALBERT C. TODD

On Modesty

When a certain genius,
                    squealing,
cried to Mandelstam
that they don't publish him,
                        the monsters,
the poet became angry,
                    the way
he would
        at a cliché.
Tactful Osip Emilevich,
as chroniclers have noted,
didn't sweet-talk the genius,
but let him go down the stairs
and, boiling over intentionally,
threw his gloves after him:
"And Jesus Christ,
did they publish him?!"

I grow bit by bit.
I am published—
                    why should I be sad,
but for Christ
getting published was more difficult.
He might even have finished
his complete works,
but Christ didn't count on
the correction of comrade Pontius.
Writing dozens of little books,
is morally nothing,

when you only think
of Christ.

1978

TRANSLATED BY ALBERT C. TODD

Monologue of a Loser

"I bid adieu to sullen time
with its lost game.
What sort of game,

                what sort of nonsense—
It's not the time, perhaps, to say,
and maybe, it's simply scary,
but I'm not yearning to explain.
My modest loss was this:
dozens of tons of verses,
the whole globe,

           my country,
my friends,

       my wife,
I myself—

      but on that account, however,
I'm not very upset.
Such trifles

        as honor
I forgot to consider.
I didn't lose?

        How can one know—as long
as the click of a trigger doesn't confirm it,
here the trigger jammed—
that, in general,
I played a semi-risky game
to no good end.
For this charity—
I'm punished with semi-death."

1978

TRANSLATED BY ALBERT C. TODD

To Charlie Chaplin

In parting with Chaplin—
                    there's no parting with Charlie.
He freezes, he starves—
                    he's alive, as in the beginning,
when in preposterous shoes,
                    shedding their soles,
he pounded out against Klondike frosts
                    a tap dance of mortal sadness.
And, too eager,
          for the ludicrous,
                    for the spicy,
boring holes
          through the screen
                    with its eyes,
a world drowning in blood
                    grasped for Chaplin's cane,
                              like a straw.
They darned the screens.
                    The generations changed.
Why
     laugh
          at tormented Charlie?
They should have
          guffawed
                    murderously
at Hitler
     in time—
who might never have grown
                    from a clown
                              into a führer . . .
And laughter at tragedy
                    became unredeemable guilt.
So little is funny
          when the hideous
                    for us is humor.
Comic sparks,
          as though real,
                    flashed in millions of retinas.

465

And the one man not laughing at Charlie—

                            was Charlie himself.

And Chaplin got an answer from Charlie,
why a never-ending callous laugh
pursued the little man?
Because he was for all that a man.
I froze and hungered.

                 Both tanks and dogs

                          snarled at me.

I saw fascism—

              and not the living Christ.

But if there had not been

        the sorrowful little black-haired imp, Charlie—

I would not be the same

               and the era would not be the same.

Parting with Charlie—

              is parting with a whole era,

and how good it is

           that now no one finds this funny.

Abandoning the alien movie

             of lying sounds,

he departs for death

            into a silent film that's his alone.

Without Chaplin people already

             have started to be a little bored,

but Charlie remains,

           and we will wait a little,

until for Chaplin

        Charlie clicks glasses

                  with the universe,

his empty shoe

        filled with Klondike rain.

1978

TRANSLATED BY ALBERT C. TODD

The Art of Ingratiating

Where did we learn
                the shameful art of ingratiating,
how to poke our noses
                with a note from someone
into the window of a theater administrator,
as if he were a Roman tyrant!
In hotels
        we anxiously proffer
with a humiliated hand,
                moist from fear,
our passports
        with a ten spot,
                tenderly inserted,
as though we were tramps without kith or kin...
We fawn all buttery
                before a bouncer,
as if he
        were better than Byron.
We truckle
        with a self-induced droop
in front of the samovar-shaped waitress,
in front of the cocky Aeroflot cashier,
disdainfully squinting her eyes at us.
Ingratiating himself
                in a furniture store,
a great sprinter
                moves like a tortoise.
The genius of our age,
                a physicist,
fawns before a plumber from the housing board.
Sweating,
        a godlike violinist
grovels before an arrogant motel maid.
Who among us has not become a stutterer,
when, like someone dying of hunger
begging from ladies on the porch steps,
we mealymouth:
                "I want to call long-distance..."
How petty authorities
                propagate themselves!

467

How they embody
                    a supreme insolence!
The art of ingratiating solves nothing.
Equality
        has been replaced
                        by obsequiousness.
By breeding
        bulldogs
                from mutts,
we ourselves
            have fostered
                        our own boors.
I have a nightmare
                that in the Volga
our groveling
            has begotten
                    a crocodile.

1978
TRANSLATED BY ALBERT C. TODD

"O Georgia . . ."

To D. Betashvili

O Georgia,
            wiping our tears,
you are to Russia's muse
                        a second cradle.
O Georgia,
            carelessly forgetting,
in Russia it's impossible
                    to be a poet.

1978
TRANSLATED BY ALBERT C. TODD

"No, literacy is not..."

No, literacy
         is not in reading newspapers
not even in books,
             which have transcended time.
Staring at letters
         is natural for eyes,
but there is another,
             inner sense of sight.
And doesn't it frighten you,
when,
     like a saucy strumpet,
impudent illiteracy of the spirit
puts on airs with a lying literacy of the eyes.

1978

TRANSLATED BY ALBERT C. TODD

Russians and Jews

It was a single epoch
for both Russian and Jew,
when Russia raised them up,
breaking history like bread.

The foundation for moral justice
is that Jew and Russian,
united together in formation,
died for their common land.

Playing from phantasmal fields
Sholom Aleichem accompanied
on his fragile fiddle
Ryazan's morning peasant pipes.

Now gone far away from us,

without quarrel or swagger,
Kachalov* and Mikhoels† are
in a single theater forever.

1978

TRANSLATED BY ALBERT C. TODD

*Kachalov: Vasilii Ivanovich Kachalov (1875–1948). Outstanding Soviet actor of the Moscow Arts Theatre. Stalin Prize (1943).
†Mikhoels: Solomon Mikhailovich Mikhoels (1890–1948). Soviet Russia's greatest Jewish actor. Stalin Prize (1946). Murdered, apparently on Stalin's orders.

Ivan the Terrible and Ivan the Fool: A Poem (Excerpt)

2.

Lord Ivan Vasilievich* the Terrible
seldom risked a dewy constitutional.
More often across carpets, marble floors,
over corpses he squelched and tramped through gore.
Lord Ivan Vasilievich the Terrible
seldom listened on a starry eve to nightingales.
No nightingale's, the tsar's nocturnal birdsong
was the screams of folk in towers and in dungeons.
But one night the dreaded sovereign was aroused
not by his upset stomach—
                              this was soused
in mead and bloated from fish patties—
but by a nightingale's anonymous ditty.
Thin was that voice but animate,
as after an execution, on the chipped ax blade,
a stray hair stirs—
                        and the tsar heard its lament
in the deep shadows:
                    "Repent,

                        repent . . ."

And in his nightshirt the monarch left the chamber,
barefoot into the garden went, and listened
fearfully to the song's accusation
issuing thence as if by miracle.
And the tsar thought, tearing away convolvulus:
"Aye, it is true that nightingales have other passions.
I'm not endowed with what the nightingale has.
What's mine is power, exercised by right, God-given.
And if it's not from God, this power, but rather
the Devil?"
    He shuddered:
        "Heresy ...
You're an apostate, nightingale,
          a wretched liar.
Power is divine.
      I'll not lose faith in that!"
The tsar, entangled in the garden, as in a thicket,
hunted the singer with claws drawn,
breathed hard and said to the nightingale:
           "I'm sick at
heart, believing in no one at all ..."
And colliding on the narrow path with his tsar,
Viskovatii,†
    clerk to the council of boyars,
pretended that he hadn't heard a thing
(though, in the end, it's true, this did not save him).
And the oprichniks,‡ stinking of raw vodka,
shook the apple trees and birches in the hue
and cry, hacking away with poleaxes to no purpose
at amethystine pearls of dew.
Viskovatii made a cunning attempt
to end this avicular torment.
If, hound-like,
    you can sense a monarch's wrath,
then even a nightingale may be put on the spot.
"My Lord,"
    said the clerk Viskovatii,
with his furtive air,
      and falsely hearty,
"I have my doubts about the printing trade:
We must be careful not to overlook mistakes."
Now, Lord Ivan Vasilievich the Terrible
was, after all, godfather to Ivan Fyodorov.§
He'd personally lay the paper on the press

and, hiding a childlike smile, examine it
and show it to his guests from overseas,
saying: "See what Ivans our Russia breeds..."
So the tsar scowled now:
                              "What did you have in mind?"
"Well,
          it is really the whole enterprise.
If books are to increase faster and faster,
then the serfs will grow to be just like their master.
And if Ivashka suddenly decides
to print subversive writings on the side?
There's a danger
                    in every handwrit word,
but printed,
                it wings louder than that bird—
it would not give you any peace at all..."
The tsar thought hard:
                          "I'll hear no idle talk...
Clerk, are there subversive texts or not?"
"There may be...
                    Tsar, close down the shop!"
"And our Ivan?
                  My hand's too tired to beat him."
"We can drop a hint
                      and on his journey speed him!"
Lord Ivan Vasilievich the Terrible
was clever,
              though he wasn't reckoned so.
That night he drank and drank,
                                  his face was sullen,
but the red wine from France bought him no comfort.
If you govern ignorant folk
                              you yourself become a
                                              blockhead.
But if they're literate,
                          you're better off dead.
Should he cut down the apple tree
                                    and cherry,
so the bird should no more offend his hearing?
It would repair
                  to broom and willow,
                                          if he did.
The tsar was kind.

He said:
                    "Then drop a hint."

And so they did.
                    Fyodorov Ivan
bade farewell to the royal printing house
and quickly slipped the type into his bag—
that it was spared showed quite uncommon lenience.
He smoothed out the edges of a stray sheet—
on it was laid the nailed impression
of an oprichnik's metal heel,
mark of his sovereign lord's appreciation.
They had not found subversive documents,
but for the oprichniks the alphabet
itself was subversive,
                    containing salt
rather than the cunning of delusive mead.
Cruelly wounded, consumed by grief,
Ivan procured a cart,
                    and left the court,
and maybe for the first time in his life
allowed himself to think his secret thoughts:
"How happy I was in my tsar to trust,
bending my head before him dutifully!
I did not irritate the State, nor judge,
but that has not stopped it from judging me.
In the State's limpid gaze, I swear—
though I do not expect a just and fair trial—
such perfidious treatment's not deserved,
for I myself have never been deceitful.
I tried to love you, State, my one desire
to be of service, but I knew
that I would cease to be if I
cringed like a cowardly dog before you.
State, you are serfs and nobles, domain
of denunciation, fawning, enmity.
The serf can't simultaneously entertain
feeling for State and country . . ."

Great Gutenberg,
                    would you have understood
the joys life offers to your Russian colleague
who, banned from Moscow, sits atop his cart,

the letters of the alphabet for luggage?
You would have understood, kirsch drinker, in your cups,
Ivan unheard, sobbing into his sleeve,
when he was shooed away, just like a pup—
lucky for him

                he was let off so cheap!
But where was he to drag his typeface, where
now his homeless printing plaques?
Ivan grimaced, in dumb despair,
like so many other unknown namesakes.
Who can accept abroad,

                    who grasp
that Russians are not simply beasts of burden?
Prince Kurbsky?"

                No. He's but a counter-tsar.
And the Swedes are Swedes,

                      when all is said and done.
Mud, mud everywhere,

                  you wade through mud.
Freedom, under suspicion, is locked in jail.
And even Russians cannot live in Russia,
though without Russia, life's intolerable.
The clouds, like psaltery players, strayed above
the road, which, smelling of damp earth,
meandered on and on, with twists and turns,
like the tortuous story of Ivan the Fool.
Suddenly from the thicket rose a whistle
and horsemen swept in at a gallop,
leaping onto the road before the printer—
no brooms, however,

                no dog masks# at their saddle.
One of these riders,

              evidently their head,
so badly scalded, it looked like the mange,
snorting through torn nostrils,** said:
"If it's gold you have,

            . deliver up, make haste!"
Hotly slashing the sacking with his sword,
he saw the lead:

          "What's that?"

                  "It's letters."
"What for?"

        "For books."

              "And books, what are they for?"

"For you, you fool..."
                        the printer muttered.
"For me, oho!"
                The chief laughed out aloud.
"I'd have been at my wit's end
if, with my ragged piece, I'd tried to sniff out
the sense of what your letters meant.
But this lead you've got here's fine—
we'll make bullets from it for our harquebuses..."
"Never!"
                "Prepare to die, then."
                                "All right. I'll die—
and you'll never be free of your troubles."
"Who's free? Even the thief's not free.
Nor is an unfrocked priest—
                        ask this one here.
So in what manner can I be free?..."
"What manner? Why, through books, through letters..."
It struck the chief at last,
                        this was no merchant.
Gold such as this he'd be ashamed to seize.
Lead, not earth
                soiled the printer's hands.
This lead, however,
                was his soil, it seemed.
"Live..."
        said the chief, climbing back on his horse.
"Let these—what d'you call them—letters be loosed,
and not from harquebuses, but so
there's blood to tell the tale,
                        not cranberry juice!..."
"You'll never settle anything with blood..."
the printer sighed.
                "Well, me, I don't eat grass,"
grinned the chief.
                "My name is Vanka Shish."
"I'm Ivan too."
                "So's our accursed tsar.
The news has reached us wandering folk
that there's been sent, from across the ocean,
an Ivangel—or some such book.
Is it about the tsar or all Ivans?"
"E-vangel's what it's called..."
                        "A fraud, I see...

We are not good enough for books, my guess is.
Print us some books, Ivan, and maybe we
will learn one day to use those letters..."
They galloped off,
                              lashing their horses' flanks,
and this is what it signified—
illiterate as they were, their anger
made the people want to read and write.
"Ivangel too will one day have its turn..."
Ivan thought. "The people will rise..."
while behind him
                              the letter in the wagon
rumbled,
                    centuries ahead of time.

1976

TRANSLATED BY DANIEL WEISSBORT (NOTES REVISED)

---

*Lord Ivan Vasilievich: Ivan IV, the Terrible (1530–84). First grand duke of Muscovy to assume
the title of tsar of Russia.
†Viskovatii: Ivan Viskovatii. Member of the Chosen Council (which effectively governed Russia
in Ivan IV's name up to 1560) who functioned as the tsar's personal secretary, secretary for foreign
affairs, and chief diplomat. He was nevertheless executed in a horrible manner in 1570, having
bravely petitioned the increasingly psychopathic monarch to put an end to the bloodshed.
‡oprichniks: The tsar's bodyguards; from the old Russian word for "special" or "apart." From
1565 till his death, the increasingly distrustful Ivan entrenched himself within reserved parts of the
state comprised of certain towns and districts, and even sections of Moscow, the oprichnina. Initially
it was composed of some one thousand carefully selected nobles.
§Ivan Fyodorov: Russia's first printer (d. 1583). In 1563 (over a hundred years after Gutenberg) a
special printing press was set up in the Church of St. Nikolai in the Kremlin, where Ivan Fyodorov
had been deacon. In 1564 Ivan Fyodorov and Piotr Mstislavtsev produced the first printed book
in Russian, *Apostol* (*The Apostle*). They were harassed by church copyists or ecclesiastical authorities
who accused them of heresy, and fled to Lithuania.
"Kurbsky: Prince Andrei Kurbsky (1528–83). Politician, soldier, and humanist writer and translator;
leader of the boyar opposition to Ivan. Previously one of Ivan IV's closest friends, a member of
the Chosen Council, an exalted functionary and general. However, fearing imminent arrest in 1564,
he fled to Lithuania, where the Polish king granted him lands. The same year, he actually led a
Polish army against Russia.
#brooms...dog masks: Reference to the oprichniks, who wore dog masks and carried brooms,
attached to their saddles, as a symbol of their role as destroyers and sweepers-away of traitors.
**torn nostrils: Common form of torture for captured bandits.

A Dove in Santiago: A Novella in Verse

Can I ask my book if I wrote it?
—Pablo Neruda

I.

Fatigue of the weariest body weighs so little
compared with the soul's, but if the two join forces
you haven't the strength even to cry ... And when
you are too tired to cry, then is the time
you especially want to ... That's how tired I was
one time ...
                    Of what?
                                    Of life? No, not of life,
it's above accusations. I was tired of all
I had found in it that resembled death, not life.
A man doesn't die all at once, but gradually,
of other people's diseases—indifference,
cruelty. And pitiable is the man
who slowly dies, infected by such ills—
for he not only dies himself but, dead,
can spread the infection to others. Many small deaths
hide in a telephone receiver where
it's shameful to phone, and yet there's no way out—
you've got to. In my wretched telephone book
there are many numbers like that; it's loathsome, sticking
your finger in the dial, as if the number
you're calling is death's, as if you were opening
a heavy safe you know to be empty except
for a few skulls and bones. That day, I remember,
I had to make several phone calls that were pointless
yet necessary. That word stinks of a privy
where you tread in something foul. Later you can't
scrape it off your shoes, that shit you've trodden in.
And I phone, stumbling on voices, sadistically sweet
as honey sometimes, a thick buzzing of flies
had fallen into it, feet upward; and sometimes babbling,
like dough afraid of the pan and giving out
cowardly bubbles. Oh, the vile, elegant art

of avoiding a decision and thereby
deciding people's fates by not deciding.
And every time, I hopelessly put down
the telephone—the dumbbell of the weak.
I still had to make one call. The telephone
revolted me suddenly, like a plastic toad.
I couldn't make the call . . .

I dragged myself

to the sofa, and fell on it facedown, too tired
to take my shoes off, forced my hand to pick up
a book from the chair and open it, but the words
swam. And it wasn't just any book, it was Pushkin.
Are even immortals incapable of helping
us mortals? Is the voice down the receiver
really stronger than Homer, Dante, and Shakespeare,
and Pushkin?

Oh, if even Pushkin can't help,

that's a bad sign. And the thought of suicide crept
into me from the holes of the receiver,
like the snake from the horse's skull, the death of Oleg.*
I hate this thought in me. It came, like a flirt,
to me in my youth, pleasantly gratifying
my vanity: "Suicide won't kill you—
it will only make you famous. Get yourself known
by killing yourself. Then they'll appreciate you."
(They, they . . . a helpful word for the feeble-hearted,
and, incidentally, for those who come,
themselves, under the comforting heading of "they.")
Now this coquettish thought had become a hag,
appearing to me at times, with yellow-stained teeth,
hiding the snake's subtle venom, and taunting me:
"Don't try, my sweetheart, you can't get away . . ."
I've grown accustomed to the hag,
and got the better of her, by despising her,
and possibly by knowing her so well.
I don't suppose there's anyone on earth
who hasn't considered taking his own life.
Mind you, I did know a songwriter who was stuffed
with joviality like straw, and I recall
him chuckling about a certain tragic affair
that ended with a bankrupt's bullet: "The fool!
I'd never do that. It's never entered my head."
But then, in general, nothing had entered his head.

I lay in the broad daylight as in darkness,
not seeing the letters of the open book,
but feeling with every wrinkle of my brow
the cold gaze of the old hag's colorless eyes
fixed on me; she bided her time in silence.
And suddenly, I felt something warm on my forehead,
as if an invisible sunbeam were striking me
from a mischievous boy's mirror. The darkness vanished,
and with it the hag. What brought about the change?
The apartment was empty.
                              Only a dove
outside, scraping at my window with its beak;
like a patch of the sky, or maybe a shade darker,
it was perched on the window ledge; its eyes were almost
human, and not a feather of it resembled
the well-fed parasites in the square below;
but like a little ruffled friend
who had flown to save me from death.
And perhaps it had flown from Chile?

2.

The word *Chile* evokes pain.
Alas, the more beautiful a country,
the greater the pain when enemies of beauty
take possession of it. Envious and malicious,
incurable moral cripples lust to own
at least the body of beauty.
Seducers don't care about the soul.

Let's return to Chile, in '72.
I was staying at the Hotel Carrera
opposite the presidential palace.
"Allende" and "palace" contradict each other.
Allende contradicted many things,
and what was perhaps most dangerous—
he went against the narrow-minded concept
of what a president should be.
That contradiction killed him.
Allende was a fine man.
Perhaps too fine. There are those who can't forgive this,
for whom anything good is dangerous.

They fear an intelligent man, and forgive the fool.
Allende was more intelligent than his killers,
but he lacked the intelligence of the tyrant,
who knows one must stop at nothing.
Allende was destroyed by his own virtue,
which makes him a survivor, an immortal;
dead, he is stronger than when he was alive.
When some extremists came to see him
with a list of ten thousand
who had to be got rid of instantly
(Pinochet was among them), he explained:

                                        "It's easy to shoot people,
but what if even one is innocent?
I don't think you or I
have the gift of resurrection.
You can't make mistakes with another's life
when you can't resurrect him if mistaken . . ."
"That's suicide!" shouted an extremist,
reeking of tobacco and dynamite.
"If we don't kill them, they'll kill us.
Permit us one percent of a mistake;
you don't make revolutions in kid gloves."
"As you can see, I don't wear gloves,
but I keep my hands clean.
Lightly to kill someone—that's suicide.
All the tyrants in the world have killed themselves.
I won't commit a suicide of this kind.
Ninety-nine percent of human justice
is tainted by that one percent of crime.
Innocent blood on the right road
changes the course of that road,
and then it can't be right . . ."
Their comrade, the president, spoke to them calmly,
in his cheap check shirt, with his face
of a country doctor, sure of his remedies,
so unlike his official portrait, dress suit with sash;
only the sash was really right,
that deep red presidential sash,
that honest sash no drop of blood had stained
disreputably. But the extremists
wouldn't listen to Allende, nor had they read
Dostoyevsky's *Devils*. Their homegrown terror
began to seem like the face of socialism,

a face that terrified the bourgeoisie.
Everything split apart. People would go
quietly into cinemas, courteously,
but as soon as Allende appeared
in documentary images on the screen,
half the audience in the shadowy darkness
whistled, howled, stamped their feet, booed,
the other half clapped so loudly
I knew their cause was doomed.
The lights went on. Instantly the storm
that had blown up in the dark subsided.
Everything is less clear in the blazing light;
everything in life is clearer where it's darker.
I saw a meeting near the palace
where there was also rather too much light
to make out clearly who was on whose side.
Hands waving torches, and projectors,
created the light in darkness; but even the hands
in a vast square aren't everyone's hands.
There are hands in reserve, to betray and murder.
Such hands, if the hour has not yet struck,
will caress cats and children
and even heartily applaud
those they intend to kill—in gratitude,
as it were, for not being killed.
Allende was no orator, he lacked
the showman's sleight of hand the crowd adores,
wishing to be deceived. Allende had no wish
to deceive either the square or the country.
He tried to deceive himself by affirming too often,
in that speech which was inevitably his last,
his dying words, how loyal his generals were,
by repetition trying to make them so.
They stood behind him, their hairy hands tensed
to applaud him and betray him.
The square lifted its torches toward the sky,
torches made out of rolled-up newspapers;
and suddenly I saw in one hand,
raised high in honor of the president,
his slowly disintegrating photograph
edged with golden black ash,
as if in a shrinking memorial frame.
The frame grew smaller, and the face vanished.

I shivered and grew uneasy,
although Allende was standing on the rostrum
alive, but with the alarming reflection of flares
flickering in his glasses. Afterward
the square emptied swiftly; only the dead rostrum,
knocked together in a hurry, creaked in the darkness,
only the street doves wandered
among the ash left by the crowd's flares,
cautiously pecking at it, as if
they might find something in it . . .

It was one of those doves, perhaps,
that flew to my rescue in Moscow?
There are too many small histories
lost within the history of the world
for historians to be able to cope with them.
We need more historians. It's suicidal
to know everything,
but ignorance is suicidal too,
and worse—cowardly. Life without knowledge
is a dead rostrum. Life is made up of lives,
and history is the link between them all.

3.

The morning after the meeting in the square,
I was telephoned in my room.
                              A woman's voice,
with a Spanish accent on *ch*, was asking if
she might speak with Comrade Señor Yevtuchenko;
"Forgive me, am I too early? May I come up?
I've a manuscript I'd like to show you." I thought
with horror—a poetess. I never know what
to say to them. Whether Russian or Chilean,
they scare me, these strange creatures who put words
into neat metrical patterns and twist rhymes
the way they put their hair into curlers at night.
There are too few women poets in the world,
but all too many of these poetesses.
I fill with animal fear
as I wait to be sprayed by emotion like a shower.
But the woman who entered my room

didn't look like a poetess. I had avoided
that particular peril. But then another unease
took possession of me—what if I was faced
more fearfully still

                  with a woman novelist?
My visitor saw that I was apprehensive
and, guessing the reason for it, she hurriedly said:
"I don't write myself . . . I've brought you a diary
to read—all that is left of my only son,
who took his life, and he was only twenty . . ."
She was, I guessed, in her early forties, still
almost beautiful, with a dark Creole beauty,
in a black mantilla, a severe black dress,
and a Catholic cross was glittering on her neck
where there were no betraying wrinkles,
and the gray streak in her black hair
sparkled like the curl of a waterfall.
The woman came closer to me, sighed, warily
extended a hand in a black transparent glove
as if she was afraid to give to me,
the exercise book, which was also in mournful black.
I said to her: "You can leave it with me . . . I'll read it."
The woman was firm: "Please read it while I'm here.
I'm not in a hurry. I'll wait. My son loved you.
He heard you reading with Neruda.
When you open it, you will understand everything,
and perhaps you'll write a poem
saying how wrong it is to take one's life,
how self-deceiving. It's something that must be said."

And I opened the diary and commenced reading
the anguished story of a stranger's soul,
yet is there such a thing as a stranger's soul
when, so often, there isn't a soul around? . . .
The purest of souls laid itself bare to me.
The dead boy was, as they say, thin-skinned,
transparent and defenseless; I could see
through his diary the pulsing of every fiber,
the slightest quiver of his heart,
like a dove, born for the sky,
but trapped in a cramped rib cage; my fingertips
felt they were touching jagged nerves, not lines,
as the letters vibrated under my head.

483

4

Enrique was only eight years old
when his father, a linguist and a womanizer
(which sounds milder in Spanish—*mujeriego*),
left his mother and married a woman
whose husband was a diplomat
and not a linguist, but also a *mujeriego*;
and in desperation his mother hurriedly married
an antique-furniture dealer, who,
as fate would have it, was also a *mujeriego*.
His father at first seemed happy,
but gradually his new wife, like a new toy,
began to bore him; with cruel curiosity
he cracked open his not-so-new toy
and found, inside, her simple mechanism,
and the springs of stupidity and affectation,
which were so rosily disguised
by the smooth, celluloid, well-cared-for skin.
It was then he began to miss his son.
Enrique's mother realized her new version,
in the person of the antique dealer, was old,
made worse by the fact that he went after women,
and was, moreover, jealous. Most of all
he was jealous of his stepson. Taking her son,
she'd climb into her Volkswagen, and visit the ocean,
whose face was changeable but never betrayed,
like the face of Neruda's poems,
which she read aloud to her son. The heavy green breakers
hurled at their feet, as they walked across the sand,
mane-like seaweed, jellyfish parachutes,
dark bottle fragments, so gently rounded by
the sea you could mistake them for emeralds,
and pebbles whose value
was hidden in their shapes, not in their names.
Enrique's mother started to collect pebbles—
simply, at first, to put them in a saucer,
with the water that transformed them, to create
a little of the ocean in her home.
Then she took lessons in stone polishing
from a craftsman and a drunkard, and the pebbles
talked to her, then, as no one else had done.
More than pebbles, Enrique loved the ocean,
the sea you couldn't capture in a saucer,

strong in that it didn't know its strength,
and never knew what it might do next.
It's a drag—always behaving well.
It's a bore to behave badly on purpose.
But it's wonderful not to know what you'll do next.
Quite simply, you should live as the ocean does.
As a child, Enrique began to draw, and he liked
the way his brush did not know how to behave
and didn't know what to do next, either.
But his mother was the first to interfere,
saying of her portrait in watercolor:
"I'm not so old as that, you know . . .
I didn't know you could be so cruel.
Art should make life more beautiful, but you . . .
but you . . ." And his mother ran off crying
to seek refuge at her alcoholic craftsman's,
to polish beach pebbles. And the boy's stepfather,
crammed with ideas about furniture, including
beds and their warm contents, muttered, "Crap! . . .
You'd do better to draw money, kid."
Everyone's a connoisseur of art;
the ignorant don't dabble in chemistry,
microbiology, or quarks. Restraining
her tears, the mother of an astronaut
can only say, "Take care in space, Son . . ."
But everyone knows the way it shouldn't be done,
how not to do it, in literature and art,
though harder for them to say what should be done.

And strangely enough, the first to like Enrique's *crap*
was the man who had first inflicted a wound
on the little boy's heart—his father. Only when
he'd abandoned his son did he really begin to love him.
He aged. He immersed himself in Sanskrit,
divorced his wife, and lost his mistresses
gradually, as they noticed his bald pate,
expanding paunch, or general lack of prospects.
And he clung to his son as a sign of hope
that he could love someone and be loved;
but people who are egoists in love
are egoists as fathers, too. Remembering
him only with his pocket for ten years,
one day he saw a student, a young man
with his family's almond eyes,

who had grown up without him;
and rather belatedly he began to want
to instill in him all that had grown musty,
moldy, rotten, in him—the father . . .
but *had* been in him truly; so long ago
that hardly anyone remembered it.
He wanted to remind his son
how talented he once had been, himself,
and to convince him that his talent
came from his father's genes, and not his mother's.
Enrique's mother, not altogether fairly,
was outraged by this flare-up
of fatherly affection, calling it
hypocrisy, not altogether fairly.
She gave the womanless *mujeriego*
a piece of her mind, forbidding him
to see her son. And he responded that his son
should come to live with him,
his stepfather being so insensitive,
as wooden as the furniture he sold.
When two adults batter each other's heads
with their child, the child's head gets broken.
The mother was frightened. They made peace.
It was agreed the object of their fight,
while continuing to live at home,
would spend each Saturday with his father.
Enrique knew he'd been
abandoned by his father, but because
he sensed his father's desolation
he loved his father with a father's love;
and every time he left for home, his father
watched him go out of sight, with a dog's gaze;
and sometimes Enrique stayed, killing his mother,
and went away early on the Monday morning,
and killed his father by leaving, so
becoming a murderer against his will.

5.

Enrique was eighteen when a forty-year-old
actress friend of his mother looked at him
suddenly in a special way, as if

she had not noticed him before, and said:
"How tall you've grown!" Onstage, or at receptions,
she managed to disguise her fading beauty,
but knew that what she could conceal today
would be less easy to conceal tomorrow.
In the beauty parlor, wearing a strawberry mask,
she would lie on a hard couch, and the mulatto
masseuse's muscles were as disciplined
as boxers' when her two slippery black fists
pounded on the vulnerable back:
"Calm yourself, señora, it's only rain . . ."
Then her fingers penetrated into
the neck folds, seeking out the nerve ends . . .
"Señora, you must relax; it's only lightning!"
But the youth's awkward gaze seemed suddenly
a lightning flash when—in an unchildlike way
for the first time in his life—his eyes met hers.
As we inevitably age, the adulation
of a young man or woman works on our vanities
like a massage. At first like gentle rain,
but as the body weakens and gives way,
the lightning pierces it. We're blinded by
that light and—for however short a time—
are happy to be blinded, not to see
the horror of our aging. There's a price
we have to pay—others may fall out
of love with us, just when we can't stop loving.

One day she rang him, saying she was ill
in bed, and asking him to bring a book,
if possible, a nineteenth-century Russian
novel. He brought *The Brothers Karamazov*
to her, amid shouts of "Allende for president!"
He rang the bell. He heard a soft call: "It's
not locked." He entered, in confusion, holding
before him, with both hands, the novel, which
seemed suddenly very heavy. But of course
he didn't know its real weight as yet.
He saw her lying on a sofa, covered
by a thin sheet that traced her body's outline,
and her head was wrapped in a wet towel.
A strange, dull light shone in her eyes; her hands
twitched feverishly at the sheet, under her chin.
"Sit down . . ." Her eyes directed him to a chair.

"So that's the book you've brought me. Have you read it?"
"I've started it . . ." "You're only at the start
of everything in your life . . . How lucky you are
not to have read that book for the first time.
My eyes are aching. Will you read to me?
—from anywhere at all: about Aliosha . . ."
"I couldn't read it with expression."

                                    She laughed,
like one of the witches in *Macbeth*, her face
hidden beneath the sheet. Nothing betrays
wrinkles so much as laughter. "Who taught you that?
What does it mean—with expression? Expression
is in the words themselves, when they have meaning.
You've picked it up from some teacher. I suppose,
or some idiotic ham-actor.
How can you improve a work of genius
by reading it with expression, for God's sake?
It's quite enough if you don't spoil the meaning."
Enrique grew even more confused. She made
him draw his chair up closer, and began
to read to him, as if the book was not
in her hands, as if the words were being spoken
for the first time. He found himself wishing to kiss—
not her lips, but the words; and leaned toward her
so maladroitly his mouth caught her chin
and he leaped back in fright. She let the book
fall slowly, took his face between her hands,
drew it gently toward hers, toward her eyes,
which seemed so huge, and opened his lips with hers,
and the boy's breath was lost in her moist breath.
For ages, sitting beside her, he breathed her warm
and scented breath, and burned with shame because
he wanted her so much. "Lie down with me . . ."
she said. He wondered, horrified, how he
was going to unlace his shoes, and unzip his trousers,
without becoming an object of ridicule.
She, as if sensing by instinct how he felt,
gently and matter-of-factly helped him.
Shivering with cold, his teeth chattering,
he felt embarrassed at his nakedness
before the enigma of a naked woman.
Quivering with love and fear, he realized
he wasn't able to do anything.
He had wanted to, too much. He sobbed, disgusted

with himself, and huddled his head against
her small, empty breasts. A single wounding word
from her, and everything might have been changed
for him, it might have sown a hatred of women.
But a woman in love can't help but feel maternal
toward her man. "Why are you crying, darling?
Everything will be all right... Don't worry..."
she whispered, and so made it possible
for him to love the women he'd not yet met,
in whom she would be loved again by him
when he had completely ceased to love her.
Without the irksome clumsiness of the body,
she nestled so lovingly against him that
her gentleness made him strong
and he experienced for the first time the wonder
of a man and a woman becoming one.

There is a lesson in our first act of love
that's more important than a lesson for the body—
because the body teaches the soul in it.
When I observe the repulsive chill in the eyes
of a cynic, I suspect he learned his cynicism
from the first woman with whom he slept.
But then, who made that woman cynical
if it wasn't the cynic who first slept with her?
It's a marvel the whole earth is not cynical...
All the good and noble qualities of men
come from our mothers, and from our first women,
in whom there is also something from their mothers.

Enrique was grateful to his first woman.
His gratitude made her afraid, and he was afraid
that he was simply grateful to her. A woman's
last love is sorrow pretending to be hope,
and there is nothing more hopeless in the world
than sorrow trying to be hopeful.
She loved him fatally, and understood
its fatality, trying to comfort herself
by murmuring, "What's meant to be, will be...
Another five years... And then... and then...
and then..."

The laws of time, stronger than divination,
elected Allende president.

Victor Hara† with his blazing eyes,
sang at Che Guevara's monument.
Allende didn't know he was going to be killed.
The immortal hero's statue didn't guess
that it would be destroyed and melted down.
The hands on the guitar did not foretell
that they would be cut off. Enrique
didn't know what would happen to him. But someone knew,
hiding his face, because of the heavy knowledge,
in the clouds hanging above the swaying mass
of people, and his expression was sensed by a dove
perched on the hero's bronze shoulder; and suddenly
it shuddered for everyone and for itself.

6.

When we are young, we're drawn to someone older.
As we grow old, we cleave to someone young.
And yet, if we would reach self-understanding,
we need to be with someone our own age.
We start as children in the shadow of
some other person's rich experience,
and later—our experience becomes
unwilling father to the innocence
we have elected to take under our wing.
But two innocences create experience,
beautiful in that neither spirit lies
in the shadow of the other.

                        One morning Enrique
was walking through the city park,
gathering leaves, with veins, which seemed to vibrate
alive in his hands, and suddenly he saw,
running powerfully through the russet alleys,
over the leaves, over thrown-away proclamations,
through lacy shadows, over cigarette butts,
a girl, with a serious expression,
in a clinging-wet white T-shirt bearing
the inscription "University of Chile,"
in ragged short jeans and gym shoes.
Pushing something invisible out of her way
with her strong elbows, and hitting something
invisible with the caps of her scratched knees,

breathing intently, as if on sports results
depended the whole history of the nation.

And the girl leaped in the air as she ran along
and tore off an autumn oak leaf.
She put the twig between her teeth,
twirling it for a second like a gold propeller,
before continuing her earnest run.
Robust, athletic, confident, she was
a little too large, but even that was good.
Enrique didn't stop to think
but turned in his tracks and ran after her,
at first seeing only her back, the notches of
her spine rippling through the snow-white
transparent T-shirt. Combs and hair clips lost,
her hair streamed after her large powerful body
like a Patagonian horse being chased
by its black, wiry tail. Enrique,
through some incomprehensible superstition,
tried to jump over her footprints
in the morning alley where the sand was patterned
by her checkered soles. Inside each print there seemed
a fragile sandy town, on no account
to be destroyed. Then he drew level with her,
with her shoulder, almost as thick as a wrestler's,
with her tense cheek to which a mole adhered
like a coffee grain, with her strong aquiline nose,
with her large, wind-cracked lips,
within which each tooth sparkled
like a freshly washed white baby.
Enrique wanted to look her in the eyes,
but could only see her profile, her right eye
—which was just like her mole
except for its slightly scornful expression,
which moles fortunately don't have.
"Isn't it hard-going in a suit and shoes?"
she asked without slowing. Enrique, sweating as if
from a steam bath, panted, "It is a bit."
"Ten miles to go," she warned him with a laugh.
"I'll make it," Enrique assured her;
"But what's at the end of the run?"

                              "The end of the run,"
said the girl with a grin. Enrique took off
his jacket and threw it onto the cracked wings

of a poor marble angel, took off his shoes
and left them in the grass, having tucked his socks
hurriedly into them, and ran on barefoot
as he had done in childhood, running through
the ebbing foam at low tide. "Won't they get stolen?"
she asked when, puffing and panting, he caught up with her.
"I'm counting on the angels being honest.
We live in a Catholic country, don't forget."
"You believe in God?" At once both eyes,
under their thick, imperious brows, were fixed
mockingly on him. "In something . . ." "But what
do you mean by something?" "I don't know exactly.
Something above us . . ." "Then, you're a mystic?"
"I'm just an artist." "What do you mean by just?"
"Just that and nothing else." "So you're one of those
who arm themselves with a paintbrush, are you? That's
not much of a weapon for a man."
"At least it's a clean weapon." Her elbows working
like pistons, she asked him sharply, "Don't you think
Che Guevara's rifle was clean, then?
Which party are you in?" "El Greco's, Bosch's . . ."
"I can't say I know it. Which party's that?" "It's good,
but not very large. What party are you in?"
"None at present. But I want to get things moving."
"So do I. But can't art get things moving?"
"Depends how you look at it." "And how do you?"
"I don't, very often. Haven't liked museums
since I was a kid. Look, take your Picasso,
who's so great, and calls himself a Communist,
but he sells his paintings to the bourgeoisie . . ."
"Picasso gives away half of his earnings
to Spanish underground fighters . . ."
"And the other half—to Chile, I suppose!
Oh, come on! His battle is just a game.
How can you expect a millionaire
to turn against other millionaires?
I prefer Gorky's storm petrel to the dove
of peace with absolutely everyone . . ."
"I'm also against that kind of peace. I'm sure
Picasso is too . . ." He could hardly keep pace with her,
scorching his bare heels on the park's stone path,
and then the grit road leading from the city.
But the girl was tireless, and brusque
like her arm strokes. She said, "I'm studying medicine,

not dentistry or pediatrics: surgeons
are what the revolution needs..." "Our teeth,"
he said, "are second-class citizens,
and don't serve the revolutionary cause?
What if they become decayed and fall out
and the fighters can't chew their food?"
"Well, you don't have that problem to worry about.
You've still got your milk teeth, muchacho..."
and she shrieked, suddenly stumbling,
and started hopping, holding on to one foot;
then she stopped and sat down. "This is my weak spot..."
Her face screwed up, she nodded at her ankle.
"Good lord! I'd never have imagined you'd
have any weak spots!" "I know what spots
you so-called men are interested in.
Just remember, as far as mine are concerned,
they're quite intact... Hey, get your hands off me!
I can kick just as well with a lame foot..."
"Calm down, I'm not going to eat your foot.
Every artist should know a little about
anatomy, so he should be able to set bones.
Let's take a look. Gently now. Don't kick.
Your foot's not exactly Cinderella's, is it?
It wasn't intended for a crystal slipper."
"Don't think I'm made of crystal, either."
"I can see that... What size do you take? Eleven?"
He twisted her foot in his hands, and,
through her tears, she said, "Are you crazy? Size six!"
He tore up his handkerchief and bound her foot
swiftly and tightly. "This is unusual—
bandaging a surgeon..." "You'd be better off
bandaging your tongue..." She laced her gym shoe
with difficulty, for her foot had swollen
a whole size, and when she tried to run again
her foot, cruelly injuring her vanity,
brought her up short. "Okay, we'll take a rest.
I can see you're tired, muchacho." He sat down
and she fell into the grass, laughing: "Muchacho,
you're sitting on an anthill!" He jumped up,
and looked down at the cone of teeming life
he'd crushed... And it was someone's work, love, struggle.
But the girl went on laughing: "Now you know
what was at the end of the run—an anthill!"
Hiding his confusion, giving his trousers

a vigorous shake, he snapped: "We're also someone's
anthill, when they squash us with their behind . . ."
"We mustn't allow it!" She sternly raised
her finger above her head. "We must neither be ants
nor someone crushing ants with his behind!"
"Well, at last, that's something I agree with."
Enrique also lay down on the grass
and saw, through the grass, a brown butterfly
a couple of steps away settle on one
of the two knolls sharply rising from her T-shirt,
which was already slightly grass-stained.
Enrique rolled over three times
and spun head over heels, chasing away
the startled butterfly from her breast,
and drew between his lips first the T-shirt and ants,
and then T-shirt and skin,
pressing fingers against fingers, ribs against ribs,
winning her arms with his arms,
her eyes with his eyes, her lips with his lips,
and her youth with his youth.
Tearing her arms twice out of his,
she twice pushed him away,
but the third time she couldn't tear away
and embraced him. She no longer wanted to scream.
She had liked him from the moment he threw his jacket
over the angel's wings
because it was stopping him from running.
At thirteen, she had turned against the church
when an old priest with a trembling, feverish hand
had fondled her breast in the confessional.
She hated the feelings that had been aroused,
and her virginity, and all the men
who wished to deprive her of it on the sly.
The legal sale of one's virginity
by being called wife she also found disgusting.
But her body was terribly curious,
it was aching and yearning, and reducing her
to such a state that, no matter what the shame,
like a prostitute, she considered throwing herself
at the first man to come along,
so that she could find out what it was like—
then she would drown herself, or join a convent.
She tried to cure herself of these desires
of the body, which her reason judged immoral,

494

by studying the revolution and by running,
but suddenly all this was overthrown.
She wanted to. Only not with just anybody
but with this funny discarder of shoes and jackets,
who possibly had acted in that way
so that the angels could be shod and clothed.
She wanted to. Not sometime later. Now.
Through her spine the grass told her to go ahead,
there was nothing wrong in it. Was she already
in love? Perhaps. Everything in her
suddenly became a weak spot. It flashed through her:
"If you've got to fall,
make sure it's first from a good horse."
The sky plunged on to the grass-blades,
without bending them at all, and the two were doubled
by nature; and from the silent anthill
millions of spectators watched them.

7.

Did you at nineteen love a nineteen-year-old?
Still green, their union made them ripen swiftly,
yet this maturity was doubly youthful.
Everything in the world became multiplied
by two: eyes and arms, hair and lips,
breathing, resentment, hope,
the wind's bite, the sea, sounds, smell, color.
Nature flung them together in such a way
it became impossible to tell apart
the boy, the girl, and nature,
as if their crazy run without an end
went on as it had begun. Their run
together was a run away from something
that bored them to death, suffocated them.
Their run together was a run over ditches,
toward something that had never existed
but which ought to exist
although it probably never would.
Their run together was through the age of hurry,
when everyone was running about on business,
glancing askance at two young people running
without an aim in view, censuring them
for their lack of purpose, as if anything in life

495

is more important than becoming oneself.
It's beautiful to be running without an aim,
and for the two who were running what mattered most
was not what they were running to—but through.
Through all the tips on how they ought to run,
who to run after, when they ought to stop.
Through the dense crowd. Through bullets and explosives.
Through right and left wing; those who tried to trip them.
Through other people's terrors, and their own.
Through whispers that it's better to stand still.
Through all the warnings that they'd break a limb
running at such a speed. Through the clutching
rapacious hands on all sides, telling them:
"This way! This way!" But what is happier
than to have nowhere to go, and everywhere?
They ran, falling together
on anything—it didn't matter what:
on the first inviting grass; iodine-scented
seaweed; the tilted seat of a Mercedes
abandoned in a cemetery of cars;
on the bed of a shabby hotel
in which the bedbugs, transparent from hunger,
converged on them from the tattered wallpaper.
Enrique didn't breathe a word
to his first woman. He was too afraid.
Also he was too afraid to tell
the girl he loved about the other woman.
He now saw both of them.
He tore himself in two, rushed to and fro,
and an agonizing lie was created
when he lied to one that he was busy,
and then lied to the other. He lied all the time.
It's impossible to be truthful with a woman,
but you can't deceive her in anything.
Women have an animal's scent for other women.
When women's nostrils quiver, no pumice stone
will rub off us the alarming smell
of another woman.
The two women, the older and the younger one,
although they did not know about each other,
by instinct guessed the other one existed.
When she was driving by the sea one day,
out of the car window the older woman
caught sight of Enrique lying beside the younger

in the sand. With a bottle of ice-cold lemonade,
smilingly she was stroking Enrique's forehead,
cheeks, chest, and stomach. Everything dimmed
and tears welled in the eyes
of Enrique's first woman, not the kind of tears
that freely spring, but the kind that linger,
and flow treacherously inward.
Somehow or other she managed to drive home;
she got hold of her bottle of tranquilizers,
and, wrenching off the lid, she whispered:
"You fool . . . It serves you right . . ." tossing
all the pills into her mouth.
She was saved. Enrique went to the hospital,
stunned, shattered, broken,
feeling like a murderer again,
and, his tears falling into her waxen hand,
promised her something—another lie.
A lie to save oneself is a cowardly truth,
but fear of facing the cruel truth is crueller.

8.

And meanwhile at the art school he attended
he was likewise split in two. His teacher there
was an old man with a soused Bohemian charm
who never came to work without his flask.
His strict views on the classical laws of art
were as unchanging as the brand of cognac
sticking out of his pocket. Never diluting
his drink with food, and unbelievably thin,
he used to joke: "When God made frames for people,
He left me in the portfolio . . ."
His coat was scorched in places, and layered with ash
like Pompeii; and dandruff sprinkled his collar.
But in his art he was meticulous.
The least attempt to change the bounds of form
evoked his caustic and sarcastic wit.
Art ended for him where our century
began. He'd cry: "You want to be progressive?
Then study science or technology
or politics, but leave art well alone.
In art, my friends, there's no such thing as progress.
But you will say—Picasso, there's progress for you.

What does that make El Greco, then—regressive?"
He worked his students till they sweated blood,
making them draw—exact in every detail—
now, a tomato he had brought from home,
tobacco-flaked, bruised by his pocket flask
—now, shivering yawning models, coyly asking
for a five-minute break to take a pee.

Enrique loved his first teacher,
for rightly insisting on strict discipline,
but Enrique also had a secret teacher,
old like the first, but with the difference
that he was meticulous about his clothes,
never touched alcohol, and despised all drunkards,
but in his paintings he was a subversive.
In his attic, fiery explosions warped
his canvases, and there among them mincing
—in moccasins, a dazzling white starched shirt
with the most delicately spotted tie,
a formal suit, the only one he had,
without the slightest trace of a double crease
in trousers razor-sharp as his hair-parting—
was the stormy old man, no taller than a doll,
the great, unrecognized demolisher
of all established classical foundations.

He made the most incendiary speeches
so gently and velvetly, his razor-thin
parting sparkled and blazed like a safety fuse.
"Drawing from nature is *mierda*!"—shit:
but notice how much gentler the word sounds
in Spanish. Raising his childishly small fists,
clenching invisible hand grenades,
he appealed to Enrique: "You're being ineptly taught!
An artist who copies vegetables and fruit
is committing a criminal act. They're to be eaten,
not copied. Copying women is also stupid.
Nature's already drawn them to be slept with,
not drawn again! . . . Under everyone's skin,
in a lump we call the heart, there's a whole world.
The only one worth wasting paints on.
A photographer can't get in there.
You must imprint the invisible. An artist
is not an observer of life—he's its creation

and creator. An artist builds by making explosions..."
Enrique respected both his teachers,
listening first to the one and then the other,
but wanted a third way for himself.
He thought: "Realism is dead, it's paid the price
for immortality. And abstractionism
has committed suicide by blowing itself up."

Enrique spent a whole year painting a canvas
ten feet square. He called it "Watermelon."
In it, thirteen faceless pig-eyed mugs,
armed with long predatory knives, thirsting
with all their steel for the blood of a watermelon,
not yet a human victim, posed like mafia
over the first gash, spilling startled seeds.
His first teacher, opening his flask,
said: "You've betrayed all the laws of beauty.
You've begun your way in art with a betrayal.
Well, that's a dangerous start.
I know you've got another teacher,
a Lilliputian megalomaniac.
You'll have to choose between him and me..."

The second, velvetly raging, said to him:
"You haven't reached the heights of an explosion.
You're still a slave to verisimilitude.
Figurative... Figurative again...
I didn't suspect that you were such a coward...
I know you've got another teacher.
Hasn't he choked himself with brandy yet?
You'll have to choose between him and me..."

The world is so obsessed with suspicion,
without betraying a soul
you can easily end up as a double Judas.

9.

Enrique had two friends he'd known since boyhood.
One of them belonged to the large brood
of a worker in a canning factory.
The other was the only son of the owner
of a rather peculiar factory making mirrors,

which also manufactured men's braces.
The three boys had been drawn together by football.
They had chased after a battered ball,
with other children like themselves,
on a patch of waste ground, their school satchels
democratically thrown down to make the goals.
But the satchels were of varying quality.
Some were made of imitation leather,
which soon wore out, others were rough pigskin,
and others still were made of the softest kid;
while the satchel of a wealthy banker's son
was even made of crocodile skin
and its lock was reputed to be real gold.
Football softens the edges of class distinction
but doesn't eradicate it, and the contempt
of the crocodile skin for the sensitive and proud
imitation leather's shoddiness
expressed itself in arrogant back-passes,
and, plagued by the contrast, the imitation
leather didn't try to hide its grievance.
The pigskin hovered between the two.
Contemptuous of the pigskin, the kid
was attracted to the arrogant crocodile
yet squeaking with secret envy. But they shared
the same pitch, the same game, the same ball.
Adults can't share the same ball—
they tear it to shreds; and the pitch ceases
to be shared—everyone wants it for himself:
and they can't share the same game
because they don't have the same rules.
When the rules differ tempers get lost,
and the players start shouting: "Ref, are you blind?"
Everyone's a foul player and the referee.
The three friends drifted apart,
but still tried to remain friends.
They went to football matches together
—football more and more becoming
the only thing they had in common.
One of them, who had followed his father
into the canning factory, would clearly
go on being a tinsmith. The other friend,
seeing no point in his father's mirrors and braces,
was studying for the priesthood; and Enrique
was, in his own eyes at least, a budding artist.

Sitting on a bench together, munching
their sandwiches and uncorking a bottle of wine,
they turned from a discussion of the match
they had just watched to current politics.
Talking about football they were boys again,
arguing about politics killed what was left of childhood . . .
The tinsmith said: "Allende's being too cautious.
You can't fight a battle slowly . . ." The priest:
"Many people would say he's going too fast . . ."
Tinsmith: "He's only giving the monopolists
a bit of a fright—which is all to the good.
I'm just afraid that's all they'll get—a fright . . ."
Priest: "And what about the frightened housewives?
They're only monopolists in their kitchens,
but they're scared to death of what tomorrow may bring.
They're buying twenty bars of soap at a time . . ."
Tinsmith: "It will take more than twenty bars
to wash off their petty-bourgeois prejudices . . ."
Priest: "All the same, people do have to wash.
When housewives feel that things are out of control,
the situation's hopeless." Tinsmith: "Your
situation's hopeless . . ." Priest: "I don't understand—
what's 'your'?—what's 'our'? There's only the people . . ."
Tinsmith: "Don't lump me with swinish civil servants,
secret-police thugs, cadging scheming priests,
cutthroat generals, stinking thieving salesmen . . ."
Priest: "*Muchas gracias, amigo*,
for not forgetting us scheming priests . . ."
Tinsmith: "You asked for it, *amigo* . . .
The people, the people . . . A highly convenient word
to use for those who squat on other's necks:
spouting from their pulpits how much they love us . . .
There's not a *people* anywhere in the world.
In any people there are always two peoples:
those who squat on other people's necks
and those who hold out their necks to be sat on.
But we've got to learn not to. Marx left us
a pretty good instruction manual."
Priest: " 'Existence determines consciousness'—
how simplistic! Doesn't consciousness also
determine our existence? Jesus Christ
brought people together, but Marx has split the world
into two camps." Tinsmith: "It's always been split.
But, as a matter of fact, who drove the merchants

out of the temple? Marx? In his private life
Marx was more mild and civilized than Jesus..."
So they went on arguing
and banged their young fists on the peeling bench
outside the stadium, without knowing
that very soon it would become
a prison for them both and for others,
after Allende's death.
(The young priest hid the tinsmith in his home
and was thrown into prison with him,
and then they both disappeared for good,
and their arguments vanished with them...)
The tinsmith had been jailed before, under Allende.
He had joined a far-left group
assembling homemade bombs,
to give the capitalists a real fright,
not realizing that such explosions
played into the hands of the cutthroat generals,
giving them a pretext to suppress
Red terror with their own color of terror, brown.
And at the time of the tinsmith's first arrest,
a vicious rumor started
that none other than the priest had turned him in,
"For friendship's sake." The terrible rumor grew.
Curling their lips in disgust, the far-left
students from the seminary
passed the priest by on the other side of the road.
And what provided a wry coda—his father,
the owner of the curious mirror-factory,
which also produced braces, a man
who declared openly that in these times
you'd be advised to make a loop in your braces
and hang yourself in front of your mirror—
clapped his son on the shoulder, saying:
"I hear you've betrayed the tinsmith? Splendid!
I didn't think you had the guts. But I can see
you've grown up. The whole lot should be arrested,
all the Reds, with the president leading the way!"

Then the priest came to Enrique, with a hunted look,
swaying a little, avoiding his friend's gaze,
he muttered somberly: "Are you a friend?"
"Of course I am! You're innocent, I know."
"Then who could have spread this rumor?

Who heard us arguing after the football match,
and made quite sure he didn't get involved?"
"I wasn't afraid to speak, if that's what you think.
It was just that sometimes he seemed right,
and sometimes you, and sometimes you both did,
and sometimes neither..." The young priest shook his head,
his brow pale, sweating and feverish, and moved close
to Enrique. "No, it was you who did it.
You like to think you're cleverer than us,
you want to rise in the world, and how better
than by dragging your friend down with a lie?
You proudly stand aside from Christ and Marx.
You're the everlasting odd man out.
You've said to yourself: I'm a genius,
and geniuses are lifted above sin.
But these lesser mortals are capable
of any atrocious action—like informing.
And remembering my quarrels with our friend,
you assumed I'd come to hate him,
that he was my enemy, and surely it's no great sin
to betray an enemy?... That's what you thought."
"I didn't, I swear..." "Don't add another lie.
What you did not know was that I love him
far more than I love myself,
and it's only for that reason
that I've argued with him so much.
I've been afraid for him, as for a brother.
He wanted to change everything overnight.
He could blow up in his own hands
like a homemade bomb, and with the splinters
maim or kill those dearest to him, whom
he never meant to hurt—his mother, me, you...
Yes, I wanted to make him stop his madness,
but I'm not one of those hypocrites in a cassock.
—To warn a friend by turning him in!
How does it feel—being a stool pigeon?
You've betrayed me to the mob.
How thirsty it is for slander of this kind,
how it loves getting its fangs into
an innocent man labeled an informer!
But worse than the mob howling for your blood
are the people who praise you for informing...
My own father, my braces-and-mirror-flogging dad,
offered me his congratulations...That's

what you've done for me, Enrique..." "I swear I've not."
"Maybe you've done it and it's slipped your mind.
You're a genius. You didn't mean to do it.
Geniuses are notoriously careless.
A single word slipped out, perhaps. But now
it's branded on my forehead. And on yours!"
The door slammed painfully like a face-slap.
Enrique stood, shaking from the lie
of his tormented friend, who'd conjured it
out of the air to drug the pain a little.
When we're insultingly accused of crimes
we haven't done, we start accusing others
and enter the vicious circle where every guiltless
face bears the look of guilt.
Enrique jumped out of his skin—the phone rang
with an insistent, shrewish jingle.
His hand, still shaking, picked up the receiver.
"Oh, it's you, father..." "You remember my voice?
I thought you might have forgotten it
as you forgot that yesterday was Saturday.
I waited for you all evening. Are you ill?"
"No, but Mother is..." "It's remarkable
how often your mother manages to fall ill
on Saturdays and Sundays, don't you think?..."
"She really is sick." "Couldn't you have rung me?"
"I tried to, Father, but I couldn't get through.
I think your phone must have been out of order."
"There was nothing wrong with my phone. Must have been
    yours.
Caught the flu from its subscriber, I expect
phones can get ill too, you know, when it suits them."
Just then his mother, carrying a pipette,
walked in in her dressing gown. "Enrique,
help me put in my nose drops. I don't seem
to be able to control my hands." And instantly,
seeing the raised receiver, she guessed right
with her female's instinct: "Oh, it's your so-called father!
Give me the phone!" She snatched it from his hand,
and in a voice booming like Ella Fitzgerald's
said: "Would you mind not ringing when I'm ill?"
She slammed the phone down and as it quivered
she turned on Enrique: "Go on, go to him!
Leave your sick mother.
He abandoned you—do you realize that?

But you've forgiven him. Aren't you kind?
Daddy's played on your sympathy because
he's all on his own, and you've fallen for it,
forgetting that I, your own mother,
who didn't abandon you, am so lonely
life isn't worth living. You don't need me anymore.
Who am I, my God? Just a useless woman,
whom her own son doesn't want..." And with a tragic
bow of head, she stuffed the pipette
up her nose, squeezed exactly the right amount,
and, sniffing back her sobs, went back to bed.
The phone, as if it had waited for her to leave,
rang again. This time it breathed the well-known
odor of his teacher's cognac and classicism:
"Here's what I've got to say to you, Enrique:
Whoever becomes friendly with a Lilliputian
gradually becomes a dwarf himself.
You were too weak to choose between him and me,
but in art you can't be of two minds.
So I suggest that you forget me, and I
will forgive your forgetfulness, don't worry..."

For a minute or two he stared at the silenced phone
in his hand, but the smell of brandy
evaporated. Now it smelled of plastic.
That's a dead smell. Strictly, not even a smell.
He squeezed in his fist the impassive short pips,
but no sooner had he put the phone down than
the plastic means of noncommunication
shuddered again.

               With a sigh, he picked it up,
and heard: "Greetings from a terrorist! Don't worry,
I'm not in jail. They let me out today.
On bail. I've been a good boy and signed a paper
promising not to make those dreadful bombs.
But I can still make phone calls.
So here I am. A little whisper tells me
our mutual friend, the fourteenth apostle,
our friend whose motto is, Thou shalt not kill,
squealed on me... Is it possible, Enrique?"
"No, it's absurd. He'd never do such a thing..."
"What a coincidence, I agree with you.
His conscience is too sensitive. Besides,

he's never tried to hide his opposition,
and obvious opponents don't betray.
It's those with no opinions who betray.
You see what I'm getting at?" "I'm sorry, no."
"Of course, you'd rather not see it. You recall
the day you paid a visit to my home
and saw the dynamite? Now, in your shoes,
the apostle would have raised the roof.
But you said nothing; you just took it in
with that inscrutable artistic look.
What do you do, while the fight is going on
all around you? You continue drawing!
But perhaps you took it into your head
to put aside your oils and watercolors
for a short while, and try your hand at ink?
Such as, writing a denunciation?"
"I?" "You. Or some other artist like you
who's listened carefully to his friends'
political wrangles, and kept amazingly quiet?
A good listener can be a good talker too.
Forgive me, I must be honest. I'm not sure
it was you, Enrique, but I'm not sure that it wasn't..."
How heavy a phone is...Its weight could drag one
not toward the hook nor toward the ground but into
    the ground.
Enrique put down the phone again,
but clinging with its icy black body
to his palm, the secret lines of destiny,
the lowered receiver wouldn't let go of his hands.
The young man knew it hadn't stuck for nothing.
For a time it was ingratiatingly silent,
relaxing its invisible muscles,
getting ready to pounce on his temples.
And then it pounced...In it was the same voice
that had asked him cheerfully in the park:
"Isn't it hard-going in a suit and shoes?"
But this voice no longer belonged to her
but to the two-headed phone
in whose two heads was the same spiteful thought:
It's time to finish this off. "I'm ringing
to tell you that I've spoken to your other
woman. What a line you've spun us both!
I'd guessed something of the sort for ages.
A heart divided like yours can't be a heart.

Don't worry, I shan't try to keep you
by taking an overdose like her. I'm strong.
I'm sorry for you, actually. You wished to run
along two tracks at the same time. Poor boy,
you must be well and truly exhausted.
You've run yourself out. Ruined your health.
Find yourself an anthill to rest on,
although one's probably not enough for you,
you'd better find two, and sit between them.
That's what you like doing, isn't it?
Now you know what is at the end of the run."
She was just slightly too large
for this world in which everything is cramped.
But how can she have shrunk
to this standard size in the hand of a clenched phone
pounding on his temple with words?

Death has many faces . . .
                    Suicide
cannot have only one cause.
We're not finished while there's something to cling to,
but when there's not—we've had it! Death may wear,
at one and the same time, the face of the crowd,
the fact of the age itself, of a newspaper,
telephone, friend, the face of our father,
our teachers' faces. Death may have the face
of our beloved, and even our mother's face.

                    10.

And Enrique wrote in his diary:
"I'm twenty. Life's just begun, as they say.
What's to come, though, when it's started like this?
A man is only given one soul,
but he isn't allowed to keep it for himself.
Everyone wants to slice it into shreds
as though it were meat, and each diner
smacks his lips over his own portion
and puts his own favorite sauce on.
But while they're eating a man's soul
they're also glancing to each side jealously.
In fact, they don't just want a bigger piece,
they want the lot. And after they've eaten

they still feel hungry and bad-tempered,
and they demand another soul to carve up,
and if they can't have it they start gnawing
their own souls, they're so hungry and spiteful.
No, I'm wrong ... People aren't to blame.
It's the soul itself that carves itself up
and sends off the bits like magnets to draw in
other souls, and the soul cuts these up
into little pieces too. But why?
One soul alone can't hope to bring happiness
to all other souls at once. How good,
how easy it must be for those without souls.
But if you have a soul, there's no way out.
I've come to understand that life is a crime.
To live is to give hurt to those you love.
On any path, we tread on ants without thinking,
and on the path of life we kill our loved ones,
quite without meaning to, against our will,
treading on bodies that we do not see.
Hurting people is unbearably painful.
But it's inevitable. Once you realize that,
it's logical to wish you hadn't been born.
But what do you do if you've already been born?
The most humane thing, then, is to kill yourself.
Kill yourself, to avoid killing others.
Forgive me, everyone I've killed,
read my diary and you'll understand
that I didn't mean to, I didn't hate you,
any of you, nor betray any of you,
that I loved you all, and love you,
and that I'm leaving you in order to express
my misunderstood love for you ..."

Then carefully he washed his brushes,
left his diary open on the table,
calmly put on a clean shirt,
stuffed his swimming-trunks sewn with a smiling penguin
into a cellophane bag and, going out,
walked up to say good-bye to the watermelon
whose bloody wound seemed still wet on the canvas
under the predatory knives; the pig-eyes winked
at one another, and as if in a mocking gesture
of farewell to him, the smug phone started ringing.

·   ·   ·

Enrique walked blindly through the city,
staring down at the gleaming pavement,
not noticing the purposeful-looking eyes
and tumors on the general's face,
possibly General Pinochet's,
in the Ford racing along the street
and almost knocking him down.
Enrique walked to the Hotel Carrera.
The shadow of his death preceding him
opened the doors hospitably, and in
the air-conditioned elevator he pushed the button
marked 23. Superbly situated,
the rooftop, faintly chlorine-scented pool
was shimmering. Strewn on air mattresses
were bodies in bikinis, slowly sipping
Tom Collinses. He grew less agitated,
for everybody spoke in English there.
One's native language sometimes is the last
foothold preventing us from dying. But,
thank heavens, it isn't possible to clutch
the straws of cocktails held in total strangers'
falsely occupied hands. Having got changed
in a tiny cubicle, he plunged into the pool.
He didn't swim much. He lay on his back,
his arms stretched out; but from all sides, the arms
of other swimmers kept on striking him,
preventing the sky from looking him in the eyes.
These strangers seemed deliberately to be trying
to jostle him to left or right, even here.
Pulling himself from the pool, with drops on his skin,
which dried immediately in the bright sun,
he paused for a moment on the very edge of the roof,
and with his tanned and tensely arched back, heard:
"How handsome! Charming boy!" Lightly he swung
over the rail, lightly pushed off from the edge,
jumping as from a springboard into water.
He was a long time flying, it seemed to him.
The asphalt approached so slowly he had time
to notice, on the asphalt, a silver blaze
of doves, and realized that he was flying
toward them, but too late. He caught onto
some wire, and then another, then straightway
another, finally torturing his body
with an electric current before he died,

but those wires broke, knowing the shock was fatal.
By chance Enrique died not on the ground,
but in the air, and falling onto the road,
he who had wanted so much not to murder
when living, killed a dove with his dead body.

II.

I had been to that pool many times,
where the water was changed so regularly,
not only, perhaps, because of germs, but so that
the water, vainly growing agitated,
might not betray the secrets it had heard.
I read, in the Hotel Carrera,
the diary left by the self-murderer,
and his mother filled me in on other facts,
and some I worked out for myself.
Taking back the diary, his mother said:
"My son believed that by taking his own life
he would save himself from killing others.
But look what happened: With his dead body,
senselessly, for no reason, he killed a dove.
He killed his father, who for the first time
in years I had started to feel sorry for.
He killed me. He killed the two women together.
He killed his two teachers, he killed his friends
and his talent, which was just beginning to flower.
All of us are guilty of his death,
but he, also, is guilty of killing us.
Do you have children?" I replied: "A son."
"Then it's easier for you to understand.
You, Señor, might hurt your son, without
intending to, of course, by being too busy,
or not understanding him. You and his mother
may argue, pulling him in two directions,
forgetting that it's tearing him apart.
And what would happen to his mother and you
if he took his revenge by taking his life?
Oh yes, we are all guilty of his death,
but heavens! how we have paid for it. Forgive me
for touching on your personal life, Señor.
There are no personal lives in the world.

Everything is linked. You are linked to me,
and linked to my dead son, although you mightn't
have known it if I hadn't made up my mind
to come and see you. I beg you to write something
to expose the false glamour of suicide.
Art has made it glamorous. We're all so stirred
when the hero dies by his own hand, encouraging
the shameful wicked myth that it's something brave
and beautiful, and all the more appealing
because the stage directions make it sound
so simple: 'Stabs himself in the heart . . .'
'Shoots himself in the temple . . .' I could throttle
those dramatists, but unfortunately most
are beyond my reach, their throats protected by
a bronze buff collar. So write something.
If you can save a single living soul
by doing so, you will save your own . . ."
She went away; since then
she has never left my memory.

12.

Snow was falling in Chile; so native to Russia,
it was alien and frightening for the Chileans.
The sentries outside La Mondeda‡ froze,
draping their blue ears with their handkerchiefs.
Mercurio observed with satisfaction:
"This snow is a present to us from the Kremlin."
Surprised by the snow's weight, the roofs of plywood
shanties collapsed and crashed on children's dreams.
Cars floundered through the snow to die in drifts.
The president hovered in a helicopter
over the chaos, over the panic and cries,
the paralyzed highways, and the buried roads,
and, landing where the snow had drifted deepest,
Allende, haggard and unshaven, seized a spade
in his awkward hands and, staggering, cleared the road
himself, chewing the snow from his mustache
furiously—the way he cleared the past
like a mountain of rubble blocking the horizon;
and thus he swayed, clearing away the corruption,
without seeing through his dirt-splattered glasses

that worms had been burrowing into the spade's tip
for so long it had crumbled, nor hearing the jibes:
"Clear it away . . . You won't clear it all away . . ."

I traveled around Chile with Pancho,
a gray-bearded drinker, an overgrown *niño*,
a one-time whaler and *mujeriego*.
Confessing his sins, he would grow softer-eyed
than a whole drawing room of maiden aunts.
I adored him like all the wonderful
pure-hearted drinkers of the planet—
they are leviathans bearing on their shoulders
the earth and all its narrow-minded abstainers.
This leviathan (and ex-harpoonist) was
so powerfully gushing with stories one only needed
to attach him to a good writer. The problem was—
it turned out that he wrote on the sly himself!
His stories were now about an iceberg
on which there was a frozen grand piano,
and sometimes penguins pecking with their beaks
the slighty stiffened keyboard extracted sounds;
now about his first, late love—Matilda,
a prostitute with a consumptive flush
who was his fiancée, only she died
before the wedding; and her friends in the brothel
collected enough money to erect
two marble doves on her untimely grave.
In the fishing village of Punta Arenas
we spent a whole day searching for that grave,
but for some reason couldn't find it,
and went off instead to see Matilda's friends,
whom Pancho embraced, and then he cried for a long time,
but no longer wanted to visit the grave.
Pancho's two basic instincts were anger and tears.
While we ate with the girls, and drank *colamono*
(literally, "monkey's tail"), a hellish concoction
of vodka and milk, Pancho suddenly flew
into a towering rage against us both:
"Eujenio, while you and I sit gorging ourselves
on food and drink, our Chilean people are starving!"
And, as unexpectedly, he burst into tears,
obliging Matilda's friends to ease his pain.
Although his gluttonous appetite was amoral
from a social point of view, and dangerous

from a medical one because of an old ulcer,
he confessed his sinfulness and ate—ate everything:
frogs, sparrows, molluscs, but most of all
he loved *erisos*—see urchins fresh from the ocean;
raw with lemon juice, salt, and pepper,
they squealed in your stomach, Pancho said.
On the fishing quay at Portamona,
he bought them by the dozen, straight off a boat,
and gulped them down, with spasms of delight,
then doubled up with pain. Resorting to
the old method of two fingers, he brought them up
and swallowed them again, exclaiming, with
their caviar in his beard: "Eujenio,
erisos are so wonderful! A life
without *erisos*—can you call it life?"

When he had lain for three days
in the local hospital, having convulsions,
and, being unable to indulge in confession,
was unexpectedly able to listen,
I took advantage of the moment
and told him the story of young Enrique,
who by committing suicide had killed
his mother and many of his dearest ones,
and the dove on the dusty road.

Seizing hold of his stomach with both hands,
as people often do when they're laughing
but now because of lacerating pain,
my friend had a fit of anger and tears:
"What villains!" "Who?" I asked, surprised,
straightening suffering Pancho's crumpled pillow.
"All of them are villains," he bellowed. "They all
pushed him off the roof together..."
"But what about the dove?" Avoiding an answer,
the old man groaned: "I want *erisos*!"
We visited Tierra del Fuego together
when he had recovered from his *erisos*.
Swaying on mangy horses, he and I rode
past tens of thousands or maybe millions of geese
flying in for the winter, but Pancho muttered,
over and over, a single word: "Dove...Dove..."
We paused by a rusty dredge, leaning over a river.
Pancho said: "You know, this river is called

Rusfin, for some strange reason. A Russian gold-
prospector who came to Chile, God knows how,
got drunk here, they say, and the dredge caught his sleeve
in its teeth and dragged him in. He was ground up
with the rocks. Before he died, he shrieked:
'Rus fin!' which roughly means, in broken Spanish:
'The Russian's a goner'... But perhaps it was suicide...
Who knows?... It happened so long ago...
Have you ever thought of suicide, *amigo*?"
"Yes, I did once... How about you, Pancho?"
"Ah! I love *erisos*, Eujenio.
They're a unique experience, not only
to eat, but even also to vomit them up.
I couldn't forgo them. I thought you were made
of sterner stuff, Eujenio. I'm ashamed
to have drunk *colamono* with such a weakling.
A man should never have such thoughts. You want
to help those scum who hide their fascist leanings,
but dream of you and me together jumping
off roofs, or putting pistols to our heads,
hanging ourselves, or rotting our livers with drink?
You want to do their dirty work for them?
Remember, you Russian scoundrel, there's no such thing
as a hopeless situation. There's always an answer.
Nooses, bullets, jumps—they belong to a circus.
Don't you forget it. If you ever kill yourself
I'll kill you, *amigo*, I promise!"

                              His anger changed,
without an interval, to a fit of tears:
"I'm lying to you, damn it! I too have thought
of suicide, at times. I just didn't want
to let you think so, even for a second..."
Pancho and I embraced and fell silent
by the rusty dredge in whose teeth lurked
the lost secret of someone's life,
And it grew quiet all around,
As if the dead dove soared above us.

                              13.

In my apartment that was no longer mine,
where even the things looked at me
as if at something completely obsolete,

I once had an ultimate, dead, wistful yearning
for *erisos*, like a last wish before death.
But I remembered they weren't to be found
in Moscow's stores and restaurants.
Everything had been so shattered in my life,
I knew it could never be stuck together again.
Divorce. The loss of my son. Insults
from the mouths of former friends.
The magistrate's sympathetic, yet curious, look.
And the stream of other judges,
all of whom considered themselves "the people,"
but who showed not a hint of fellow feeling
in their quietly gleeful, accusing eyes.
Everyone there accused me of egoism,
self-interest, moral corruption, and conceit,
of inattention, and of not appreciating
those whom I ought to have appreciated
yet failed abjectly to do. No one there,
except myself, thought of accusing me
of murder. I was so tired of hurting people—
relatives, women, friends. At every step
forward or step back, to right or left,
or even if I just stood still, it seemed
I was killing someone. And on that day
when the yearning for *erisos* overcame me,
I gritted my teeth, like a bad provincial actor
in a Chekhov tragedy, tipsily slurring:
"My friends, my dears, how can I make you happy?
How can I help you to breathe more easily?
I know I am the reason for your tears,
although perhaps I'm not altogether at fault;
but certainly I have hurt you, and I think
it's better that I quietly withdraw..."
But something wouldn't let me die.
The apartment was empty. Only a dove
with almost human eyes
was perched outside my window.
But perhaps it was the one that was killed
in Santiago under the Carrera hotel,
and dead, it had flown to my rescue,
so that I shouldn't let myself die?
There are no "foreign" disasters.
When people understand that, they will fly
across frontiers to the rescue, like this dove,

515

and then there will be happiness on earth.
And then, if someone, somewhere, is unhappy—
in Santiago, Khimki-Khovrino, New York—
he still won't have the right to kill himself.
When I was young, a great poet, who amazed
everyone by surviving into his seventies,
said to me: "Mayakovsky and Yesenin
criminally predicted their own deaths.
Poetry has an autosuggestive force.
My advice to you is, write whatever you like,
about whatever you like, only avoid
predicting your own suicide."
Since then, I have placed my writing desk
as a barricade against death. And I shall not
be intimidated by you two
glib salesmen—you prophet
of pessimism, hawking despair and death;
and you merchant of lying hopes,
pseudo-optimist. You are not really rivals,
you are in league to lure us to the edge
and crush the future with dead bodies,
like the dove in Santiago.
Murdered Allende, I am not your judge,
I only claim to judge your murderers.
With the reprisal of immortality,
transform the extremists to self-slaughterers.
Decree with your presidential power that none
but hangmen hang themselves, and only those
who have executed freedom on this earth
may turn their rifles on themselves, in fear.

Epilogue

It's suicide to believe that we are mortal;
rotting under the ground's so tedious.
More shameful than lies, more ignoble than slander,
is to make others believe that death exists.

I hate death, like Tsiolkovsky,§
who longed to reach the stars because

he wanted to populate the whole universe
with people, all equally immortal.

You will come to look upon life
as a thread that the centuries have woven.
Resurrected, as in Fyodorov's# vision,
our ancestors will come to us.

They will float to us in boats and triremes.
Romulus and Remus will climb into rockets with us.
And if I die, it will only be for a short while.
I will be everywhere. Everyone. Everything.

And on the ice crust of a distant star,
sending signals to people in space,
I will celebrate life like the dead dove,
soaring immortally over the earth.

1978

TRANSLATED BY D. M. THOMAS

*Oleg: Prince of Kiev and Novgorod (d. 912 or 922) celebrated in Pushkin's poem "Song of Prophetic Oleg." When it was prophesied that he would receive his death from his own horse, he parted with his steed. Many years later he came to where his horse's bones were scattered. A snake crawled out of the skull and stung him to death.
†Victor Hara: Chilean poet and singer. Imprisoned in the stadium after Allende's overthrow, he continued to play and sing. His hands were cut off so that he could no longer play his guitar.
‡La Moneda: Presidential palace.
§Tsiolkovsky: Konstantin Eduardovich Tsiolkovsky (1857–1935). Russian scientist, teacher, philosopher who pioneered research in rockets and space travel, motivated significantly by the extraordinary teachings about immortality of N. F. Fyodorov.
#Fyodorov: Nikolai Fyodorovich Fyodorov (1828–1903). Russian philosopher and librarian who wrote in his two-volume, posthumously published work, *The Philosophy of the Common Task*, how mankind should unite in the struggle to conquer death and resurrect the dead through science and technology.

1979⁄1985

A half blade of grass in the teeth—
there's my whole secret

"Moscow believed ..."

To I. Gutchin

Moscow believed my tears,
when at the entrance to a squalid magic door for bread
I lost in the muddle my sacred ration card
as though through a hole in my hand.

A short-haired old woman—typhus had trimmed her—
whispered:
> "My old man gave up his soul to God.
But some days still remain on his card.
Though a dead man's bread you can eat a little.
>> But don't blab!"

Moscow believed my tears,
and I didn't jump off the tail ends of her streetcars,
carrying in my mitten another's right to bread ...
I ate for a dead man. I couldn't let myself be killed.

Moscow believed my tears
and her tears I've believed forever,
when widowed by unnumbered soldiers,
Moscow howled like a farm wife.

Womanly Moscow creaked with its homespun ...
It all happened as if it were the mesozoic age.
The magic doors have expanded, together with the muddle,
and again something troubled my hand.

Again I'm spasmodically squeezing something,
like ration cards for bread, when I was small,
but I lost it in the river of people,
what, I don't know, but again there's a hole in my hand.

After so many years I've blurted it out,
when there's neither ration cards, nor old women.
I'm headed toward squealing brakes ...
Moscow, will you believe again my tears?

1979

TRANSLATED BY ALBERT C. TODD

Designers of Spiderwebs

Who are the solicitous fathers
of binding sticky routines?
Designers of spiderwebs,
exalted creative masters.

When he dangles on saliva
deep in his spidery world
a spiderweb designer considers
that he's even being daring.

Designers of spiderwebs
take pride in the creation
of almost weightless masterpieces
that ensnare people.

The torment of this particular creativity
is to give birth to this thread from themselves,
in order to bind our hands
by a spiderweb that's as beautiful as possible.

But there's also the spider error.
Designers tell themselves the lie:
"The more exquisitely I torture a victim,
the more my labor is valued . . ."

But how with sight that's dying
can one crave such beauty,
and how can you find delight
in a design that has entrapped you?

1980

TRANSLATED BY ALBERT C. TODD

Directness

"There is a directness
                    that's like something crooked.
It is hunchbacked inside itself.

Before it
        life is guiltlessly guilty
that it is not a simple drawing.
Be afraid of making life straight,
                        without understanding
that by straightening you can bend.
Sometimes in history the straight line
between two points
                is the longest route.

1980
TRANSLATED BY ALBERT C. TODD

Two Pair of Skis

Two pair of skis
                nestled tenderly against a house,
silent,
        almost without life.
But in the house,
                you and I are alive.
I'm not asleep.
                You are.
Our sole guardians are
two pair of skis,
                offended
that we didn't let them lean inside the house.
On each ski is a shallow white groove,
like the Milky Way.
Danger roams crunchingly across the frost.
Everything is fragile—
                from icicles even to us,
and, as if the skis feel the threat,
they focus on the stars.
You remember—
        the snowy woods full of the sun and in the snow
    the inscription written with the ski pole:
                        "G. Savel'iev."

Inside the letters a white spruce had shed its needles,
and, as if wolves had eaten him,
                              Savel'iev himself
disappeared.
And something made me fear
                              for the life of Savel'iev,
for a son
              with a birthmark on his fragile fontanelle.
And you and I,
              and the skis,
                              and the universe—
on a tiny thread.
I am so afraid
                 for the crystal silence,
for the moonlight
                        on the slopes of sleeping roofs . . .
And did the two pair of skis
leave for long a ski track from us?
Coziness,
           health—
                        the pitiful little grabs
at so-called life . . .
                        Only
if they press the button,
              not even a splinter of you will remain—
two pair of skis.
Beneath every roof—
                        is also mankind.
Absolutely no less valued than Paris
is our home,
              where on a porch lit by the moon
are two pair of skis.
And listening with keen attention to the endlessness,
where you move your lips in sleep,
two pair of skis
support
           eternity
                        on their tips.

1981

TRANSLATED BY ALBERT C. TODD

Back Then

Back then,
      back then,
the palisade wept resin,
the crosses wept resin
at the cemetery in the undulating heat,
and resin dripped through
the knotholes in the dacha walls.
The night pleaded for lightning
to help itself,
and, raising branches to the sky,
"Rain! . . ."
      whispered the night,
              "Rain!"
Jasmine intoxicated the jasmine,
transforming itself through the night,
and it peered into the window
where there were rustles
      and sin,
and where, shimmering, the sheet
slithered from you,
      slithered from me,
and the glow of our bodies
made the jasmine squint
      and sweat.
We loved each other so
that the jasmine's tender pollen,
remaining on our lips,
leaped from face to face.
We loved each other so, that
in our exhaustion
only fingers
      wandered like blind men
in all directions
      along our bodies.
From your breast
      my hand
removed a moth.
I kissed again,
      again,
your slightly salty shoulder.

You rose,
         went to the window.
The jasmine recoiled into the depths,
and dissolving in the nocturnal nowhere,
"To the water! . . ."
                you whispered,
                      "To the water! . . ."
The car leaped into the murk,
while at the dacha,
            on the floor,
lay
   the sheet,
         contorted,
without you,
         without me.
It was in midnight heat,
             that a hole
in a fence led us
into the bushes—
            the kingdom of the nightingale.
We loved each other so
that the swaying willow bed
mingled with the prestorm air
where the nightingale
            swayed
and lavished songs
            from the branches,
catching bits of storm with its tongue,
unwilling to live silently
or obey, in time,
the shushing of the reeds.
It's not true
       that birds
have no faces.
They are recognized by gardens
               and forests.
Their faces
       are their voices.
Out of all others I would
recognize that prestorm nightingale.
May the singer eternally
be recognized by his voice
              as if by face!
It did not surrender to the clouds

that had taken the night in hand,
but, sitting on a twig,
called
             the storm down onto its feathers.
And the invited thunder roared
on the branches,
                     lake,
                          and house,
where once Field Marshal Paulus*
lived as a prisoner.
Back then,
          back then,
there was the war
                     and Stalingrad.
But memory
          is like a sieve.
Field Marshal Paulus
                     means nothing
to the foliage
               and the nightingale,
to the roach
             and the sheatfish,
or to the barefoot goddess
that in the hour of nocturnal triumph
in a soaked dress
                  mischievously
ran with me
            into the lake!
The rain raised bubbles
with flickering eyelets
and you were like a wave
under me,
          over me.
I didn't know
              which was the storm
                                   and which was you.
You have
         mermaid tails.
And, making kindling of lightning bolts,
the storm danced on the waves
to the crazy dance of the fish,
and two happy heads
danced,
        as if chopped off

527

to the sound of thunder . . .
Back then,
        back then,
we swam off into the distance on a whim.
Love
     is like swimming in a place unknown.
At first
      playfulness.
But where the water thickens,
becoming hard,
we crawl with such difficulty
along the bottom,
        as if under ice,
and sometimes swim
          with our children in our arms
in the accumulated spit.
All the water spirits as one
diligently pull us to the bottom
and a ghost
      through Zeiss binoculars
watches
     our legs convulse.
Now, while I'm certain, unhappily,
that old hole has been plugged,
what damned revanchist
avenges
     artistic warbling?
Could ghosts once again
attack the throat,
to block everyone
from nightingales?
Could the world have sung itself out,
could that prestorm nightingale and its voice
have withered away
under the indifferent grass?!
The world is not the same
          and we're not the same
in the dark absence of the nightingale.
But should the heat rise again,
sing, little nightingale,
       at least from the cross
in the cemetery,
      where the resin once again
seeps from crosses in the heat.

Break a hole in the fence
with your voice in the midnight heat!
How lovely the world would be
if all fences were made
                    of holes!
Sing, little nightingale,
                    I'll join in,
as befits a nightingale,
as my unnamed brother sang
back then,
                    back then . . .

1981

TRANSLATED BY ANTONINA W. BOUIS AND JAMES RAGAN

*Paulus: Field Marshal Friedrich Paulus. German commander at the battle of Stalingrad who surrendered his army to the victorious Red Army.

Maternity Floor

In Shelley Road—named after Percy Bysshe—
an Anglo-Russian child has just been born,
founder of the Lake School of Sodden Nappies.
Clean the mud off your shoes,
                    stub out your cigarettes—
this is the maternity floor!
In a woman a mother is born,
                    discovering her pain to be pleasure;
a son is born,
            creating his father's rebirth.
Everything under the sun is reborn:
Russian snow falls whirling over Bournemouth,
                            transformed into English showers;
the white spots on the stems of Dunhill pipes
                            change back into elephants' tusks.
Beefsteaks change back into cows.
                    Estuaries, long silted up, start gushing again.
Geese, resurrected from their tins of foie gras,
                            soar through the skies.
The policeman's redoubtable truncheon

                              reverts to resin
and falls from his fist like a tear.
London Bridge, which had been trundled off to the States,
                              finds its way home on the Concorde,
its moss-covered stonework
                              travels first-class and drinks Guinness!
And all this has been achieved by our son—
                              our wrinkle-faced miracle!
He demands your breast
                    with the greediest appetite—
this tiny fragile bridge
                    joining
                         our two peoples!
Darling, give him a chance to move,
                         don't wrap him up too tight!
Ah, if only all nations
                    loved one another as we do!
But why are the newborn
                    so wrinkled?
They screw up their faces in advance
                              at everything that's vile in the world!
In the ward where the women are in labor
                         a reporter already pokes about with his pen,
and jabs a political question
                    between baby and breast.
Don't curdle
          the mother's
                    milk!
I won't let you upset my son,
                    furiously sucking away,
wrapped, as if in diapers,
                    in pages of Shakespeare and Pushkin.
Descended from Irish brigands
                    and oppressed Siberian peasants,
he's also wrapped in the Jolly Roger
                         and the sail of vagabonds from Lake Baikal!
He's a moist, happy, tiny present!
                         But nearby are other presents:
Mr. Barnes, only a day old, is screaming
                         as if he's already at Speakers' Corner.
And they're all utterly clean candidates
                         who've never taken a bribe in their lives.
The largest Party in the world
                    is the Party of Children!

Of course children can also be bribed

                                 with sweets and ice cream,

but those here have had no chance

                           to be tempted!

I see an Indian in the corridor

with something strange rolled up under his arm.

Unrolled, it turns out to be a carpet.

He kneels down with a sigh, discarding his shoes,

and, shy and alone, whispers

a prayer for his son who was born next to mine.

And to make sure there will never be, neither an English

                                 nor a Russian Hiroshima,

let the earth of the whole planet

                         be a prayer carpet

for all children

                 as well as for my son!

On the maternity floor

                    a triumphant cry rings out—

the cry of an Anglo-Russian wrinkle-faced miracle

                       clasped in the hands of Nurse Wilson!

And God in a white coat, concealed

                    under the pseudonym of Doctor Sid,

lifts up our son,

              naked as truth itself!

We live too briefly on this earth.

                 Three hundred years minimum are needed!

Oh, if only everything could be resolved

                          on the maternity floor!

1981

TRANSLATED BY ARTHUR BOYARS (REVISED)

On What Is Life Spent?

April casts icicles,

             mints them,

and the crackling sky

             has turned so blue,

and the garage guard mooches money
for a drink from me.
The gurgling of the brook
                        under the icy crust,
in which someone's cigarette butt has grown,
and the April fir tree
                    with snowy trim,
its needle landing under my collar,
and the chorus of rooks
                            with its febrile gabble—
all pose a question
that contains all questions in one:
On what is life spent?
Really, on what?
                    On what is it spent?
Tell me, garage guard! . . .
                        Are you deaf, old man?
Perhaps no more than those
who educated their ear with symphonies?
We are often deaf to those far from us.
                    And deaf to those near,
especially
while squeezing them dry.
We talk with friends,
                    yet do not hear them,
holding our own words
                    most high.
While she is alive,
                we are deaf to our beloved—
we'll only hear an old woman's death rattle.
We've made conscience
                        intentionally hard of hearing,
stuffing cotton in its ears—
such is the way of pretended innocence.
And how much time lost
                        in the past
for stuffing ears,
                    our own and others'!
Death will remove the cotton,
                            and find no ears.
Skulls don't hear.
                    God will judge them.
Worm, don't dig around
                    in a former ear!

On what is life spent?!
The world is in a fatal arms race,
it is so deaf
                    to the gurgle of earth's ferment,
to the brooks in April race of disarmingness
in their seeming childishness
                                        and unneededness.
Don't die, nature,
                    hold out!
On what is life spent?
We are deafened
                    by damned wars' explosions.
Let us not be deaf to the dead,
                                        to those who are alive.
Heal wounds!
                    Blood, spurt only under the skin!
On what is life spent?
Life is spent
                    on our false fame.
In ignominy glory will grow later.
Life is spent
                    on something externally complex
that suddenly turns out
                                        to be simple theft.
Life is spent
                    on something externally modest,
but modest cowards should be tried!
On trifles,
                    one would think, bloodless.
But trifles are bloody.
                                        Its blood they suck.
We will all one day become
                                        incorporeal,
but how will we save our souls?
For if I have to die—
                    I'd like to know:
On what is death spent?

1981

TRANSLATED BY ANTONINA W. BOUIS

Final Faith

Is it possible that we are so twisted
there is no salvation for any of us,
and that ideas have become wingless
in an age of winged rockets?

Is it possible that a crippled birch,
bending over to the last river,
will see the last man
in its boiling water?

Is it possible there'll be no Big Ben,
Saint Basil's, or Notre Dame
and that neutron foam will gush
over our final steps?

But that the planet, cherry trees,
birds, and children will perish,
I don't believe. This disbelief
is my final faith.

Skull after skull will not
be piled up in towers again.
The final Nuremburg approaches us
before, not after the war.

And the last soldier on earth
will throw his shoulder strap in a stream,
and watch how peacefully
dragonflies sit on it.

All rascality will end.
All people will understand—we are a family.
The last government
will abolish itself.

The last exploiter,
opening his toothless mouth,
will gobble the last money
furtively like a delicacy.

·   ·   ·

The last cowardly editor
will be doomed forever
to read from the stage in sequence
everything that he destroyed.

So that the last bureaucrat
can rest and be silent,
his gullet will be stuffed in payment
with the last rubber stamp.

And the earth will turn
without fear of the last years,
there never will be born
the last great poet.

1982

TRANSLATED BY ALBERT C. TODD

Momma and the Neutron Bomb:
A Poem (Excerpt)

Momma,
            I've been reading today's newspapers
through the transparent-from-hunger children of Leningrad
who have come to the global Christmas tree for murdered children.
Tiny shriveled hands from Piskariovskoe Cemetery*
reach out for the yellow lanterns
                                of tree decoration tangerines,
but when they pluck them
                                they don't know what to do with them.
Children of Auschwitz,
                        with convulsed blue little faces,
choking on gas,
                ask Santa Claus for a gift from the tree
of a glass bauble,
                    inside of which
there's just a tiny bit of oxygen.
Unborn babies from My Lai
                            ripped from their mothers' wombs

535

crawl
      to a sobbing Big Bad Wolf.
Little Red Riding Hood
                        struggles to glue together pieces
of children blown up by bombs
                        in Belfast and Beirut.
Children of Salvador,
                    who had been crushed by a vindictive tank,
recoil in horror
          from a toy one.
The dancing circle of murdered children
                  round their global Christmas tree is endless.
But if a neutron bomb goes off
                      there will be no children at all:
there will only be kindergartens
                  where teddy bears will howl
as they tear with plastic claws
            their chests of plush right to the sawdust inside,
and inflated elephants
              will trumpet a belated alarm ...
Thank you, Samuel Cohen,†
                and other humanitarians,
for your new "toy"—
not one for children to play with,
but one that plays with children,
until there isn't a single child left ...
For the disappearance of the line in Children's World store,
for the end of the shortage of paper diapers,
for Disneyland,
        where now
                no one
                    will break anything,
for the dolls,
            whose pigtails will never be cruelly pulled off,
for the windows,
              that will never be broken by rude footballs,
for the forever riderless
              merry-go-round ponies,
creaking in the worldwide emptiness.
for children's tights,
carefully hung out on wash lines,
                  which never will be torn
in a game of hide-and-seek amid the brambles ...
A final worldwide hide-and-seek game will take place.

There will be no children.
                    There will be no adults.
Safe and sound streets
                    will be strewn with safe and sound wristwatches
with fastened straps and bands
still retaining the shape of vanished wrists,
with wedding rings fallen from fingers,
with turquoise and other earrings
                    fallen from women's lobes,
and only safe and sound empty gloves
                    will grip
safe and sound steering wheels of safe and sound cars.
The whole international display of women's legs in Perugia
will vaporize:
          only empty shoes will remain
with a handful of ash imprinted in gold on the insoles,
and between the suede and patent leather urns
a half-fused small chain
                    from the ankle
of a vaporized Peruvian girl
                    will crawl and sniff about the heels.
There will be no Momma either.
                    Only her newsstand will remain,
on which an atomic wind will leaf through
moldy editions that have become antiques:
Football and Hockey,
          America, and *Health*.
And the ghost of Momma's butcher
                    turned into vapor
will by habit leave
          for Momma's ghost
the ghost of a frozen chicken—
                    a fellow countryman of Maupassant
from a country
          where safe and sound Maupassant is on the bookshelves
and not a single fellow countryman is safe and sound.
And a new Major Firby,
                    after pressing a Hiroshima button,
will see how Europe is turned into
                    a dead Euroshima,
and the major won't be able to go crazy,
                    since he's become a ghost himself.
Momma rarely talks about politics,
but this is what she once said

upon return from a wallpaper store
on Star Boulevard,
where her buttons were torn off by accident
in the scramble for wallpaper from East Germany:
"My God,
                what people won't do out of greed for things.
That's probably why
                        they invented the neutron bomb..."
And I imagined
                millions of stores all over the world
packed with wallpaper,
                        mink coats,
diamonds,
        Italian shoes,
Japanese stereos,
                cans of Danish beer,
where there will be everything
        but the one thing that's disappeared—
a customer.
Pillows will start looting
                        Neanderthal skulls from museums.
Shirts
    all alone
                will pull themselves on statues and skeletons.
Children's strollers will rock
                        babies bottled in alcohol from medical labs.
Razor blades
        will want to slit their own throats
                                from loneliness.
A mass hanging of neckties from trees
                        will take place.
Books, longing for eyes and fingers,
                        will organize self-immolations.
Things, it is possible, will adapt themselves.
            By themselves things will start going to stores
and, very likely, will create universal havoc
when an unverified rumor gets started
that in some store in the suburbs
                        a man had suddenly appeared on sale.
Things are bound to come to political blows
and, probably, some eager-beaver refrigrator
will devise a new neutron bomb,
which destroys
            only things

and leaves people
            safe and sound . . .
But what will remain
            if people don't remain?
He who takes up the atomic sword
                  will perish by it.

1982

TRANSLATED BY ALBERT C. TODD

*Piskariovskoe Cemetery: Burial place in Leningrad of many of those who perished in the blockade of the city during World War II.
†Samuel Cohen: The American inventor of the neutron bomb.

Guardian of the Hearth

To Jan

Barely back from the road
I repossess my scattered self
and cross the threshold
of the country called "family."

Even while there's no absolving me,
here I will be understood and forgiven,
and in this country I am ashamed
of that from which I've just returned.

A lion stuffed with sawdust
seizes my coat by his teeth,
tears it off and demands I stand
in the corner, and knows his reason.

A much-darned sullen giraffe
licks me all over,
tugging my sleeves with his lips
to the cave where our sons are sleeping.

You—eternal woman
are the unsleeping timeless hearth

with the gas blue eyes
of a Moscow kitchen stove.

A poker stirs the coals of years
in the golden cinders
gilding the silhouette
of this, my guardian of the hearth.

The breast our child sucks,
full and deep, is edged in gold.
All the bombs in the world
won't frighten you from nursing.

More fearful with the years
and intimidated at times
is the once happy play of color
in your violet eyes.

Fate carried you afar,
while like a golden bee,
you know your own craft,
my guardian of the hearth.

Without thinking at all,
trampling everything on the way,
I've destroyed two hearths
and guard the third trembling.

I can hear the pounding of feet
of those who trample hearths
and march in universal bedlam
over the bodies of women and children.

On the roadways of women's wrinkles
they advance. In the eyes
of humanist males
S.S. ice flashes.

But the smoldering embers
of ravaged hearths
cling to their heels
and burn such enemies in sleep.

. . .

But how the essence of it all
becomes clear, inside and out,
when the road is illuminated
both by woman and the hearth.

Family is an amalgamation of I's.
I ask, in the country
called "family," when will
oppression and hostility end?

Answer me in the silence of night,
hearth guardian, wife—
is it really possible in this country
there ever could be war?!

1983

TRANSLATED BY ALBERT C. TODD AND JAMES RAGAN

Flowers for Grandmother

I came to the cemetery in the hazy heat of autumn,
where the crosses creak as they split,
to my grandmother—Maria Iosefovna—
and bought flowers at the gate.

In the era of silent movies Grandmother's braids
were formed into a tight wreath,
and neighbor ladies in the smoke-filled kitchen
called her the Commissar.

My grandmother beat me very little.
A shame that her hand grew tired of beating,
for, in the opinion of a bathhouse attendant,
I deserved nothing but boiling water.

I teased her cat in utter bliss
to be sure no one called me a sissy.
I swapped her eight volumes of history
for three volumes of *Man and Woman*.

.   .   .

A great soccer game was at hand—
Yugoslavia versus the USSR—
I filched her gold wedding ring
after hiding secretly in the chiffonier.

And that ring, heavy and reddish,
from Grandfather's finger, who is no more,
got into the clutches of a speculator
for a mere standing room ticket.

My grandmother Maria Iosefovna,
by merely biting the edge of her lip,
so chilled the soup on the table
it was covered with Siberian ice.

In front of a Robert Taylor poster,
back in ration card times,
she slipped on the ice by the bakery
and lost consciousness.

And with two fingers raised,
white-faced like the Old Believer Morozova,*
she repeated only one thing:
"Be thou accursed!"—and I was.

Hiding behind the primus stove, I thought
that Grannie, for sure, from spite
only pretended to be dying . . .
She punished me—and died.

To the neighbor's record *Rio Rita*
she fixed her stare straight up,
and all the relatives implored me:
"Confess . . . Confess . . . Confess . . ."

They continued to curse without stopping,
from right and left—I was fed up!
But Grandmother's curse
alone stuck in my heart.

And the ring, staring through the loamy soil,
torments, avenges, and glitters from out of the bones . . .
Remove your curse from me, Grannie,
don't be sorry for me, but for my children.

· · ·

The guilty, gentle flowers I
place on the grave in silence.
It never enters my mind
that their stems are suspiciously short.

By the small gray gravestone,
knowing all that goes on with people,
Mother whispers, so Grandmother won't hear:
"They steal flowers for resale here . . . Break the stems . . ."

All of us are caught up in resale.
Perhaps, I had brought as my gesture
flowers, whose stems had once been broken,
but which had been cut clean at the break.
It makes one shudder in the subway or on a trolleybus
to see a couple, cheek to cheek,
with all the stems in the young girl's happy hand
covered with cemetery clay.

All broken stems get cut off,
and in the shadow of departed shadows
tragic is the sale of suffering,
but the resale is yet more tragic.

If there is a tiny mercenary drop in me,
then I don't belong to my family.
Put a curse on me once more, Grandmother,
and never take that curse away.

1983

TRANSLATED BY ALBERT C. TODD

*Morozova: Feodosiia Prokofevna Morozova (d. 1672). Aristocratic supporter of Archpriest Avvakum during the Russian Church schism. Her banishment to a monastery was immortalized in V. I. Surikov's painting *Boiarina Morozova*.

"A small dish . . ."

A small dish darkens in the shadows,
dripped with wax that did not burn . . .

A candle, melted on the table,
will not return.

Deft technicians can plane verse
into curls and fancy turns,
but the charm of Pushkin's curls
will not return.

After so many lips, like a bitter trace,
only the taste of a poisoned urn,
but the taste of watermelon in childhood
will not return.

He who breaks up a family,
another one will never earn,
and friendship trampled underfoot
will not return.

On leashes in alien hands
great nations each other spurn,
and people—even from the heavens
will not return.

On fat mugs with honeyed lips
bloodstained traces we discern.
A face once turned into a fat mug
will not return.

Only with a revolt of shame
against shamelessness
will we escape the Day of Judgment—
honestly, more or less.

Only with the revolt of the face
against facelessness
will life return again
in all its divine mess.

Shamelessness can devour children—
and never cease to yearn.
But shame is not frightening. Shame is not death.
Everything will return.

1983
TRANSLATED BY ALBERT C. TODD

Afghanistan Ant

A young Russian lad lies on Afghan ground.
A Moslem ant circles his cheekmound.

Crawling is difficult, the dead too long unshaven,
the ant speaks softly, not the least bit craven:

You don't know exactly where from wounds you die.
You know one thing only—Iran is nearby.

Why with his gun is he like a scapelamb,
hearing for the first time the word *Islam*?

What will you give to our poor, barefoot motherland,
if you can't give your own people the things they demand?

Thinking is done not just where the HQ flag waves.
Those who march as slaves, get carted off to graves.

Is it possible there's not enough dead for you?
To add still more to twenty million, can't be true.

A young Russian lad lies on Afghan ground.
A Moslem ant crawls across his cheekmound.

In order to be raised up, resurrected,
he wants to have Orthodox ants selected.

But in the northern motherland of orphans and widows
very few such ants remain in the meadows.

1983
TRANSLATED BY ALBERT C. TODD

My Universities

I learned not only from those
                      who brightly beam out of golden frames,

but from everyone whose ID photo
                              didn't come out quite right.
More than with Tolstoy
                    I sensibly learned from blind beggars
who sang in train cars about Count Tolstoy.
From barracks
          I learned more than from Pasternak
                              and my verse style was hot "barracko."
I took lessons on Yesenin
                        in snack bars from war invalids
who tore their striped sailor shirts
                          after spilling out their plain secrets.
Mayakovsky's laddered verse
                        didn't give me as much
as the dirty steps of staircases
                        with handrails polished by kids' pants.
I learned in Zima Junction
                      from my most untalkative grannies
not to be afraid of cuts, scratches,
                            and various other scrapes.
I learned from dead-end streets that smell of cats,
                        from crooked spattered lanes,
to be sharper than a knife
                    and simpler than a butt end.
Empty lots were my shepherds.
                          Waiting lines my nursing mothers.
I learned from all the young toughs
                      who gave me a whipping.
I learned
        from pale-faced great little poets
with fatal content in their verse
                        and empty content in their pockets.
I learned from all the odd balls in attics,
                            from the dress cutter Alka,
who kissed me
            in the dark of a communal kitchen.
I was put together out of the birthmarks of the motherland
                            from scratches and scars,
cradles and cemeteries,
                hovels and temples.
My first globe was a rag ball,
                      without foreign threads,
with brick crumbs sticking to it,
and when I forced my way to

the real globe,
I saw—it was also made of scraps
                                and also subject to blows.
And I cursed the bloody soccer game,
            where they play with the planet without refs or rules,
and any tiny scrap of the planet,
                        that I touched,
                                    I celebrated!
I went round the planet
                        as if it were a gigantic Zima Junction,
and I learned from the wrinkles of old women,
                            now Vietnamese, and now Peruvian.
I learned folk wisdom,
                    taught by the worldwide poor and scum,
the Eskimo's smell for ice,
                    and the Italian's smiling non-despair.
I learned from Harlem
                not to consider poverty poor,
like a black
            whose face is only painted with white skin.
And I understood that the majority bends
                        their necks on behalf of others,
and in the wrinkles of those necks
                        the minority hides as if in trenches.
I am branded with the brand of the majority.
                        I want to be their food and shelter.
I am the name of all without names.
                        I am a writer for all who don't write.
I am a writer
            created by readers,
and readers are created by me.
                    My debt has been paid.
Here I am,
            your creator and your creation,
an anthology of you,
                a second edition of your lives.
I stand more naked than Adam,
                        rejecting court tailors,
the embodiment of imperfections—
                        yours and my own.
I stand on the ruins
                of loves I destroyed.
The ashes of friendships and hopes
                        coldly fly through my fingers.

547

Choking on muteness
     and the last man to get in line,
I would die for any one of you,
      because each of you is my homeland.
I am dying from love
     and I howl with pain like a wolf.
If I despise you—
    I despise myself even more.
I could fail without you.
      Help me to be my real self,
not to stoop to pride,
    not to fall into heaven.
I am a shopping bag stuffed
      with all the world's shoppers.
I am everybody's photographer,
      a paparazzo of the infamous.
I am your common portrait,
      where so much remains to be painted.
Your faces are my Louvre,
     my secret private Prado.
I am like a video player,
      where the cassettes are loaded with you.
I am an attempt at diaries by others
      and an attempt at a worldwide newspaper.
You have written yourself
     with my hard-nibbled pen.
I don't want to teach you.
     What I want is to learn.

1983
TRANSLATED BY ALBERT C. TODD

Violets

I look for a haystack in a needle,
and not a needle in a haystack.
I look for a lamb in a gray wolf
and a rebel inside a dead log.

   .   .   .

But a wolf is a wolf irreversibly.
A wolf isn't a future sheep.
And Pinocchio's rebellious nose
won't sprout from blocks of wood.

As in an extended drinking spree,
I believe, somewhere in the scrap heap
on a spit-spattered fence
violets will grow one day.

But the fence will hardly blossom,
rotted through to the extreme,
if on its aromatic planks
are piss showers and not flowers.

But violets have grown into my skin
and I'll not pull them out or cut them.
The more I get punched in the face
the happier the faces in my dreams.

The gates of paradise are too narrow
for a rich man and a brown nose,
but I will pass through the eye of a needle
riding on a camel's back.

And, longing for new friends,
like a sworn brother,
from the heads of others, so wooden,
I carve myself a Pinocchio.

Amid global ashes and clashes,
I drag to my beloved heap
of violets grown on spittle
on all the pissed-on fences of the world.

And the wolf kisses me like a brother
in a dead-end street's lively pub.
And whose brazen nose uninvited
already pokes from a piece of wood?

1983

TRANSLATED BY ALBERT C. TODD

Meditations at the Back Door

Zina Priakhina from Siberia,
like a Lady Paul Bunyan at tryouts for drama school,
read Nekrasov's verse so thunderously
that Stanislavsky fell off the wall nail.

The horrified examining directors
contemplated her face of a thousand freckles,
her size-eleven Amazon sandals,
and her typhoon-blown wig.

But behind her stood her lumbermill,
her worker's amateur drama club,
her Siberian switchman mom,
and Mom's patched little signal flag.

No one had ever abused Zina with words,
but with her nuclear explosion in verse:
"Find me one safe place of asylum..."*
the Dean pressed his temples in despair.

And departing like a warm snowflake in a blizzard,
she sobbed in a corner fast-food store.
Though thirsting for the stage and applause,
she seized hold of a Moscow broom.

Zina Priakhina became a street cleaner
and brusquely chipped ice on the Arbat,
mixing Shakespeare with Albee,
whispering roles with doomed hope.

She stands alone now with her heavy iron bar,
drowning in theatrical dreams,
in front of a prominent food store,
but, at its no less important back door.

Overwhelmed Zina watches in a dream
how into the fresh snow from the back door,
real-life celebrities emerge
as if from a gala show.

. . .

The Adidas sport bag of hockey's
superstar furtively stinks
of back door black caviar
and, VIP only, smoked sturgeon.

Now comes a vampirish lady pop singer,
who always throws her groupies into a trance,
and buckwheat, nowhere available, leaks betrayingly
through a hole in her bag with the label "Air France."

Now comes the celebrity fortune-teller,
but from his diplomat's briefcase drips flesh blood.
What's the mystery? Hidden inside diplomatically
a juicy filet is weeping red tears.

So transparently wanting to feast on
everything in their nontransparent bags—
out come barbers and pedicurists,
psychiatrists and television emcees.

And now the street sweeper, the ice chipper,
whispers in Mom's old-fashioned worn scarf:
"Find me one safe place of asylum . . ."—
Zina Priakhina with her heavy iron rod.

The rod never bends nor does Zina,
but in this kingdom of marketing miracles
there are privileged people—the back-doorites,
in the privileged world of back-door land.

Zina, I'm no master at procuring delicacies,
but even my hands grow shamed by the traces
of olive oil smeared on the handles
of their slippery back doors.

Long ago as a homely, skinny boy,
lining up with Siberian war widows,
I wore on my transparent palm the honest
violet-inked number of my place in line.

And from which black year
was our age infected by
the psychology of the black back door
and this black market enterprise?

. . .

Like worms, tsars of pickles and smoked salmon,
kings of salami and Italian shoes
would like to drill
their black back door into our Red banner.

It would be a crime against people
if someone's unhappy mother,
only through the black back door,
could get medicine for her suffering child.

They climb on the shoulders of relatives with influence,
squeezing into the future as though it were a food store,
with their black back door diplomas stabbing
as though with iron rods through so many Zinas.

Zina, is it possible they'll manage
to squeeze into their poacher's Adidas bags
the Red flag of our land
and even your Mom's patched little flag?

Zina Priakhina from Siberia,
do you remember drama school windows shaking with your basso?
You didn't read that poem to the end.
Don't be shy! Raise your voice to full crescendo!

You will break through onto the stage, you will,
through the main entrance and not the black back door . . .
remembering how into the Nazi's Reichstag years ago,
we did not enter through a black back door!

1983

TRANSLATED BY ALBERT C. TODD AND JAMES RAGAN

*"Find me one . . .": Line from Nekrasov's poem *Razmyshlenie U Paradnogo pod"ezda* (Meditations at the Main Entrance), whose title and subject are carefully echoed in this poem.

Murder

No one sleeps more beautifully than you.
But I am afraid
          that you will waken just now,

and touch me with an indifferent glance, lightly passing,
and commit the murder of beauty.

1984
TRANSLATED BY ALBERT C. TODD

You Still Haven't Returned

You still haven't returned
all my letters
        and haven't thrown them out in the trash,
but you distance yourself,
as if the block of ice, where we live—
              were cut in two.
You sleep most innocently,
as if you were beside me—
          only an arm's length away,
but this fissure
grinds the deathlike starch of the sheet.
You distance yourself,
and it is terrible, that it's done bit by bit,
             without haste.
You shut yourself off
from me as though
        from a still not dead
           soul.
You take away everything—
both so many shared years
         and our two children.
You are pulling away
like living skin
        from my living bones.
The pain of estrangement
cuts carelessly,
      brutalizes.
          On our ribs there's blood and slime

along the fracture line
of two souls,

553

which had almost grown together.
Oh, that double-damned
almost impossible to overcome "almost"!
How can
          everything crucified
or almost already crucified
                    be saved?
Easily,
     skillfully,
like piranhas, leaving only a skeleton on the bottom,
petty little things devoured
still one more unrelivable love.
But devouring
is contagious,
               like the black plague,
and love that's been betrayed
                    turns to treason on its own.
And some howling thing
clutches at the children,
                    without hiding its claws in fur.

Love is a monster
that devours even its own children.
For all the time I spent pub crawling,
for devouring of the best years of your life,
I beg with most Christian humility—
forgive me,
          don't devour me in revenge.
There is a trite expression:
A woman has, as they say, no past.
I am
     your past,
and, that means, there's no me.
                    I am my own skeleton.
I carry in horror
my remains to the hostile bed.
For the nonexistent
it's no easier to exist.
My beloved,
resurrect me,
          your own child,
mold me,
     mold me,
from all the remains,

from yourself,
from nothing.
You are
my future,
my momentary and eternal star.
Perhaps loving,
but forgetting how one loves...
Forever?

1984
TRANSLATED BY ALBERT C. TODD

"What right..."

What right did I have to mock,
to have the doubtful right
to crush left and right
talent,
like clumsy chalk?

1984
TRANSLATED BY ALBERT C. TODD

Eight-year-old Poet

On the platform, in Pasternak's unerased footprints,
leaving behind your own print,
you stand a moment with me in farewell,
eight-year-old poet.

I can't understand your origins
or from which kind of rain you come.
Created almost in a vacuum, Nika,
you part the rain with a mere glance.

. . .

You simply stopped being a child,
burning, tormenting yourself.
As soon as you learned to stand,
you spat your pacifier into the fire.

A secret little queen,
you and your crown have grown into one.
Each illness you've survived
is a heavy jewel in your tiara.

I fear that you will suddenly shatter,
and the invisible ring
of the freshly forged white-hot crown
will scorch your childish bangs.

A pencil in your fingers is heavier than a scepter;
your notebook has iron pages.
If a chasm opens at your feet,
you have nothing to lose but your childhood.

Might this be our salvation from a lack of poets,
when children as if from a cliff
leap directly into the poetry-abyss
to fill up the gap?

If elders fear this profession,
children will avenge them.
Will a nursery bring forth a Homer
and kindergarten a Shakespeare?

Children are secret grown-ups. This torments.
All of us are secret children,
and we'll never grow up completely,
because we fear the children within.

On the platform, in Pasternak's eternal footprints,
leaving behind your own print,
you sigh a deep moan inside,
eight-year-old poet.

With a burst you skip and run down the platform,
flying with girlish delight,
but when you stumble on your dropped crown
you are no longer a child.

. . .

And from the footboard your eyes call me
into a life where there is no age.
Farewell! It's too late for me to jump on your train,
eight-year-old poet.

1984
TRANSLATED BY ALBERT C. TODD AND JAMES RAGAN

Being Late

Something dangerous
               is beginning:
I
 am coming late
             to my own self.
I made an appointment
             with my thoughts—
the thoughts
        were snatched
               from me.
I made an appointment
             with Faulkner—
but they made me
        go to a banquet.
I made an appointment
             with history,
but a grass-widow
        dragged me into bed.
Worse
    than barbed wire
are birthday parties,
            mine and others',
and roasted suckling pigs
            hold me
like a sprig of parsley
           between their teeth!
Led away for good
to a life absolutely not my own,
everything that I eat,

557

eats me,
everything that I drink,
                              drinks me.
I made an appointment
                              with myself,
but they invite me
                              to feast on my own spareribs.
I am garlanded
                    from all sides
not by strings of bagels,
                              but by the holes of bagels,
and I look like
                    an anthology
                              of zeros.
Life gets broken
                    into hundreds of lifelets,
that exhaust
                    and execute me.
In order
          to get through to myself
I had to smash my body
                              against others',
and my fragments,
                    my smithereens,
are trampled
                    by the roaring crowd.
I am trying
                    to glue myself together,
but my arms
                    are still severed.
I'd write
          with my left leg,
but both the left
                    and the right
have run off,
                    in different directions.
I don't know—
                    where is my body?
And soul?
Did it really fly off,
without a murmured
                    "good-bye!"?
How do I break through
                    to a faraway namesake,

waiting for me
                in the cold somewhere?
I've forgotten
                under which clock
I am waiting
                for myself.
For those who don't know
                who they are,
time
        does not exist.
No one is
                under the clock.
On the clock
                there is nothing.
I am late for my appointment
                                with me.
There is no one.
                Nothing but cigarette butts.
Only one flicker—
                a lonely,
                        dying
                                spark . . .

1985
TRANSLATED BY ALBERT C. TODD

Trumpet

To R. Bykov

And will you remain yourself
when you come into the world
                            with a trumpet,
to summon to righteous battle,
but they order you
                to sound retreat?
You
    can't be
            your own man,

if you make retreat
                    your destiny.

And will you remain yourself,
when a trumpet with somebody's saliva
is forcefully shoved in your mouth,
to trumpet the reverse?
A trumpet with someone else's saliva
will play someone else's lies.

And will you remain yourself
when, with a battered lip,
they push you away,
                    after changing the tune
and sticking
          a gag
                    in the trumpet?

And will you remain yourself
with a trumpet stuffed with sugar,
when
        they begin to feed you with love,
gently preparing you for slaughter?
I damn those who would like to turn
a rebel trumpet into a singing slave,
banning all sounds with cunning taboo,
letting it
          only "boo, boo, boo!"?

And will you remain yourself,
when there is dissonance and discord
in the jealous world of trumpeters
and you can't tell
                    who is who,
and who already long ago
was crushed along with his tinfoil trumpet . . .

And will you remain yourself
even beneath a gravestone,
shoving
          your trumpet
like a golden fist
                    through the grass?

They will break

the trumpet
even with snot,
if you surrender
and grow old.
And will you remain yourself?
If you are yourself,
you will remain yourself.

1985

TRANSLATED BY ALBERT C. TODD

Disbelief in Yourself Is Indispensable

While you're alive it's shameful to put yourself into
the Calendar of Saints.
Disbelief in yourself is more saintly.
It takes real talent not to dread being terrified
by your own agonizing lack of talent.

Disbelief in yourself is indispensable,
indispensable to us is the loneliness
of being gripped in the vise,
so that in the darkest night the sky will enter you
and skin your temples with the stars,
so that streetcars will crash into the room,
wheels cutting across your face,
so the dangling rope, terrible and alive,
will float into the room and dance invitingly in the air.

Indispensable is any mangy ghost
in tattered, over-played, stage rags,
and if even the ghosts are capricious,
I swear, no more capricious, than those who are alive.

Indispensable amid babbling boredom
are the deadly fear of uttering the right words,
and the fear of shaving, because across your cheekbone
graveyard grass already grows.

. . .

561

It is indispensable to be sleeplessly delirious,
to fail, to leap into emptiness.
Probably, only in despair is it possible
to speak all the truth to this age.

It is indispensable, after throwing out dirty drafts,
to explode yourself and crawl before ridicule,
to reassemble your shattered hands
from fingers that rolled under the dresser.

Indispensable is the cowardice to be cruel
and the observation of the small mercies,
when a step toward falsely high goals
makes the trampled stars squeal out.

It's indispensable, with a misfit's hunger,
to gnaw a verb right down to the bone.
Only one who is by nature from the naked poor,
is neither naked nor poor before fastidious eternity.

And if from out of the dirt,
        you have become a prince,
                but without principles,
unprince yourself and consider
how much less dirt there was before,
when you were in the real, pure dirt.

Our self-esteem is such baseness . . .
The Creator raises to the heights
only those who, even with tiny movements,
tremble with the fear of uncertainty.

Better to cut open your veins with a can opener,
to lie like a wino on a spit-spattered bench in the park,
than to come to that very comfortable belief
in your own special significance.

Blessed is the madcap artist,
who smashes his sculpture with relish,
hungry and cold—but free
from degrading belief in himself.

1985

TRANSLATED BY ALBERT C. TODD

To Incomprehensible Poets

I always envy
all those
        who write incomprehensibly,
whose verse,
        like half a stain,
        half a cloud,
        half-smoke and half-ice,
are half of something and half of nothing.
I adored the Formalists,
my eyes popped out with rapture,
but, a coward, I always avoided
charming abracadabras and gibberish.
I went all out like a warrior
        in the fight
with common sense,
but with secret horror I never found
        inside myself
even a little drop of craziness.
I was deeply ashamed.
        Sometimes it takes hard labor
        to look crazy.
I worked at craziness
        with honest sweat,
but the only reward
        for my soggy efforts,
was life turned
        into a madhouse.
My plastic ivory tower
        I transformed
into a tower of sarcastic tortures.
But somehow I underplayed it
and failed to invent
        anything as immortal
as three famous words:
        "dyr, bul, shchyl."*
Oh, you incomprehensible poets!
You are the only subject
        of my greenest, but cleanest, envy.
My guilt is in my simplicity.
        My crime is my clarity.

I am the most comprehensible of worms.
No restraint frightens you.
No one has bridled you with clear ideas.
And someone's petty
              "I don't get it"
for you is sweeter than a virgin's kiss.
Creators of abracadabras,
              beyond today's fleeting moment,
you live with overabundant faith
              that someday
you'll be understood
              by others.
Happy creatures!
All the same it is frightening
to be understood like me,
              in the wrong way,
all of my life
              to write comprehensibly
and depart
so hopelessly uncomprehended.

1985

TRANSLATED BY ALBERT C. TODD TOGETHER WITH THE AUTHOR

*"dyr, bul, shchyl": Alexei Eliseevich Kruchionikh (1886–1968), Russian poet and theoretician of Futurism, became celebrated partly because he invented those three meaningless words in a poem of that name, "*Dyr, bul, shchyl.*"

Comradesbutwhatifers

Not every idea sprouts,
                    not every seed breaks through the asphalt.
With his fist Archimedes
                    pounded the globe like the Almighty:
"Give me the right fulcrum
                    and I will lift the whole earth,"

but they didn't give it to him, saying:
                              "But what if..."

"But what if . . ."
                    they had put sticks through the wheels
of the first locomotive—
                    pushing it off the track,
and blacksmiths had grabbed
                    the scalpel of the surgeon,
who for the first time
                    opened a heart to save it.
"But what if . . ."
                    some sated smug mugs
had grumbled against flying machines
                    and Edison's lamp.
"But what if . . ."
                    banned by their fears,
Bulgakov's *The Master and Margarita**
                    was published later by twenty years.
Saying good-bye to rotgut
                    is torture for an alcoholic.
Pretzels forgotten by drinkers
                    sadly drown in borscht.
But there are alcoholics of cowardice—
                    a special breed apart.
They are "comradesbutwhatifers,"
                    a juicy new word.
Their hands tremble,
                    as though they had the d.t.'s,
when asked to sign their names
                    to poems, plans, and designs,
and even water pitchers
                    bubble alcoholically
in the hands of alcoholics of cowardice,
                    the rotgutters of lies.
And inside telephone wires,
                    crawling from ear to ear,
as through oversweetened tubing,
                    comes the verbal rotgut.
Instead of worries about wheat
or meat
        or steel,
we hear a sticky mumbling:
"But what . . . if . . . but . . . what . . . if . . ."
The Russian Doubting Thomas,
copulating with the telephone,
like a society samovar,

in the Russian Tea Room,
boils with civic doubts.
His copper forehead comes unsoldered.
A stream of steam spurts through the seam
but it's all for him ridiculously simple:
"But . . . what . . . if . . . what . . . if . . ."
It's high time to exhibit Filonov
so that even Paris might swoon.
But for them this great name smells
                     like a lit fuse:

"But . . . what . . . if . . ."
While great truths are seeking proof,
our days, our years,
disappear into nowhere,
sucked out by quiet vampires,
by comradesbutwhatifers . . .
How much has been burned out,
                as in a great drought,
                          by this butwhatiferism.
It's shameful to try to catch
              belated rain with a sieve!
Some give their whole lives
              to create at least something,
and there are drones whose sole labor
                  is to create nothing.
Their look is aimed
              like a double-barreled shotgun,
as though a trembling petitioner
                  were a hungry timber wolf.
That safe, crammed with so many undecided fates,
                      is a coffin of red tape
whose steel-trap teeth
              wolfishly crunch human souls.
Knights of procrastination,
            in the armor of resolutions,
masters
      of circular files,
where even long-nosed Nessy
                could never find the bottom,
are no better than Colorado beetles,
              like hoof and mouth disease,
they ravage wheat and cattle
              as well as innocent farmers.

Our Mother Earth is widowed,
                            deprived of loving hands that plant,
stalks of buckwheat languish,
                        and clover sags in sadness,
and tormented sheaves of wheat
                        are cut down at the roots
by a falsely great
                state biology,
and in order to dodge pitiless taxes
                        poor chickens have learned to croak like frogs.
In his button-bursting tunic
                        Comrade Butwhatiferinsky,
to protect his dear fellow citizens
                            from so-called harmful tricks
saw in all of cybernetics
                    only obscurantism and mysticism
and robbed computers
                    from our future children.
And denying everything that's new,
                        the procrastinators,
                                    the shoverouters,
menacingly wave their rubber stamps:
                        "But there is no precedent,"
forgetting that
                with Granddad's old rifle,
                            in lice,
                                barefoot,
                                    in rags,
the October Revolution also had no precedent!
I look forward to the time
                        when, by the laws of ballistic science,
our dear comrades butwhatifers,
                    who in place of ideology
                                use only armchairology,
will be catapulted head over heels
                        out of their cozy armchairs.
O great land of ours,
                throw them out
                            from their headless headquarters.
Let them at long last breathe the fresh air
                            of our enormous expanse.
When censoring pencils
                    are in the cowardly hands of comradesbutwhatifers

567

there is an enormous chasm
between a red banner
and a red pencil.
On this banner is embroidered
only a hammer and sickle
and not somebody's craven
"But . . . what . . . if . . ."

1985

TRANSLATED BY ALBERT C. TODD TOGETHER WITH THE AUTHOR

*Bulgakov: Mikhail Afanasievich Bulgakov (1891–1940). His most important novel, *The Master and Margarita*, was written in 1928, with corrections dictated just before he died in 1940. It was published in the Soviet Union in a considerably censored version in 1966–67. The uncensored version was published only in 1973.

A Half Blade of Grass

Death is still far off
and everything is so hard,
as if the way up is on rotted stairs.
Life is getting bitter,
like overheated milk
with foam burned black.
They say to me, sighing:
"Feel sorry for yourself,"
but I'll take a half blade of grass in my teeth
and already I'm more cheerful
from this gift of the field—
from the sourness
and from the bitterness.
I'll take a gentle bit
in summer or in spring,
and I am made happy by this green trifle,
and my people
must have taken pity on me in advance,
because they don't spoil me with pity.
If they smash my ribs smartly in a fight,
I consider
that's how it's supposed to be.
They jab me in the back
and don't understand—

why I'm not smiling.
In those who were pitied in childhood,
there is no strength,
                    but pervasive weakness.
A half blade of grass in the teeth—
                        there's my whole secret,
and in the earth still growing—
                    there's a half blade of grass.

1985
TRANSLATED BY ALBERT C. TODD

A Distant Relative, or Désespoir: A Poem

There are some distant relatives in our soul,
who almost don't exist for us at all,
but suddenly turn up
                    like ghosts of pain,
to whom we prefer
                    painless ease in vain.
I was once a guest at a chic party,
but not as an active member
                    of "this" party,
whose purpose was purging
                    all painful thoughts
like washing garbage
                    from drowning boats.
A Parisian producer attended,
                    no one knew why,
by world reputation
                    a real nice guy.
He chomped his food
                    and swilled his drink,
prepared to drink anything,
                    even ink.
But now I must interrupt my rhymes
because the changing situation
                    will make them look like crimes.

And suddenly the bell rang . . .
                                    Barely poking eyeglasses through,
some "thing" got stuck in the door,
                            all hung with shopping bags
on her arms, her back, and chest.
Familiarly they said:
                        "What are you standing there for, come in!"
This guest,
            this bespectacled old woman,
had a string of bagels hanging from her shoulder,
which probably
                didn't fit
in her pouch
                or canvas backpack.
When dropped,
                the bags rang with the sound
                                    of frozen meat.
"Don't worry, niece,
                I'll leave the pouches on the balcony
                                        till morning.
Grumbling:
            "Oh, our marsupial Russians,"
the hostess closed the door reluctantly.
"Get acquainted—
                    my aunt,
                        Maria Kirillna.
Or as I usually call her—
                    Auntie Masha."
The hostess was a bit out of sorts.
She whispered,
            squeezing my elbow:
"But not my own aunt.
                    As the saying goes,
about seven times
            removed."
The conversation was global and way up in the clouds
about Felliniism
                and Coppolaism,
but Auntie Masha came in
                    quiet as a ghost
in her peasant polite wool socks.
With her silver braids in a knot
she sat down decorously,
                not touching the goblets,

and rubbed her bag-stretched hands
furtively under the table.
She looked at us with curiosity,
                          not detached,
but girlishly,
            not at all like an old woman,
her eyes gleamed blue from beneath cracked glasses
with the sly naiveté of cornflowers.
The shopping bags,
                witches of oilcloth and Leatherette,
in a sad, modern fairy tale,
had turned her into an old woman,
but with the bags gone from her shoulder
                          all the aging went away.
Holding the producer's lapels,
a fellow from Mosfilm insisted loudly:
"What's your Fellini got,
                  or Bertolucci?
Nothing but despair . . .
                  Where is the conflict?"
The translator began to fidget,
                  and breathe heavily through his nose:
"Despair—now, how do you say that in French?"
Auntie, who was a guest, suddenly moved closer
and suggested in a whisper:
                  "Désespoir!"
The group was stunned
by this unexpected discovery,
as if the whole Soviet nation
all at once had begun to speak Sanskrit.
"Well, there's seven times removed for you . . ."
I thought,
        and this guest Auntie explained:
"I teach French in the city of Oriol.
I've translated Ionesco."
"Well, you are, so to speak,
                  right from the heart
                          of Russia,"
the Mosfilm man growled,
                  "What good,
for example, is this 'désespoir' to you?"
The hostess interrupted:
                  "Have something to eat . . ."
But maintaining her restrained dignity

571

the guest Auntie said,
                              furrowing her eyebrows still more:
"Well, it's true,
                    I have despaired too.
And so I teach . . .
                        I hope it's of some use . . ."
"For some reason you come to see us so seldom,
                                          Auntie Masha . . ."
The hostess made an effort to turn over a new leaf,
but Auntie grinned:
                      "I am a coward . . .
I do come,
              but I am afraid to ring the bell."
The producer spilled something on the floor,
and as the translator had his wits about him
he tried to explain gently:
"Cette vielle dame de la ville fameuse
de chevauxs de trot Orloff . . ."
"Your memory apparently is a bit off . . ."
Auntie Masha paused for a breath with sensible restraint,
"That name is
                  from the stables of Count
Orlov . . .
              not from the city of Oriol . . ."
The hostess served the producer guest her pie,
beaming:
"C'est un pirojki russe,"
and the look of an unrealized terrorist girl
under the old woman's brows scorched through everyone,
as if an underground prerevolutionary group
had just dropped in on postrevolutionary Moscow high society.
And nineteenth-century intellectuals in youthful beards
with cornflowers on their Russian blouses
stood sternly behind her back
with their silent indictment of guilt.
The old woman became a teenage girl
as if inside of her,
squeezing the pages
                      dripped with wax,
a young coed began reciting antiestablishment verse.
Oh, Lord,
            but standing in a gloomy line,
amid the cursing, would I have recognized
in this old woman,

innocently draped with shopping bags,
the Teacher,
the Mother of Mother Russia?
Let all the archangels,
trumpeting above us in the clouds on Judgment Day,
accept you among the Saints,
you, the Intelligentsia of Russia,
with tragic shopping bags on your arms.
The strings of every shopping bag sting me.
There is no such place as the provinces.
God is scattered among all kinds of faces.
There are souls everywhere
that are like capital cities.
The provinces are
everything that devours and lies.
Like a pellet in my wing,
you sear me, Russian heartland,
and, biting deep in my feathers,
you don't let me fly
criminally high . . .
I ran out onto the street.
I was
confused by the snow beating madly in my soul,
like a howling foray
of incomprehensible white forces.
The blizzard tore space into tatters
and the sky smiled from above,
and there was no Orlov trotter
on which to ride away.
How can I look
this old woman in the eyes,
I,
a nineteenth-century Russian of the atomic age?
What discotheque is large enough
to hold
the voices of all the ghosts of Russia?
And I whispered in terrible frenzy:
"Even I am in despair,
everything's been swept away,
but, maybe, honest despair is better
than false hopes,
the handicraft of cowards?
I've been knocked off my feet,
and everything is swaying in my eyes,

and there is no friend,
and no father to be found.
Don't I have the right at last to despair,
don't I have the right
not to hope?"
But something shone blue like a cornflower
while I walked
and wheezed through the blizzard
like a forgotten distant relative of the sky:
"Désespoir."
And the snow spat out:
"Désespoir . . ."
From the
desperate, impenetrable sky
I had not heard man's word of God
but a woman's living God word:
"Well, it's true,
I have despaired too . . ."
And suddenly it penetrated once and for all:
Despair is
not the worst misfortune.
There are things more despairing than despair—
a soul
that is incapable of despair
means no soul at all,
but simply a storehouse
of false hopes
in which there is only poison.
All nice little smiles are dressed
in false hopes
concealing the essence.
Despair
is a shyness of hope,
when it is afraid to deceive
the hopeful,
which someday . . .
So these were the thoughts
given to me
by this not quite so simple old woman,
when as a forgotten distant relative
she suddenly appeared out of a blizzard.
How terrible
if, with illusory conception,
we grow accustomed to consider frivolously,

as forgotten distant relatives—
$$\qquad\qquad\text{conscience}$$
and honor—
$$\qquad\qquad\text{seven times removed.}$$
How terrible if during the snow-drifted night,
irreparably far from us,
like a forgotten distant relative, our Motherland
is afraid to touch the bell.

1984

TRANSLATED BY ALBERT C. TODD

Fuku: A Poem (Excerpts)

Knocking innocence from me,
$$\qquad\qquad\text{a kid,}$$
they sprinkled wisdom over my borscht
$$\qquad\qquad\qquad\text{along with the cockroaches.}$$
Wisdom was whispered to me,
$$\qquad\qquad\text{in a murmur,}$$
by the fleas
$$\qquad\text{sewn into the seams}$$
$$\qquad\qquad\text{of my patched shirt.}$$
But poverty is not wisdom,
$$\qquad\qquad\text{and money is not wisdom,}$$
yet, inch by inch,
I grew up clumsily,
$$\qquad\qquad\text{in a jerking motion,}$$
after they punched me in my empty stomach.
I used the high-flown argot of knives.
I smoked cold saliva in somebody's dropped cigarette butts.
From my guts I learned the hunger of war.
My ribs taught me the geography of Russia.
Nobody gave me
$$\qquad\text{so-called fame,}$$
I snatched it myself
$$\qquad\qquad\text{by the neck, like a chicken.}$$
My soul filled up
$$\qquad\qquad\text{like a wartime train station}$$

with screaming,
                    clambering,
                              crying people.
In my soul are more than seventy countries,
all the concentration camps,
                         all the monuments,
and the cardsharps
                    and the presidents.
Swallowing the epoch and choking on it,
but never puking out of squeamish disdain,
I know no less than dust or dirt,
and more than all the ravens with their doubtful wisdom.
But I grew too proud,
                    too cocky for my own good.
I became so impossibly vain
you'd think I wore a special stamp
                              across my forehead
with the confidential phrase:
                         Top Secret.
In vain I turned my nose up to the ceiling,
taking pleasure in the childish thought
that they'd bump me off soon—
                              because
I knew too much.
In Hong Kong I tried to land on a knife,
in Vietnam I flirted with bullets.
I'd been impatient to be killed,
                         to be a hero,
but they punished me skillfully,
                              by postponing my death.
And I remained alive—
                    humiliatingly—
externally unwounded,
                    hurt only inside.
They hassled and harassed me,
                         they ate me alive,
cunningly torturing me to death
                         with nondeath.
Shamefully whole,
               I'm not decorated
with pleasant battle scars
                    or other gifts.
There may be a reason why they haven't killed me:

What if my knowledge doesn't scare them at all?
That bitter thought took away my swagger
and the remnants of my former conceit:
my deeds lag behind my inner needs,
my words lag behind my inner worlds.
If you grab life's mystery by the tail
it slips through your hands so smoothly.
The more mysteries we understand,
the more the main mystery becomes bottomless.
We ourselves have buried so much on the bottom,
and the accursed abyss of knowledge
has swallowed up such famous ships,
gobbled up such mighty states.
And I have lost myself on this earth,
from a torturing lack of talent,
feeling like a gnome crushed by the burden
of a weary and crippled Atlas.
Probably in the same way Christopher Columbus
lost himself with his desperate drunken crew,
setting sail over blood into the depths of the mystery,
the taunting mystery melting in fog . . .

And I went into the streets of Santo Domingo
clutching the year '41 to my breast,
and some sweet childish fear resurrected inside me
was expecting somebody's switchblade knife.

And again I was that kid who got away from pursuers,
who didn't scare easily, who still doesn't,
jumping down from the policeman's palm, so sticky,
before his palm would become a fist.

And I went into the streets of Santo Domingo,
clutching the year '41 to my breast,
while a Siberian ground-wind blizzard
like witch's breath followed and ran ahead.

I was followed by a crowd of sorrows,
as if a Trans-Siberian track ran past these Dominican palms,
and women rubbed one felt boot against the other,
lined up for bread under Columbus's bronze stare.

.   .   .

And behind me, through magnolia *avenidas*,
like ambassadors of old but endless war,
stood widows, orphans, wounded invalids,
carrying on their faces the unmelting Russian snow.

Lobsters moved their claws in stalls so easily,
pineapples lay dreaming, heaped in the shade,
and I couldn't believe that there was no line,
that people weren't writing numbers on their hands.

But through everything that seemed exotic and luxurious
and begging for color film or an easel,
unshaven faces came, like ghosts,
with a sadness of blurred, half-Indian features.

Pus oozed from eyes under straw sombreros.
Pleading, begging for at least a penny,
crooked fingers with broken nails
flocked around me like Hitchcock's birds.

I was like a white crow. I was a stranger,
and they were tearing me apart.
The kids all tried to shine my *zapatos*,
and the whores all dragged me into the bushes.

And like a clot of universal blackouts,
near the entrance to the glittering hotel,
a Haitian boy who had fled here
tried to sell me one of his naive paintings.

How lonely he must have been,
self-taught and not quite fifteen,
if he had escaped from Baby Doc's paradise
to this land where all artists were hungry.

Who invented this global barter market?
"Abyss for abyss, madhouse for madhouse."
What a choice—to flee from one hell with hope
and to land in a different hopeless hell.

Here the aggression of begging poverty
clobbered me in street after street.
My sleeve was plucked, pulled, and grabbed,
and finally the pursuit wore me down.

· · ·

And to the sobs of distant Siberian accordions,
and the song "Glorious Sea, Holy Baikal,"
I ran from the vile word *money*!
I ran from my brothers in hunger.

For so many years the line fed me nothing
but wartime black bread eked out with wormwood—
and now at my heels, all the hungry, all the starving,
stood in line for me, as for bread.

These panting people did not know
that I myself was once a hungry kid,
that the war hit me hard,
making two childhoods and two of me.

I went into the slums. Two Creole nymphs
were my bodyguards, risking their bodies.
Their wigs from Taiwan, their shapes under tight dresses
aroused the drinkers in the sleazy bars.

Here the aggression of poverty vanished:
only the kids fought, brown skins naked,
and a cripple in rags offered me *cerveza*,
straight from the bottle, unafraid of my plague.

And they posed for my Nikon, without hiding;
they didn't reach for my pockets or threaten with knives.
I was a guest, and with me were *dos buenas muchachas*,
and no one asked me for anything.

The mothers were strict, though it was Saturday,
picking up the children playing in the dust,
and sighing, instructed, "Time to go to work ..."
And the children went off to beg again.

And on a fence, grinning triumphantly
like an ad for a tailor who makes tuxedos,
fluttered a torn poster: "Everything for the Poor!"
and under that, a fat-faced, pre-election jester.

I asked one of the nymphs, "Who's that guy?"
and she laughed like I was crazy.
She covered her lips with a finger, which stuck to the lipstick,
and whispered a strange word: "Fuku!"

. . .

579

I asked carefully, "Fuku is a name?"
and she, now convinced I was stupid,
laughed harder, swayed her tight hips,
and slyly replied, "Just the opposite."

And all the poor folk, with teeth of steel
and with toothless mouths teasing the stranger,
turned to the poster and laughed,
repeating, as if blowing out a candle, "Fuku!"

The jester on the poster squirmed, one of the gang
of other thugs who promised miracles,
thugs, who with the knives of false beggars
extract votes from the hoodwinked poor.

Those guys, multiplied on every fence,
mint medals out of the people's hunger,
make bombs out of the people's hunger,
make tuxedos out of the people's hunger.

I cannot contemplate poverty calmly.
What can I do to turn my body or spirit
into the bread of salvation, into millions of crumbs,
chunks, pieces, and loaves?

In the Gothic cathedral of Santo Domingo
two sisters, two creatures of Creole nights,
unexpectedly shy, with a quiet hesitation,
lit ten candles before the Madonna.

One of the sorrowful pair explained,
as a wax drop hardened on her sleeve,
"For our dead sisters and brothers.
Ten died. We two survived."

And the expected voice from heaven did not thunder,
only a tear glistened on the Creole cheek,
and my childhood Siberian hunger
drew close to the hunger of the world ...

ـــــــ

It was so unbearably hot in Santo Domingo that it looked as if Columbus's
statue, unable to stand it any longer, would tear off its bronze doublet, but the
grave marker in the cathedral, where, if the sign was to be believed, the admiral's
bones reposed, gave off a damp cemetery chill. That marker was like a fin-

gerprint file for the world, for every tourist felt duty bound to touch it. Local black marketeers, appearing like ghosts from behind the peeling columns, offered tourists a more hospitable rate of exchange in tactful whispers. Columbus lived in that cathedral as if in four dimensions, because in the four corners of the cathedral several guides simultaneously told various stories about his life to the rustling accompaniment of dollars, francs, and West German marks. In one corner Columbus had just explained his idea to Queen Isabella's confessor, who was pretending to be deaf; in another he was already sending the queen gold and slaves from the New Indies with this humane note: "And even if slaves die in transit—not all of them face that fate"; in a third he was being sent back, put in irons by his own cook, the shackles still bearing the caked blood of Indians; and in the fourth, already mad, with a pen skipping on parchment, he wrote a hymn to the metal that destroyed him: "Gold creates a treasure, and he who has it can do anything he wants and can even lead human souls into heaven." But whose souls did he lead into heaven when he couldn't transport his own there?

Here's what amazed me: Not one of the guides called the admiral by name—only *almirante*.

"Why?" I asked my Dominican friend.

"Fuku!" he replied with a shrug.

And suddenly a gust of wind from the sea, stale and hot, rushed into the cathedral, and whirled bank notes that it had torn from someone's hands over Columbus's vault, repeating in a multilingual rustle: "Fuku! Fuku! Fuku!"

We are those islanders
who came in canoes
bearing branches to the sails
and watched from the boats
as mango juice streamed down the mustaches
of the hungry gods.
The white gods gave us
the pigskin of the Bible,
but that skin does not save from hunger,
and horrible is the god who
can with a sharp spur
rip open a pregnant belly.
They nailed hooks into our backs
and used hot irons on our feet,
threw us into snake pits,
strung us up,
and gave gonorrhea
to our wretched wives and sons.
We are those islanders
to whom Columbus

brought the wheel and then broke us on the wheel.
We were stupefied by rum,
killed by thunder,
thrown facedown on anthills.
We were conquered by the cross
and called savages,
and promised the freedom to get drunk.
Who was more treacherous?
The most savage savagery
is civilization.
Columbus, is that why
you came to our lands,
where you dug your own grave too?
By what right
did you eat our guava
and by what right did you discover us?
Europe wasn't sleeping,
it was busy capturing slaves,
and Africa wept like a widow
when, lashed by whips,
black flesh filled
our cursed isles.
The slaves broke their shackles
and ran for boats,
but a noose on a branch awaited them.
It was during the capture of people
that the word was born,
that African word *fuku*.
Fuku is not naive.
Fuku is a taboo
on a name that has brought misfortune.
You use the name
and trouble will follow—
that's the work of the name.
Like the rust of retribution,
fuku eats through shackles,
and the first "Fuku!"
invoked here
was on the bones of the Genoan
who rotted with his sword at his side.
No Dominican—
priest, tramp,
shoemaker with nails in his mouth,
drunkard from the tavern—

Would ever say out of superstition
"Cristóbal Colón" or "Columbus."
A Creole mother can't frighten
her kids with threats of a wolf,
so she whispers, in fear of body's wrath:
"If you don't stop crying
el almirante will come!"
In museums even sweating guides
with oily smiles
won't say "Columbus,"
but only "Come closer.
Here are the bones of *el almirante*."
No one will utter the name.
Killers and crooks erect monuments
to other killers,
and that's clear to any fool.
But the point of folk wisdom
is to shake them out of memory
and put on all killers a fuku.
You, celebrated bones,
stop knocking at the door
of the poor man who fell asleep with a sigh,
if, vainglorious,
you creak out whose bones you are,
the poor man's answer will be: "Fuku!"
We are those islanders
who are more Christian
than all the killers in the name of Christ.
You can't scrape the injury from our genes.
Fuku on the bones of that Antichrist
who came with a fake cross!

ـﺴـــــﻄ

The sea took its revenge:
                            it scattered
the admiral's bones
                    after his death.
Gray tangles of hair crept from the skull
and the bones began wandering the seas.
Secretly
        on the queen's orders
they were transported by caravels.
Keeping his eye out,
                    an empty eye,

at night the skeleton climbed from his coffin
and raised a periscope over the world,
pressing it to gaping sockets,
and from his decayed boots,

                      without support,
with a clatter,
            the spurs fell.
His fingers,
        fleshless,
               did not tire:
they grabbed
           the stars
                 as if they were gold.
But they,
         grasped by bones,
turned spitefully to glass beads.
Without its plumage,
              battered and alone,
the skull attempted to shout, "I am Columbus!"
but the wind moaned,
               "Fuku!
                   Fuku!"
and back to the lousy hold would go
the discoverer of the false India.
From island to island the bones sailed
like uninvited guests.
It's said they are in Santo Domingo.
Of course, that is very doubtful.
Perhaps, in the vault smelling of decay,
there is just emptiness
                and Trujillo's dust?
It's said those bones are in Seville.
Tourists poke their walking sticks at them.
And once,
        with unexpected agility,
the skeleton grabbed a stick:
apparently the tip was gold
just like the rings of the chieftains' daughters.
It's said
        those bones are in Havana,
as if alive,
         writhing in anger,
quivering and clicking, they desperately want
to discover and conquer someone else.

If the admiral has three vaults,
does it mean there were three skeletons?
Or did the thirst for fame,

                        the thirst for power

tear the bones

                into three parts?

The thirst for glory

                    is the path to ignominy,

if that glory is bloodstained

                          redder than rust.

Such is the glory that has ignominiously besmirched

                                  the admiral's bones.

The Spanish conquistadors got Indians drunk on "fire water," the Indians later
sharpened the pieces of broken bottles and made arrowheads out of them.

Oh, how I would like to bury forever
in the mud, beneath the remains of their statues,
the new name for killers, "occupier,"
and the old one, "conquistador."

Why did you carry chains in your holds?
Tell me, what kind of courage is it
to turn all the blank spots on the map of the world
into bloodstains?

When you were dying, Admiral,
and turning from side to side,
rasping, you tore at the blood
of Chief Kaonabo on your gouty hands.

Blood binds the world together
and the blood of the murdered chief
lay like a brand on Columbus's grandson,
who paid for the sins of his grandfather.

But my own *Santa Maria*
was an oily fish barrel on Lake Baikal.
Why am I fated to suffer this guilt?
I'm ashamed to play the good guy.

I didn't nail anyone to the cross
or put anyone behind barbed wire.

But my hands burn with the crust
of all the blood spilled by men.

The fires of the Inquisition are now legends.
Now the whole planet is an execution block,
and like typhus-bearing fleas
shivers of fear go crawling about the world.

And the Middle Ages, roaring like a bear
under somebody's tasseled banner,
reappear as a "witch-hunt" someplace
or as a *conquista* called a "peace-keeping mission."

A poet in our age is the age itself.
All the countries are like wounds on his body.
The poet is an ocean cemetery for everyone,
those in bronze and those unknown.

The poet is despised by the people
when out of pitiful conceit
he betrays the poor for his own profit
and eats at the expense of the hungry.

The poet understands in all times
that each age is ruthless,
that immortality is doomed to be part of war
as long as oppression is immortal.

The poet who has not surrendered to the Middle Ages
is the ambassador of all the oppressed.
Not eternal glory but eternal shame
to those who are glorified by bloodshed.

In every border post
                there's something insecure.
Each one of them
                is longing for leaves and for flowers.
They say
        the greatest punishment for a tree
is to become a border post.
The birds that pause to rest
                        on border posts
can't figure out

                    what kind of tree they've landed on.
I suppose
            that at first, it was people who invented borders,
and then borders
                    started to invent people.
It was borders who invented police,
                                armies, and border guards.
It was borders who invented
customs men, passports, and other shit.
Thank God,
            we have invisible threads and threadlets,
born of the threads of blood
                        from the nails in the palms of Christ.
These threads struggle through,
                            tearing apart the barbed wire,
leading love to join love
                    and anguish to unite with anguish.
And a tear,
            which evaporated somewhere in Paraguay,
will fall as a snowflake
                    onto the frozen cheek of an Eskimo.
And a hulking New York skyscraper
                        with bruises of neon,
mourning the forgotten smell of plowlands,
dreams only of embracing a lonely Kremlin tower,
but sadly that is not allowed.
The Iron Curtain,
                unhappily squeaking her rusty brains,
probably thinks:
                "Oh, if I were not a border,
if jolly hands would pull me apart
and build from my bloody remains
                        carousels, kindergartens, and schools.
In my darkest dreams I see
                    my prehistoric ancestor:
He collected skulls like trophies
                        in the somber vaults of his cave,
and with the bloodied point of a stone spearhead
he marked out the first-ever border
                        on the face of the earth.
That was a hill of skulls.
                    Now it is grown into an Everest.
The earth was transformed
                    and became a giant burial place.

                    587

While borders still stand
                    we are all in prehistory.
Real history will start
                    when all borders are gone.
The earth is still scarred,
                    mutilated with the scars of wars.
Now killing has become an art,
                    when once it was merely a trade.
From all those thousands of borders
                    we have lost only the human one—
the border between good and evil.
But while we still have invisible threads
joining each self
                    with millions of selves,
there are no real superpower states.
Any fragile soul on this earth
                    is the real superpower.
My government
                    is the whole family of man, all at once.
Every beggar is my marshal,
                    giving me orders.
I am a racist,
                    I recognize only one race—
the race of all races.
How foreign is the word *foreigner*!
I have four and a half billion leaders.
And I dance my Russian,
                    my death-defying dance
on the invisible threads
                    that connect the hearts of people.

———

The Kolyma River
                    in cold and in fever
beautiful river,
                    infamous river.
The Kolyma River
                    roars and jumps,
a liquid grave for inmates of the camps.
One night under a random roof
in Siberia I find Paris,
                    chic and aloof.
I rub my eyes,
                    is this really true?

Oui?

It's "French Week"
                    on the local TV.
Aznavour from the screen
                    sings into the room
of former camp barracks,
                    full of whispering gloom.
Could you,
            as you listen to Dalidas,
remember the watchdogs on leashes?
                            Da?

Could you,
            as you watch Gilbert Bécaud,
not forget Comrade Beria & Co.?
But a nineteen-year-old driver,
                            in his truck,
hung a portrait of Stalin,
                    for good luck.
And next to this mustache,
                    a Playboy bunny attempts
to turn Siberian pants
                    into tents.
"Why are you bugging me,
                    Pops,
                            with the past?

In a pair of real Levi's
                    I could be
                            twice as fast."
Wake up, you silly unremembering son,
it's your grandfathers and fathers
                            you're driving on.
Barbed wire will remind you of the past,
                            as it aspires
to burst all of your stupidly speeding tires.
You won't get far
                    in any jeans
if you forget
            what history means.
If you forget the victims
                    of yesterday's sorrow
you could become
                    a victim of tomorrow.
Overcoming my sadness,
                    like an inner night,

is unending arm wrestling,
                              an unending fight.
My opponent's arms
                    are incredibly able,
pushing camp topics
                    from our table.
"Here, have a glass,
                  join our repast."
For those who don't think,
                              there is no past.
How stupid you are
                    to feel no alarm,
and to be blind followers
                          of a strong arm.
If you forget the victims
                          of yesterday's sorrow,
you could become
                  a victim of tomorrow.
In a chic dress, Mireille Mathieu
                                  is on the screen.
In Siberia such rags
                    are never seen.
If Kolyma girls could dress
                            that way,
they'd learn to sing better
                            in half a day.
The table under our elbows shakes.
My opponent fights
                    without mistakes.
He argues
          the camps never caused any harm,
he simply wants
                to bend down my arm.
My arm,
        why are you so weak,
like the arm of a prisoner
                            who will die in a week?
But with a splintering crunch
                              growing through the tabletop,
hundreds of dead blue arms
                            come to make the wrestling stop.
And bend
          to the songs from Paris-town

that

almost victorious arm

down.

⁓——⁓

There is a third choice—to choose nothing,
when two lies are being slipped to you,
not to change, in someone's dirty games,
into an ass-licker or a slanderer.

It is more honest to die in a ditch
than to prefer the dubious honor
of escaping from your own bastards
only to be embraced by bastards abroad.

It is shameful for a true writer
who is proud of his unrecruited soul
to break with homemade reaction
just to be reactionary elsewhere.

When your enemy is a jackal, the shark is not a friend.
There is a third choice: amid all the biting,
to sit between two chairs, if both,
in their own way, are dirty.

I despise licking both asses.
I consider it equally foul
to fawn, bowing your back before your native country,
and to turn your back indifferently on your homeland's pain.

⁓——⁓

It's too early to say my last word—

I speak almost at the end,

like a half-vanished ancestor

dragging my body between two eras.

I am

an accidental scrap,

an apple core of this century

that left no leftovers.

History choked on me,

gnawed on me,

but didn't swallow me.

Almost at the end:

I am
          a cracked but exact
                              living death mask of wartime evacuation,
and to be recognized,
                    I need no name tag.
In a blizzard I was sculpted
              by the rusty hands of the Trans-Siberian—
                              the scraping buffers of train cars.
Almost at the end:
In pants rough as the devil's hide
                              I walked like a son of hell.
Each pant leg thundered in the frost
                              like a frozen drainpipe,
and the "Devil's hide" grew on my own
                              and wouldn't pull off.
and in fights saved my backbone,
                    fragile but unbreakable.
Almost at the end:
Once I cried
          in the shadow of spattered, roadside branches,
leaning my head
              on the red and yellow "No Thruway" sign,
and everything that they tried to squeeze down my throat,
                    at their gluttonous banquets,
I puked from my guts,
                    turning them inside out.
Almost at the end:
History danced on me many times
                    in muddy boots and ballet slippers.
I was not on the stage,
          I was the stage in the blood of my epoch,
                              in the vomit of this age,
and everything in my life,
              which seemed to you not my blood,
                              but just the thirst for fame,
I do not doubt
              someday you'll call heroic deeds.
Almost at the end:
I am just the ragtag voice of all the voiceless,
                    I am just a faint trace of all the traceless.
I am the half-scattered ashes
                    of somebody's unknown novel.
In your respectable entrance halls
              I am the ambassador of all dead-end streets.

I am a ghost of barracks and plank beds,
                bedbugs,
                        lice, flea markets,
                                and thieves' dens.

Almost at the end:
Half my life
        I searched hopelessly with a bent fork
                for even a hint of meat
                        in canteen cutlets.

Once, when not even ten,
                I screamed a mother oath
                        in front of my horrified aunt.

I will come to my successors
                as though in Lermontov's epaulets,
police hands on my shoulders,
                with their polite suggestion:
                        "Let's go, buddy!"

Almost at the end:
I am
    the same age to all ages.
I am
    the countryman to all countries
                    even to faraway galaxies.
Like an Indian in the rusty handcuffs of Columbus,
                before my death I shall rasp out:
"Fuku!"
        to those falsely immortal tyrants.

Almost at the end:
A poet today,
        like a coin of Peter the Great,
                        has become really rare.

He even frightens his neighbors on the globe.
But I'll find understanding with my successors
                        one way or another.

Almost candid.
        Almost dying.
                Almost at the end.

1963–1985
Havana — Santo Domingo — Guernavaca — Lima —
Managua — Caracas — Venice — Leonding — Zima
Junction — Gul'ripsh — Peredelkino
TRANSLATED BY ANTONINA W. BOUIS
"ALMOST AT THE END" TRANSLATED BY ALBERT C. TODD

1986/1990

"We can't go on this way!"

"We should be stingier . . ."

We should be stingier
breathing out and breathing in—
then, perhaps, the epic
will lie down in neat quatrains.

We have to be more generous,
louder, like the outcry "Follow me!"
stronger, coarser—
with the earth's coarse globe.

I envy the relics of space,
compressed by the word in layers,
but brevity is the sister of ineptitude
when it springs from emptiness.

Not all conciseness is priceless.
Rhymed oil cakes are stiff and brittle,
and someone's square hay,
I wouldn't eat if I were a horse.

I like hay by the armful,
with the dew still not dried out,
with red whortleberries, with mushroom caps,
clipped by a scythe.

All sentimentality with form is sloppy,
hurl the epoch into rhythm,
tear it up the way an invalid in despair
tears up his striped sailor's shirt!

Should we place in a woman's cap and dress
along with other old-fashioned rags,
the divine tatters
that we call life?

Handicraft taste is not art.
A great reader will grasp
both the charm of the absence of style
and the splendor of longeurs.

1986

TRANSLATED BY ALBERT C. TODD

Antedeluvian

The woman walked past Execution Block

                               on Red Square

carrying rolls of toilet paper,

                     twenty at least,

not in her arms,

               but on twine hanging from her neck.

These are the necklaces of Mother Russia today!

And this woman—

             my God!—was almost proud,

while my head all but pounded

                  the cobblestones,

ashamed that in the Russia

              of Gagarin and Shostakovich

trials and torments

        of getting necessities

                 are so demeaning!

Why brains and courage enough

           for the cosmos,

but not

      for toilet paper?

We heroically build difficulties.

Antedeluvian—

        I can't say it otherwise—

              antedeluvian.

From Execution Block

        in consternation

the severed skull of Stenka Razin watches

              a brawl over track shoes

in the Moscow Mall.

His gouged eyes stare,

        inside out,

at the Russian woman

        bearing her antedeluvian yoke

like a Mongol captive.

Right in front of the Kremlin

        someone hauls a pedal sewing machine,

another,

     a Persian rug,

        with no Persian princess, for sure.

If each day

this antedeluvian deluge appears,
it's hard for Stenka's severed head to grasp
                    who are the boyars and who are the serfs.
We live in a land
                    that's not comfortable,
the first in some things,
                              but in others antedeluvian,
and our antedeluvianism has
a putrid spirit, half boyar
                              half serf.
When our bedraggled quasi-boyars
deposit grain
                    in a storehouse with a rotten roof
and throw computers out
                              to perish under snow—
it smells like a raid by Genghis Khan.
Quasi-boyars stare arrogantly,
                              boorishly,
but if you dig into them—
                    there's the batting
                              of servility.
It was they who put into parks,
                    empty and sexless,
antedeluvian plaster discus-throwers.
Their discus-throwers crumble at the slightest touch.
Their alarm clocks won't wake up
                              without an alarm clock.
Don't try to dress up
                    in their stores,
where there are no dresses—but curses,
                              no shoes—but abuse.
Their vegetable bins—
                    are pits for mortals.
A store can't be a temple
                    for those who turn temples into stores!
It's their necklaces
                    of spools of toilet paper
our suffering women wear,
                              certainly not pearls.
How I want to believe:
                    The unsung song will be sung.
Like a spring flood
                    we'll wash away all antedeluvianism,
and around the necks of our loved ones,

we will place
>   the real necklaces
>   they deserve!

1986

TRANSLATED BY ALBERT C. TODD AND JAMES RAGAN

Zoya Osipova

Zoya Osipova is
>   a telegraph operator
with sadness
>   in her fingers.
The earth's pole is nearby
yet happiness
>   is at full distance.
Zoya, a single mother, has burned out.
Her fatherless son is sick.
His golden bangs
>   could set fire
to their barrack walls.
A live wedding ringlet
>   full of life's
misfortunes and abuse
>   curled up like a puppy
on two chairs,
>   he sleeps in the post office.
Mother sings lullabies when she can,
and in a hundred teletype styles,
now happily,
>   now sadly, she taps out
death,
>   birth,
>   and love.
Her fingers fly across the keys
punching their way throughout the globe,
yet Zoya never manages to type out
an apartment for herself.
Clumsily, never getting through,

she struggles to find the tiniest room
where she,
   and her tiny son,
      and tiny kitten
might live a tiny bit easier.
But when she bothers
those who know not how to feel,
they say to her fatherly:
"Well, your family is so small . . ."
Indifference
   is aggression.
Zoya Osipova
   is not a state,
not a Vietnam,
    not a Lebanon, and not a Chile,
but she also needs defending.
It's possible,
   even after hanging posters
with Picasso's dove of peace,
by indifference
   to smash to pieces
the downtrodden and lonely.
In the name of motherhood
let us be the ones to banish
this undeclared war
of militarism in daily life.
How very little is needed,
    Lord,
by each of us,
   and by the country,
so Osipova, the telegraph operator,
may call me to the window in the morning,
her blue eyes won't shout for joy,
but for just a moment
    her two newborn keys
will surface in her palm.

1986

TRANSLATED BY ALBERT C. TODD

Siberian Wooing

In Siberia there once was what at first seemed a barbaric but canny custom.
During wooing the bride was required to wash the feet of the groom and then drink
the water. Only in this way was the bride considered worthy to be taken as a wife.

The bridegroom of forty-one,
                  who tomorrow goes off to war
                                  in a heated van,
is planted by his Zima relatives
                  on a creaky stool,
and new, still pale, bootstraps
                      stick out of his smashing kid boots
where the wickedly elegant upper part
                    is turned back
and where a golden
            kerosene light plays.
The bride of forty-one
                 enters with a heavy washbowl
                    painted with roses,
in which the softly steaming water
                    shifts uneasily,
and pulling the groom's boots off,
                    soiling both hands at once
                          with shoeblack,
she unwinds his leg wrappings,
                  all without shame.
Now she immerses
             his bare feet with their little-boy red spots
so that when he winces in reflex
                water spills over the rim
                          onto the patterned floor mat,
and caresses his feet with water
                  and the female tenderness
                        of shaking girlish fingers,
diamond after diamond
             dropping from her eyes into the washbowl.
She stands on her knees
             before her future dead husband,
washing him in advance, so that if he is killed—
                he is cleansed,

and the tips of her fingers
                    caress on his feet
                              each tiny hair,
the way a peasant woman's fingers caress
                              every tiny ear of corn in the field.
And her future husband sits there—
                    neither alive
                              nor dead.
She bathes his feet,
                    but his cheeks and Cossack forelock are soaked.
He breaks into such a sweat
                    that his eyes spend tears,
relatives
          and icons
                    break into tears.
And when the bride bends over
                    to drink the water of her beloved,
he jumps up,
          raises her up in a single motion,
                              sits her down, as his wife,
falls on his own knees,
     and instantly pulls from her
          the garishly painted, combed felt boots,
and thrusts her feet into the washbowl,
                    shaking as in a chill of fever.
How he washes her feet—
                    each toe,
                    each nail!
How he kneads
          her sweet-apple ankles
                    in his trembling palms!
How he washes her!
                    As though she were his yet unborn daughter,
whose father,
          after his own future demise,
                    he will become!
And then he raises the washbowl
                    and presses his teeth—biting
                              until the enamel crunches
and his adam's apple dances on his neck—
                    drinking that cup to the bottom,
and across his face,
          across his chest,

quivering, like a transparent flag

of greatest purity,

flows the water from the feet of lovers,

water from the feet of lovers . . .

1986

TRANSLATED BY ALBERT C. TODD AND JAMES RAGAN

Aldan Girl

Aldan* girl, well-done girl,
look at me, who am I?
A guest? A thief from the wildest west,
so ragged is my vest?
I just try to do my best.

In her hand, a hunter's gun.
Watch your step, you hooligan!
She checked me out—I am a guest.
Yet in her eyes, still one request.

She scraped the moss with her boots
as she was trying to find my roots.
She's as graceful as a sable.
Not to love her, I'm quite unable.

From woodcock feathers she'd made a fan.
Come my lovely, we'll have some fun.
Señorita from Siberia
sitting softly on the porch,
brushing off those courting mosquitoes,
tasting blood as though hot borscht.

And her mosquito net mantilla
trembles cautiously on guard.
Though I am silent and boyish,
an old Siberian bard.

. . .

I construct with clumsy fingers
a hand-rolled butt from last year's *News*.
I joke with words though I am trying
to share with her my wordless views:

"I've almost reached the end, my dear,
all addresses I forgot.
I've returned to the shadow of your tear
from Buenos Aires, oh my God!

One, who's burned two family houses
is happy now in just a tent.
My third's inflamed in tears and collapsing.
To save it now, I don't attempt.

I'm not one of those tit grabbers,
not one of those liars, but
don't open your door, which squeaks so softly,
else I'll burn out your blameless hut.

Who am I, what kind of creature?
A full disaster looking for cuddles?
I didn't fall from a pink cloud.
I am out of pits and puddles.

I am a walking fallen tree. I tease
the other, lying fallen trees.
I'm tasty to some men's wives
and to some men's friendly knives.

I'm from those special hoboes,
I'm hoboing inside myself,
in my own bird cage encaged.
And my guts are my bed shelf.

So many sucking swamps inside me.
So many uncuttable jungles.
But something blue and defenseless
flowers, whispers, bangles.

All my life—such a mess, my honey.
All I've done—a false kind of bliss.
But I'm made from forget-me-nots.
I can't forget a single kiss!

· · ·

Please believe me, the crier-liar,
I destroyed everything—it is done.
But I've never unloved anybody.
I will never unlove anyone.

Even wildflowers are dying,
I am wild, but to die is not clever,
love is not only love, it's something.
Love is also unloving never!

You are so beautiful now,
Aldan girl, well-done girl, in your blue.
Like a queen's train behind you gliding,
the mosquitoes with pleasure taste you.

I am a little bit old for you, sweetie.
I'll not find any grace in disgrace.
But allow me just to stand a moment
as close as possible to your face."

1986
TRANSLATED BY ALBERT C. TODD WITH THE AUTHOR

*Aldan: The Aldan River is a major tributary to the great Lena River in Eastern Siberia.

Farewell

Listen, sweet little girl,
                    forgive my bazaar podium style
of speaking,
            but after all you are young,
and because I'm rusted through
                        time already is chucking me
                                        into the scrap heap,
but scrap metal,
            resmelted,
                    is salvaged for propellers and bridges.
Like a broken crowbar,
            I have been turned into scrap iron.

Why did I break?

    The wall turned out harder than I am,

but what I broke through

      won't stay in the past,

and beyond the walls I shattered

        my sons will force their way.

They will enter the future

      as a fortress captured,

having forgotten

    how much boiling tar

       was poured on our heads.

With my knucklehead

     I smashed it, broke the hole through,

and they can't patch it over

      with imprisoning cement.

Listen, sweet little girl,

     you foolishly made one mistake,

for simply due to youth,

     in haste

you married not a man—

      but a crude brute of a crowbar

in the hands of history

     and Russia.

Listen, sweet little girl,

     I thank you.

Forgive me,

   if I was unintentionally harsh.

A crowbar

   doesn't get screwed

      submissively

       into the wheel

of a peaceful sewing machine,

      chirring like a cricket.

I don't want to find myself

among nauseatingly domestic

      "normal husbands,"

who, outside the house,

     squirming like snakes,

betray their wives, not with women,

      but with a despicable so-called job.

Listen, sweet little girl,

    no, I'm not Pushkin

      and you're not d'Anthes.*

Nor are you
                    perfidious
                              or wicked.
But the weight of imagined metal
                                        won't redeem a crowbar.
A home can be destroyed by a needle.
Listen, sweet little girl,
                         I understand I'm at fault.
I wanted to change.
                    It didn't work out,
                                        I couldn't.
A handle can be changed only on a shovel.
A crowbar is a whole thing.
                          It doesn't need a handle.
And someday,
             stopping on excursion
                                    by the ruins of the fortress,
you will understand,
                    how I loved,
because for you,
                and our children,
together with that fortress wall
                            I smashed myself.

1986

TRANSLATED BY ALBERT C. TODD AND JAMES RAGAN

*d'Anthes: Baron Georges-Charles d'Anthes killed Aleksandr Pushkin in a duel.

Fireflies

The house has been taken out of the house
                                        that was abandoned by you.
A languid Black Sea night,
                          but Baikal howls along the coast,
and only your ghost,
                    remaining faithful,
                                        has not been taken
from the Black Sea,
                    from the depths of the mirrors

that tremble in the storm.

Like a departed soul you have abandoned
                    a body that seems still to be.

But even it is gone,
                as though washed away
                            by the sea—

I am only an outline of myself.
                Fireflies fly through me—
                            the Georgian seaside *tsitsinateli**—

as though I were
                only the thickened twilight,
                            just barely.

Of rivals near or far, fair or foul,
                    I am not jealous.

I'm jealous of myself,
                when I was so young and foolish,

and the air above the sea,
                like the land

where kisses remain alive
                and live on,

but only apart from our lips
                    that were stolen by others.

There is no strength for pledges,
                    in love no rights of damning.

Baikal or Black Sea
                senselessly beats the air,

and the *tsitsinateli,*
                are like sequins
                            on the slyly rustling black gown

of the grand, unthinkably old actress
                            whose name is night.

With that actress
                we played no short run

on the stages of damp cellars
                    and cobwebbed attics.

She didn't disappear.
                She held on in the eyes of other generations,
                            and never failed.

I didn't stand my ground.
                    I am only one of her fireflies.

Like a firefly I got enmeshed,
                    not in the mane of Pegasus,

but in the mane of a rocket
                of new atomic Attilas.

609

It is no less frightening
                    than to be snuffed out altogether.
But I still haven't shown all my light,
                              haven't glowed all the way.
Why, deceiving both yourself and me,
                                  did you one day fly off
above the croaking of sleepy frogs
                          into the starless black height?
Why did you set yourself and me afire
                                snuggling close
                                          like the *tsitsinateli*
and why did we give birth
                        to two defenseless fireflies?
Why, in air
          where radiation has become more frightening
                                        than bullets,
rising into a false heaven
                        from a similarly false earth,
did we so blindingly and blindly
                            and momentarily glow
and helped not our children,
                        and did we help the darkness?

1986

TRANSLATED BY ALBERT C. TODD

tsitsinateli: Georgian for "fireflies."

Requiem for *Challenger*

This white tragic swan
                    of farewell explosion,
this white swan of death
                      made from the last breath
                      of seven evaporated souls,
shook the gravestones of Arlington,
                              the Kremlin stars,
                              and the ancient armless statues of Rome.
The already gray
            Pyrenees,

Caucases,
        and Everest
now are become even more gray forever.
Gagarin's brotherly shadow
                    shuddered,
immortally crucified on the stars,
and his widow
            began to walk over the ocean
            to her American sister-widows.
The Statue of Liberty,
                crying the green tears of a mermaid,
tried to reach the cosmos
                to save her children,
                but could not.
Our life is a challenge.
                Our planet is our common "Challenger."
We humiliate her,
            frightening each other with bombs.
But could we explode her?
                    Even by mistake?
                    Even by accident?
That would be the final mistake,
                which could never be undone.

8 March 1986
TRANSLATED BY ALBERT C. TODD WITH THE AUTHOR

The Last Attempt

The last attempt to become happy,
after falling before all the twists and turns
of babbling trembling whiteness
and intoxicating elderberries.

The last attempt to become happy,
as though my ghost stands before a precipice
and wants to leap from all the injuries
into the place where long ago I was smashed.

· · ·

There on my broken bones
a dragonfly sits relaxing,
and ants come calmly to visit
in my empty former eyes.

I have become a ghost. I've gone from my body,
I slipped out of the medley of bones
but I've had it among the ghosts,
and I'm drawn again to so many abysses.

A loving ghost is more frightening than a corpse.
But you were not frightened, and understood,
and together we leaped, as though into an abyss,
but the gaping abyss stretched out white wings
and lifted us on mist.

And you and I lay not on a bed,
but on mist that held us just barely.
I am a ghost. I won't break anymore.
But you're alive. I fear for you.

Again the raven with funeral hues circles about
and waits for fresh fare, as on a field of battle.
The last attempt to become happy.
The last attempt to love.

1986
Petrozavodsk
TRANSLATED BY ALBERT C. TODD

Stalin's Funeral

On that day,
                that arduous, foaming, terrifying day,
when trucks squashed against people,
they fought for life
                        in hand-to-hand combat,
and old men perished underfoot.

Vertebrae were crushed by heels.
The pellucid square lay off to our right,

and on breath formed into clouds
played shadows of March branches.

We won't wrong the leader with false accusation.
But judgment was passed on the day of the funeral,
when people came to Stalin over people,
for *he* taught them to walk over people.

5 March 1953—1987
TRANSLATED BY ALBERT C. TODD

The Peak of Shame

"Well, step aside,
                    old man!
We are young,
                    which means, right..."
"Where are you going, youngsters?"
                                        "To the peak
of fame..."
"Hold on!
            I too clambered up there,
gouging out
                steps
                        with an ice ax,
till I became
                a sculpture of ice,
glorified,
            but unloved.
And is this my peak?
                        No smoke,
                                    no flame,
neither a kind word,
                        nor a sprig of green,
only somewhere,
                    torn from me,
my children
                scream.
It's not true,
                that upward means
                                    ahead.

Even when palaced with gold,
to hell with the top,
where tin cans
                    and condoms
freeze in ice.
On the peak of fame
                        there's a faint smell
of murder.
To be a genius
                    is to ignore caution.
In ruthless hands
                    an alpenstock
can do you in.
When,
        half hidden in clouds,
murderers ascend to power,
dismembered corpses
are concealed in their rucksacks..."
"Trying to spoil our mood,
                            old man?!"
"For your general enlightenment.
The peak of fame
                    easily changes to a peak
of shame.
The raped horizon
                    wails,
and mountain lakes
                        shy away and shudder,
when rubbish alpines its way
to the peak of shame.
The summit
            is at the same time a dead end
and an executioner's block,
                            where the blade
is God's eye.
There are colossuses
                    on the peak of shame,
so icy,
        only made of clay—
plasticine kings
                wretchedly
disintegrating.
There, like frozen spittle,
decorations and medals,

those sordid throwaways,
are given to cowards with contempt.
In its graveyard of rusted crowns—
both of Ancient Rome
                    and Russian empires,
there are piles of names
                    and banners,
eaten by the moth of infamy.
It's dangerous when fog deceives the eyes
to confuse labels foolishly,
shamefully calling
                    a peak of decay
a peak of blossoms.
When will we rid ourselves
of all this clambering
                    and sweating
of our infamous degradations,
and squalid false summits?"
"Old man,
            are there really no true summits?"
"There are.
                Young people, they're ahead of you.
But together
            we'll accomplish more.
I'm going with you,
                with the young."

1987

TRANSLATED BY ALBERT C. TODD AND JAMES RAGAN

Russian Koalas

Oh, Russian koalas!
Dozing away on tree trunks,
the era's yes-men with a nose
in every idea and deal.
My contemporary, my slumber-mate,
like a scoundrel, you wipe
your eyes only a third open—
afraid to rub them clean.

No,
            it's not a cataract.
Your sleepy character is at fault,
my dear fellow citizen, on whose wrist
one can't even feel

                        a social pulse.
You weren't awakened by *Avrora.**
In a pre-Petrine stupor,
you came to in long johns
when the fire gnawed your bed.
Marxism for you was a book of dreams:
not to live by—

                        but to tell fortunes.
Open-hearth furnaces,

                        blooming mills,

                                    cofferdams—
your breed of idols.
Physically you lived without sleep.
Morally you were

                        sleeping cowards.
When the arrests went on at night
and you stuffed the gag in your own mouth,
the bands played marches,
like the shameful snoring of conscience.
Somnolent and yawning,
you dozed through the war
and yawned through Sorge's† ciphers
to dreams of victories.
Like a member of the bureaucratic army
of all the nasal singing choirs,
you snored out Chernobyl in a dream,
and the *Admiral Nakhimov*‡
noisily breathed out your nostrils.
A cheeky aerochick,§
missed by drowsing koalas in Air Defense,
nearly knocked over

                        the Kremlin.
And didn't you sleep through
the hounding of Pasternak,

                        grumbling in your sleep:
"I didn't read the novel,

                        but
I am extremely outraged by it ... ?"
You gave out medals, not for nothing,

keeping your own collection as well,
to memoirs that yield nothing
of our harvest of total shame.
In order not to be disgraced now,
you accuse everyone
                                in civic sorrow
but yourself:
"We slept through,
                            we missed so much ..."
When will we all wake up?
You,
        my fellow citizen,
sleep
        like Gogol's snoozy Osip"
and brag
            like old Khlestakov.
Here's what your "healthy sleep" means:
A country will be blown with the wind
when, to a two-nostril whistle,
it stupidly oversleeps.
But will you suddenly—
                                weak with a hangover,
after sleeping tipsy through the war—
wake up naked
                on a naked
earth that's stripped of words?
And without any sort of orders,
and without any sort of chains
permit me
            the audacity of suggesting
a single,
            most plain:
            "Don't oversleep!"

1987

TRANSLATED BY ALBERT C. TODD AND JAMES RAGAN

Avrora: the firing of the guns of the warship *Avrora* at the Winter Palace in St. Petersburg was the signal for the Bolshevik seizure of power in the 1917 Revolution.
†Sorge: Viktor Sorge was a renowned master spy for the USSR in the Far East. He was caught by the Japanese during World War II and executed.
‡*Admiral Nakhimov:* Soviet cruise ship that suffered a major disaster in the Black Sea.
§aerochick: In 1986 Mathias Rust, a young German pilot, managed to fly his light aircraft through the Soviet defense warning system and to land on Red Square in Moscow.
"Osip: Osip and Khlestakov are characters from Nikolai Gogol's novel *Dead Souls.*

The Accidentless Captain

The Lena caresses the shore
with restraint,
        Mississippi-like,
and protects the captains:
It doesn't knock the sand out of them.
They become teachers,
and don't mock new salts,
and chat,
like the Lena,
        leisurely,
"How many years have you sailed,
                gramps?"
"Fifty,
     and it seems to have suited me."
"How many accidents?"
              "Not a one.
I don't drown,
        like Neptune."
In the storms and squalls of our years
no accidents
        is a rarity.
What a lucky bearded fellow!
And he looks and feels young.
He'll dance at a party,
and on his chest he wears
           a batch of ribbons,
and they called him
Mr. Superquota.
But why,
     when you are drunk,
accidentless captain,
do you lie wildly?
Do you want me
        to tell?
In '37 you piloted
a barge along the Lena,
with prisoners in the hold.
Shouts came from below:
          "Open the hatch!
We can't breathe!

We're dying!"
But you kicked the hatch and said,
"I'll deliver you,
                    enemy bitches,
like grains in sacks."
Things grew quiet in the hold,
                              the sailors got sick.

The hold,
          like a battlefield,
was stuffed with swollen meat.
Accidentless captain,
you trampled so many lives.
You were almost not to blame,
and you became almost a butcher.
You thought that they were enemies.
Lord,
      help the misled!
Your only god was the plan.
There is no god more treacherous.
Accidentless captain,
your whole life was an accident.

1987

TRANSLATED BY ANTONINA W. BOUIS

Monuments Still Not Built

Monuments still not built
                    stride across the reindeer moss tundra
all the way to the permafrost of blood,
                              packing down the Kolyma* snow,
and pass
        from one sleeve to another,
                              by an old practice in the camps,
a hand-rolled butt
              licked together from newspapers of '37—
                              only one for everybody.
Monuments still not built
                    exhume with ice saws our perished brothers,

who from the cold have become sculptures

                                           inside nameless graves,

and with logger's mittens frozen together

                                           almost as hard as marble,

pound at night on all the doors

                                    of those who have forgotten about them.

Bliukher's† bloody tears

                           are still cast in metal.

From a pedestal Yakir‡ extends

                            his granite arm to the country.

Let us rear a monument to everyone

                               who wrote out on a wall

the ABCs of the Revolution

                           with a finger whose nail was torn out.

Monuments of the coming future,

                            you advance on us by yourselves.

I hear the cast-iron tread.

                          I hear the voice of bronze.

There can be no rebuilding

                        without rebuilding memory,

and without rebuilding monuments

                          to those who built us.

Now is your time, monuments,

                        the time of honest marble.

From all that's slandered

                       the sludge is being stripped off forever,

and the once crushed violin

                     of Marshal Tukhachevskii§

grows together piece by piece,

                     becoming marble.

1987

TRANSLATED BY ALBERT C. TODD

*Kolyma: Site of an infamous Siberian prison camp.
†Bliukher: Marshal Vasili Bliukher. Executed in Stalin's 1937 purges.
‡Yakir: Marshal Yona Yakir. Executed in Stalin's 1937 purges.
§Tukhachevskii: Marshal Tukhachevskii. Executed in Stalin's 1937 purges.

Personal Letter from the Generalissimo

Beyond Baikal
         above the Selenga River
people no longer smell of Stalin,
just one
        old gossip
with a stubborn Stalin stench,
a feeble
        war veteran
with a cedar peg leg full of cracks.
"It's all coming apart,
           everyone's become loose.
What can save Russia?
         Another Stalingrad.
If Stalin were alive,
        people would know fear
and without fear
        Russia will collapse ..."
On his gate
        the Generalissimo himself stares
like a sovereign eagle
in tin graveyard flowers under glass,
so that women balancing yoked buckets
muffle their idle chatter while passing.
Beyond Baikal
        above the Selenga River
was once a prison camp
        with the harshest regimen.
And to the war veteran
came a veteran of the camps,
        an innocent man,
who had come from Moscow with a cough
to this non-cemetery cemetery
where his comrades were buried.
He said:
        "I don't want to offend you,
but to speak from my heart—

veteran to veteran.
Why do you need him on your gate,
a man who kept people in pens
                              like cattle?"
The war veteran took offense:
"His portrait hangs inside me.
He was a harsh leader, but that's what we needed.
In the war he knew all his soldiers by name.
He knew my name and patronymic,
and sent me a letter himself from the Kremlin..."
His chest swelled out.
                         The veteran
suddenly seemed taller
                         as if on a pedestal:
"The Generalissimo wrote me
a personal letter!
                    And signed it personally!"
And he led
           the veteran of the camps
to his secret treasure-house.
First he opened
                 a forged chest.
Inside was a locked safe,
                          also forged as of old,
and inside was a box for hard fruit candy,
and in the box
                a letter,
                          and in the letter
words of gratitude for the battle of Oriol,
his name, patronymic, surname
                               written in ink,
and Stalin's signature—
                         only a rubber stamp—
a lie of flattery to a trusting heart.
How blind is
             a soldier's sincerity!
The personal letter of the Generalissimo,
the personal impersonal letter,
how easy the betrayal.
The veteran of war wept with pride
over the false signature.
The old prison camp veteran

turned the letter over in his hands,
allowing no smile.
This is what they keep concealed.
This is what they love him for—

deception.

Fortunately

veterans of the prison camps
have grown wiser

than veterans of the war.

1988

TRANSLATED BY ALBERT C. TODD AND JAMES RAGAN

Provideniia Bay*

Hoarfrost doesn't form

on wolverine fur,
and they use the fur to make

diapers for Chukchi† babies.
There is no love more primitive,

no tenderness more animal,
than here, where even furs

roar with the cold.
The local divorcée's breasts swell,

painfully,
lonely beneath her deerskin shirt,

like yellow fruit.
But, people here do not get mean.

The cold makes them warmer.
People made of ice will never

survive on these icy shores.
I live in Provideniia Bay

like the ghost
of a forgotten poet,

the one

from the mainland.
Lucky in other people's eyes,

623

                              like snow fallen into a bra,
I am actually only probably happy,
                                    but not for sure.
That is the certainty
                    of my uncertain fate.
I'm not dependable.
                I cause bad dreams.
I'm like the divorcée,
                    like a kayak frozen in the ice,
and dogs rub up against me
                              as they whimper.
Sniffing into the distance better
                              than any Chukchi in the tundra,
a sable stands upright on
                    a whale vertebra,
and seems to be complaining
                        that here at the tannery,
if they skin you,
                the finish won't be as good.
Beyond the silently sleeping
                        strip of water
an American soldier
                listens and hears.
A heavy explosion thuds.
                        Must be a moonshine still.
It didn't make it to the holiday,
                        November seventh.‡
The border patrol band,
                    brick red in the face,
rehearses for the parade,
                    hitting a few false notes,
and our tykes,
                dressed in sheepskin jackets,
snuffle their noses
                under the nose of the U.S.A.
And the sable, the sable, the sable,
                              with special tread
circles on the ice floes in the bay,
                        tail puffed up,
between two systems,
                and chrysanthemum floes,
between two radars,

> between two blows,
>
> running from ice to ice
>
> without a tremble . . .

1988

TRANSLATED BY ANTONINA W. BOUIS

*Provideniia Bay: Located at the easternmost end of the USSR at the bottom tip of the Chukotskii Peninsula.
†Chukchi: Nationality inhabiting northeastern regions of Siberia.
‡November seventh: Anniversary of the Russian Revolution, the most important state holiday in the USSR.

We Can't Go On

When the country almost went off the rails,
we grabbed her wheels with our teeth,
and understood,

as we tried to apply the brakes:
"We can't go on this way!"
How did *he* make his way to power

through party cells,

through the whole cadre network—

their cadre

not some other?!

"We can't go on this way!"

—was the guide,

gnawing at *his* whole conscience.
There is a peak to the shame of moral venality.
Icons cannot be hung in a bordello.
Life

was able to go on only,

with a huge

"We can't go on this way!"

1988

TRANSLATED BY ALBERT C. TODD

Vendée

Reaction comes in Panzer "swine" formation,
the way the Teutonic menace came,
and in the reaction in our very own nation
there's the stench of manure of Vendée* fame.

Our very own national swamp hollow,
the most self-satisfied muck,
sulking like *sans culottes,* swallows
all those who think and don't suck.

The literary Vendée
doesn't wield a pen that's powerful,
a powerful ax is its way,
always ready for a pogrom sorrowful.

The literary Vendée,
in speeches much concerned about the native land,
with a sneer and hidden anger, grumbles that
it has no regrets about Pasternak's smashed piano.

It comes out with ready rhetoric
in favor of ecology in nature
but the ecology of freedom
is not understandable and frightening to it.

With brass-knuckle and tire-iron passion
it snarls that jazz is hell incarnate,
and that aerobics are sneaking in on us
like Mata Hari.

When talent is in such a sucking swamp
it's enough to bring on tears,
but the false saviors of Russia
play at Vendée for keeps.

Here is where there is danger for the country,
when a real bone breaker
comes out from behind glasnost
with brass knuckles and tire irons.

. . .

To be a progressive little swine
is shameful in that hour when
with snorting and with squealing
reaction is at war in Panzer "swine" formation.

1988

TRANSLATED BY ALBERT C. TODD

*Vendée: The Vendée province in southwestern France gave its name to the reaction of peasants who, ignorant of the revolutionary aims and changes taking place and resisting conscription, began the counterinsurgency of 1793 against the French Revolution.

The Apple Trees of Drobitskii

Tiny tender pink petal,
more transparent than maiden's skin,
you're guilty
        of nothing—
shed no tears with the dawn.

Hover as you fly from the branch,
flutter about—
           if only for a moment,
Ukrainian, and Jewish,
God's
      common tiny petal.

Why the tears,
        Ruvin Ruvinovich!?
In May Drobitskii Yar*
            is so lovely!
To be a Jew
       and to be so easily wounded
is impossible—
       you can't make it through life!

If into the earth
       endowed by the dead,
in this ravine

you stick
your cane
all polished—
it will be an apple tree in the morning.

Over Drobitskii Yar
tiny apple petals
are strewn
like an aerial
wedding dress
torn in shreds.

Mankind,
listen,
see—
here
by the little sister's
bloody well.

Sarah—little apple tree
whispers in Yiddish,
Khristia—little apple tree
in Ukrainian,
the third little apple tree—
Russian
Manechka
stands on tiptoe
stretching upward,
and the fourth—the little Armenian,
Dzhan.
All the skeletons
embrace one another in the ground.

Bones underground
never quarrel,
bones
lack sordid passions.
There are no "Pamiat'" society
members',
no anti-Semites'
bones.

Tell us,
Ruvin Ruvinovich,

how, as a teenager,
                 naked as the day you were born,
all smeared with blood,
                 your face drained bloodless,
you crawled out from under,
                 shoving bodies aside.

Was this why
                 you made your way into the sun
and were the son of the regiment
                 through all the war,
so that someday
                 they could charge your gray hairs
with Jewish Freemasonry?!

We all have fallen
out of our cradles
                 to be shot.
We all have crawled out
from under dead ideas
                 and bodies.

We were swaddled
                 as the dead.
Corpse on top of corpse,
                 and on top of everything
pressing us down
                 was the dead body of Stalin;
we are barely able to get out
                 from under him.

Above Drobitskii Yar
                 in autumn,
when leaves are burning,
                 like brocade,
this collective state apple tree
is guarded by shepherd dogs,
                 growling.

More precious to me
                 than the authorities' power
is the lightness of an apple tree's
                 tiny petal.
I love nothing that comes with shepherd dogs—

elite orchards,
            or elite troops.

Why the tears,
                Ruvin Ruvinovich?
Life is
        a sequence of Chernobyls.
Could it be
            we are all beneath great ruins
and we'll never crawl out ever?

We are working our way out.
                            An ignominious task,
though enormous!
                Only don't let
the demolition shovel
                    succeed again
in finishing off
                those who are trying to crawl out!

Tiny tender pink petal,
paler than maiden's skin,
you're guilty
            of nothing—
shed no tears with the dawn.

Hover as you fly from the branch,
fly about—
            if only for a moment,
Ukrainian,
            and Jewish,
and Tbilisian,
                also our own,
also God's tiny petal . . .

8 May 1989
On the Moscow-Kharkov train
TRANSLATED BY ALBERT C. TODD

---

*Drobitskii Yar: *Yar* in Russian means "ravine." Site near Kharkov of yet another mass murder of Jews and others by the Nazis during World War II.

A Striking Heart

To the memory of A. D. Sakharov

The heart went on strike,
                as if it were a mine.
Just yesterday,
          hair even whiter in the snow,
he left the Kremlin, hatless,
                shaky,
through ghosts of boyars,
             tsars,
                 and leaders.
Maliuta* spied on him in the powdery snow,
and so did Beria,
              and that pock-marked butcher ...†
His last words to his wife
and the world were:
                "Tomorrow there will be a battle ..."
History's most peaceful rebel,
in dying, he
            did not come down from a cross,
but he left a horrifying hole
in the moral fabric of the world.
Death.
      There is no strike more terrible.
But in defiance of advancing death
stoop shouldered,
              face whiter than a leaflet,
he raised his fists
             above the congress's jeers.
Not vengeance,
          not personal spite,
but reason led him to save the country
from rule by arrogance,
              self-genocide,
which long ago turned into war against the self.
He understood, in premonition of the end,
boos still ringing in his ears:
that unenlightened semi-freedom
was just a step away from enlightened freedom.
O Homeland!

Weary of tears and groans,
lines,
           and prisons,
                      and hospitals,
don't grow accustomed
                      after the murder of millions
to the loss of individual geniuses.
The pivot of a nation
                      is an individual.
A nation is made up of people,
                      not zeros.
O Homeland!
           To keep from freezing over,
learn at last to be warmer toward your geniuses.
We're too closely enmeshed
                      with the base and the unclean,
and by solving complexities crudely,
                      head on,
we will have to weep over the idealists
we hound to the grave.
Will we be able
           to avert apathy
and keep up our spirits and our conscience,
and worry how to earn our freedom
where power belongs to everyone
                      and the only authority is conscience?
Let's unite at the fateful mountain pass!
As long as our hearts
                      bear up under the load
and do not tire,
           do not go on strike . . .
As long as there is a tomorrow,
                      tomorrow there will be a battle.

15 December 1989

TRANSLATED BY ANTONINA W. BOUIS

*Maliuta: Maliuta Skuratov (d. 1572). Chief of Tsar Ivan IV's (the Terrible) security guards and one of the principal military leaders of the privileged, brutally abusive oprichniki created by Ivan as a force to nullify the power of the traditional boyar aristocracy.
†pock-marked butcher: Stalin's face was heavily pockmarked.

Half Measures

Half measures
   can kill
when,
   chafing at the bit in terror,
we twitch our ears,
     all lathered in foam,
on the brink of precipices,
because we can't jump halfway across.
Blind is the one
   who only half sees
      the chasm.
Don't half recoil,
    lost in broad daylight,
half rebel,
   half suppressor
of the half insurrection
     you gave birth to!
With every half-effective
    half measure
half the people
   remain half pleased.
The half sated
   are half hungry.
The half free
   are half enslaved.
We are half afraid,
    halfway on a rampage ...
A bit of this,
   yet also half of that
party-line
   weak-willed "Robin Hood"*
who half goes
   to a half execution.
Opposition has lost
    its resolution.
By swashbuckling jabs
    with a flimsy sword
you cannot be half
   a guard for the cardinal
and half

a king's musketeer.
Can there be
                    with honor
a half motherland
                    and a half conscience?
Half freedom
            is perilous,
and saving the motherland halfway
                              will fail.

1989

TRANSLATED BY ALBERT C. TODD

*"Robin Hood": The Russian is Stenka Razin. See listing of historical figures.

RUSSIAN WRITERS AND HISTORICAL FIGURES FREQUENTLY REFERRED TO IN THE POEMS

Vissarion Grigorevich Belinsky (1811–48). Powerful and passionate literary critic. His advocacy of social criticism in art had a profound influence on the development of Russian literature.

Lavrenti Pavlovich Beria (1899–1953). Head of Stalin's security police organization under the Commisariat of Internal Affairs (NKVD) and responsible for directing massive arrests, executions, and savage tortures.

Aleksandr Aleksandrovich Blok (1880–1921). Russia's great symbolist poet who embraced the Revolution with his poems: "The Twelve," full of stark images of Red Guards patrolling the snowy night city, and "The Scythians," which ominously warns of Russia's ancient Asiatic might that now challenges the world anew. He later grew disillusioned with postrevolutionary developments in the Soviet Union.

Gavrila Romanovich Derzhavin (1743–1816). Poet, governor of a province, later secretary to Empress Catherine the Great, and for a short time minister of justice under Tsar Aleksandr I. Though didactic, most of his poetry is lyric, and his sonorous and majestic odes made him the leading poet until Pushkin and his contemporaries eclipsed the older generation.

Aleksandr Ivanovich Herzen (1812–70). Highly respected and widely influential Russian political thinker in the nineteenth century and a gifted revolutionary writer. He left Russia in 1847 to live abroad and in London published the most important organ of the revolutionary emigration, *Kolokol (The Bell)*.

Mikhail Iurevich Lermontov (1814–41). Leading Romantic poet and novelist who was considered to be the successor to Pushkin in poetry and in the struggle against tyranny. He was arrested and banished by military assignment for a scalding poem attacking those near the throne whom he blamed for Pushkin's death. Like Pushkin he was killed in a duel which was foreshadowed in his writing.

Osip Emilevich Mandelstam (1891–1938). One of Russia's greatest poets in the twentieth century, who perished in prison for an irreverent poem about Stalin.

Vladimir Vladimirovich Mayakovsky (1893–1930). Leading Futurist poet who enthusiastically embraced the October Revolution, but committed suicide in both political and personal disillusionment.

Nikolai Alekseevich Nekrasov (1821–78). Poet of radical political views who as a

635

major publisher was often in conflict with the government over censorship. His poems express great compassion for the suffering of the peasants.

Boris Leonidovich Pasternak (1890–1960). Major lyric poet and novelist who survived Stalinism. Awarded the Nobel Prize in 1958; however his celebrated novel *Doctor Zhivago* was banned in the USSR and he was not allowed to leave the Soviet Union to receive the award. His life in the suburbs of Moscow was a sometime theme of his poetry.

Aleksandr Sergeevich Pushkin (1799–1837). Russia's greatest poet, who first raised the banner of freedom from tyranny. Often exiled from St. Petersburg, he was killed in a duel laced with political intrigue. He gave (in the face of official censorship) a surprisingly sympathetic portrait of Pugachov in his story "The Captain's Daughter" (1836). He also wrote the history of the rebellion.

Stepan (Stenka) Razin (ca. 1630–71). Don Cossack who led a mixed Russian and non-Russian peasant rebellion (1670–71) that engulfed the southeastern steppe region. This formidable uprising was one of the periodic frontier rebellions against the serf-based regime of the centralizing state and was suppressed with great difficulty. Celebrated in folk-songs and -tales, he was finally captured and taken to Moscow, where he was publicly quartered alive.

Igor Severianin (1887–1941). Poet of the Ego-Futurist and Cubo-Futurist movements renowned for the beauty of his poetry reading.

Maliuta Skuratov (d. 1572). Chief of Tsar Ivan IV's (the Terrible) security guards and one of the principal military leaders of the privileged, brutally abusive oprichniki created by Ivan to nullify the power of the traditional boyar aristocracy.

Sergei Aleksandrovich Yesenin (1895–1925). Russia's "hooligan" unschooled poet who wrote simple, touching, mellifluous lyric verse about the country landscape, village life, work, and holidays. He sometimes touched on religious themes and frequently used the image of Russia's symbolic birch tree. He committed suicide by hanging himself in a Leningrad hotel after writing a farewell poem in his own blood.

RIVERS AND GEOGRAPHIC NAMES FREQUENTLY REFERRED TO IN THE POEMS

Aldan: The Aldan River is a major tributary to the great Lena River in eastern Siberia, which flows into the Arctic Ocean.

Amderma: Tiny port on the Iugorskii Peninsula in the Karskii Sea of the Arctic Ocean west of the northern end of the Ural Mountains.

Don: The Don is the major river west of the Volga; it flows into the Black Sea and is now connected to the Volga by a canal allowing navigation through the enormous system.

Euinki: Small nationality located principally in northern Siberia.

Kama: The Kama River flows west from the Urals into the Volga just east of the city of Kazan.

Kolyma: Located in northeastern Siberia, the Kolyma River flows northward into the East Siberian Sea of the Arctic Ocean. It is the site of infamous labor camps of the Stalin era.

Lena: The Lena River begins north of Lake Baikal in Siberia and flows northward into the Arctic Ocean.

Oka: The Oka River lies south of Moscow and flows east to the Volga at the present city of Gorky.

Pechora: The Pechora River rises in the Ural Mountains and flows west and north to its delta to empty into Pechora Bay of the Barents Sea and the Arctic Ocean.

Rus: Ancient Russia. The name of the eastern Slavonic tribe became in the ninth century the name for the emerging nation and the early feudal state.

Taiga: Subarctic coniferous forest of Siberia beginning where the tundra ends.

Ugra: The Ugra River is located southwest of Moscow.

Vilyui: The Vilyui River in Siberia lies north of Lake Baikal and flows into the Vilyui Reservoir.

Vitim: The Vitim River lies east and north of Lake Baikal and flows into the Lena River.

Yaik: The Yaik is the ancient name of the Ural River, which flows south from the mountains into the Caspian Sea east of the Volga.

Zima Junction: Small Siberian station on the Trans-Siberian railroad where Yevtushenko was born and where he spent years of childhood wartime evacuation.

PREVIOUS TRANSLATION
SOURCES

Almost at the End. Translated by Antonina W. Bouis, Albert C. Todd, and Yevgeny Yevtushenko. New York: Henry Holt, 1987.

Bratsk Station and Other New Poems. Translated by Tina Tupikina-Glaessner, Geoffrey Dutton, and Igor Mezhakoff-Koriakin. Melbourne: Sun, 1966. New York: Doubleday, 1967. New York: Praeger, 1967.

A Dove in Santiago: A Novella in Verse. Translated by D. M. Thomas. New York: Viking, 1982.

The Face Behind the Face. Translated by Arthur Boyars and Simon Franklin. London: Marion Boyars, 1979.

From Desire to Desire. Translated by Albert C. Todd, Lawrence Ferlinghetti, John Updike, Stanley Kunitz, Richard Wilbur, James Dickey, Geoffrey Dutton, Edward Keenan, George Reavey, Herbert Marshall, Robin Milner-Gulland, and Peter Levi. New York: Doubleday, 1976.

Ivan the Terrible and Ivan the Fool. Translated by Daniel Weissbort. New York: Richard Marek, 1979.

Kazan University and Other New Poems. Translated by Eleanor Jacka and Geoffrey Dutton. Melbourne: Sun, 1973.

The New Russian Poets 1953–1966: An Anthology. Translated by George Reavey. New York: October House, 1966.

Poems Chosen by the Author. Translated by Peter Levi and Robin Milner-Gulland. London: Collins, 1966.

The Poetry of Yevgeny Yevtushenko. Translated by George Reavey. New York: October House, 1967.

Stolen Apples. Translated by James Dickey, Geoffrey Dutton, Lawrence Ferlinghetti, Anthony Kahn, Stanley Kunitz, George Reavey, John Updike, Richard Wilbur, Edward Keenan, Albert C. Todd, Igor Mezhakoff-Koriakin. New York: Doubleday, 1971.

Yevtushenko: Selected Poems. Translated by Robin Milner-Gulland and Peter Levi, S.J. New York: Dutton, 1962.

Yevtushenko Poems. Translated by Herbert Marshall. New York: Dutton, 1966.

Yevtushenko's Reader. Translated by Robin Milner-Gulland and Peter Levi, S.J., George Reavey, Albert C. Todd, John Updike, Stanley Kunitz, Vera Dunham, and Herbert Marshall. New York: Dutton, 1972.

BIBLIOGRAPHIC DATA

Bibliographic information is provided in the following format: The English title, the date of composition, then the title in transliteration (in quotes), followed by the place and date of first publication (most often a journal or newspaper). The final line identifies the poem's location in Yevtushenko's three-volume collected works (*Sobranie sochinenii*, abbreviated here as *Sob. soch.*) when possible, or the place of first book publication, which is the fair copy unless otherwise noted.

1952–1955

Lies
1952
"He nado govorit' nepravdu detiam"
Tretili sneg: Kniga liriki (Moscow 1955), pp. 25–26.

Train Car
1952
"Vagon"
Tretii sneg: Kniga liriki (Moscow 1955), pp. 30–32.
Sob. soch., vol. I (Moscow 1983), p. 27.

The Depth
1952
"Glubina"
Komsomol'skaia pravda, 9 Dec. 1954, p. 3.
Sob. soch., vol. I (Moscow 1983), p. 32.

You Are Great in Love
1953
"Ty bol' shaia v liubvi"
Tretii sneg: Kniga liriki (Moscow 1955), pp. 84–85.
Sob. soch., vol. I (Moscow 1983), p. 33.

The Third Snow
1953
"Tretii sneg"
Oktiabr' no. 2 (1955), pp. 127–28.
Sob. soch., vol. I (Moscow 1983), pp. 36–37.

"I wander ..."
1954
"Ia shataius' v tolkuchke ..."

Shosse entuziastov: Stikhi (Moscow 1956), p. 89.
Izbrannye proizvedeniia vol. I (Moscow 1975), p. 39.

"In every instance ..."
1954
"Pri kazhdom dele est' ..."
Stikhi raznykh let (Moscow 1959), p. 150.
Sob. soch., vol. I (Moscow 1983), p. 43.

Boots
1954
"Sapogi"
Stikhi raznykh let (Moscow 1959), pp. 10–12.
Sob. soch., vol. I (Moscow 1983), pp. 47–48.

Weddings
1955
"Svad'by"
Oktiabr', no. 9 (1956), pp. 128–29.
Sob. soch., vol. I (Moscow 1983), pp. 51–52.

"The window looks out onto ..."
1955
"Okno vykhodit v belye ..."
Shosse entuziastov: Stikhi (Moscow 1956), pp. 50–52.
Sob. soch., vol. I (Moscow 1983), pp. 76–77.

Last Side Street
1955–1975
"Poslednii Pereulok"
Druzhba narodov no. 7 (1975), p. 85.
Sob. soch., vol. I (Moscow 1983), p. 80.

On a Bicycle
1955

"Na velosipede"
Shosse entuziastov: Stikhi (Moscow 1956),
pp. 90–93.
Sob. soch., vol. I (Moscow 1983), pp. 81–83.

Envy
1955
"Zavist'"
Novyi mir no. 7 (1955), p. 46.
Sob. soch., vol. I (Moscow 1983), p. 84.

Prologue
1955
"Prolog"
Obeshchanie: Stikhi (Moscow 1957), pp. 5–
7.
Sob. soch., vol. I (Moscow 1983), pp. 85–86.

"I am a purse ..."
1955
"Ia kosheliok"
Obeshchanie: Stikhi, (Moscow 1957), pp. 64–
65.
Sob. soch., vol. I (Moscow 1983), p. 87.

Idol
1955
"Idol"
Nezhnost': Novye stikhi (Moscow 1962), pp.
23–24.
Sob. soch., vol. I (Moscow 1983), p. 95.

Fury
1955
"Zlost'"
Under the title "Mne govoriat, kachaia,
golovoi ..." in *Literaturnaia gazeta*, 17
July 1962, p. 3.
Sob. soch., vol. I (Moscow 1983), pp. 96–97.

Gentleness
1955
"Nezhnost'"
Kater sviazi (Moscow 1966), p. 203.
Sob. soch., vol. I (Moscow 1983), p. 98.

The Park
1955
"Park"
In the anthology *Den' poezii 1962* (Moscow
1962), p. 118.
Sob. soch., vol. I (Moscow 1983), pp. 99–
100.

"In a red woolen cap ..."
1955

"V pal'to nezimnem ..."
Molodaia gvardiia no. 1 (1956), pp. 9–10.
Sob. soch., vol. I (Moscow 1983), pp. 101–
102.

Zima Junction: A Poem
1955
"Stantsia Zima: Poema"
Oktiabr', no. 6 (1956), pp. 97–115.
Sob. soch., vol. I (Moscow 1983), pp. 103–
30.

1956–1962

"I don't understand ..."
1956
"Ne ponimaiu ..."
Obeshchanie: Stikhi (Moscow 1957) pp. 27–
28.
Sob. soch., vol. I (Moscow 1983), pp. 131–
32.

"What a rude sobering ..."
1956
"Kakoe nastupaet ..."
Novyi mir, no. 4 (1957), p. 77.
Sob. soch., vol. I (Moscow 1983), p. 140.

"Cowards have ..."
1956
"U trusov ..."
Under the title *O smelosti* in *Moskovskii
literator*, 3 Nov. 1956.
Sob. soch., vol. 1 (Moscow 1983), p. 142.

Ice
1956
"Liod"
Izbrannye proizvedeniia vol. I (1975), p.
140.
Sob. soch., vol. I (Moscow 1983), p. 145.

"I congratulate you, Momma ..."
1956
"Ia pozdravliaiu vas, mama ..."
Iabloko: Novaia kniga stikhov (Moscow
1960), pp. 6–7.
Sob. soch., vol. I (Moscow 1983), p. 150.

"Poetry is a great power ..."
1956–1970
"Poeziia—velikaia derzhava ..."

Obeshchanie: Stikhi (Moscow 1957), pp. 37–
38.
Sob. soch., vol. I (Moscow 1983), p. 152.

"My love will come..."
1956
"Moia liubimaia priedet..."
Obeshchanie: Stikhi (Moscow 1957), p. 80.
Sob. soch., vol. I (Moscow 1983), p. 153.

"Damp white imprints..."
1956
"Sledov syrye otpechatki..."
Obeshchanie: Stikhi (Moscow 1957) pp. 86–
87.
Sob. soch., vol. I (Moscow 1983), p. 160.

"I don't know what..."
1956
"Ne znaiu ia..."
In the anthology *Den' poezii* (Moscow
1956), p. 100.
Sob. soch., vol. I (Moscow 1983), p. 165.

Momma
1957
"Mama"
Obeshchanie: Stikhi (Moscow 1957), pp. 53–
54.
Sob. soch., vol. I (Moscow 1983), pp. 171–
72.

They Killed Someone!
1957
"Cheloveka ubili"
Stikhi raznykh let (Moscow 1959), pp. 151–
52.
Sob. soch., vol. I (Moscow 1983), p. 174.

"The square..."
1957
"Skver velichavo..."
Obeshchanie: Stikhi (Moscow 1957), pp. 43–
46.
Sob. soch., vol. I (Moscow 1983), pp. 175–
76.

Letter to One Writer
1957
"Pis'mo odnomu pisateliu"
Znamia, no. 4 (1987), p. 15.
Posledniaia popytka (Petrozavodsk 1988),
pp. 82–83.

"Again a meeting..."
1957

"Opiat' proshedshee sobranie..."
Znamia, no. 4 (1987), p. 16.
Posledniaia popytka (Petrozavodsk 1988),
pp. 84–85.

"Here is what..."
1957
"So mnoiu vot..."
Novyi mir, no. 4 (1957), p. 78.
Sob. soch., vol. I (Moscow 1983), p. 181.

"When I think of Aleksandr Blok..."
1957
"Kogda ya dumaiu o Bloke..."
Obeshchanie: Stikhi (Moscow 1957), p. 39.
Sob. soch., vol. I (Moscow 1983), p. 182.

My Dog
1958
"Moi pios"
Under the title "Moei sobake" in *Stikhi
raznykh let* (Moscow 1959).
Sob. soch., vol. I (Moscow 1983), p. 211.

Loneliness
1959
"Odinochestvo"
Oktiabr', no. 9 (1959), pp. 120–22.
Sob. soch., vol. I (Moscow 1983), pp. 218–
20.

"The icicles' delicate chime..."
1959
"Sosulek tonkii zvon..."
Sob. soch., vol. I (Moscow 1983), pp. 223–
24.

Smiles
1959
"Ulybki"
Nezhnost': Novye stikhi (Moscow 1962), p.
110.
Sob. soch., vol. I (Moscow 1983), p. 227.

Assignation
1959
"'Net, net, ia ne siuda popal...'"
Znamia, no. 1 (1968), pp. 65–66.
Sob. soch., vol. I (Moscow 1983), pp. 230–
31.

In Memory of the Poet Xenia Nekrasova
1959
"Pamiati Ksenii Nekrasovoi"
In the anthology *Den' poezii 1965* (Moscow
1965), p. 65.
Sob. soch., vol. I (Moscow 1983), p. 243.

Incantation
1960
"Zaklinanie"
Iabloko: Novaia kniga stikhov (Moscow 1960), pp. 23–24.
Sob. soch., vol. I (Moscow 1983), p. 248.

"I am older by . . ."
1960
"Ia starshe sebia . . ."
Nezhnost': Novye stikhi (Moscow 1962), pp. 113–14.
Sob. soch., vol. I (Moscow 1983), pp. 250–251.

The Incendiary
1960
" 'Ty nachisto pritvorstva lishena . . .' "
Ogoniok, no. 9 (1962), p. 17.
Sob. soch., vol. I (Moscow 1983), pp. 252–53.

Let's Not . . .
1960
"Ne nado"
So mnoiu vot chto proiskhodit . . .: Izbr. lirika (Moscow 1966), pp. 7–8 (*B-ka "Ogoniok,"* no. 5).
Sob. soch., vol. I (Moscow 1983), p. 254.

Secret Mysteries
1960
"Tainy"
Novyi mir, no. 7 (1962), pp. 34–35.
Sob. soch., vol. I (Moscow 1983), p. 255.

"They shuffle . . ."
1960
"V vagone sharkaiut . . ."
Vzmakh ruki (Moscow 1962), pp. 323–25.
Sob. soch., vol. I (Moscow 1983), pp. 256–57.

Pasternak's Grave
1960
"Ograda"
Iunost', no. 12 (1960), p. 6.
Sob. soch., vol. I (Moscow 1983), pp. 263–64.

Our Mothers Depart
1960
"Ukhodyia Materi"
Iabloko: Novaia kniga stikhov (Moscow 1960), pp. 32–33.
Sob. soch., vol. I (Moscow 1983), p. 265.

Honey
1960
"Miod"
Moskva, no. 6 (1961), p. 84.
Sob. soch., vol. I (Moscow 1963), pp. 273–74.

The American Nightingale
1960
"Amerikanskii solovei"
Literaturnaia gazeta, 24 Aug. 1961, p. 2.
Sob. soch., vol. I (Moscow 1983), pp. 278–79.

Encounter
1960
"Vstrecha v Kopengagene"
Under the title *Vstrecha* in *Iunost'*, no. 4 (1961), p. 7.
Sob. soch., vol. I (Moscow 1983), pp. 281–82.

Talk
1960
"Razgovor"
Literaturnaia gazeta (Kiev), 1 Sept. 1961, p. 4.
Under the title *Monolog Amerikanskogo pisatelia* in *Sob. soch.*, vol. I (Moscow 1983), p. 283.

Babii Yar
1961
"Babii iar"
Literaturnaia gazeta (Moscow), 19 Sept. 1961, p. 4.
Sob. soch., vol. I (Moscow 1983), pp. 316–18.

Irpen
1961
"Irpen' "
Posledniaia popytka (Petrozavodsk 1988), pp. 88–90.

Irony
1961
"Monolog bitnikov"
Ogoniok, no. 9 (1962), p. 17.
Sob. soch., vol. I (Moscow 1983), p. 319.

Girl Beatnik
1961
"Bitnitsa"

Nezhnost': Novye stikhi (Moscow 1962), pp. 48–49.
Sob. soch., vol. I (Moscow 1983), p. 320.

"No people are . . ."
1961
"Liudei neinteresnykh . . ."
Under the title *Liudi* in *Iunost'*, no. 5 (1961), p. 43.
Sob. soch., vol. I (Moscow 1983), p. 323.

"Professor . . ."
1962
"Professor . . ."
Nezhnost': Novye stikhi (Moscow 1962) pp. 27–28.
Sob. soch., vol. I (Moscow 1983), pp. 334–35.

The Dead Hand of the Past
1962
"Miortvaia ruka"
Znamia, no. 4 (1988), p. 43.
Posledniaia popytka (Petrozavodsk 1988), pp. 90–91.

The Heirs of Stalin
1962
"Nasledniki Stalina"
Pravda (Moscow), 21 Oct. 1962, p. 4.
Smena, no. 6 (Moscow 1986). Revised.
Posledniaia popytka (Moscow 1988), pp. 193–95.

Fears
1962
"Strakhi"
Komsomol'skaia pravda, 21 Oct. 1962, p. 4.
Kater sviazi (Moscow 1966), pp. 192–93.

1963–1964

People Were Laughing Behind a Wall
1963
"Smeialis' liudi za stenoi"
Iunost', no. 9 (1963), pp. 59–60.
Sob. soch., vol. I (Moscow 1983), p. 353.

"Early illusions are beautiful . . ."
1963
"Ocharovan'ia rannie . . ."

Iunost', no. 9 (1963), p. 60.
Sob. soch., vol. I (Moscow 1983), p. 352.

The Third Memory
1963
"Tret'ia pamiat' "
Novyi mir, no. 7 (1964), pp. 105–106.
Sob. soch., vol. I (Moscow 1983), pp. 355–56.

The Sigh
1963
"Vzdokh"
In the anthology *Den' poezii 1965* (Moscow 1965), p. 64.
Sob. soch., vol. I (Moscow 1983), p. 357.

Picture of Childhood
1963
"Kartinka detstva"
Under the title *Kartinka daliokovo detstva* in *Prostor*, no. 8 (1965), p. 75.
Sob. soch., vol. I (Moscow 1983), pp. 358–59.

Nefertiti
1963
"Nefertiti"
Moskva, no. 2 (1964), pp. 103–104.
Sob. soch., vol. I (Moscow 1983), pp. 360–61.

The Far Cry
1963
"Dolgie kriki"
Znamia, no. 1 (1965), p. 75.
Sob. soch., vol. I (Moscow 1983), p. 366.

The Hut
1963
"Izba"
Znamia, no. 1 (1965), pp. 77–79.
Sob. soch., vol. I (Moscow 1983), pp. 367–68.

The Mail Cutter
1963
"Kater sviazi"
Znamia, no. 1 (1965), pp. 76–77.
Sob. soch., vol. I (Moscow 1983), pp. 372–73.

Perfection
1963
"Sovershenstvo"

Znamia, no. 1 (1965), pp. 79–80.
Sob. soch., vol. I (Moscow 1983), p. 387.

Wounded Bird
1963
"Podranok"
Under the title "Siuda k prostoram vol'nym, severnym . . ." in *Znamia*, no. 1 (1965), pp. 88–89.
Sob. soch., vol I (Moscow 1983), pp. 390–91.

"Citizens, Listen to Me . . ."
1963
" 'Grazhdane, poslushaite menia' "
Under the title "Ia na parokhode Mayakovskii . . ." in *Znamia*, no. 1 (1965), pp. 92–93.
Sob. soch., vol. I (Moscow 1983), pp. 396–97.

"No, I'll not take the half . . ."
1963
"Net, mne ni v chiom ne nado . . ."
Iunost', no. 9 (1963), p. 60.
Sob. soch., vol. I (Moscow 1983), p. 400.

Love's Maturity?
1963
"Zrelost' liubvi!"
Moskva, no. 2 (1964), p. 102.
Sob. soch., vol. I (Moscow 1963), p. 401.

And So Piaf Left Us . . .
1963
"Tak ukhodila P'iav"
Moskva, no. 2 (1964), p. 103.
Sob. soch., vol. I (Moscow 1983), pp. 402–403.

Hand-rolled Cigarettes
1963
"Samokrutki"
Znamia, no. 4 (1987), p. 3.
Posledniaia popoytka (Petrozavodsk 1988), pp. 91–92.

A Ballad about Seals
1964
"Ballada o nerpakh"
In the anthology *Den' poezii, 1965* (Moscow 1965), pp. 62–63.
Sob. soch., vol. I (Moscow 1983), pp. 409–11.

Why Are You Doing This?
1964

"Zachem ty tak?"
Znamia, no. 1 (1965), pp. 85–86.
Sob. soch., vol. I (Moscow 1983), p. 411.

Ballad about Drinking
1964
"Ballada o vypivke"
Under the title "Vesiolaia ballada" in *Moskva* no. 6 (1965), p. 93.
Sob. soch., vol. I (Moscow 1983), pp. 424–26.

White Nights in Archangel
1964
"Belye nochi v arkhangel'ske"
Znamia, no. 1 (1965), pp. 80–81.
Sob. soch., vol. I (Moscow 1983), pp. 414–15.

Ballad about Mirages
1964
"Ballada o mirazhakh"
Under the title "Ballada o lozhnykh maiakakh" in *Iunost'*, no. 1 (1968), p. 4.
Sob. soch., vol. I (Moscow 1983), p. 421.

"We can't stand . . ."
1964
"Nam smirno usidet' "
Znamia, no. 4 (1987), p. 8.
Posledniaia popytka (Petrozavodsk 1988), p. 96.

A Very Special Soul
1964
"Osobaia dusha"
Posledniaia popytka (Petrozavodsk 1988), pp. 99–101.

Pitching and Rolling
1964
"Kachka"
Under the title "Ballada o bochke" in *Zvezda Vostoka*, no. 3 (1967), pp. 26–27.
Sob. soch., vol. I (Moscow 1983), pp. 422–23.

The City of Yes and the City of No
1964
"Dva goroda"
Under the title "Ia, kak poezd . . ." in *So mnoiu vot chto proiskhodit . . .* (Moscow 1966), p. 21–22.
Sob. soch., vol. I (Moscow 1983), pp. 434–35.

A Ballad about Benkendorf, Chief of Gendarmerie ...
1964
"Ballada o stikhotvorenii Lermontova 'na smert' poeta' i o shefe zhandarmov"
Moskva, no. 10 (1964), p. 195.
Sob. soch., vol. I (Moscow 1983), pp. 437–38.

Sleep, My Beloved
1964
"Liubimaia, spi ..."
Novyi mir, no. 7 (1964), pp. 112–14.
Sob. soch., vol I (Moscow 1983), pp. 440–42.

Bratsk Hydroelectric Station (Selections):
Prayer Before the Poem
Monologue of an Egyptian Pyramid
The Execution of Stenka Razin
Simbirsk Fair
1964
"Bratskaia ges" *(Izbrannye chasti)*
"Molitba pered poemoi"
"Monolog Egipetskoi Pyramidy"
"Kazn' Stenki Razina"
"Iarmarka v Simbirske"
Iunost', no. 4 (1965), pp. 26–67.
Sob. soch., vol. I (Moscow 1983), pp. 443–44, 451–54, 461–66, 472–77.

1965–1967

"White snow is falling ..."
1965
"Idut belye snegi ..."
Idut belye snegi (Moscow 1969), pp. 11–12.
Sob. soch., vol. II (Moscow 1984), pp. 7–8.

Mating Flight of the Woodcock
1965
"Tiaga val'dshnepov"
Znamia, no. 1 (1965), p. 89.
Kater Sviazi (Moscow 1966), p. 39.

A Superfluous Miracle
1965
"Lishnee chudo"
Under the title " 'Vsio, ei-bogu, zhe, bylo by proshche ...' " in *Znamia*, no. 12 (1965), p. 82.
Sob. soch., vol. II (Moscow 1984), p. 21.

Autumn
1965
"Osen' "
Under the title "Vnutri menia osenniaia pora ..." in *Moskva*, no. 6 (1965), p. 91.
Sob. soch., vol. II (Moscow 1984), p. 24.

"The first presentiment ..."
1965
"Predoshchushchenie stikha ..."
Znamia, no. 12 (1965), pp. 77–78.
Sob. soch., vol. II (Moscow 1984), p. 25.

Kamikaze
1965
"Ballada o smertnike"
Komsomolets (Yerevan), 12 Dec. 1965.
Sob. soch., vol. II (Moscow 1984), pp. 31–32.

Coliseum
1965
"Kolizei"
Znamia, no. 12 (1965), pp. 73–76.
Sob. soch., vol. II (Moscow 1984), pp. 36–39.

The Confessional
1965
"Ispovedal'nia"
Poiushchaia damba: Stikhi i poema (Moscow 1972).
Sob. soch., vol. II (Moscow 1984), pp. 43–44.

Procession with the Madonna
1965
"Protsessiia s Madonnoi"
Zaria Vostoka (Tbilisi), 5 Dec. 1965, p. 3.
Sob. soch., vol. II (Moscow 1984), pp. 48–49.

Letter to Paris
1965
"Pis'mo v Parizh"
Posledniaia popytka (Petrozavodsk 1988), pp. 113–15.

A Hundred Miles
1965
"V sta verstakh"
Znamia, no. 4 (1987), pp. 6–7.
Posledniaia popytka (Petrozavodsk 1988), pp. 108–10.

Letter to Yesenin
1965

"Pis'mo Ieseninu"
Posledniaia popytka (Petrozavodsk 1988), pp. 111–13.

Italian Tears
1966
"Ital'ianskie sliozy"
Novyi mir, no. 6 (1966), pp. 97–101.
Sob. soch., vol. II (Moscow 1984), pp. 29–34.

The Stage
1966
"Estrada"
Ogoniok, no. 36 (1966), p. 19.
Sob. soch., vol. II (Moscow 1984), pp. 74–76.

"Poetry gives off smoke..."
1966
"Poèziia chadit..."
Kater sviazi (Moscow 1966), pp. 115–17.
Sob. soch., vol. II (Moscow 1984), pp. 77–78.

Dwarf Birches
1966
"Karlikovye beriozy"
Untitled with a different first line: "V Iak-utni vechnoi merzlotnoi..." in *Sov. Molodiozh* (Irkutsk), 10 Sept. 1970.
Posledniaia popytka (Petrozavodsk 1988), pp. 115–17.

The Torments of Conscience
1966
"Muki sovesti"
Ogoniok, no. 36 (1966), p. 18.
Sob. soch., vol. II (Moscow 1984), pp. 79–80.

Old Women
1966
"Starukhi"
Under the title "V tot den' vysokim ob-shchestvom starukh" in *Moskva*, no. 3 (1967), p. 115.
Sob. soch., vol. II (Moscow 1984), pp. 82–83.

In Memory of Akhmatova
1966
"Pamiati Axhmatovoi"
Iunost', no. 8 (1966), p. 65.
Sob. soch., vol. II (Moscow 1984), pp. 85–87.

"I fell out of love with you..."
1966
"Ya razliubil tebia..."
Ogoniok, no. 36 (1966), p. 18.
Sob. soch., vol. II (Moscow 1984), pp. 88–89.

The Ballad of the Big Stamp
1966
"Ballada o bolshoi pechati"
Ogoniok, no. 1 (1989), p. 9.

"The old house..."
1966
"Kachalsia staryi dom..."
Ogoniok, no. 36 (1966), p. 18.
Sob. soch., vol. II (Moscow 1984), pp. 91–92.

"The snow will begin again..."
1966
"A sneg povalitsia, povalitsia..."
Ogoniok, no. 36 (1966), p. 18.
Sob. soch., vol. II (Moscow 1984), p. 93.

Yelabuga Nail
1967
"Yelabuzhskii gvozd'"
Znamia, no. 7 (1987), pp. 19–20.
Posledniaia popytka (Petrozavodsk 1988), pp. 117–18.

Belly Dance
1967
"Tanets zhivota"
Idut belye snegi... (Moscow 1969), pp. 336–37.
Sob. soch., vol. II (Moscow 1984), pp. 102–103.

The Mark of Cain
1967
"Kainova pechat'"
Ogoniok, no. 27 (1968), p. 12.
Sob. soch., vol. II (Moscow 1984), pp. 104–107.

Love in Portuguese
1967
"Liubov' po-Portugal'ski"
Poiushchaia damba: Stikhi i poema (Moscow 1972), p. 102.
Sob. soch., vol. II (Moscow 1984), p. 108.

When They Murdered Lorca
1967

"Kogda ubili Lorku"
Novyi mir, no. 3 (1969), pp. 59–60.
Sob. soch., vol. II (Moscow 1984), pp. 110–11.

Barcelona's Little Streets
1967
"Barselonskie Ulochki"
Novyi mir, no. 3 (1969), pp. 58–59.
Sob. soch., vol. II (Moscow 1984), pp. 112–13.

Happiness Andalusian Style
1967
"Schast'e po-Andaluzski"
Novyi mir, no. 3 (1969), pp. 61–62.
Sob. soch., vol. II (Moscow 1984), p. 115.

The Revue of Old People
1967
"Reviu starikov"
Novyi mir, no. 3 (1969), pp. 62–63.
Sob. soch., vol. II (Moscow 1984), pp. 117–18.

Black Banderilla
1967
"Chernye banderili"
Novyi mir, no. 3 (1969), pp. 60–61.
Sob. soch., vol. II (Moscow 1984), pp. 119–20.

"I dreamed I already ..."
1967
"Mne snitsia ..."
Znamia, no. 1 (1968), pp. 62–63.
Sob. soch., vol. II (Moscow 1984), p. 133.

Stolen Apples
1967
"Kradenye iabloki"
Znamia, no. 1 (1968), pp. 61–62.
Sob. soch., vol. II (Moscow 1984), pp. 134–35.

An Attempt at Blasphemy
1967
"Popytka bogokhul'stva"
Znamia, no. 1 (1968), p. 68.
Sob. soch., vol. II (Moscow 1984), p. 138.

In a Steelworker's Home
1967
"V dome stalevara"
Iunost', no. 4 (1972), pp. 30–31.

My Handwriting
1967
"Moi pocherk"
Iunost', no. 1 (1968), p. 4.
Sob. soch., vol. II (Moscow 1984), pp. 160–61.

Ballad of the Running Start
1967
"Ballada o razbege"
Ia sibirskoi porody: Stikhi (Irkutsk 1971), p. 183.
Sob. soch., vol. II (Moscow 1984), pp. 170–72.

"Hurry is the curse ..."
1967
"Prokliat'e veka ..."
Ogoniok, no. 27 (1968), p. 12.
Sob. soch., vol. II (Moscow 1984), pp. 173–74.

Monologue of a Poet
1967
"Monolog poeta"
Under the title "Monolog Amerikanskogo poeta" in *Znamia*, no. 1 (1968), pp. 57–59.
Sob. soch., vol. II (Moscow 1984), pp. 178–79.

Monologue of an Actress
1967
"Monolog brodveiskoi aktrisy"
Znamia, no. 1 (1968), pp. 56–57.
Sob. soch., vol. II (Moscow 1984), pp. 180–81.

A Ballad about Nuggets
1967
"Ballada o samorodkakh"
Pravda, 12 Feb. 1967, p. 3.
Sob. soch., vol. II (Moscow 1984), pp. 182–84.

New York Elegy
1967
"N'iu-Iorkskaia elegiia"
Under the title "Monolog Amerikanskogo brodiagi" in *Znamia*, no. 1 (1968), pp. 57–59.
Sob. soch., vol. II (Moscow 1984), pp. 185–86.

Monologue of a Blue Fox
1967

"Monolog golubogo pestsa"
Under the title "Monolog pestsa na ali-
askinskoi zveroferme" in *Znamia*, no. 1
(1968), pp. 54–56.
Sob. soch., vol. II (Moscow 1984), pp. 187–
88.

The Restaurant for Two
1967
"Restoran dlia dvoikh"
Literaturnaia gazeta, 21 June 1967, p. 13.
Sob. soch., vol. II (Moscow 1984), pp. 189–
90.

Cemetery of Whales
1967
"Kladbishche kitov"
Under the title "Na kladbishche kitov" in
Moskva, no. 3 (1967), p. 156.
Sob. soch., vol. II (Moscow 1984), pp. 191–
92.

Smog
1967
"Smog"
Znamia, no. 1 (1968), pp. 52–54.
Sob. soch., vol. II (Moscow 1984), pp. 193–
96.

On the Question of Freedom
1967
"K voprosu o svobode"
Literaturnaia gazeta, 21 June 1967, p. 13.

1968–1972

Monologue of a Restorer
1968
"Monolog Restavratora"
Sov. molodiozh (Irkutsk), 10 Sept. 1970.
Sob. soch., vol. II (Moscow 1984), pp. 197–
98.

Ballad about Sausage
1968
"Ballada o kolbase"
Komsomol'skaia pravda, 18 Aug. 1968, p. 4.
Sob. soch., vol. II (Moscow 1984), pp. 201–
203.

Knowing and Not-Knowing
1968
"Poznan'e i neveden'e"

Druzhba narodov, no. 9 (1969), pp. 86–87.
Sob. soch., vol. II (Moscow 1984), p. 209.

"Light died in the hall . . ."
1968
"Svet umer v zale . . ."
Znamia, no. 1 (1968), p. 63.
Poiushchaia damba: Stikhi i poema (Moscow
1972), p. 27.

The Streetcar of Poetry
1968
"Tramvai poezii"
Krasnoe znamia (Vladivostok), 31 Jan. 1971.
Sob. soch., vol. II (Moscow 1984), p. 213.

Gratitude
1968
"Blagodarnost' "
Novyi mir, no. 11 (1971), p. 45–46.
Sob. soch., vol. II (Moscow 1984), p. 216.

Russian Tanks in Prague
1968
"Russkie tanki v Prage"
Aprel': Al'manakh, no. 1 (Moscow 1990), pp.
3–4.

The Art of Flower Arranging
1969
"Iskusstvo sostavleniia buketov"
Literaturnaia Rossiia, 17 Oct. 1969, p. 17.
Sob. soch., vol. II (Moscow 1984), pp. 277–
78.

Thanks
1969
"Spasibo"
Literaturnaia gazeta, 2 July 1969, p. 7.
Sob. soch., vol. II (Moscow 1984), pp. 284–
85.

Marektinsky Shoals
1969
"Marektinskaia shivera"
Ia sibirskoi porody (Irkutsk 1971), pp. 186–
88.
Sob. soch., vol. II (Moscow 1984), pp. 298–
300.

A Special Vantage Point
1969
"Osobennaia tochka"
Nedelia, 10–16 Aug. 1970, p. 23.
Sob. soch., vol. II (Moscow 1984), pp. 303–
304.

Russianness
1969
"Russkost' "
Unpublished.

The Singing Dam
1970
"Poiushchaia damba"
Vost.-Sib. pravda (Irkutsk), 6 Sept. 1970.
Sob. soch., vol. II (Moscow 1984), pp. 310–12.

The Grave of a Child
1970
"Mogila rebionka"
Under the title "U mysa Mogila Rebionka" in *Nedelia*, 10–16 Aug. 1970, p. 23.
Sob. soch., vol. II (Moscow 1984), pp. 313–14.

Come to My Merry Grave
1970
"Prikhodite ko mne . . ."
Sob. soch., vol. II (Moscow 1984), pp. 319–20.

Unrequited Love
1971
"Nerazdelionaia liubov' "
Nedelia, 6–12 Sept. 1971, p. 13.
Sob. soch., vol. II (Moscow 1984), pp. 379–80.

The Salty Hammock
1971
"Solionyi gamak"
Novyi mir, no. 3 (1971), pp. 147.
Sob. soch., vol. II (Moscow 1984), pp. 381–82.

A Moment Half-Winter, Half-Fall
1971
"V mig poluoseni-poluzimy"
Iunost, no. 4 (1972), p. 31.
Sob. soch., vol. II (Moscow 1984), pp. 383–84.

Keys of the Comandante
1971
"Kliuch komendante"
Literaturnaia gazeta, 8 Sept. 1971, p. 15.
Sob. soch., vol. II (Moscow 1984), pp. 400–402.

My Peruvian Girl
1971

"Moia Peruanka"
Under the title "Peruanka" in *Literaturnaia gazeta*, 26 May 1971, p. 9.
Sob. soch., vol. II (Moscow 1984), pp. 408–409.

Satchmo
1971
"Truba Armstronga"
Komsomolskaia pravda, 18 July 1971.
Sob. soch., vol. II (Moscow 1984), pp. 410–11.

Son and Father
1972
"Syn i otets"
Ogoniok, no. 11 (1973), p. 14.
Sob. soch., vol. II (Moscow 1984), p. 413.

The Family
1972
"Sem'ia"
Novyi mir, no. 4 (1973), pp. 27–28.
Sob. soch., vol. II (Moscow 1984), pp. 429–30.

Tips of Hair
1972
"Konchiki volos"
Novyi mir, no. 4 (1973), pp. 29–30.
Sob. soch., vol. II (Moscow 1984), p. 433.

Pompeii
1972
"Pompeia"
Nash sovremennik, no. 5 (1973), pp. 51–52.
Sob. soch., vol. II (Moscow 1984), pp. 435–36.

A Childish Scream
1972
"Detskii krik"
Krokodil, no. 27 (1974), pp. 8–9
Sob. soch., vol. II (Moscow 1984), p. 441.

A Few Tender Days
1972
"Neskol'ko nezhnykh dnei"
Literaturnaia gazeta, 1 Jan. 1973, p. 7.
Sob. soch., vol. II (Moscow 1984), p. 444.

Kompromise Kompromisovich
1972
"Kompromis, kompromisovich"
Krokodil, no. 27 (1974), pp. 8–9.

Sob. soch., vol. II (Moscow 1984), pp. 452–53.

Vietnam Classic
1972
"V'etnamskii klassik"
In the anthology *Poèziia* (Moscow 1972), vyp. 7, pp. 108–109.
Sob. soch., vol. II (Moscow 1984), pp. 454–55.

Who Are You, Grand Canyon?
1972
"Kto ty, Grand Kanion?"
Under the title "Grand Kanion" in *Ogoniok*, no. 36 (1972), p. 14.
Sob. soch., vol. II (Moscow 1984), pp. 462–67.

Wolf House
1972
"Dom volka"
Ogoniok, no. 36 (1972), pp. 14–15.
Sob. soch., vol. II (Moscow 1984), pp. 470–75.

Two Blacks
1972
"Dva negra"
Ogoniok, no. 36 (1972), pp. 13–14.
Sob. soch., vol. II (Moscow 1984), pp. 476–77.

Saints of Jazz
1972
"Sviatye dzhaza"
Nedelia, 12–18 June 1972, p. 15.
Sob. soch., vol. II (Moscow 1984), pp. 480–81.

From Desire to Desire
1972
"Ot zhelaniia k zhelaniiu"
Doroga nomer odin: Novaia kniga stikhov (Moscow 1972), pp. 166–83.
Sob. soch., vol. II (Moscow 1984), pp. 482–86.

I Would Like
1972
"Ia khotel by . . ."
Ogoniok, no. 36 (1972), p. 15.
Sob. soch., vol. II (Moscow 1984), pp. 487–90.

Kazan University: A Poem (Excerpts):
Lesgaft
Saturday
A Tartar's Song
1970
"Kazanskii universitet poèma" (Vyderzhki)
"Lesgaft"
"Subbota"
"Tatarskaia pesnia"
Novyi mir, no. 4 (Moscow 1970), pp. 46–89.
Sob. soch., vol. II (Moscow 1984), pp. 338–42, 355–59, 359–62.

Under the Skin of the Statue of Liberty: A Poem (Excerpts)
1968
"Pod kozhei Statui Svobody": poèma (Vyderzhki)
Poiushchaia damba: Stikhi i poèma, (Moscow 1972), pp. 140–41, 144–47, 161–63.
Sob. soch., vol. II (Moscow 1984), pp. 244, 247–50, 262–64.

1973–1975

An Old Friend
1973
"Starii Drug"
Literaturnaia gazeta, 3 Oct. 1973, p. 6.
Sob. soch., vol. III (Moscow 1984), pp. 7–8.

The Drunken Cow
1973
"P'ianaia korova"
Ogoniok, no. 51 (1973), p. 12.
Sob. soch., vol. III (Moscow 1984), pp. 12–13.

Love Is Always in Danger
1973
"Vsegda v opasnosti liubov' "
Ogoniok, no. 51 (1973), p. 13.
Sob. soch., vol. III (Moscow 1984), pp. 14–15.

Wisdom and Folly
1973
"Um i glupost' "
Ottsovskii slukh (Moscow 1978), pp. 23–25.

Sob. soch., vol. III (Moscow 1984), pp. 16–17.

A Father's Ear
1973
"Ottsovskii slukh"
Ottsovskii slukh (Moscow 1975), pp. 99–100.
Sob. soch., vol. III (Moscow 1984), pp. 118–19.

The Face Behind the Face
1973
"Litso Litsa"
In the anthology Poèziia (Moscow 1975), vyp. 15, p. 52.
Sob. soch., vol. III (Moscow 1984), p. 22.

For Your Attention
1973
"K vashemu svedeniiu"
Novyi mir, no. 4 (1973), pp. 32–33.
Sob. soch., vol. III (Moscow 1984), p. 23.

Epistle to Neruda
1973
"Poslanie Nerude"
Under the title "Poslanie Pablo Nerude" in Literaturnaia Rossiia, 21 Sept. 1973, p. 6.
Sob. soch., vol. III (Moscow 1984), pp. 31–32.

Wounds
1973
"Rany"
Literaturnaia gazeta, 3 Oct. 1973, p. 6.
Ottsovskii slukh (Moscow 1975), p. 30.

Memento
1974
"Napominanie"
Nedelia, 9–15 Sept. 1974, p. 15.
Sob. soch., vol. III (Moscow 1984), p. 74.

Mother
1974
"Mama"
Izvestiia, 17 Aug. 1974.
Ottsovskii slukh (Moscow 1975), pp. 61–62.

"When I cast off for . . ."
1974
"Kogda ia v sen' vekov . . ."
Literaturnaia gazeta, 14 Aug. 1974, p. 7.
Sob. soch., vol. III (Moscow 1984), p. 66.

Lament for a Brother
1974
"Plach po bratu"
Under the title "Okhotnich'ia ballada" in Literaturnaia Rossiia, 29 Nov. 1974, p. 5.
Sob. soch., vol. III (Moscow 1984), p. 5.

Russia
1974
"A. sobstvenno, kto ty takaia . . ."
Under the title "Odnoi znakomoi" in Nash sovremennik, no. 10 (1974), p. 96.
Sob. soch., vol. III (Moscow 1984), p. 61.

Malachite Frog
1974
"Malakhitovaia liagushka"
Nedelia, 9–15 Sept. 1974, p. 15.
Sob. soch., vol. III (Moscow 1984), pp. 62–64.

Interconnection of Phenomena
1974
"Vzaimosvyaz' iavlenii"
Znamia, no. 4 (1987), p. 11.
Posledniaia popytka (Petrozavodsk 1988), p. 122.

Metamorphoses
1974
"Metamorfozy"
Literaturnaia gazeta, 14 Aug. 1974, p. 7.
Sob. soch., vol. III (Moscow 1984), p. 67.

Verbosity
1974
"Mnogoslovie"
Oktiabr', no. 11 (1974), p. 14.
Sob. soch., vol. III (Moscow 1984), p. 69.

"A drop fell . . ."
1974
"Upala kaplia . . ."
Under the title "Kogda est' drug . . ." in Oktiabr', no. 11 (1974), p. 6.
Sob. soch., vol. III (Moscow 1984), pp. 70–71.

Potato Flower
1974
"Tsvetok kartoshki"
Druzhba narodov, no. 7 (1975), p. 84.
Sob. soch., vol. III (Moscow 1984), p. 56.

Hope
1975

"Nadezhda"
Ottsovskii slukh (Moscow 1975), pp. 15–16.
Sob. soch., vol. III (Moscow 1984), pp. 125–26.

A Tear
1975
"Sleza"
Iunost', no. 6 (1975), p. 38.
Ottsovskii slukh (Moscow 1975), pp. 59–60.

The Ringing of the Earth
1975
"Zvon zemli"
Iunost', no. 6 (1975), p. 37.
Sob. soch., vol. III (Moscow 1984), p. 127.

But Before . . .
1975
"No Prezhde, chem . . ."
Iunost', no. 6 (1975), p. 37.
Sob. soch., vol. III (Moscow 1984), p. 128.

Iron Staircase
1975
"Zheleznye stupeni"
In the anthology *Poèziia* (Moscow 1975), pp. 50–51.
Sob. soch., vol. III (Moscow 1984), pp. 130–31.

The Easter Procession
1975
"Krestnyi khod"
Druzhba narodov, no. 7 (1975), pp. 85–86.
Sob. soch., vol. III (Moscow 1984), pp. 132–33.

Memory's Revenge
1975
"Vozmezd'e pamiat'iu"
Ottsovskii slukh (Moscow 1975), pp. 130–31.
Sob. soch., vol. III (Moscow 1984), p. 137.

To Beginners
1975
"Nachinaiushchim"
Iunost', no. 6 (1975), p. 36.
Sob. soch., vol. III (Moscow 1984), pp. 139–40.

Alder Catkin
1975
"Ol'khovaia seriozhka"
Literaturnaia gazeta, 30 Apr. 1975, p. 7.

Sob. soch., vol. III (Moscow 1984), pp. 141–43.

"In moments of . . ."
1975
"V mig osleplen'ia . . ."
Ottsovskii slukh (Moscow 1975), pp. 21–22.

The Wild Ass's Skin
1975
"Shagrenevaia kozha"
Ottsovskii slukh (Moscow 1975), pp. 10–11.

"Once people . . ."
1975
"Esli liudi v menia . . ."
Iunost', no. 6 (1975), p. 36.
Sob. soch., vol. III (Moscow 1984), pp. 135–36.

Safari in Ulster
1975
"Safari v Ol'stere"
Literaturnaia gazeta, 17 Mar. 1976, p. 4.
Sob. soch., vol. III (1984), pp. 162–69.

Snow in Tokyo: A Japanese Poem
1974
"Sneg v Tokio: Iaponskaia poema"
Ogoniok, no. 32 (1975), pp. 17–19.
Sob. soch., vol. III (Moscow 1984), pp. 38–55.

1976–1978

Good-for-Nothing Places
1976
"Giblye mesta"
Baikal, no. 5 (1976), pp. 36–38.
Sob. soch., vol. III (Moscow 1984), pp. 173–75.

Long Life
1976
"Dolgoletiye"
Mosk. komsomolets, 3 June 1977, p. 4.
Sob. soch., vol. III (Moscow 1984), p. 178.

Woman Midget
1976
"Karlitsa"
Under the title "U kinoteatra 'Orlionok' " in *Literaturnaia gazeta*, 5 Jan. 1977, p. 7.

Sob. soch., vol. III (Moscow 1984), pp. 183–84.

Tomorrow's Wind
1977
"Zavtrashnii veter"
Literaturnaia Gruziya, no. 12 (1977), p. 10.
Sob. soch., vol. III (Moscow 1984), pp. 221–23.

Gogol's Mistake
1977
"Oshibka Gogolia"
Oktiabr', no. 7 (1977), pp. 7–8.
Sob. soch., vol. III (Moscow 1984), pp. 225–26.

Across Eight Thousand Kilometers
1977
"Skvoz' vosem' tysych kilometrov"
Vost.-Sib. pravda (Irkutsk), 28 Aug. 1977.
Sob. soch., vol. III (Moscow 1984), pp. 228–29.

"When the clover field stirs . . ."
1977
"Zashumit li klevernoe pole, . . ."
Novyi mir, no. 8 (1977), pp. 118–19.
Sob. soch., vol. III (Moscow 1984), pp. 236–37.

Insurance Agent
1977
"Agent po strakhovaniiu"
Magadan pravda, 30 July 1977.
Sob. soch., vol. III (Moscow 1984), pp. 240–41.

Don't Disappear
1977
"Ne ischezai"
Magadan pravda, 30 July 1977.
Sob. soch., vol. III (Moscow 1984), p. 244.

Nice People
1977
"Milye liudi"
Komsomolskaia pravda, 13 Mar. 1977, p. 2.
Sob. soch., vol. III (Moscow 1984), pp. 248–49.

Moscow-Ivanovo
1978
"Moskva-Ivanovo"
Avrora, no. 12 (1978), pp. 51–53.

Sob. soch., vol. III (Moscow 1984), pp. 279–80.

The Unexpressed
1978
"Nevyskazannost' "
Sob. soch., vol. III (Moscow 1984), pp. 284–86.

Psychotherapy
1978
"Psikhoterapiia"
Utrennii narod: Novaia kniga stixov (Moscow 1978).
Sob. soch., vol. III (Moscow 1984), p. 292.

On Modesty
1978
"O skromnosti"
Utrennii narod: Novaia kniga stikhov (Moscow 1978), p. 196.
Sob. soch., vol. III (1984), p. 293.

Monologue of a Loser
1978
"Monolog proigravshevosia"
Utrennii narod: Novaia kniga stikhov (Moscow 1978), p. 197.
Sob. soch., vol. III (Moscow 1984), p. 294.

To Charlie Chaplin
1978
"Charli Chaplinu"
Sovetskaia kultura, 20 Jan. 1978, p. 8.
Sob. soch., vol. III (Moscow 1984), pp. 303–304.

The Art of Ingratiating
1978
"Zaiskivan'e"
Iunost', no. 6 (1978), pp. 87–88.
Sob. soch., vol. III (Moscow 1984), pp. 305–306.

"O Georgia . . ."
1978
"O Gruziia . . ."
Tiazheleie zemli: Stikhi o Gruzii: Poèty Gruzii (Moscow 1979), p. 20.
Sob. soch., vol. III (Moscow 1984), p. 301.

"No, literacy is not . . ."
1978
"Net, gramotnost' . . ."
Under the title "Bezgramotnost' " in *Literaturnaia Rossiia*, 6 Aug. 1976, p. 5.
Sob. soch., vol. III (Moscow 1984), p. 307.

Russians and Jews
1978
"U russkogo i u evreia"
Znamia, no. 4 (1987), pp. 12–13.
Posledniaia popytka (Petrozavodsk 1988), pp. 130–31.

Ivan the Terrible and Ivan the Fool: A Poem (Excerpt)
1976
"Ivanovskie sitsy: poema" *(Vyderzhki)*
Avrora, no. 8 (1976), pp. 7–18.
Sob. soch., vol. III (Moscow 1984), pp. 188–94.

A Dove in Santiago: A Novella in Verse
1978
"Golub' v Sant'iago: Povest' v stikhakh"
Novyi mir, no. 11 (1978), pp. 156–92.
Sob. soch., vol. III (Moscow 1984), pp. 309–54.

1979–1985

"Moscow believed..."
1979
"Moskva poverila..."
Literaturnaia gazeta, 27 June 1979, p. 7.
Sob. soch., vol. III (Moscow 1984), p. 359.

Designers of Spiderwebs
1980
"Dizainery pautiny"
Svarka vzryvom: Stikhotvoreniia i poèmy (Moscow 1980), pp. 56–57.
Sob. soch., vol. III (Moscow 1984), p. 379.

Directness
1980
"Est' priamota..."
Sob. soch., vol. III (Moscow 1984), p. 391.

Two Pair of Skis
1981
"Dve pary lyzh"
Dve pary lyzh: Novaia kniga stikhov (Moscow 1982), pp. 3–4.
Sob. soch., vol. III (Moscow 1984), pp. 418–19.

Back Then
1981
"Tomu Nazad..."

Sob. soch., vol. III (Moscow 1984), pp. 428–32.

Maternity Floor
1981
"Etazh materinstva"
In English in *Invisible Threads* (New York: Macmillan, 1981), pp. 40–41.
Dve pary lyzh: Novaia kniga stikhov (Moscow 1982), pp. 20–23.
Sob. soch., vol. III (Moscow 1984), pp. 441–43.

On What Is Life Spent?
1981
"Na chto ukhodit zhizn'"
Sob. soch., vol. III (Moscow 1984), pp. 436–37.

Final Faith
1982
"Posledniaia vera"
Sob. soch., vol. III (Moscow 1984), pp. 445–46.

Momma and the Neutron Bomb: A Poem (Excerpt)
1982
"Mama i neitronnaia bomba: Poema" (Vyderzhka)
Mama i neitronnaia bomba i drugie stikhi (Moscow 1983), pp. 20–23.
Sob. soch., vol. III (Moscow 1984), pp. 463–66.

Guardian of the Hearth
"Khranitel'nitsa ochaga"
Sob. soch., vol. III (Moscow 1984), pp. 504–505.

Flowers for Grandmother
1983
"Tsvety dlia Babushki"
Pochti naposledok (Moscow 1985), pp. 16–18.
Sob. soch., vol. III (Moscow 1984), pp. 498–500.

"A small dish..."
1983
"Pomerklo bliudechko..."
Pochti naposledok (Moscow 1985), pp. 46–47.
Sob. soch., vol. III (Moscow 1984), p. 512.

Afghanistan Ant
1983

"Afganskii muravei"
Ogoniok (Moscow), no. 1 (1989) p. 9.

My Universities
1983
"Moi universitety"
Pochti naposledok (Moscow 1985), pp. 1–7.
Sob. soch., vol. III (Moscow 1987), pp. 365–68.

Violets
1983
"Fialki"
Pochti naposledok (Moscow 1985), pp. 19–20.
Sob. soch., vol. III (Moscow 1987), pp. 355.

Meditations at the Back Door
1983
"Razmyshleniia u chernogo khoda"
Sob. soch., vol. III (Moscow 1984), pp. 513–15.

Murder
1984
"Nikto ne spit..."
Pochti naposledok (Moscow 1985), p. 39.
Sob. soch., vol. III (Moscow 1987), p. 372.

You Still Haven't Returned
1984
"Ne otdala eshchio..."
Pochti naposledok (Moscow 1985), pp. 33–35.
Sob. soch., vol. III (Moscow 1987), pp. 370–71.

"What right..."
1984
"Kakoe pravo ia imel..."
Pochti naposledok (Moscow 1985), p. 39
Sob. soch., vol. III (Moscow 1987), p. 372.

Eight-year-old Poet
1984
"Vosmiletnii poet"
Pochti naposledok (Moscow 1985), pp. 57–58.
Sob. soch., vol. III (Moscow 1987), pp. 377–78.

Being Late
1983
"Opozdanie"
Pochti naposledok (Moscow 1985), pp. 9–11.

Sob. soch., vol. III (Moscow 1987), pp. 345–47.

Trumpet
1985
"Truba"
Pochti naposledok (Moscow 1985), pp. 44–45.
Sob. soch., vol. III (Moscow 1987), pp. 392–93.

Disbelief in Yourself Is Indispensable
1985
"Neverie v sebia neobkhodimo"
Pochti naposledok (Moscow 1985), pp. 48–49.

To Incomprehensible Poets
1985
"Neponiatnym poetam"
Pochti naposledok (Moscow 1985), pp. 50–51.
Sob. soch., vol. III (Moscow 1987), pp. 394–95.

Comradesbutwhatifers
1985
"Kabychevonevyshlisty"
Pochti naposledok (Moscow 1985), pp. 78–82.
Sob. soch., vol. III (Moscow 1987), pp. 396–99.

A Half Blade of Grass
1985
"Poltravinochki"
Pochti naposledok (Moscow 1985), p. 21.
Sob. soch., vol. III (Moscow 1987), p. 369.

A Distant Relative, or Désespoir: A Poem
1984
"Dal'naia rodstvenitsa"
Pochti naposledok (Moscow 1985), pp. 84–90
Sob. soch., vol. III (Moscow 1987), pp. 386–91.

Fuku: A Poem (Excerpts)
1963–1985
"Fuku"
Novyi mir, no. 9, 1985, pp. 3–58.
Sob. soch., vol. III (Moscow 1987), pp. 400–84.

1986–1990

"We should be stingier..."
1986
"Nado by poskupee..."
Znamia, no. 4 (1987), p. 24.
Posledniaia popytka (Petrozavodsk 1988),
pp. 46–47.

Antedeluvian
1986
"Dopotopstvo"
Smena, no. 6 (1986), p. 6.
Posledniaia popytka (Petrozavodsk 1988),
pp. 165–67.

Zoya Osipova
1986
"Zoyi Osipova"
Smena, no. 6 (1986).
Posledniaia popytka (Petrozavodsk 1988),
pp. 168–69.

Siberian Wooing
1986
"Svatovstvo"
Literaturnaia gazeta, 21 Oct. 1987, p. 5.
Posledniaia popytka (Petrozavodsk 1988),
pp. 31–33.

Aldan Girl
1986
"Aldanochka"
Smena, no. 6 (1986), p. 7.
Stikhotvoreniia (Moscow 1987), pp. 320–22.

Farewell
1986
"Proshchanie"
Posledniaia popytka (Petrozavodsk 1988),
pp. 28–30.

Fireflies
1986
"Tsitsinateli"
Posledniaia popytka (Petrozavodsk 1988),
pp. 26–28.

Requiem for *Challenger*
1986
"Chellèndzher"
Unpublished.

The Last Attempt
1986
"Posledniaia popytka"

Posledniaia popytka (Petrozavodsk 1988),
pp. 23–24.

Stalin's Funeral
1953–1987
"Pokhorony Stalina"
Posledniaia popytka (Petrozavodsk 1988),
pp. 44–45.

The Peak of Shame
1987
"Pik pozora"
Literaturnaia gazeta, 21 Oct. 1987, p. 5.
Posledniaia popytka (Petrozavodsk 1988),
pp. 41–44.

Russian Koalas
1987
"Russkie koaly"
Literaturnaia gazeta, 21 Oct. 1987, p. 5.
Posledniaia popytka (Petrozavodsk 1988),
pp. 36–38.

The Accidentless Captain
1987
"Bezavariinyi Kapitan"
Posledniaia popytka (Petrozavodsk 1988),
pp. 67–69.

Monuments Still Not Built
1987
"Eshchio ne postavlennye pamiatniki"
Ogoniok, no. 37 (1987), p. 7.
Posledniaia popytka (Petrozavodsk 1988),
pp. 45–46.

Personal Letter from the Generalissimo
1988
"Lichnoe pis'mo Generalissimusa"
Posledniaia popytka (Petrozavodsk 1988),
pp. 51–53.

Provideniia Bay
1988
"Bukhta Provideniia"
Posledniaia popytka (Petrozavodsk 1988),
pp. 53–55.

We Can't Go On
1988
"Tak dal'she zhit' nel'zia"
Posledniaia popytka (Petrozavodsk 1988), p.
75.

Vendée
1988
"Vendeia"

Posledniaia popytka (Petrozavodsk 1988), pp. 58–59.

The Apple Trees of Drobitskii
1989
"Drobitskie iabloni"
Vechernii Kharkov, 9 May 1989.

A Striking Heart
1989

"Zabastovka serdtsa"
Pravda, 19 Dec. 1989, p. 3.

Half Measures
1989
"Poluvinchatost' "
Ogoniok, no. 4 (1990) p. 29.

ABOUT THE EDITORS

Albert C. Todd, who studied at Moscow University thirty years ago, has served as director of the Slavic workshop at Indiana University and chairman of the department of Slavic and East European Languages and Literature at Queens College/CUNY (where he currently teaches Russian and comparative literature and film). In addition to translating Yevtushenko and others, he adapted Chekhov's *Uncle Vanya* for the Mike Nichols production.

James Ragan is the director of the Graduate Professional Writing Program at the University of Southern California and a recent Fulbright Professor of Poetry (Yugoslavia and China). He is the author of three books of poetry, *In the Talking Hours*, *Womb-Weary*, and *Lusions*, and the plays *Saint* and *Commedia*. His poetry and plays have been translated in the Soviet Union.

891.7144 Yevtushenko, Yevgeny
YEV   Aleksandrovich,
         1933-

         The collected poems,
         1952-1990.

$29.45   49200

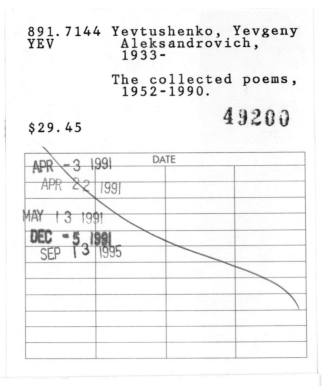

DATE		
APR - 3 1991		
APR 22 1991		
MAY 13 1991		
DEC - 5 1991		
SEP 13 1995		